*Ritual and Scripture
in Chinese
Popular Religion*

PUBLICATIONS OF
THE CHINESE POPULAR CULTURE PROJECT

Ritual Opera, Operatic Ritual: "Mu-lien Rescues His Mother" in Chinese Popular Culture. Papers from the International Workshop on the Mu-lien Operas, with an additional contribution on the "Woman Huang Legend" by Beata Grant. Edited by David Johnson. (Chinese Popular Culture Project, 1989.)

Domesticated Deities and Auspicious Emblems: The Iconography of Everyday Life in Village China. Popular Prints and Papercuts from the Collection of Po Sung-nien. Po Sung-nien and David Johnson. (Chinese Popular Culture Project, 1992.)

These books may be ordered from Institute of East Asian Studies Publications, University of California, 2223 Fulton Street, Sixth Floor, Berkeley, CA 94720.

Ritual and Scripture in Chinese Popular Religion

Five Studies

Edited by
David Johnson

Publications of the Chinese Popular Culture Project   *3*

Design & production
by Wilsted & Taylor
Oakland, California

Composition
by Birdtrack Press
New Haven, Connecticut

Printing
by Thomson-Shore, Inc.
Dexter, Michigan

LIBRARY OF CONGRESS CATALOGING-IN-PUBLICATION DATA

Ritual and scripture in Chinese popular religion : five studies /
    edited by David Johnson.
        p.   cm. — (Publications of the Chinese Popular Culture
Project : 3)
    Includes bibliographical references.
    ISBN 0-9624327-3-3 (pbk.)
1. Cults—China.   2. China—Religious life and customs.
I. Johnson, David G. (David George), 1938–   II. Series.
BL1802.R58   1994
299'.51–-dc20   93-44401
                                                           CIP

Distributed by IEAS Publications
University of California
2223 Fulton Street, Sixth Floor
Berkeley, CA 94720

Contents

Introduction

Chinese popular religion deserves serious study. Villagers undoubtedly were credulous and conservative, but in their temples and rituals they could rise to impressive heights of creativity and devotion. Religious writings directed at non-elite audiences were often hackneyed and manipulative, but they also could have a directness and honesty that are deeply moving, and in their best moments are at least as powerful as the polished, self-conscious, and restrained productions of the high literate and clerical elites. The true genius of the Chinese people found some of its best expressions in the ritual, scriptures, and art of popular religion.

The inherent attractiveness of Chinese popular religion in its many forms, its importance for our understanding of the course of Chinese history and the texture of Chinese culture, and the existence of rich collections of virtually unexplored primary sources have led to growing interest in this field among scholars here and abroad in recent years.[1] Nevertheless, the idea of Chinese popular religion is regarded with suspicion by some, who think that it implies the existence of a realm of beliefs and behaviors quite separate from elite religion, or whatever the alternative to "popular" is believed to be. Such fears are groundless, at least as far as this book is concerned, for it is based on the assumption that there were many non-

[1]See the "state of the field" article on Chinese religion, by Daniel Overmyer and others, forthcoming in the *Journal of Asian Studies*.

elite sub-cultures and, depending on one's definitions, several elite sub-cultures as well.[2] In addition, these various groupings were not isolated from each other but exercised a constant mutual influence, both direct and indirect. The terms "elite" and "popular" are simply used for the sake of convenience.

Another reason why some scholars dislike the idea of popular religion is their conviction that "everyone" in a village or town shared the same religious beliefs and participated in the same religious activities. Too little is known to be able to refute this position conclusively, and unfortunately few problems are more difficult to study. But in general those who want to dispense with the notion of popular religion are faced with two problems: first, they have to explain away the fact that members of the literate elite in China for centuries kept up a steady drumbeat of criticism against what they themselves termed popular customs and beliefs, and still are doing it today. Second, if they find a member of the gentry or a local official taking part in local religious activities they must also show that it meant to him what it meant to everyone else. This is very difficult to do, but virtually all available evidence—including that put forward in several of the chapters in this book (Chard, Cedzich, Lien)—suggests that the educated and powerful did not understand the rituals and scriptures of village religion in the same way that the uneducated and less powerful did. In fact there can be little doubt that elite and popular mentalities in traditional China differed sharply in the realm of religion, as they did in many other arenas of symbolic life. Those mentalities, however, were not isolated from each other, but on the contrary were in constant dialogue. All the chapters demonstrate this in one way or another.

As several of the chapters illustrate (Johnson, Cedzich, Chard), one of the leading characteristics of popular religion in pre-modern China was its diversity, its seemingly endless local variations. This is visible in all aspects of verbal and material culture: opera, folktales, music, dress, cuisine, and so on. For the unprepared, the variations in cultural forms from region to region, and even from village to village, can seem overwhelming—especially since there is no consensus on how to reduce this infinity of

---

[2]For details, see David Johnson, "Communication, Class, and Consciousness in Late Imperial China," in David Johnson, Andrew J. Nathan, and Evelyn S. Rawski, eds., *Popular Culture in Late Imperial China* (Berkeley: University of California Press, 1985).

difference to something approaching analytic coherence.[3] There are some practical ways of easing the burden, however. One is to work within linguistic (dialect) communities. Another is to look at specific aspects of popular religion, rather than "popular religion" as a whole.

The studies in this book are concerned with popular religious beliefs, ideas, and emotions and their expression and communication, as opposed for example to subjects like temple management, the spatial distribution of shrines, or the social function of local cults. As the title suggests, the organizing principle is the division of the subject thus delimited into two great realms, ritual and scripture. These are, of course, simple labels for extremely complex realities. It is true also that there are places where the boundaries of the two realms appear to overlap. But the distinction remains very powerful, for in practice there is a fundamental distinction in terms of effect on audiences, demands on performers, and expectations of writers between those modes of representation and communication that were predominantly verbal and those that combined words and ensemble performance. Of the papers presented here, two—Lien's and Ebrey's—are concerned with liturgies, two—Cedzich's and Johnson's—deal mostly with the "scriptural" realm (though not with scripture per se), while Chard's has much to say about both scripture and ritual.

Chinfa Lien's paper explains how to identify vernacular elements in a written text, and then shows the presence of many Min elements in an extensive collection of traditional Taoist liturgical texts from Taiwan. He demonstrates that some of the texts were written to be spoken or chanted in the Min dialect, while others were written in older Northern vernaculars, and still others were written in literary Chinese. This proves that the writers of these liturgies were concerned that parts of them at least be comprehensible to the people on whose behalf they were performed. This conclusion, which seems innocuous enough, is actually very significant, since it refutes those, like Frits Staal, who insist that rituals do not have intrinsic meanings. If this were true, why bother to adapt imported liturgies to their new linguistic context? Lien also shows very clearly that some texts written in literary Chinese were intended as meditation manuals

[3]The time when anthropologists and ethnologists could confidently appeal to universalizing schemes such as structuralism seems long past, and very little has been proposed to take its place.

and were aimed at educated readers, while others, written in the vernacular, were clearly intended for performance before Min-speaking audiences. This is strong evidence of education-based stratification in the total Taiwanese audience for these texts.

Patricia Ebrey focuses on a very different kind of liturgy: that bound up with the ancestral cult, which was celebrated by both families and lineages. She describes in detail a liturgy that was codified in the twelfth century by Chu Hsi and thereafter became a fundamental tool in the centuries-long process by which Neo-Confucian ideas about family and lineage were spread to all classes. One of Ebrey's most interesting observations is that there seems to have been an expectation that rituals could be altered to take account of local needs; that over time, and space, liturgies would need to be revised. Thus the men who formulated the rituals of ancestral worship made a basic assumption that they were meaningful, and clearly felt that enhancing that meaningfulness was more important than preserving traditional forms that had lost their relevance.

Robert Chard's chapter is concerned with ritual *and* scripture—in this case, of the domestic cult par excellence, the cult of the stove god. The central ritual of this cult took place once a year on the twenty-third or twenty-fourth day of the twelfth lunar month, when the men of the family sent the stove god off to Heaven to report to the Jade Emperor on the family's behavior during the previous year. (Women were usually but not always excluded.) In striking contrast to the Taoist and Neo-Confucian rituals of Lien's and Ebrey's papers, this and associated rituals in the cult of the stove god did not have any textual basis, but seem instead to have been a genuinely popular creation, which eventually spread all across China thanks in large part, as Chard suggests, to the circulation of woodblock-printed images of the god. There were many scriptures and other texts associated with the cult, but they ostentatiously ignored the popular rituals, instead endeavoring to popularize monthly sacrifices to the god along with constant self-examination. But this version of the cult never gained wide acceptance. In other words, the scriptural or textual side of the cult was, in part at least, used by the educated to modify popular practices and popular conceptions, while its rituals were the means by which those practices and conceptions were preserved.

David Johnson's chapter reaches a very similar conclusion. Even though the *pao-chüan* he studies were performed and were not originally intended as reading matter, he concludes that they have more in common with scriptures than with ritual. Thus Johnson's chapter is firmly on the "scriptural" side. But he shows that even didactic literature, though it was by definition in the hands of the literate, was not necessarily always a vehicle for elite attitudes and values. The story of Mu-lien as presented in prosimetric narrative changed profoundly over the millennium of its history in China, becoming less clerical and more popular in its basic messages. It may well be that the people who wrote stove god scriptures and the ones who wrote *pao-chüan* about Mu-lien were from rather different social classes.

Angelika Cedzich's chapter is also concerned with the textual side of popular religion, though her subject is not a scripture but what we call, for lack of a better word, a novel. She demonstrates that the *Journey to the South* is deeply infused with elements derived from the iconography and hagiography of the cult of the Wu-t'ung or Wu-hsien, even though it does not seem to have been designed to accomplish any particular devotional or proselytizing purpose. It is not possible to say exactly why the *Journey to the South* drew so heavily on the Wu-hsien cult, but Cedzich's painstaking reconstruction of the cult's history leaves no doubt that it did, and that it systematically put a respectable gloss on certain disreputable features of the popular cult. Here again we see that narrative is at ease with the didactic.

Two large themes appear again and again in these studies, whether they are concerned with ritual or with scripture. One is the never-ending literati campaign to reform the religious practices and beliefs of ordinary people. The other is the characteristically Chinese blurring of the line dividing religion and entertainment.

The basic thrust of Chard's chapter is to show how the stove god cult changed under pressure from elite reformers—and also how it did not change. The ancient worship of a stove goddess, which may well have been in the hands of women, was transformed early on: the goddess became a god, a god whose function it was to enforce conventional morality in the household and whose cult excluded women. Yet the annual ritual celebration of the god's departure for Heaven to make his report was celebrated not with fear and trembling but with good-natured cynicism, which centered on the symbolic bribing (or mock disabling) of the god to ensure his favorable report (or no report at all). Try though they might, the authors of the stove god scriptures never succeeded in displacing this custom, with all its unwelcome implications (unwelcome to the local elite and officials).

Ebrey's chapter deals with one of the greatest successes of the literati: the popularization of a Neo-Confucian interpretation of the ancestral cult, as embodied in the liturgies for family rituals codified by Chu Hsi and elaborated by dozens of later writers. Chu Hsi intended his book for "the general population," according to Ebrey, though no doubt he was thinking of people with at least some education and not illiterate farmers. Later writers devised even simpler versions of Chu Hsi's liturgies, evidently trying to reach a broader and broader audience. Ebrey does not pursue the point, but it is fairly clear that, in this arena at least, the Neo-Confucian literati were extremely successful: in sacrifices to the ancestors (less so in funerals or weddings) the elite model came to rule supreme.

In the long, complex evolution of the Wu-t'ung cult as reconstructed by Cedzich, one theme stands out with great clarity: the attempts by both lay and clerical elites to "domesticate" the ancient cult of Shan-hsiao and its later incarnation in the Wu-t'ung. Many different methods were used, and in the end they were successful in creating a new persona for the old spirits. However, the cult of the Wu-t'ung, disreputable as it was, did not disappear but was preserved by the people themselves in the face of elite condemnation on into the sixteenth century and beyond. This outcome reminds us strongly of what happened with the cult of the stove god.

Johnson's study speaks obliquely to this issue. The Mu-lien story was first put into prosimetric form for presentation to ordinary people as early as the eighth or ninth century, and prosimetric versions were still being produced for popular consumption a thousand years later. But Johnson argues that the story underwent a profound change over that long span of years, from a version that reflected orthodox Buddhist teachings and the interests of the clergy to one in which popular taste, shaped by operatic versions of the story, was more important. Even Lien's study, though it does not deal directly with the historical evolution of the Taoist liturgical texts it discusses, has something to say on the general subject of the interplay between literate elites and the illiterate majority, for he shows in detail how priests revised their liturgies to make them more accessible to ordinary folk without compromising the basic ideas they wanted to convey.

Lien also makes it clear that the Min segments of the Taoist liturgies he studies often were derived from folk ballads or other forms that were performed by or for the people themselves for their enjoyment, and this intermingling of the religious or didactic and the entertaining is the other theme that can be traced through most of the chapters. It appears in a minor way in Chard's, where we see that popular custom has made the annual ceremony of sending off the stove god to Heaven a rather light-hearted occasion, and it is a major theme in Cedzich's and Johnson's chapters. As noted above, Cedzich shows that key themes in the *Journey to the South* can be understood only if the novel is seen as an attempt to defend the cult of Hua-kuang and the Wu-hsien against the suspicion of impropriety, even though this does not appear to have been its *raison d'être*.[4] Evidently it seemed completely natural to a profit-minded sixteenth-century publisher to concoct a mythological romance out of materials supplied by a popular cult.

Johnson's chapter provides further illustrations of this theme. He shows that the *pao-chüan* genre, like other prosimetric performance genres before it, was equally well-suited to teaching and to entertaining, and that *pao-chüan* such as the *Mu-lien pao-ch'uan*, which he analyses, were highly entertaining, though their main purpose was didactic. He also describes in considerable detail a type of didactic or moralistic storytelling that was known by many names—*shan shu, shuo yin-kuo, Sacred Edict* lecturing, *hsüan chüan*—in which the impulse to entertain and to instruct were inextricably intertwined.

The village temples that were the locus of so much of what we think of as Chinese popular religion were often decorated with elaborate carvings not of scenes from the life or legend of the god worshipped there (though there may well have also been murals that depicted these), but of scenes from historical operas. The major ritual occasions that were celebrated in the temple invariably included operas, which quite often were performed

---

[4]There were novels that explicitly rehearsed the founding myth of popular cults, such as the *Lin-shui p'ing-yao*, translated by Brigitte Berthier as *La Dame du Bord de l'Eau* (Nanterre: Société d'Ethnologie, 1988), and that propagated specific religious teachings, such as the *San chiao yen-i* (*The Romance of the Three Teachings*), studied by Judith Berling. See her paper in *Popular Culture in Late Imperial China* (cited n. 2).

on stages that were an integral part of the temple complex. These operas were not usually religious, but instead depicted heroes and villains of past times. Farces and even romantic dramas were also presented. The symbolic world of the temple, and of village religion generally, was closely related to the symbolic world of village opera, storytelling, ballad singing, and the like. It is impossible to understand Chinese popular religion without understanding this fact, as several of the studies in this volume illustrate.

Chinese religious thought was not dominated by a fundamental dichotomy between the secular and the sacred. Because the sacred was always compromised and imperfect, dogma and doctrines, which give intellectual form to the sacred, were of little importance. There were no formal creeds in Chinese popular religion, and no excommunication. Indeed, there was no ecclesiastical organization at all and hence no enforcing of theological orthodoxy. As a result, local variants flourished luxuriantly, and were never criticized merely for departing from theological orthodoxy—because in a very real sense there was none.

This is why the long struggle between popular cults and literati values usually took the form not of violent campaigns to extirpate heretical doctrines but instead of a quiet contest over control of symbolic resources. The Wu-t'ung cult was not extirpated, it was re-defined. The stove god was not banished from households, but given a changed identity. Sacrifices to popular deities were not forbidden, but were modified (for example, "blood sacrifices" came to be less and less frequent), and their objects re-defined (inhuman deities humanized, goddesses changed into gods). Obviously there were persecutions, most commonly when popular religious beliefs began to have political implications. The fundamental concern of educated reformers was with ethics, not theology, that is to say with behavior, not doctrine. Given all this, it is hardly surprising that elite efforts to purify popular religion so often took the forms described in this book: cooptation, not extirpation; modification rather than prohibition; and the use of popular entertainment genres. Conversion was not the goal; reform was sufficient.

This volume grew out of a 1990 conference organized under the aegis of the Chinese Popular Culture Project and sponsored by the Joint Committee on Chinese Studies of the American Council of Learned Societies and the Social Science Research Council, with funds provided by the National Endowment for the Humanities and the Andrew W. Mellon Foundation. The CPCP was at that time supported by grants from NEH, the Rockefeller Foundation, the JCCS, and the University of California at Berkeley. The indispensable support of these institutions is acknowledged with gratitude. Publication was delayed because of the need to complete work on *Domesticated Deities and Auspicious Emblems: The Iconography of Everyday Life in Village China*[5] while Professor Po Sung-nien, whose collection was the basis of the book, was still in this country. I would like to thank the authors for their patience, and the participants in the original conference, both paper writers and commentators, for their valuable contributions. Special thanks are due to Jason Parker of the ACLS, whose calm competence and good judgment make him a pleasure to work with, and to his assistant, Louise Medby, who combines efficiency and tact in equal measure.

D. J.

---

[5]Published by the Chinese Popular Culture Project in 1992.

*Ritual and Scripture
in Chinese
Popular Religion*

Rituals and
Scriptures
of the
Stove Cult

ROBERT L. CHARD

*T*he New Year is unquestionably the greatest of all Chinese popular festivals. Taken in its entirety, it is an enormous topic of investigation, leading from ancient state rituals to the vast wealth of living practice, folklore, and art preserved in most parts of the Chinese world today. The modern festival includes an elaborate schedule of events—family reunion, feasting, rites of cleansing and renewal, observances to ancestors and other deities—spreading over two weeks and more. It is an occasion of particular importance in the context of Chinese popular religion, specifically for those cults observed within the household. The present study is concerned with one of these cults, one that forms a distinctive feature of the traditional New Year rituals throughout China: the observances to the god of the stove.[1]

---

[1]For a more comprehensive account of popular religion in the New Year festival, citing many previous studies, see the chapter "The Annual Apocalypse" in Stephan Feuchtwang, *The Imperial Metaphor: Popular Religion in China* (London: Routledge, 1992), pp. 25–60.

The best general accounts of the stove god and stove cult are: Yang K'un 楊堃, "Tsao shen k'ao 竈神考," *Han Hiue* 漢學 1 (1944), pp. 108–168; Tsuda Sōkichi 津田左右吉, "Shina no minkan-shinkō ni okeru sōjin シナの民間信仰における竈神," *Tōyō Gakuhō* 32 (1949), pp. 127–58; and Kubo Noritada 窪德忠, *Okinawa no shūzoku to shinkō: Chūgoku to no hikaku kenkyū* 沖繩の習俗と信仰——中國との比較研究 (Tokyo: Tōkyō Daigaku Shuppankai, 1971), pp. 313–79. See also Chard, "Master of the Family: History and Development of the Chinese Cult to the Stove" (Diss., University of California, Berkeley, 1990), which will form the basis of a forthcoming book on all aspects of the stove deity and stove cult.

Religious observances to the stove god are found in two sharply contrasting spheres. One is the real cult as practiced in most homes until quite recently, in which various observances are made to a paper image maintained in the kitchen. The high point in this cult is the New Year, when the image is burned and later replaced in two rites that vary little in their basic form through most of China. Alongside this is a tradition of scriptures and moral tracts associated with the stove god going back at least to the early Ming period, if not much earlier. Such texts always contain ritual instructions for the worship of the stove god: taboos guarding the sanctity of the stove from such things as noise and filth, a schedule of regular offerings, and invocations of atonement to be recited in times of trouble. Significantly, New Year observances are not mentioned in the majority of these works. A comparison of the nature of the rituals prescribed in the texts and the popular New Year observances reveals a fundamental difference in attitude, a demand for sincere, constant observance on the one hand, and the reality of an annual ceremony, celebrated widely but with little reverence, on the other.

POPULAR NEW YEAR OBSERVANCES TO THE STOVE

The stove god in China seems to have existed since very early times. Stove or hearth deities are found throughout Asia, and some scholars have tried to show that the form of the graph *tsao* ('stove') proves the existence of a frog or toad deity in "primitive" society.[2] Ritual observances to the stove

---

A substantial portion of the current study is based on research conducted in China between 1986 and 1988, supported by the Committee for Scholarly Communication with the People's Republic of China. Most of this research was documentary. It was supplemented by informal interviews with Chinese informants, but this should not be regarded as systematic fieldwork in any sense.

[2] For accounts of the stove god elsewhere in Asia see Kin Kyōkei (Kim Hyŏgyong) 金孝敬, Sōjin ni kan-suru shinkō 竈神に關する信仰," *Minzokugaku Kenkyū* I.I (1935), pp. 138–40 (Japan) and 140–43 (Korea); Ofuji Tokihiko 大藤時彦, "Kamado-gami かまど神," in *Sekai dai hyakka jiten* 世界大百科事典 (Tokyo: Heibonsha, 1972), vol. 6, pp. 262–63 (Japan); R. A. Stein, "La Légende du foyer dans la monde chinoise," in Jean Pouillon and Pierre Maranda, eds., *Échanges et communications: mélanges offerts à Claude Lévi-Strauss à l'occasion de son 60ème anniversaire* (The Hague: Mouton, 1970), pp. 1280–1305 (Vietnam and Tibet); Kubo, *Okinawa no shūzoku to shinkō*, p. 343 (Mongolia). For the frog or toad see Yang K'un, "Tsao shen k'ao," pp. 110–19, though the evidence cited therein is not particularly convincing.

are first documented in the *Lun yü*, and later as one of the "Five Sacrificial Cults" (*wu ssu*) or "Seven Sacrificial Cults" (*ch'i ssu*) in the *Li chi* and other ritual texts, but these sources provide little detail.[3] The *Chuang-tzu* and *Shih chi* mention a stove "ghost" (*kuei*) of uncertain gender in the teachings of occult specialists (*fang shih*) in the state of Ch'i.[4] Esoteric sources of the medieval period describe the "stove ghost" as a malign entity that causes disease, or a frightening figure with unbound hair who emerges from the stove at night, bringing death to those who see it. Those with the proper knowledge can subdue this entity, and harness it to exorcise and protect the home.[5]

More direct antecedents of the modern popular cult may be seen in a Han period story of one Yin Tzu-fang, a man of the first century B.C., ancestor of the Yin family of Nan-yang, powerful in later Han. This story must have been widely known, as it is reproduced in several sources: the *Feng-su t'ung yi*, *Hou Han shu*, the *Sou shen chi* of Kan Pao, Tu Kung-chan's commentary to the *Ching Ch'u sui shih chi*, the *Yü chu pao tien*, the *Yi wen lei chü*, and the *Ch'u hsueh chi*.[6] The following version is from the *Feng-su t'ung yi* of Ying Shao (died between A.D. 196 and 220):

> The *Records of Han* (*Han chi*) says: "Yin Tzu-fang of Nan-yang amassed a store of kind deeds and was fond of charity; he also took delight in making offerings to the stove. On the *La* day[7] as he cooked at dawn, the god of the stove appeared to him. He made repeated obeisance to receive his good for-

---

[3]*Lun yü*, *Shih-san Ching chu-shu* ed. (Shanghai: Shang-wu yin-shu-kuan, 1935) 3.7b; discussed in Yang K'un, "Tsao shen k'ao," pp. 122–28, and Tsuda Sōkichi, "Shina no minkan-shinkō ni okeru sōjin," pp. 138–41. For the *wu ssu* 五祀 and *ch'i ssu* 七祀 see *Li chi* (*Shih-san ching chu-shu*) 46.12b–13a (*Chi fa* 祭法 chapter), and the *Yueh ling* 月令 in the *Lü shih ch'un ch'iu* (*Chu-tzu chi-ch'eng* ed., Peking: Chung-hua shu-chü, 1954) 4.34 and *Li chi* 15.18b.
[4]See *Chuang-tzu chi shih* (*Chu-tzu chi-ch'eng* ed.) 19.286–87, and *Shih chi* (Peking: Chung-hua shu-chü, 1972) 12.458, 28.1387.
[5]Sources that describe a demonic stove deity include the lost *Tsa wu-hsing shu* 雜五行書 quoted in *Yi wen lei chü* 藝文類聚 (Shanghai: Shanghai ku-chi ch'u-pan shê, 1985) 80.1375, and *Teng chen yin chüeh* 登眞隱訣, *Cheng-t'ung Tao tsang* 正統道藏 (Shanghai: Shang-wu yin-shu-kuan, 1923–1926), HY 421 (vol. 193), 17a–b.
[6]*Feng-su t'ung yi chiao chu* 風俗通義校注 (Peking: Chung-hua shu-chü, 1981) 8.360–61; *Hou Han shu* (Peking: Chung-hua shu-chü, 1965) 32.1133; *Sou shen chi* 搜神記 (Peking: Chung-hua shu-chü, 1979) 4.54; Moriya Mitsuo 守屋美都雄, *Chūgoku ko-saijiki no kenkyū* 中國古歲時記の研究 (Tokyo: Teikoku shoin, 1963), p. 367; *Yü chu pao tien* 玉燭寶典 (*Ku-yi ts'ung-shu* 古逸叢書, ed. of 1884), vol. 29, 12.17a; *Yi wen lei chü* 80.1374; and *Ch'u hsueh chi* 初學記 (Peking: Chung-hua shu-chü, 1985), vol. 1, 4.85.
[7]In Han times, according to the *Shuo wen chieh tzu*, the *La* day was the third day with the

tune.[8] He had a brown sheep at that time, and offered it in sacrifice.[9] His grandson [Yin] Shih held the office of Bearer of the Gilded Mace (*chih chin wu*), and was enfeoffed as Marquis of Yuan-lu. [Yin] Hsing was Commandant of the Guard (*wei wei*), and Marquis of T'ung-yang. Their family in all produced two marquises and several tens of Shepherds and Protectors. [Yin Tzu-fang's] descendants regularly sacrificed a brown sheep to the god of the stove on the *La* day."[10]

This story most likely derives from Yin family legend, but does not reveal whether these year-end sacrifices were peculiar to them or a custom widespread in their native area.

One of the most characteristic attributes of the modern stove god appears first in the *Pao p'u tzu* of Ko Hung (A.D. 283–343), quite possibly based on Han dynasty sources. The following is part of a discussion on the spirits responsible for watching over the actions of mortals: "Also, on the last day of the month, the god of the stove ascends to Heaven and reports on man's transgressions. For major ones a Period (*chi*) is taken away [from one's allotted life span]; a Period is three hundred days. For minor ones, a Counter (*suan*) is taken away; a Counter is three days."[11] Transgressions that merit such punishment include killing or injuring men and animals, dishonesty and deceit, and insulting gods and holy men. Also included is "stepping on [or "straddling"] the stove and well" (*k'ua ching tsao*), an act of disrespect quite like those prohibited in later texts and in modern popular belief. In addition, early stove taboos appear in the pre-T'ang *Tsa wu hsing shu*, which warns of disastrous consequences if chicken feathers and dog bones are burned in the stove. The *Tsa wu hsing shu* also advises sacrificing a pig's head or a chicken on days with particular stem-branch character combinations, saying that this will bring financial success or general good fortune.[12]

---

cyclical character *hsu* 戌 after the winter solstice; see Derk Bodde, *Festivals in Classical China* (Princeton: Princeton University Press, 1975), pp. 51–52.

[8]Following the suggestion of the modern commentator Wang Li-ch'i 王利器 that *shou shen* 受神 should be read as *shou fu* 受福; *Feng-su t'ung yi chiao chu* 8.363, note 6.

[9]"Brown sheep" (*huang yang* 黃羊) is understood by some commentators as being a kind of dog; see *Feng-su t'ung yi chiao chu* 8.363, note 7.

[10]*Feng-su t'ung yi chiao chu* 8.360–1.

[11]*Pao-p'u-tzu* 抱朴子 (*Chu-tzu chi-ch'eng* ed.) 6.27 (*Wei chih* 微旨 chapter).

[12]Quoted in *Yi wen lei chü* (cited n. 5), 80.1375.

The sixth-century *Ching Ch'u sui shih chi*, a compendium of popular customs in southern China compiled by Tsung Lin (c. 500–565), records: "On that day [the *La* day, here identified as the eighth day of the twelfth month], people make sacrifices of pork and wine to the stove god."[13] Tu Kung-chan's early-seventh-century commentary quotes the story of Yin Tzu-fang and adds: "This [story] is the reason why the vulgar vie to venerate [the stove god]."[14] The Yin family home of Nan-yang was in Ching-chou, part of the area covered by the *Ching Ch'u sui shih chi*; the legend might have inspired the popular stove cult, as Tu says, or the Yin family cult itself might simply have been a well-known example of a cult already widespread in much earlier times. Nothing is said about the god's reports to the celestial authorities, though given the testimony of Ko Hung, another southerner, this cannot be ruled out. Certainly the story of Yin Tzu-fang makes it clear that the sacrifices were thought to bring good fortune, just as the New Year observances are today.

Sources from the T'ang dynasty suggest further development and increased activity in the stove cult. The ninth-century *Yu-yang tsa tsu* has a fairly detailed entry describing the god's origin, deities subordinate to him, and his monthly reports to Heaven. It also mentions reports to Heaven on the day *chi ch'ou* in every cycle of sixty, and advises sacrifices on these days to ensure good fortune.[15] New titles for the god appear in various T'ang sources: "Lord of the Stove" (*Tsao Chün*), "King of the Stove" (*Tsao Wang*), and "Overseer of Destiny" (*Ssu-ming*), suggestive of the god's increased importance.[16] Evidence for an active popular cult in the south comes in an essay titled "Explication on Sacrifices to the Stove" (*Ssu tsao*

[13] Moriya Mitsuo, *Chūgoku ko-saijiki no kenkyū* (cited n. 6), p. 366.

[14] Ibid., p. 367.

[15] *Yu-yang tsa tsu* 酉陽雜俎 (*Ts'ung-shu chi-ch'eng* ed., Shanghai: Shang-wu yin-shu-kuan, 1936) 14.104.

[16] *Tsao Chün* already occurs in the *Tsa wu hsing shu*, as quoted in *Yi wen lei chü* 80.1375. *Tsao Wang* appears in T'ang poems titled *Ching t'ing tz'u* 鏡聽詞 ("Canto on Listening with a Mirror"), which describe a form of popular divination with a mirror and invocation of the stove god, used by lonely women seeking news of absent husbands at the New Year; see samples by Wang Chien 王健 (late eighth and early ninth centuries) and Li K'uo 李廓 (early ninth century) in *Ch'üan T'ang shi* 全唐詩 (Peking: Chung-hua shu-chü, 1985) 298.3386 and 479.5457 respectively. *Ssu-ming Tsao Chün* appears in *Cheng yi fa wen hsiu chen yao chih* 正一法文修眞要旨, *Cheng-t'ung Tao tsang* (cited n. 5), HY 1260 (vol. 1003) 19b–20a. *Ssu-ming* also appears in the *Nien-hsia sui-shih-chi* 輦下歲時記, which will be covered in greater detail below.

chieh) by the famed recluse Lu Kuei-meng (died c. 880), in which he refutes the notion that sacrifices made to the stove god will bring good fortune. The relevant part of the passage runs as follows:

> It is also said, "The stove ghost (*tsao kuei*) records at fixed times the merits and faults of men, and ascends to report them to Heaven. One should sacrifice to it in order to make supplication for good fortune" (*tang ssu chih yi ch'i fu hsiang*). This is of recent derivation, from the words of Gentlemen of Techniques (*fang shih*) in the time of Emperor Wu [of the Han]. If one actually practices this, is it not an example of confusion? If I follow the way of a gentleman (*chün-tzu*), supporting the aged with respect, nurturing the young with kindness, being cold when others are cold, being sated [only] when others are sated; [showing] grief in bereavement, and respect when making sacrificial offerings; restricting myself by not forgetting the rites, harmonizing my mind by not forgetting music; not cheating others even in a darkened room, and not being ashamed even if the house is shabby; then even if I make not a single observance to the stove during a year, will [the stove god] speak deceptively of me? If I practice the way of a petty man, and always do the opposite of the actions of a gentleman; if father and son, older and younger brother, and husband and wife maintain a single stove so as to get rice gruel into their mouths (*hu k'ou*), but arrogate all advantage to themselves and practice deception, esteem treachery, and become hardened in wrongdoing, then even if I make a hundred observances to the stove during a year, will [the god] be partial toward me?[17]

Lu does not specify who was responsible for these beliefs in his own time, but it seems unlikely that he would have been moved to write the piece unless they were widespread. His biography in the *Hsin T'ang shu* identifies him as a native of Ch'ang-chou (southeast of modern Soochow), and says that he spent most of his life living and wandering through the Lower Yangtze area.[18] The earlier *Ching Ch'u sui shih chi* describes popular offerings to the stove in the south, and as will be seen below, there are particularly detailed descriptions of popular observances to the stove deity in the Lower Yangtze region during the twelfth century, all of which suggests that Lu witnessed a thriving popular cult in the late T'ang. The senti-

[17]*Ch'üan T'ang wen* 全唐文 (1814 ed., rpt. Taipei: Hui-wen shu-chü, 1961) 801.10a–b.
[18]*Hsin T'ang shu* 新唐書 (Peking: Chung-hua shu-chü, 1975) 196.5612–13.

ments he expresses are remarkably similar to those of educated men in later times.

Popular year-end observances to the stove appear in a fragment from a lost text called the *Nien hsia sui shih chi*, a compendium of customs in the T'ang capital Ch'ang-an: "On New Year's Eve the people of the capital ask Buddhist monks to read sutras (*k'an ching*), and prepare wine and fruit to send off the god. They attach stove god images (*tsao ma*) above the stove, and rub wine dregs (*chiu tsao*) on the stove door. They call this 'intoxicating the Overseer of Destiny' (*tsui Ssu-ming*). At night they burn a lamp inside the stove, calling it 'illuminating the wasting consumption' (*chao hsü hao*)."[19]

This passage contains what appears to be the earliest surviving reference to the image of the god. It is not described in detail, but it is called a *tsao ma*, one of the terms applied to the image of modern times, and the verb "attach" or "adhere" (*t'ieh*) suggests that it was of paper. The date of the *Nien-hsia sui shih chi* is unknown; the latest date mentioned in the few fragments preserved in the *Shuo fu* is in the K'ai-yuan reign period (713–741), which might suggest that the passage on the stove observance dates from the mid-T'ang. Unfortunately a similarly worded passage appears in the Sung-period *Tung-ching meng hua lu* (see below), and one cannot be absolutely certain about the authenticity of this fragment. Still, it is not implausible that a New Year observance quite like that of modern times was being observed in the T'ang capital at approximately the time that Lu Kuei-meng wrote his essay.

Descriptions of the popular stove cult in Sung times give far greater detail than is available for earlier periods, and reveal New Year stove observances strikingly similar to those of modern times. The earliest account is in the *Tung-ching meng hua lu* (compiled 1147), a description of daily life in Kaifeng during the Northern Sung: "The twenty-fourth day of the twelfth month is the 'Meeting of the Years' (*chiao nien*). The people of the capital ask Buddhist monks and Taoist priests to read scriptures, and prepare incense, tea, and wine to send off the god. They burn effigies of the entire family and paper money.[20] They attach stove god images (*tsao ma*) above

---

[19]Moriya, *Chūgoku ko-saijiki no kenkyū* (cited n. 6), p. 461 (taken from *Shuo fu* 說郛).

[20]"Effigies" is *t'i tai* 替代, a term used elsewhere to refer to the paper image of the god. It is

the stove, and rub wine dregs on the stove door. They call this 'intoxicating the Overseer of Destiny.' "[21] The twenty-fourth day of the twelfth month is the date for the modern sendoff ceremony in much of China.

The late Southern Sung *Meng liang lu* gives a more detailed account of the New Year in the capital of Lin-an (Hangchow): "On the twenty-fourth day, everyone, whether poor or rich, prepares vegetable foods, malt sugar (*hsing*), and beans to sacrifice to the stove. On this day in the markets, streets, and squares, people hawk five-colored rice snacks, flowery confections, tooth-gumming malt candy (*chiao ya hsing*), and winnowing-basket beans.[22] Their cries boil like a cauldron."[23] Further on in the same passage we are told that "as the day of the [New] Year approaches, a hundred goods appear in the shops and on the mats. They paint gate gods, peachwood charms, and welcoming plaques. The paper-image shops (*chih ma p'u*) print images of Chung K'uei, the Wealth [God], and 'Turning Head' images,[24] and give them to their major customers."[25]

The first passage stresses the widespread observance of the New Year ritual to the stove across the social spectrum, and mentions the sticky malt-sugar candy widely used in the modern cult. The second passage, though it does not include the stove god, proves the existence of specialized purveyors and printers of paper images. It is clear that these early New Year prints were an important part of the New Year festival, and perhaps of year-round popular cults as well.

Perhaps the most valuable accounts of popular year-end observances to the stove god during the Southern Sung were left by the noted writer and statesman Fan Ch'eng-ta (1126–1207). Fan was a native of Wu County,

---

possible that the text is garbled at this point, and should read "the entire family burns the effigy [of the god] and paper money."

[21] *Tung-ching meng hua lu wai ssu chung* 東京夢華錄外四種 (Shanghai: Ku-tien wen-hsueh ch'u-pan shê, 1957) 10.61.

[22] *Chi tou* 箕豆. I have been unable to identify this.

[23] *Tung-ching meng hua lu wai ssu chung, Meng liang lu* 夢粱錄 6.181.

[24] *Hui t'ou ma* 回頭馬. The *Tung-ching meng hua lu* mentions *hui t'ou lu ma* 回頭鹿馬; see *Tung-ching meng hua lu wai ssu chung*, p. 61. The term is reminiscent of the custom of "burning returning incense" (*shao hui t'ou hsiang* 燒回頭香) described by Nagao Ryūzō. This involved going around to different temples to make offerings and burn incense, then "returning" to burn incense to one's own household deities, including the stove god, to report that fact. See Nagao Ryūzō 永尾龍造, *Shina minzoku shi* 支那民俗志 (Tokyo: Shina Minzoku Kankōkai 支那民俗刊行會, 1940), vol. 1, p. 200.

[25] *Tung-ching meng hua lu wai ssu chung, Meng liang lu* 6.181.

west of modern Soochow. He is the author of the *Wu chün chih*, an early
local history of the Wu area that contains a brief notice of sacrifices to the
stove god on the twenty-fourth day of the twelfth month, which stresses
in particular that women were not permitted to participate.[26] Much greater
detail appears in one of Fan's literary works, a set of verses titled "Music
Treasury Poems on Villages and Fields during the *La*-month" (*La yueh
ts'un t'ien yueh fu*). A preface says: "The third [in the set] is the 'Canto on
Sacrificing to the Stove' (*Chi tsao tz'u*). On the night of the twenty-fourth
day of the *La*-month, [people] make offerings to the stove. They explain
this by saying that on the next day the stove god pays court in Heaven to
report on the affairs of the entire year, thus they pray to him in advance of
this time."[27] The poem reads:

> Of old it has been transmitted that on the twenty-fourth of the *La*-month,
> The Lord of the Stove pays court in Heaven to speak of [the family's] affairs.
> On a cloud chariot with horses of wind he has little reluctance to leave,
> [So] the family makes rich ceremonial offerings to him in cups and on plates.
> A pig's head is [cooked] tender and hot, twin fish are fresh;
> Bean paste is sweet and soft in the stuffed rice-flour dumplings (*fen erh t'uan*).
> The boys ladle out offerings, the girls stay away;
> They pour libations of wine and burn money, and the Lord of the Stove
>   is delighted.
> "If the bonded maidservants bicker and contend, do not listen, Lord;
> If cats and dogs touch and foul the stove, do not be angry, Lord.
> We send you, Lord, drunk and sated, to mount to Heaven's gate,
> If the ladle [or "handle"] is long or short, speak no more of it;
> We beg you to obtain benefit and a profitable market (*li shih*) and return to
>   divide it [among us]!"[28]

The first line, "Of old it has been transmitted . . ." (*ku ch'uan*), takes on
added significance in the light of Lu Kuei-meng's comments on stove
observances in a nearby locale three centuries previously. The details given
in this account show remarkable similarities to the modern New Year observance, except that there is no mention of sticky confections, and the
preponderance of meat offerings is now unusual in most areas. Fan's ren-

[26] *Wu-chün chih* 吳郡志 (Kiangsu: Kiangsu ku-chi ch'u-pan shê, 1986) 2.14.
[27] *Fan Shih-hu chi* 范石湖集 (Peking: Chung-hua shu-chü, 1962) 30.409.
[28] Ibid., 30.410–11.

dition of the invocation to the god, if it has any relation to what was actually said, would suggest that the stove taboos were known in popular belief at this time. The most important thing not mentioned is the paper image, though this does not necessarily mean it was not used.

Further accounts of the stove cult appear in local histories and other sources of the Yuan and Ming periods, but these add nothing of significance not already found in the Sung, and are too sparse to give any sense of the cult's spread. Ch'ing-period histories record the New Year stove offerings with far greater frequency, and prove their near-universal distribution throughout China.[29] It is difficult to know whether this is due merely to a change in the nature of the records kept, or whether there was a sudden upsurge in the popularity of the cult.

Descriptions of the stove cult in late Ch'ing and modern times give an enormous wealth of detail not found in earlier sources. The god is most commonly known as "Grandfather King of the Stove" (*Tsao Wang Yeh*) or "Lord of the Stove" (*Tsao Chün*). Numerous Western and Japanese accounts of Chinese popular customs describe him as one of the most ubiquitous of household gods, and even now he survives in many rural areas.[30] In Western studies he is frequently called the "Kitchen God," but this is misleading. *Tsao* signifies "stove," in particular the traditional stove, a large box-like structure built of mud, bricks, or tiles, and it is clear that the deity was thought to dwell within it, or at least to be directly associated with it.[31] The stove scriptures specify detailed lists of taboos against noise,

[29]For the accounts of the stove god in the local histories see Chard, "Master of the Family" (cited n. 1), pp. 103–7 (Yuan and Ming) and 10–46 (Ch'ing).

[30]For accounts of the god in recent times see Justus Doolittle, *Social Life of the Chinese* (New York: Harper & Brothers, 1867), vol. 2, pp. 74, 75, 81–85, 330; Lewis Hodous, *Folkways in China* (London: Arthur Probsthain, 1929), pp. 214–19; Clarence Day, "Studying the Kitchen God," *Chinese Recorder* 57 (1926), pp. 791–96; Juliet Bredon and Igor Mitrophanov, *The Moon Year* (rpt. New York: Paragon Books, 1966), pp. 74–76; Nagao Ryūzō, *Shina minzoku shi*, vol. 1, pp. 81–91; Henri Maspero, *Taoism and Chinese Religion*, Frank A. Kierman, tr. (Amherst: University of Massachusetts Press, 1981), pp. 112–13; Wolfram Eberhard, *Chinese Festivals* (New York: Henry Schuman, 1952), pp. 17–26; V. R. Burkhardt, *Chinese Creeds and Customs* (Hong Kong: South China Morning Post, 1953), vol. 1, pp. 75–76, vol. 2, pp. 1 and 52; and Kubo Noritada, *Okinawa no shūzoku to shinkō* (cited n. 1), pp. 353–76. For regions in which the god is still to be found, see Chard, "Master of the Family," p. 51.

[31]In some cases food offerings to the god were placed on top of the stove, smeared onto the door, or cast into the flames inside; see Doolittle, *Social Life of the Chinese*, vol. 2, p. 84; *Wu-*

filth, clutter, nakedness, and licentious behavior near the stove, lest the deity be offended, and in some places an awareness of these rules seems to have existed in the popular cult as well.[32]

The primary function of the stove god is to observe and record the merits and misdeeds of the family. According to popular belief, he has direct access to the supreme monarch of Heaven, the Jade Thearch (*Yü Huang Ta Ti*), and ascends at the end of each year to report all that he has seen and heard. Rewards and punishments are then dispensed by the celestial authorities, or the stove god himself. In this way the deity holds considerable authority over the fate of each family member, a belief reflected in certain of his titles, such as "Overseer of Destiny of the Eastern Kitchen" (*Tung Ch'u Ssu-ming*), i.e. the fate-controller who rules the kitchen, and "Master of the Entire Family" (*Yi chia chih chu*). He is not just the god of the stove, or of the kitchen, but of the household as a whole.

The stove cult is second only to the ancestral cult within domestic observance, and, as several anthropologists have observed, it frequently delineates a smaller group, specifically the most basic family unit.[33] The territory or space governed by the stove god would in administrative terms coincide more or less with a "household" (*hu*). Households headed by different brothers might share an ancestor cult but maintain separate stove

---

hu hsien chih 蕪湖縣志, *Chung-kuo fang-chih ts'ung-shu* 中國方志叢書 (Taipei: Ch'eng-wen ch'u-pan shê, 1970–), Anhwei 715 (ed. of 1807) 1.21a (unless otherwise noted, all citations of local histories will be to the Ch'eng-wen reprint series, citing province, number in the series, and the date of the edition reprinted); *Nan-ch'ang hsien chih* 南昌縣志 (Kiangsi 103, rpt. ed. of 1935) 56.8a; and *Wan hsien chih* 萬縣志 (Szechuan 379, ed. of 1866) 12.5b. There are also instances of a single kitchen shared by two families with two stoves and two stove gods; see Maurice Freedman, "Ritual Aspects of Chinese Kinship and Marriage," in Freedman ed., *Family and Kinship in Chinese Society* (Stanford: Stanford University Press, 1970), p. 165. The stove god is frequently abandoned when the large traditional stove is replaced with the small gas-burning ranges in common use today; see Liu Chih-wan 劉枝萬 (Ryū Shiman), *Chūgoku dōkyō no matsuri to shinkō* 中國道教の祭りと信仰 (Tokyo: Ofūsha, 1983), vol. 1, p. 637.

[32]The stove taboos in the scriptures will be discussed below. For their counterpart in popular belief, see Fei Hsiao-tung, *Peasant Life in China: A Field Study of Country Life in the Yangtze Valley* (London: George Routledge & Sons, 1939), p. 100, and Kubo Noritada, *Okinawa no shūzoku*, pp. 346–47 and 365–67.

[33]See Emily Martin Ahern, *The Cult of the Dead in a Chinese Village* (Stanford: Stanford University Press, 1973), p. 95, and Maurice Freedman, "Ritual Aspects of Chinese Kinship and Marriage," pp. 164–65. Here and below I have benefited from conversations with John Lagerwey and Michael Szonyi.

gods.[34] Setting up a stove establishes the independence of a family; to "divide stoves" (*fen tsao*) entails the separation of a household and the division of property. Occasionally the role of household god so overwhelms that of stove god that the deity is kept in the main hall with the ancestors.[35]

Families who maintain the stove cult keep a paper image of the god (called a *chih ma* or *tsao ma*) which is the focus for all observances to him.[36] This is mounted in the kitchen, in a special niche or on the wall near the stove. Sometimes the niche is made to look like a small altar, with a railing in front and roof above; often there is at least a small shelf or ledge below the image for incense offerings.[37] At its simplest, it is not an image at all, but just a piece of paper with the names or titles of the god.[38] The image itself varies somewhat from region to region. In the north it is larger and more elaborate, with the god's wife, called "Grandmother King of the Stove" (*Tsao Wang Nai-nai*), a calendar, various officials and other figures in attendance, and usually a chicken and a dog. In other areas, particularly the middle Yangtze region and the southwest, the god is accompanied by two female figures, said to be the god's principal wife and concubine. In the southeast the god is alone, often with five or six children grouped under him, surrounded by various symbols of wealth and fecundity, and the words "Determining Good Fortune" (*ting fu*) or "Palace Where Good Fortune is Determined" (*ting fu kung*) above. On the image, or on paper scrolls above and to either side, are displayed various attributes, descriptions, and titles of the god, such as "Overseer of Destiny of the Eastern Kitchen," "Master of the Entire Family," "Star of Heaven, the god Lord of the Stove" (*T'ien Hsing Tsao Chün Shen*), and, the most common of all, "Ascend to Heaven and Speak of Good Things,/ Descend to

[34]See Arthur Wolf, "Gods, Ghosts, and Ancestors," in Arthur Wolf, ed., *Religion and Ritual in Chinese Society*, p. 133, and Freedman, "Ritual Aspects," p. 165.

[35]See *Wan-yuan hsien chih* 萬源縣志 (Szechuan 363, ed. of 1934) 5.37b, and Ahern, *The Cult of the Dead*, pp. 95–96.

[36]Photographs of the altar appear in Hodous, *Folkways in China*, facing p. 114, and V. R. Burkhardt, *Chinese Creeds and Customs*, vol. 1, p. 75 (both cited n. 30).

[37]For a general study of New Year prints see Po Sung-nien and David Johnson, *Domesticated Deities and Auspicious Emblems: The Iconography of Everyday Life in Village China*, Publications of the Chinese Popular Culture Project 2 (Berkeley: Chinese Popular Culture Project, 1992), especially the section on the stove god on pp. 23–59.

[38]See the illustration in Kubo, *Okinawa no shūzoku* (cited n. 1), p. 353. See also the descriptions in Doolittle, *Social Life of the Chinese*, vol. 2, p. 82; Bredon and Mitrophanov, *The Moon Year*, p. 75; and Burkhardt, *Chinese Creeds and Customs*, vol. 2, p. 52 (all cited n. 30).

Earth and Preserve Peace and Tranquility" (*shang t'ien yen hao shih / hsia ti pao p'ing-an*), a standard prayer or invocation to the god recalled by almost everyone familiar with the cult in childhood.[39]

The paper image is absolutely crucial to the existence of the popular stove cult. As with any statue or image in Chinese religion, it is seen as the primary manifestation of the god in the human world. Once installed, the image is not only the focus for offerings and other observances, but also a constant reminder of the god's presence to those who spend time in the kitchen, the women of the household. Maurice Freedman has argued that the stove cult was the embodiment of the male authority within the family, in which case the tangible presence of the image would enforce domestic discipline in the women's sphere of activity, preventing disruptive strife and insubordination.[40] The iconography of the image and the inscriptions are a sort of shorthand for important items of belief, in particular the divinity of the god, his function as spirit inspector, and the promise of domestic prosperity. Illiteracy is no barrier to these messages. Even the written scrolls are brief, and within any given locality largely standardized; most of those who cannot read will know what they say.

Many families make daily or twice-monthly incense offerings to the stove god's image, and larger food offerings on days of particular importance during the year,[41] but the most important observances are those

---

[39]See the images reproduced in Po and Johnson, *Domesticated Deities and Auspicious Emblems*, pp. 26–59; for the southeastern *ting fu* images see the descriptions and illustrations in Chard, "Master of the Family" (cited n. 1), pp. 53–72, based on images and inscriptions collected in contemporary mainland China.

[40]For Freedman's argument see "Ritual Aspects of Chinese Kinship and Marriage" (cited n. 31), p. 183. The subordination of the daughter-in-law to her husband's family, represented in the person of the stove god, appears in folktales and popular performance genres; rebellion against the husband and/or husband's family is expressed in acts of violence against the deity. Stove god moral tracts lay great stress on the docility and obedience of the daughter-in-law, enforced by the god's authority. See Chard, "Folktales on the God of the Stove," *Chinese Studies* 8 (1990), pp. 174–78, and "Master of the Family," pp. 326–29.

[41]For the daily offerings see Arthur Wolf, "Gods, Ghosts, and Ancestors" (cited n. 34), p. 133, and Doolittle, *Social Life of the Chinese*, vol. 2, p. 81. For the twice-monthly observances see Maspero, *Taoism and Chinese Religion* (cited n. 30), p. 113; Doolittle, vol. 2, p. 81; DuBose, *The Dragon, Image, and Demon, or, the Three Religions of China, Confucianism, Buddhism, and Taoism* (London: S. W. Partridge, 1886), p. 323; *Yung-chou-fu chih* 永州府志 (Hunan 298, ed. of 1828) 5.41b; Kubo, *Okinawa no shūzoku*, p. 360, and Fei Hsiao-tung, *Peasant Life in China* (cited n. 32), p. 99. Fei also gives a chart of important activities which shows other days when the stove god is worshipped; see Fei, pp. 152–53.

performed at the New Year, the sendoff before the god's ascent to Heaven, and the welcome on his return.

The rite of propitiation performed to the stove god before his ascent is usually called "Seeing Off the Stove [God]" (*sung tsao*). It takes place either on the twenty-third or twenty-fourth day of the twelfth month, depending on the area, and ensures that the deity does not submit an unfavorable report to the celestial authorities. This is unquestionably the single most important observance of the stove cult, and the one most frequently recorded in local histories and other sources on popular customs. The day on which it takes place is in many places called "Small New Year's Eve" (*hsiao nien, hsiao nien yeh,* or *hsiao ch'u*), a lesser counterpart of New Year's Eve proper, and it usually marks the beginning of the New Year festival period as a whole.[42] The other main event of the day is a thorough cleaning of the house, a custom still observed in places where the stove cult has long been abandoned.[43]

The mood surrounding the sendoff ceremony presents something of a paradox. On the one hand, the propitiation of the god is an important matter, with implications for the family's fortunes during the upcoming year. This is evident from the fact that it used to be so widespread, and some sources emphasize that it was performed with great solemnity. But in most cases the occasion seems to have been dominated by an atmosphere of amusement and good humor. As will become evident below, the rite itself was tinged with an element of mischievous deceit. People in China today recall the stove god with a smile, and express surprise that something so quaint or frivolous would be the object of scholarly inquiry. In some respects, though certainly not in all, he might be compared to Santa Claus.

[42]All three of these terms appear with great frequency in the local histories. Examples that suggest a comparison with the New Year proper include: Ch'ang-hai Hsien Chih Pien-chi Wei-yuan-hui 長海縣志編輯委員會, *Ch'ang-hai hsien chih* 長海縣志 (Ch'ang-hai Hsien: Ch'ang-hai Hsien Chih Pien-chi Wei-yuan-hui, 1984), p. 693 ("pass the Little New Year," *kuo hsiao nien* 過小年); *Ling-ling hsien chih* 零陵縣志 (Hunan 309, ed. of 1875) 5.14b ("they call it the Little [New] Year . . . it is somewhat like New Year's Eve"); and the *Tao-chou chih* 道州志 (Hunan 294, ed. of 1877) 10.4a, where the twenty-fourth day is called the "Little [New] Year festival" (*hsiao nien chieh* 小年節), and New Year's Eve the "Big [New] Year festival" (*ta nien chieh* 大年節).

[43]Based on personal observations in Wenchow, Shanghai, and Nanking between 1986 and 1989. See also Kubo, *Okinawa no shūzoku,* pp. 373–74.

The basic form of the sendoff ceremony varies little in most parts of China. Food offerings are set out, usually on a table, and candles and incense lit on the ledge or other space immediately below the image. Various candies and confections are always prominent among the offerings. The head of household leads the family in bowing to the god (*pai*), either standing with sticks of incense held between the hands, or kneeling on the floor.[44] In many places the women are not allowed to participate.[45] A prayer is made to the deity, entreating him to conceal the bad things he has seen, report the good, and bring good fortune on his return. Then the paper image is taken down and burned, the god being thought to ascend to Heaven with the smoke. The sweet offerings almost invariably include something that is soft and sticky: a chewy, jelly-like candy called *hsing*, soft barley, sorghum, or other grain sugar (*yi t'ang*), or glutinous rice cakes (like Japanese *mochi*). In the southeast and elsewhere these are sometimes referred to as "stove candy" (*tsao t'ang*); in many parts of the north the grain sugar is called "candy melons" (*t'ang kua*).[46] These are often smeared directly onto the god's mouth before the image is burned, or onto the door of the stove. They are said to sweeten the god's mood, or, more commonly, to glue his jaws shut and enforce his silence in the presence of the Jade Thearch.[47]

[44]In a reenactment of the sendoff ritual I observed in Ou-hai County 甌海縣 north of Wenchow in 1987, the family members bowed while standing, but other informants both there and elsewhere (Shanghai, Soochow, and Nanking) told me that as children they had been required to kneel.

[45]This point is discussed in Freedman, "Ritual Aspects of Chinese Kinship and Marriage," pp. 173–75, where he cites several other sources in which the same phenomenon is noted. See also Kubo, *Okinawa no shūzoku*, p. 367.

[46]Sweet offerings are documented in Ma Hung-chih 馬宏知, *Nien-chieh ch'ü hua* 年節趣話 (Sian: Shan-hsi jen-min ch'u-pan shê, 1982), p. 124; Ho Ch'i-chang 何錡章, "Tsao shen k'ao yuan 竈神考源," *Ta-lu tsa-chih* 大陸雜志 35.12 (1967), p. 381; Cheng K'ang-min 鄭康民, "Chung-kuo ssu tsao te ch'i-yuan yü fa-chan 中國祀竈的起源與發展," *Tung-fang tsa-chih fu-k'an* 東方雜志復刊 1.8 (1968), p. 56; *T'ai-p'ing fu chih* 太平府志 (Anhwei 236, ed. of 1903) 5.4a; *Wan hsien chih* 萬縣志 (Szechuan 379, ed. of 1866) 12.5b; *Wen-chou chiu su shih-liao* 溫州舊俗史料 (an undated anonymous ms. in two vols. in the Wenchow Municipal Library, probably completed not long after 1949), vol. 1, p. 62 (here it is called "Stove Buddha candy," *tsao fo t'ang* 竈佛糖); Kin Kyōkei (Kim Hyŏgyong), "Sōjin ni kan-suru shinkō" (cited in n. 2), p. 135; *Wei-hai wei chih* 威海衛志 (Shantung 82, rpt. ed. of 1929) 1.10a; and *Yen-an fu chih* 延安府志 (Shensi 294, ed. of 1802) 39.3b.

[47]For examples of the intended effect of the sweet offerings, see *Fang hsien chih* 房縣志 (Hupeh 329, ed. of 1865) 11.7b (causing the god to speak "sweet words," *kan yen* 甘言), and *Chiu-chiang fu chih* 九江府志 (Kiangsi 267, ed. of 1874) 8.3a ("to sweeten the god's

Another ceremony, called "Receiving the Stove [God]" (*chieh tsao* or *ying tsao*), welcomes the god back from his journey to Heaven. This usually takes place on New Year's Eve or early on New Year's Day, though it can come as early as the twenty-sixth day of the twelfth month or as late as the twenty-fourth of the first month.[48] At this time a new paper image of the god is installed, and offerings of food and incense placed before it. Most sources describe this observance in much less detail than the sendoff ceremony, partly because the occasion commands less urgency, and partly because it is only one of many events held on New Year's Eve. The offerings are similar to those made at the sendoff ceremony, except that the tooth-gumming candy is no longer prominent.[49]

This general structure of the New Year stove rites was largely similar through most of China, but actual practice was much embellished with details that varied considerably from region to region. The food offerings in particular differed, depending on local tastes and special foods. In the past the offerings were exclusively vegetarian in the overwhelming majority of places, but in northwest China chickens were sacrificed (in one instance placed live before the god and not killed, however), and in Fukien and Taiwan the deity was treated to meat and alcoholic beverages.[50] The inclusion of certain foodstuffs sometimes had a peculiar significance within the context of local folklore. For example, one Canton source describes sugar cane leaned against the stove to provide the god with a "ladder to Heaven."[51] In one Chekiang village one of the main offerings was steamed

---

mouth," *t'ien shen chih k'ou* 甜神之口). A larger proportion of the sources that explain the sweet offerings say that it is to keep the god from talking; see the citations in note 46.

[48]The twenty-sixth of the twelfth month was reported to me by a woman of about sixty recalling her childhood in a village in central Chekiang. The twenty-fourth of the first month is recorded in the *Ying-shang hsien chih* 潁上縣志 (Anhwei 710, ed. of 1753) 12.12a, though a note in this text says that the custom in the area was changing, with many people now performing the rite on New Year's Eve.

[49]Many local histories say that the welcoming ceremony is "similar" to the sendoff ceremony; see, for example, *Ling-ling hsien chih* 零陵縣志 (Hunan 309, ed. of 1875) 5.14b.

[50]Chickens are mentioned in *Yen-an fu chih* 延安府志 (Shensi 294, ed. of 1802) 39.3b and 5a, *Ching-ning chou chih* 靜寧州志 (Kansu 333, ed. of 1746) 3.12a, *Wu-liang ch'üan chih* 五涼全志 (Kansu 560, ed. of 1749) 2.34a and 3.24b, and *Ya-chou fu chih* 雅州府志 (Sinkiang 28, ed. of 1739) 5.44a. The live chicken is described in *Ling-chou chih* 靈州志 (Ninghsia 4, ed. of 1788) 1.31a. For Fukien offerings see Doolittle, *Social Life of the Chinese* (cited n. 30), vol. 2, pp. 82 and 85; for a detailed list from different parts of Taiwan see Kubo, *Okinawa no shūzoku*, p. 368.

[51]See *Hui-chou fu chih* 惠州府志 (Kwangtung 3, ed. of 1881) 45.5b.

buns (*man-t'ou*) with four red dots to symbolize the fire of the stove; if the dough failed to rise, it was a sign that the god would submit a bad report and that a year of misfortune was in store.[52]

Other aspects of the ritual might also vary. Women were frequently excluded from the sendoff ceremony, but in a few places were in charge of the offerings.[53] In some accounts from Fukien the stove god is only one of "the Hundred Spirits," all the gods with any connection with the household, who are all sent off to Heaven at the same time.[54] There were innumerable variations in procedure. The image might be burned outside the gate, or in an urn next to the table with the food offerings.[55] In many areas a paper palanquin made from a lantern was burned along with the image, sometimes complete with paper bearers; elsewhere a straw horse or a paper boat was provided.[56] Sometimes there was paper money for travel expenses and paper clothing, or even fodder and water for the god's horse.[57] The list of such details is endless; extensive field research into surviving practices and folk memories would be necessary to account for the full range of diversity that occurs on this level. For the purposes of the present study it is sufficient to show that variations existed, and contrast this with the trans-regional standardization that characterized the basic form of the observance.

The most important element in this basic form is the disposition of the

[52]Described by the informant in note 48 above.

[53]*P'u-an chih-li t'ing chih* 普安直隸廳志 (Kweichow 276, ed. of 1884) 4.2b; *Fang hsien chih* 房縣志 (Hupeh 329, ed. of 1865) 11.7a–b; *Chih-li Ho chou chih* 直隸和州志 (Anhwei 720, ed. of 1901) 4.35; and Georg Stenz, *Beiträge zur Volkskunde Süd-Schantungs* (Leipzig: R. Voightländer, 1907), pp. 62–63.

[54]See, for example, the entry in the *T'ing-chou fu chih* 汀州府志 (Fukien, ed. of 1762) 6.8b, and Kubo, *Okinawa no shūzoku*, p. 359.

[55]See, for example, *Ch'ing chia lu* 淸嘉錄 (Kiangsu: Kiangsu jen-min ch'u-pan shê, 1986), 12.216–17 (outside the gate), and Hodous, *Folkways in China* (cited n. 30), p. 217 (in an urn).

[56]See Henri Maspero, *Mythologie asiatique illustrée* (Paris: n.p., 1928), p. 270; Kano Naoki 狩野直喜, "Shina no sōjin ni tsuite 支那の竈神について," *Shinagaku bunsō* 支那學文藪 (rpt. Tokyo: Misuzu Shobō, 1973), p. 83; *Hsia-men chih* 廈門志 (Fukien 80, ed. of 1839) 15.4b; and *P'eng-hu chi lüe* 澎湖記略 (Taiwan 17, ed. of 1771) 7.13b–14a.

[57]For references to travelling money see *Wu-chou fu chih* 梧州府志 (Kwangsi 119, ed. of 1873) 3.6b; *Su-sung hsien chih* 宿松縣志 (Anhwei 671, ed. of 1921) 8.4a; Clarence Day, "Studying the Kitchen God" (cited n. 30), p. 794; Doolittle, *Social Life of the Chinese* (cited n. 30), vol. 2, pp. 82, 83, and 84; and Maspero, *Mythologie asiatique illustrée*, p. 270. For the paper clothing see *Ling hsien chih* 酃縣志 (Hunan 308, ed. of 1872) 7.14a. The offerings to the horse appear in many sources; see, for example, *Ch'ing chia lu*, 12.216–17, Hodous, *Folkways in China*, p. 218, and Doolittle, *Social Life of the Chinese*, vol. 2, p. 83.

paper image. The image, together with orally transmitted lore regarding its use, is the vital core of the popular cult. It has provided a vector for the transmission and perpetuation of cult observances and established a degree of standardization that would not otherwise exist. This standardization can be traced back to the Sung period, and it is striking that the growth of the popular cult, as best as can be determined from the available sources, closely parallels the evolution of printed paper spirit images in China.[58] Detailed descriptions of popular observances to the stove in the Sung dynasty come at approximately the same time as the first appearance of printed images. The dramatic increase in records on the stove cult in local histories of the Ch'ing period follows a time of great growth in the printed *nien-hua* industry during the late Ming.

Both the spread of the cult and the uniformity of certain stove god rituals all across China were almost certainly due to the central role of printed images of the god. The process of transmission might have taken place as follows. A paper image of the stove god was brought to an area where the stove cult did not previously exist (or perhaps existed in very different form) by a returning merchant or other itinerant. Those adopting the cult, persuaded of the god's power to determine domestic prosperity, would see the image as his manifestation in the mortal world, and want to know exactly how it should be used. This knowledge might be acquired either by personal observation or word of mouth. These unwritten instructions on the proper use of the image would be transmitted with it; the more significant points—that the image should be burned on the twenty-fourth or twenty-third day of the twelfth month to send the god on his way, and replaced on New Year's day—would be easily remembered and less likely to vary. Less important details would be more susceptible to alteration as the image was transmitted over great distances or used over a long period of time. This would result in the pattern that actually existed in recent times, rituals universal in basic outline but varied in detail.

It should be stressed that the image and the way it is used are a primary characteristic of the popular cult, as distinct from the ritual practices pre-

---

[58]See Po and Johnson, *Domesticated Deities and Auspicious Emblems* (cited n. 37), p. 12. Here and below I have also benefited from conversations with Po Sung-nien concerning his research on the history of printed *nien-hua* in China.

scribed in the stove god texts, where the image is never mentioned. Many stove texts were created and circulated with the intent of standardizing popular rituals to the stove, but the rituals they prescribe are in fact strikingly different in form and attitude from the New Year observances, and seem to have had little or no effect on actual practice.

THE STOVE TEXTS

No account of the scriptures of popular religion would be complete without some mention of the texts associated with the stove cult. The tradition of such texts extends as far back as pre-T'ang times, though the earliest surviving specimens are to be found in the *Tao tsang*, probably dating from Sung or early Ming times. More recent stove god texts and appended materials come in many forms: scriptures (*ching*), invocations of atonement (*ch'an*), moral tracts (*shan shu*), "treasure scrolls" (*pao chüan*), invocations or prayers (*pao kao*), and divination slips (*ch'ien*), designed to be used in different ways by householders or ritual specialists, but sharing certain essential features. All propound the belief that the god ascends to Heaven to report on the family's merits and faults, and warn that he should be honored and his precepts obeyed; to this extent the textual teachings agree with popular belief. But beyond this the contrast between the texts and actual practice is striking. Detailed instructions in the scriptures for ritual observances to the stove god rarely include the New Year, a point that reflects the different nature and purpose of the scriptural rituals. The remainder of this study will examine the rituals and practices stipulated in the texts, with the aim of uncovering as much as can be known of their origin, intended function, and actual effect. This will serve to highlight the fundamentally popular nature of the New Year stove observances, and demonstrate to what degree they are at odds with the teachings of the texts.

The *Sui shu* bibliographic treatise records a "Scripture of the Stove" (*Tsao ching*) attributed to Hsiao Kang (Emperor Chien-wen of the Liang dynasty, r. 550–551). This is possibly the same as a "Book of the Stove" (*Tsao shu*), from which a brief sentence giving the names of the stove god and his wife is quoted in the *Yü chu pao tien* of Tu T'ai-ch'ing (died c. 600).[59] The *Sui shu* also lists a "Book on Observances to the Stove" (*Tz'u*

---

[59] *Sui shu* 隨書 (Peking: Chung-hua shu-chü, 1974) 34.1038; *Yü chu pao tien* 玉燭寶典 (*Ku yi ts'ung shu* ed.) 12.17a.

tsao shu), perhaps the same as a "Scripture on Observances to the Stove" (*Tz'u tsao ching*) recorded in the *Chiu T'ang shu*.[60] In the Sung period, a "Yellow Thearch's Scripture of the Divine Stove" (*Huang Ti shen tsao ching*) is listed in the twelfth-century *T'ung chih*; a Southern Sung commentary to the *T'ai-shang kan ying p'ien* quotes briefly from a similarly titled work, the "Yellow Thearch's Scripture of the Stove" (*Huang Ti tsao ching*) on the subject of the stove taboos: "In front of the stove one may not sing or chant, cry, weep, curse, scold, yell, or shout."[61] This is quite like injunctions in stove texts surviving in the *Tao tsang*, which suggests that the *Huang Ti (shen) tsao ching* might have been similar in content. Unfortunately, nothing more remains.

It is quite possible that the content of early stove texts was similar to material on the stove god in other contemporary sources, and in fact the extracts from the *Pao p'u tzu*, *Tsa wu hsing shu*, and *Yu-yang tsa tsu* already cited on the deity's monthly report to Heaven, stove taboos, and sacrifices at specified times all find more elaborate counterparts in later stove texts. Another source in which the stove god appears is the *T'ai-shang kan ying p'ien*, a moral tract probably compiled by the Northern Sung. This work was an important early prototype for many tracts, including stove god texts, that were in circulation in late imperial times. The text is grounded in the same tradition as the *Pao p'u tzu* chapter in which the stove god appears, and seems to have a mainly Taoist orientation; a version with extensive commentary is included in the Taoist canon.

The stove god is mentioned early in the text as one of many deities charged with keeping watch over the actions of mortals. The description of him is taken almost verbatim from the *Pao p'u tzu*, continuing the tradition of reports on men's faults to the celestial authorities at the end of each month.[62] Like the *Pao p'u tzu*, the text makes no recommendations as to ritual observances to the stove. It also includes three stove taboos: "Chanting, singing, or crying to the stove; also burning incense in the fire of the stove; preparing food with polluted firewood. . . ."[63] All of these are identical to stove taboos in later texts.

---

[60]*Sui shu* 34.1038, *Chiu T'ang shu* 舊唐書 (Peking: Chung-hua shu-chü, 1975) 47.2044.
[61]*T'ung chih* 通志 (Shanghai: Shang-wu yin-shu-kuan, 1937) 67.792c; *T'ai-shang kan-ying p'ien* 太上感應篇, *Cheng-t'ung Tao tsang*, HY 1159 (vol. 838) 28.2b.
[62]Ibid., 1.17a.
[63]Ibid., 28.2b–5b.

Much more appears in the *Tao tsang* edition commentary, attributed to one Li Ch'ang-ling (938–1008), though this is suspect.[64] It must in any case have been compiled by the thirteenth century, as each note has attached to it a rhymed encomium by Cheng Ch'ing-chih (fl. 1227). The following is offered on the stove god: "With regard to the stove god's nature as a deity, it is called the 'Overseer of Destiny' (*Ssu-ming*). It controls the destinies of the entire family, free (*liang*) and bonded (*chien*) [members] alike. No matter whether hidden or revealed, the most intimate of details are reported."[65] The commentary explains that the god ascends to the Celestial Departments (*t'ien ts'ao*) at the end of each month to report on the transgressions of men. Then something different appears:

> Another [source] says that there are thirty-six deities in the stove, who can turn disaster into good fortune, remove death, ensure life, drive out monsters and evil, cause one to be transferred to higher office, and increase one's emolument. If at the proper time one sacrifices to them and prays for what one wishes, they will invariably accord with [one's request]. Some people clean the stove on the dark of the moon, and set incense, flowers, wine, and fruit before it to apologize (*hsieh*) to it. This is also auspicious.[66]

The advice to clean and make offerings to the stove at the end of the month is more elaborate than the simple notices of auspicious times for sacrifice in the *Tsa wu hsing shu* and *Yu-yang tsa tsu*, but the import is the same. Nowhere in this commentary, or in the *T'ai-shang kan ying p'ien* itself, is there any hint of the New Year observance that by Sung times had become firmly established in popular practice.

The earliest complete independent stove texts are preserved in the *Tao tsang*. These are the *Most High Cavern Perfected's Scripture for Securing the Stove* (*T'ai-shang tung chen an tsao ching*, HY 69, hereafter referred to as the *An tsao ching*), the *Most High Numinous Treasure Scripture on Supplemental Apologies to the Stove* (*T'ai-shang ling pao pu hsieh Tsao Wang ching*, HY 364, hereafter referred to as the *Pu hsieh Tsao Wang ching*), and the

---

[64] Li Ch'ang-ling was a prominent statesman of the early Sung who was criticized for corruption while holding office. There is no hint in his biography that he took any interest in Taoism or the *T'ai-shang kan ying p'ien*. See *Sung shih* (Peking: Chung-hua shu-chü, 1985) 287.9652–3.

[65] *T'ai-shang kan ying p'ien* 1.17a.

[66] Ibid., 1.17a–b.

Lamp Ritual to the Overseer of Destiny of the Eastern Kitchen (*Tung Ch'u Ssu-ming teng yi*, HY 208). The teachings in these texts are set within a Taoist framework. (The first two are said to have been transmitted by the "Primal Celestial Exalted One" [*Yuan-shih T'ien Tsun*] or equivalent deity.) Like the *T'ai-shang kan ying p'ien*, they draw on elements of earlier esoteric lore, most notably the god's monthly ascent to Heaven as set out in the *Pao-p'u tzu*, and the stove taboos. From the point of view of the Taoist pantheon as a whole, the position of the stove deity was a minor one; the production of these texts must have been a response to the needs of the laity as the stove cult grew in importance during the Sung and after.

No information on date or authorship is provided in any of the texts themselves. As far as can be determined from internal evidence, the *An tsao ching* and *Pu hsieh Tsao Wang ching* seem to have been intended for use by householders, which suggests that, like the stove texts of Ch'ing times, they were directed toward a general lay audience. The third text, the *Tung Ch'u Ssu-ming teng yi*, is a script for a confession ritual probably to be recited by a priest during the course of a Taoist *chiao* or similar ceremony. All three of the texts are brief, but they were influential; they provided the prototypes for much of the material in later texts, and at least one of them, the *Pu hsieh Tsao Wang ching*, continued to be circulated up into the twentieth century as part of other compilations. In none of them is there any mention of the New Year.

In structure the first two texts, the *An tsao ching* and *Pu hsieh Tsao Wang ching*, resemble each other, and many of the same elements are incorporated in a different way into the *Tung Ch'u Ssu-ming teng yi*. A primary component is the myth of the stove god, an account of how a celestial or primordial deity of great power was transformed into the myriads of individual stove gods on earth. This myth will not be discussed here because it has no direct bearing on the ritual prescriptions of these texts, but its function within the scripture should be noted. In the *An tsao ching*, the stove god is said to be a transformation of a primordial mother goddess who invented cooking, the "Divine Mother, Mother of Cooking" (*Ch'ui Mu Shen Mu*); in the *Pu hsieh Tsao Wang ching* he is a transformation of the "Mother Who Seeds Fire" (*Chung Huo chih Mu*), an omnipotent goddess who resembles the Eternal Mother (*Wu Sheng Lao Mu*) of Ming sectarian religion. The purpose of the myth is to establish the divinity of the stove god and his absolute power over the family, and thereby to inspire sincere devotion to the stove god among the people. This devotion is expected to be expressed in the ritual observances set out in the texts.[67]

The second important component of the stove scriptures is the taboos, moral precepts, and regular observances that express people's devotion and that must be followed if the god's goodwill is to be maintained. As these are an attempt to prescribe certain behavior from the standpoint of religious practice, they will be discussed in some detail here.

The third component of the scriptures is a script for an invocation of atonement (often called a *ch'an*), designed to convey the respectful devotion and confession of those who are suffering misfortune, or are in imminent danger of suffering misfortune, as a result of not following the stove god's taboos and precepts. The *Tung Ch'u Ssu-ming teng yi* is entirely a script for such an invocation, though unlike the others it is meant to be recited by a ritual specialist rather than lay householders. The basic intent of the invocation and accompanying ritual trappings is in many respects similar to that of the popular New Year observances, though in form and application they are quite different. As these invocations of atonement are an important part of the ritual prescribed in the texts, they will also be discussed below.

The *An tsao ching* is extremely brief, covering barely two traditional pages of the *Tao tsang*. Certain elements in it are less developed than in the other texts, and it is probably the earliest of the three. It is impossible to determine the precise date of composition, but its contents show points of similarity with the *T'ai-shang kan ying p'ien* commentary, and so could date from the Sung. It is also possible that it is even earlier; many of its features, including the "Divine Mother, Mother of Cooking" from whom the male stove god is derived, are already attested in the T'ang period.[68]

The expression *an tsao* in the title here signifies something like "pacify the stove [god]." Recitation of the scripture or the invocation in it was supposed to appease the deity when householders had violated the taboos

---

[67]For more on the stove myth see Chard, "Folktales on the God of the Stove," *Chinese Studies* 8 (1990), pp. 149–82.

[68]This goddess is mentioned in the T'ang dynasty Cheng-yi 正義 commentary to the *Shih chi*; see *Shih chi* 28.1378. Kubo says that the *An tsao ching* gives the "impression" of being later than the T'ang; see *Okinawa no shūzoku* (cited n. 1), p. 342.

and risked misfortune.[69] The teachings of the scripture are delivered by the "Supreme High Primordial Most Exalted One" (*T'ai-shang Yuan-shih chih tsun*), almost certainly the same as the "Primordial Celestial Exalted One" (*Yuan-shih T'ien Tsun*), the paramount Taoist deity from whom all spiritual teachings originate.

The scripture begins with the primal avatar of the stove god, the Mother of Cooking, addressing the Most Exalted One. She explains her history, which is how the stove myth in this text is introduced. Her responsibilities include watching over the actions of everyone on earth and submitting a report to Heaven on the last day of each month. Then she reports that she suffers from the "affronts and violations" (*ch'u fan*) of vulgar mortals. The Most Exalted One replies with an exposition of the stove taboos; the stove must be protected from sharp implements, feathers and fur, and unclean firewood and water. He then adds, "If one violates these taboos, [the god] can cause the house and home to be insecure, and the people to suffer violent illness."[70] Then he offers instructions for a once-monthly observance to the deity:

> The ceremony to him is a regular sacrifice to the stove each month. On the good [lucky] evening of an auspicious day, one may put pure water in the pot and scatter the fragrant *mao* plant in it.[71] Set out a table, burn incense, and make offerings of wine and fruit. Summon and invite the Master Overseers of Destiny of the Five Thearchs (*Wu Ti Ssu-ming chih chu*) and the numinous spirits of the Divine Women of the Six [Celestial Stem] *Kuei* (*Liu Kuei Shen Nü chih ling*). Pray [to them] as you would to the numinous spirits of the Perfected, and invoke them as follows:

> O Supreme Numen of the Thearch of the North,[72]
> O Divine Women of the Six *Kuei*,

---

[69]Normally *an tsao* has the sense of "install the stove," referring to its construction, which had to be performed according to precise rules. Such rules are still included in popular almanacs; see, for example, *Chü pao lou t'ung sheng jih-li yueh-li* 聚寶樓通勝日曆月曆 (Hong Kong: Chü pao lou yin-shua-ch'ang, 1988), *Tung Kung hsuan-tse jih yao-lan* 董公選擇日要覽 section, p. 10a (*An tsao chueh* 安竈訣), and 10b (*Hsiu tsao chi hsiung jih* 修竈吉兇日 and *Yi tsao chi hsiung* 移竈吉兇).

[70]*An tsao ching, Cheng-t'ung Tao tsang,* HY 69 (vol. 32), p. 1a–b.

[71]*Mao* 茆 is *Brasenia schreberi*, a water plant said to resemble a lotus.

[72]Earlier in the text, in the exposition of the stove myth, the stove god/goddess is said to be a subordinate of the Thearch of the North, a major fate-controlling deity.

> Your Servant now makes sacrifice,
> And is qualified to act as host.
> Vast are the divine waters,
> Incense and lamps are raised in ranks.
> I lift my head and behold the numinous chariot,
> Coming, approaching the site of the *chiao* ceremony.

When the invocation is finished, dip a willow branch in the water and sprinkle it over the *chiao*-ceremony mat. Then make invocation again:

> Cool and pure is the monthly food we lay out,
> Exquisite viands beyond imagining.
> Clear, pure water, with the Five Aromas:
> With fragrances the willow scatters it.

If one repeatedly makes recitation according to the scripture, and prays to the Sacred in this way, one can assure that fathers are kind and sons filial, that husbands lead and wives follow, older brothers are respectful and younger brothers obedient, the exalted and base are in their proper order, and that the younger inherit from the older. In man's baleful [?][73] they will be delighted and pleased, the Way of the family will prosper and thrive, [one's] flesh and blood will find a secure resting place, and sleeping and eating will be harmonious and peaceful. What fear will there be that numinous spirits and foul demons will cause disasters and injure men? But take care to avoid talking loudly in a high voice, offending against the taboos and risking disaster. Do not allow the disgusting and filthy, the rank and the foul-smelling, to violate and offend [the stove]. This will immediately cause demons and devils to be attracted [or "immediately cause the god to attract demons and summon devils"; *chi ling yin kuei chao mo*] and one will likely suffer disaster.[74]

It is evident that this monthly ritual was conceived of as a simple version of a *chiao* purification ceremony, as this word is used in the invocation. The invocation is not addressed directly to the stove god, but to the Thearch of the North (*Pei Ti*), under whose authority the Mother of Cooking carries out her office, and to the "Six *Kuei* women," who are either the

---

[73]The word *hsiung* 凶 in the text at this point seems at odds with the context, and may be a corruption.
[74]*An tsao ching*, pp. 1b–2a.

god's daughters or other goddesses associated with the stove.[75] The last paragraph stresses the benefits of performing the ceremony, and once again warns of the consequences of violating the taboos, which here include a prohibition against noise.

The *Pu hsieh Tsao Wang ching* is slightly longer than the *An tsao ching*, but still less than three pages of the *Tao tsang*. It is more elaborate than the *An tsao ching* in many respects, and is almost certainly of later date, perhaps composed not long before the compilation of the *Tao tsang* in the fifteenth century. The expression "supplemental apology to the King of the Stove" in the title indicates a retroactive act of atonement for violations of the stove taboos. The expression "apologize to the stove" appears in the *T'ai-shang kan ying p'ien* commentary, where it applies to the monthly offerings made to the stove, but in the *Pu hsieh Tsao Wang ching* the ritual is to be performed in times of trouble and misfortune rather than at fixed intervals, a point that also sets it apart from the *An tsao ching*.

As in the *An tsao ching*, the teachings of the *Pu hsieh Tsao Wang ching* are revealed by a "Celestial Exalted One" (*T'ien Tsun*), who in this case may be the "Numinous Treasure Celestial Exalted One" (*Ling Pao T'ien Tsun*).[76] First comes an exposition of the stove myth, in which the stove god is identified as a transformation of the "Mother Who Seeds Fire," an all-powerful goddess involved in the operation of the basic forces of the cosmos, who manifests herself in Heaven as the "Thearch of Heaven" (*T'ien Ti*) and on earth as the "Overseer of Destiny" (*Ssu-ming*). The Celestial Exalted One then expounds a set of stove taboos, which prohibit subjecting the stove to pollution from sharp implements, chicken feathers, dog bones, human hair, and other unclean objects, and warns what happens if the rules are violated:

> The god of the stove will immediately cause discord between men and women, losses in business, disease and ailments, sores and wounds, mad-

---

[75]In the stove myth as presented in the *Yu-yang tsa tsu*, the god is said to have six daughters (*Yu-yang tsa tsu* [cited n. 15], 14.104). The same is said in the *T'ai-shang kan ying p'ien* commentary, where a note identifies them as the six *kuei* 癸 women (*T'ai-shang kan ying p'ien* [cited n. 61], 1.17a).

[76]A "Celestial Exalted One" appears in the text immediately following the *Pu hsieh Tsao Wang ching* in the *Tao tsang*, the *T'ai-shang shuo li yi Ts'an Wang miao ching* 太上說利益竈王妙經, and in this case is identified as the *Ling Pao T'ien Tsun* 靈寶天尊. The two texts are roughly similar in style and content, and may be related.

ness and insanity, miasmic diseases, dimness and darkness of the eyes, reversals of dreams and [waking] thoughts, barrenness of fields and silkworms, and wasting and exhaustion among the six domestic animals. He will allow strange demons to enter the house fearlessly and at random, monstrous prodigies to appear among chickens and dogs, thieves and bandits to intrude and harass, wild quarrels to break out, men and women to be deluded by wickedness, official authorities to put them in custody, and the family property to be scattered and lost. All of this is brought about by violating [the taboos].[77]

If such misfortunes occur, "It is urgently necessary to apologize to him." This involves "inviting" (*ch'ing*) a great list of subordinate stove deities and delivering an invocation of atonement:

Your disciples so-and-so, husband and wife, and relatives great and small, are all ordinary folk, and knew nothing of the prohibitions and taboos. Many were our violations, but we were unaware of them. Sometimes we made things to east and west, or built things to the north and south, and pointed knives toward the stove, startling the exalted deities. We shouted noisily after drinking wine, spoke recklessly and talked loudly, put our feet up to the fire, displayed our naked bodies, [subjected the stove to] the filth and pollution of man and woman and to foul and rank smells from cooking; we sang and chanted inside the kitchen, and shouted and called before the stove; this all has caused the Three Calamities to arise in unison,[78] a hundred monstrosities to come to life together, wealth to be exhausted and scattered, illness to continue unbroken, fields and silkworms to bring no yield, promotions in official rank to not be bestowed, buying and selling to be without profit, the house and lodging to fall into disrepair, evil men to plot harm, the six domestic animals to not bear young, dreaming and [waking] thoughts to be reversed, and all that we seek not to succeed. Thus we piously and sincerely wish to express our repentance and apologies.[79]

The inclusion in the *Pu hsieh Tsao Wang ching* of an invocation of atonement designed to dispel misfortune after it has struck suggests that it was designed for circulation among a wide general audience. The text would have been attractive to those seeking remedies for evil fortune, precisely

[77]*Pu hsieh Tsao Wang ching, Cheng-t'ung Tao tsang*, HY 364 (vol. 180), 1b–2a.
[78]The "Three Calamities" (*san tsai* 三災) here refers to warfare, illness, and starvation.
[79]*Pu hsieh Tsao Wang ching*, p. 2b.

the people who are often the most receptive to religious and moral teachings. The phrase "your disciples so-and-so, husband and wife . . ." (*ti-tzu mou fu-ch'i . . .*) confirms that this invocation was for the use of the householders themselves. Moreover, the *Pu hsieh Tsao Wang ching*, like the *An tsao ching*, is written in relatively simple literary Chinese, which clearly suggests that both texts were designed for a wide general audience rather than just Taoist or other ritual specialists. If this assumption is correct, they would have been intended for actual use within domestic religious rituals, introducing new elements into the framework already existing within the popular stove cult.

But there are important differences between the prescriptions in these texts and popular belief in the Sung and after: the god makes his reports monthly, and there is no mention of the New Year. Nor is there any mention of the paper image; as far as can be determined all observances are made directly to the stove itself. These two texts, then, prescribe practices that are at odds with general custom, probably with the aim of modifying the ritual observances of the popular cult.

Not all the domestic rituals of the scriptural cult were to be performed by the householders themselves. Sometimes it was necessary to call upon the services of a ritual specialist, as is advised at the end of the *Pu hsieh Tsao Wang ching*: "If the men and women of the latter generation have offended the Lord of the Stove, and there are disasters and suffering, they must all cleanse, sweep, and sprinkle [water], light a bright lamp and burn incense, and summon a Taoist priest to read the scriptures repeatedly, call upon the names of the Stove Lord and his family members, and make a report of their having presented money and wealth, or provided food and drink for the benefit of others."[80] This appears to be an addendum of some sort, one that contradicts the main body of the text, in which the householders are expected to perform the invocation of atonement themselves. It may have been included by someone who felt that the ritual was a Taoist one and should not be performed by the laity, or perhaps only as a last resort if the householder's invocation was ineffective.

It is precisely within the context of a ritual performed by a religious specialist that the third *Tao tsang* stove text, the *Tung Ch'u Ssu-ming teng yi,*

---

[80]Ibid., pp. 3a–b.

is intended to be used. This text is not a scripture like the other two, but entirely a script for the performance of an invocation. Within the text of the invocation the person reading it is called the *"chiao*-ceremony officiator so-and-so" (*chiao kuan mou jen*) rather than "husband and wife so-and-so" as in the *Pu hsieh Tsao Wang ching*. The *Tung Ch'u Ssu-ming teng yi* is one of a series of *Teng yi* ("lamp ritual") texts within the *Tao tsang*, and it might have been used in one stage of a longer *chiao* purification ritual. It is written in a terse and allusive style much more difficult to read than the simple prose of the other two texts, and obviously was not designed to be accessible to a general audience. As this work was not a prescriptive text for observances performed by the householders themselves, it will not be discussed here. It is worth noting, however, that although it is considerably more elaborate, it is a script for an invocation similar to that contained within the *Pu hsieh Tsao Wang ching*, and all of the basic features of the scriptural cult—stove myth, taboos, atonement, and appeals for good fortune—are alluded to within the invocation itself. As it was recited by a religious specialist, something of its content might have been conveyed to the listener despite the complexity of the language, in particular the apologies for breaking the stove taboos, in which the taboos themselves are explicated in some detail.

RECENT STOVE TEXTS

A considerable number of stove texts of one sort or another have been in circulation from mid-Ch'ing times (and probably earlier) to the present. Some of these are primarily moral tracts, in which the trappings of the scriptural stove cult are included to enhance the effectiveness of the central message, and even in many others that are called "scriptures" the moral content is much more pronounced than in the *Tao tsang* texts. Still, the stove taboos and prescriptions for domestic observances remain prominent, and it is this element that will be discussed here.

Following is a list of titles and brief discussions of the texts used in this study:[81]

1. *Ching tsao ch'üan shu* ("The Complete Book on Revering the Stove"), edition cited here published in 1924 in Shanghai;

---

[81]For a longer list of stove god texts see Chard, "Master of the Family," pp. 532–33.

original preface dated 1819. This is a collection of various writings: prayers, testimonials, divination slips, and scriptures. A primary component of the compilation is a text called the *Tsao Chün ching* ("Scripture of the Stove Lord"), postface dated 1788. This contains lists of rules and ritual prescriptions, the complete text of the *Pu hsieh Tsao Wang ching*, and an invocation of atonement called the "Most Supreme Purple Tenuity Jade Case Treasure Confession for Extinguishing Disasters, [Addressed to] the Primeval Pacifying and Suppressing Overseer of Destiny of the Eastern Kitchen" (*T'ai-shang Yuan-shih an chen Tung-ch'u Ssu-ming tzu wei yü chi hsiao tsai pao ch'an*). Following the *Tsao Chün ching* in the *Ching tsao ch'üan shu* is a brief vernacular scripture called the *Ch'u shen Tsao Chün ching* ("Scripture on the Origin of the Stove Lord"), which is similar in form and content to the stove god *pao chüan*.[82]

2. *Tsao Chün ching* ("Scripture of the Stove Lord"), no date given, probably published in the twentieth century. This is not the same text as the *Tsao Chün ching* in the *Ching tsao ch'üan shu*, but a short, widely circulated vernacular scripture, written in verse, with a strong moral message. The version used here is from the collection of Wu Xiaoling and was acquired by him in a Peking used book market in 1988.

3. *Tsao Wang chen ching* ("True Scripture of the Stove King"), edition dated 1941, date of original compilation not given. This is a vernacular scripture written in verse, with a strong moral message underscored by the theme of impending world dissolution. This text is also from the collection of Wu Xiaoling, acquired by him in a Peking used book market in 1988.

4. *Tsao Chün pao chüan* ("Treasure Scroll of the Stove Lord"), collated and printed in 1884 from a manuscript compiled

---

[82]Different editions of the *Ching tsao ch'üan shu* seem to have been widely circulated. A version collected by Kubo contains two items not in the edition used here, but does not include the *Ch'u shen Tsao Chün ching*; see Kubo, *Okinawa no shūzoku* (cited n. 1), pp. 343–47. A text called the *Tsao shen chen ching* 竈神眞經 published in Canton (no date, most recent prefaces written in 1850 and 1855) collected by David Faure is in fact a much-abbreviated version of the *Ching tsao ch'üan shu*.

sometime after 1846; also published under the title *Ssu-ming pao chüan* ("Treasure Scroll of the Overseer of Destiny") in Tainan in 1941 (in the collection of Gary Seaman). This is a vernacular text intended for oral presentation, written in alternating simple literary prose and seven-syllable rhyme. It has a strong moral content, and incorporates various testimonials describing the miraculous salvation the stove god brings to those who give up evil ways and do good.[83] The second half of the text is a separate document, an exhortation to turn to the Buddha, and is entirely unconnected with the stove god.

5. *Tsao Huang pao chüan* ("Treasure Scroll of the August One of the Stove"), a manuscript of uncertain date in the Shanghai Library. This is another vernacular text intended for oral recitation, written in alternating vernacular or literary prose and seven-syllable verse. The first part of this work is roughly similar to the *Tsao Chün pao chüan*, except that the emphasis is less on moral edification than on the spiritual efficacy of the performance of the text itself. It incorporates parts of the *Pu hsieh Tsao Wang ching* and a script for an invocation of atonement not unlike that of the *Tung Ch'u Ssu-ming teng yi*, neither of which appears in the *Tsao Chün pao chüan*.

6. *Ssu-ming Tsao Chün ch'üan shih wen* ("Writings to Persuade the World from the Overseer of Destiny, Lord of the Stove"), published in Taiwan in 1985 or later, and available in temples. A collection of stove texts, including a *Tsao Chün chen ching* ("True Scripture of the Stove Lord"), a rhymed vernacular scripture said to have been revealed in 1930; a *Tsao Wang chen ching* ("True Scripture of the Stove King"), different from no. 3 above, but also with a strong millenarian bent, date not given; the *Tsao Chün pao chüan*; and two other very brief documents, one a message from the stove god revealed through spirit writing in 1985.

---

[83]A study of this text appears in Cheng Chih-ming 鄭志明, *Chung-kuo shan shu yü tsung-chiao* 中國善書與宗教 (Taipei: Hsueh-sheng shu-chü, 1988), 161–84. The text is also reproduced entire in Kubo, *Okinawa no shūzoku*, pp. 504–530.

7. *Tsao Wang ching ch'an ho k'o* ("Combined Publication of the
   Scripture and Atonement of the Stove King"), supplemented
   and published in 1903 in Szechuan, copy in the D. C. Graham
   collection in the East Asian Library of the University of California, Berkeley. This compilation includes a *Tsao Wang ching*
   ("Scripture of the Stove King"), further divided into a "Scripture," patched together from a number of different sources
   (including the *Pu hsieh Tsao Wang ching*), and a "New Scripture"
   written in simple literary Chinese; and a *Tsao Wang ch'an* ("Confession to the Stove King"), the script of an invocation of atonement patched together in alternating segments from a vernacular
   rhymed stove scripture (originally not a confession) and a true
   confession document written in literary prose.

8. *Tsao Wang pen yuan ching* ("Scripture of the Original Vow of the
   Stove King"), reprinted in 1887, available in an English translation by D. C. Graham.[84] The theme of the stove god's mercy
   and power to bring salvation is particularly strong; the reader of
   the text is encouraged to make a vow to save all living things,
   similar to the vow by which the stove god himself achieved divinity. Such a vow, it is claimed, will bring miraculous protection
   against evil and other benefits. Moral teachings are given less
   emphasis in this text than in most of the other works.

9. *Ssu-ming chih kuang* ("The Light of the Overseer of Destiny"),
   published in Taichung, Taiwan, in 1982 by the Sheng-te Pao
   Kung and distributed in temples. A collection of documents and
   transcripts of conversations with the stove god through a spirit
   medium. This text presents a latter-day version of traditional
   stove god teachings modified for modern life.

To make sense of texts such as these, obviously it is desirable to find out
as much as possible about the context in which they were created, disseminated, and put to use. Unfortunately, such information is disappoint-
ingly scarce. In the case of the *Tao tsang* scriptures, one can only assume

[84]D. C. Graham, "The Original Vows of the Kitchen God," *The Chinese Recorder* 61 (Dec.
1930), pp. 781–88, and 62 (Jan. and Feb. 1931), pp. 41–50 and 110–16. I have not found a
copy of the original Chinese text.

on the basis of content that they were produced by Taoists for the use of ordinary householders in times of misfortune. In the recent texts, at least there sometimes are prefaces that give some idea of who produced them, and what their motives were. In the *Tsao Chün pao chüan*, for example, a colophon notes that the original manuscript, riddled with textual errors, was in the possession of a certain "Master K'ung" (K'ung Chün). The unidentified writer of the colophon was impressed by the text's moral message and the Buddhist teachings appended to it, and felt it should be more widely disseminated. He corrected the text, and persuaded K'ung to provide the funds to have it printed. This leads one to the conclusion that the two men between them had a fair level of literacy and the financial means to publish a book.[85] Kubo Noritada also says that stove texts were collected by educated men, not necessarily to disseminate them, but as prized rare books.[86]

The clearest information on the publication of the stove texts covered here appears in the *Ching tsao ch'üan shu*. The Shanghai bookseller who printed it in 1924, the Hung-wen t'ang shu-chü, distributed moral tracts (*shan shu*) in large lots for "virtuous gentlemen" to disseminate to others.[87] The preface to the *Tsao Chün ching* in the *Ching tsao ch'üan shu* expresses the hope that "kind people and gentlemen" (*jen jen chün-tzu*) will help transmit it far and wide.[88] Most revealing, however, is the 1819 preface to the *Ching tsao ch'üan shu* as a whole, which refers to the social backgrounds of both the compiler and the intended audience, and how it was hoped the text would be spread and used. The preface is divided into two parts, the first written in an allusive and educated style for highly literate readers, a message from the compiler to other like-minded "gentlemen" who might be inclined to join in the work of disseminating the text for the moral edification of the lower classes. The following is an extract:

> The gentleman (*chün-tzu*) reads this compilation, and copies and prints it so
> that it will circulate and be distributed, causing all those throughout the

---

[85] *Tsao Chün pao chüan* (ed. of 1884, text in the East Asian Library of the University of California, Berkeley), pp. 47a–b.

[86] Kubo, *Okinawa no shūzoku*, p. 357.

[87] Publisher's advertisement in *Ching tsao ch'üan shu* (Shanghai: Hung-wen-t'ang shu-chü, 1924), p. 1a.

[88] *Ching tsao ch'üan shu* (*Tsao Chün ching* section), p. 3a.

towns and cities, and the remote fields and distant corners, to place a copy in their homes. Fathers will give teachings and elder brothers will give encouragement. I know that when the desire of people of the middle level and below (*chung jen yi hsia*) to do good burns like oil, there is invariably one who watches over from above, admonishes from the side, and gives protection and aid in silence.[89]

The assumption here is that "those of the middle level and below" are in need of moral guidance, and that works such as the *Ching tsao ch'üan shu* can provide this. The writer stresses moral guidance rather than the religious teachings that lie behind the ritual prescriptions of the scriptural stove cult, but since both moral teachings and ritual prescriptions appear in his compilation, the same social implications must have applied to both.

No other information of this sort appears in our texts, though a little more may be said on the origin of their content. It is obvious that they were based in part on their predecessors in the *Tao tsang*, and probably also on similar texts from other sources. The entire *Pu hsieh Tsao Wang ching* is included in the *Tsao Chün ching* of the *Ching tsao ch'üan shu*, and parts of it are reproduced verbatim in the *Tsao Wang ching ch'an ho k'o* and *Tsao Huang pao chüan*.[90] The stove god myth in a number of texts, particularly the two *pao chüan*, shows obvious links with the *Tao tsang* scriptures.[91] The compiler of the *Tsao Chün ching* within the *Ching tsao ch'üan shu* says that he drew upon the "stove scripture and stove confession from the scriptures of the Canon(s)" (*tsang ching chung tsao ching tsao ch'an*) to create a text for general circulation.[92] The scripture is the *Pu hsieh Tsao Wang ching*, which is in the *Tao tsang*, but the confession text, also a Taoist work, is not. In a section of the *Tsao Chün ching* called the *Ching tsao p'ien* ("Piece on Revering the Stove"), the same compiler says of the stove taboos: "Recently I encountered an eminent gentleman (*kao shih*) who bestowed

<hr>

[89]*Ching tsao ch'üan shu*, p. 2a.
[90]*Ching tsao ch'üan shu* (*Tsao Chün ching* section), pp. 3b–4b; *Tsao Wang ching ch'an ho k'o* 3b–4b; *Tsao Huang pao chüan* (undated manuscript in the Shanghai Library), pp. 10b–11a.
[91]For the stove god myth in the *Tsao Huang pao chüan*, quite similar to that in the *Tao tsang* scriptures but considerably more elaborate, see Chard, "Folktales on the God of the Stove" (cited n. 40), pp. 163–64.
[92]*Ching tsao ch'üan shu* (*Tsao Chün ching* section), pp. 8a–b.

upon me a number of prohibitions and taboos recorded in the scriptures of the Canon(s)."[93] Whoever the "eminent gentleman" may have been (perhaps a priest or monk?), it would seem that the taboos were taken from pre-existing religious works, though these particular lists do not seem to be in any text of the *Tao tsang*.

Also important is the question of how the scriptures were intended to be used. Like any other scripture, they were to be recited—on days of special significance, in times of trouble, or at any time for one's own spiritual and material benefit. The act of recitation itself was a ritual of considerable efficacy, above and beyond what the document might actually say. Like other scriptures, the texts were sacred objects; notices on their covers warn that they must be kept in a clean place, and that sullying them or failing to respect them will bring on supernatural retribution.[94] Some texts, particularly the *pao chüan*, were performed in the home by ritual specialists. This is confirmed by the *Tsao Huang pao chüan*, which recommends that Buddhist monks or Taoist priests be summoned into the home to hold a "Full [or "Sacred"] Meeting of the August One of the Stove" (*Tsao Huang sheng hui*), an expression used to denote the performance of the *pao chüan* for the relief of families suffering misfortune.[95] Chün-fang Yü has found a woman in the lower Yangtze city of Yi-hsing who performs *pao chüan*, including a *Tsao Wang pao chüan* ("Treasure Scroll of the Stove King"), in the homes of people suffering from illness or about to give birth.[96] Texts other than the *pao chüan*, however, seem to have been intended to be read by the family members themselves. This is made explicit in the case of the confession invocation in the *Ching tsao ch'üan shu*, where the invocator excuses his neglect of affairs in the kitchen by saying that as head of household his normal sphere of activity is in the main hall far away.[97]

Several of the texts specify particular occasions on which they should

<hr>

[93]Ibid., p. 3a.

[94]See, for example, the preface to the *Ching tsao ch'üan shu*, p. 2a.

[95]*Tsao Huang pao chüan*, p. 10b (where *sheng hui* is written 勝會; on p. 1a the ritual of performing the text is called a *sheng hui* 聖會).

[96]Personal communication. For more information on the performance of *pao chüan*, see David Johnson's chapter in this volume.

[97]*Ching tsao ch'üan shu* (*Tsao Chün ching* section), p. 7a.

be recited, as this passage in the *Tsao Chün ching* of the *Ching tsao ch'üan shu* indicates:

> Whenever you wish to chant the scripture and perform the ritual of confession (*sung ching li ch'an*), you must first fast and observe the precepts, bathe, and change clothes. In a Pure Chamber (*ching shih*), concentrate the spirit and fix your thoughts, burn incense, bow, and chant. On the [stove god's] Sacred Birthday, the new and full moons, and *feng ssu* [?][98] this can insure the good luck and felicity of the household and the peace and security of the family members; a hundred good fortunes will come side by side, and a thousand auspicious manifestations will gather like clouds.[99]

The preface to the *Tsao Wang ching ch'an ho k'o* stipulates a single monthly recitation at the new moon.[100] Other texts, such as the vernacular *Tsao Chün ching* and *Tsao Wang chen ching*, specify no particular occasion, and instead advise that they be recited as often as possible, and, better yet, copied and circulated to others. The *Tsao Wang chen ching* says:

> If you read the *True Scripture of the King of the Stove* once,
> Good fortune and longevity will be achieved in full measure.
> If you read the *True Scripture of the King of the Stove* ten times,
> The entire family will be secure and at peace.
> If you read the *True Scripture of the King of the Stove* a hundred times,
> The whole village may be protected.
> If you read the *True Scripture of the King of the Stove* a thousand times,
> The width of an entire county will be aided.
> If someone can transmit the *Scripture of the King of the Stove*,
> Then North, South, East, and West,
> All places, through the Eight Directions, the Buddhas will know it clearly;
> Everyone will have much merit.
> If you transmit one *Scripture of the King of the Stove*,
> The myriad of illnesses cannot arise.
> If you transmit ten *Scriptures of the King of the Stove*,
> The whole family is guaranteed to be secure and tranquil.
> If you transmit a hundred *Scriptures of the King of the Stove*,
> You may escape water, fire, and wind.

---

[98]逢四; I have been unable to discover the significance of this term.
[99]*Ching tsao ch'üan shu* (*Tsao Chün ching* section), pp. 8a–b.
[100]*Tsao Wang ching ch'an ho k'o*, p. 1a.

If you transmit a thousand *Scriptures of the King of the Stove,*
You can escape baleful and slaughtering stars.
If you transmit ten thousand *Scriptures of the King of the Stove,*
Your name will be great on the announcement board of Heaven.
If you transmit twenty thousand *Scriptures of the King of the Stove,*
Your merit will be great, your good fortune not insubstantial.
If you transmit several tens of thousands of *Scriptures of the King of the Stove,*
It will always be green through summer and winter.
If you can forever transmit the *Scripture of the King of the Stove,*
You will not age, and will always have extended life;
Your good fortune will be as the sea, your longevity like the pine,
The gods and Buddhas will guarantee your peace,
You will sit on the Lotus Platform of the Nine Degrees,[101]
Happiness and good fortune will be infinite.[102]

The *Tsao Wang pen yuan ching* advises that its miraculous powers may be activated if one burns incense, lights a lamp, makes offerings, and recites the text while kneeling over a period of twelve hours.[103] In most works ample incentive is given for recitation, either as part of a scheduled observance, or at any time for one's personal spiritual advancement and material benefit. The New Year is never mentioned as being one of these ritual occasions.

Like the *Tao tsang* texts, recent scriptures devote considerable space to various observances that should be made to the stove. The significance of such observances is frequently summed up in the phrase "revere the stove" (*ching tsao*). The *Tsao Chün ching* and *Tsao Wang chen ching* give extravagant descriptions of the benefits of revering the stove; one can expect to get anything one desires, expressed in the promise: "If you seek anything, there will invariably be a response" (*yu ch'iu pi ying*).[104] What "revering the stove" entails is sincere adherence to all the teachings of the particular text—observing the stove taboos that guard the sanctity of the stove and performing ritual observances to the god at specified times.

---

[101]The nine grades of rewards in the Pure Land; see Soothill and Houdous, *A Dictionary of Chinese Buddhist Terms* (London: Kegan Paul, 1937), p. 16.
[102]*Tsao Wang chen ching* (n.p., 1941, in the collection of Wu Xiaoling), pp. 6b–7b.
[103]Graham, "Original Vows of the Kitchen God," *The Chinese Recorder* 62 (1931), p. 116.
[104]See, for example, *Ching tsao ch'üan shu*, p. 2a.

The stove taboos vary little from text to text. The following list from the *Tsao Chün ching* is a representative example:

I will transmit to you the "Ten Precepts Within the Kitchen"
(*Ch'u chung shih chieh*).
O multitudes of good people, every one of you, remember them firmly in
your hearts.
The first thing not permitted: scraping the pot and grinding in front
of the stove;
Rapping spoons and chopsticks, striking bowls and saucers—the family will
be broken and the people impoverished.
The second thing not permitted: being before the stove naked and exposed;
The dirty, slovenly body offends and desecrates the gods.
The third thing not permitted: fouling, defecating, and urinating in front
of the stove;
Basins with blood and sweat, and implements with smelly urine should be
kept far from the kitchen.
The fourth thing not permitted: sniveling, weeping, crying, and sobbing
before the stove;
This ruins the family, wrecks the house, and disturbs the spirits.
The fifth thing not permitted: cursing, swearing, making oaths in front
of the stove;
Hating Heaven and Earth, resenting the Buddha, and deceiving the gods
and spirits.
The sixth thing not permitted: brooms before the stove, and making food
with polluted firewood;
Do not put onion and garlic skins, chicken feathers, and bones into the stove.
The seventh thing not permitted: drying smelly clothes, toasting shoes, and
heating socks;
Burn fragrant coal and pure water—it should be immaculate and clean.
The eighth thing not permitted: casting away the Five Grains, throwing
away rice, and scattering flour;
If you have extra tea and leftover rice, give it to a hungry man.
The ninth thing not permitted: killing chickens and slaughtering ducks
without reason;
People who eat vegetarian food must do good, shun killing, and release
living things.
The tenth thing not permitted: eating beef and dog meat;
Oxen till the fields and dogs guard at night; they have important tasks.

O multitudes of good people, remember these "Ten Precepts Within
  the Kitchen";
You will eliminate disasters and be exempt from trouble; good fortune and
  longevity will be increased.
If you can also heed my encouragement to respect and value written paper,
You will give birth to exalted sons, become a high official, and be wealthy,
  honored, and distinguished.[105]

The *Tsao Chün ching* calls its list the "Ten Precepts" (*shih chieh*), presumably inspired by the "Ten Precepts" of Buddhism. Other texts call
them by other names, such as the "Twelve Prohibitions" (*Shih-erh chin
yueh*) in the *Tsao Chün pao chüan*, and the "Taboos on the Stove" (*Tsao
shang chi*) in the *Tsao Chün ching* of the *Ching tsao ch'üan shu*, or by no
particular name at all. In addition to the old rules of the sort found in the
Tao tsang texts, the modern prohibitions usually include killing and eating
animals (especially dogs, cattle, and water creatures such as turtles and
shellfish), spilling and wasting grain, and showing disrespect toward paper with writing on it (which had to be disposed of by burning, but not
within the stove). Other taboos have to do with particular days during the
month when the god is active (called "days when the god is in power";
yung shih chih jih), when, for example, the pot may not be scraped; these
days vary depending on which source is consulted.[106]

Many of the stove taboos are obviously inspired by simple consider-
ations of hygiene, and there are wider social implications beyond their
religious import; in part they seem to have been an effort to impose more
refined manners on the lower classes. Here, however, it is sufficient to
note that adherence to the taboos entails a constant awareness of the sanctity of the stove and a sensitivity to the presence of the god. The key word
is "constant"—a general moral tract called the *Ching hsin lu* (not listed
above) includes a section on the stove in which responsibility for the observance of the stove taboos rests with the head of household, who is
advised to explain them regularly to his family, or write them on wooden
plaques and display them prominently in the kitchen.[107]

<hr>

[105]*Tsao Chün ching* (undated printed text in the collection of Wu Xiaoling), pp. 6b–8b.
[106]Different systems appear in sections titled "Taboo Days for Scraping the Pot" (*Kua kuo
chi jih* 刮鍋吉日) in *Ching tsao ch'üan shu*, pp. 5a–b, and *Tsao Chün pao chüan*, p. 2a.
[107]*Ching hsin lu* 敬信錄 (Fukien ed. of 1844, held in the Library of the School of Oriental and
African Studies, London), p. 84a.

In addition to the taboos, most of the stove texts stipulate regular observances of one sort or another. A typical example appears under the heading "Several Rules for Revering the Stove" (*Ching tsao shu tse*) in the *Ching tsao ch'üan shu*:

> Every morning and evening, burn one stick of incense before the stove. [The stove] should always be clean and immaculate. Before using the stove, one must always wash one's hands.

> At the new and full moons each month, burn a lamp and offer a cup of pure water.

> Every month on the seventh, seventeenth, twenty-third, and twenty-seventh days, clean the kitchen, stove, and the central pot. Place a lamp inside the door of the stove. Put seven wicks in it, with a pattern of coins on them to hold them down. Fill it with rapeseed oil so that the light of the lamp burns constantly through the night, corresponding to the seven stars of the Northern Dipper above.[108] Merit accumulates easily, and the good fortune reaped thereby is very great (*kung yi chi erh huo fu shen ta*).

> The thirtieth day of each month is the appointed time for the Lord of the Stove to ascend and report. When it reaches the hours of *hsü* [7–9 P.M.] and *hai* [9–11 P.M.], the entire family should sincerely and piously make respectful ritual. The purity and good luck of the household and the tranquility of its members may thus be assured.

> The third day of the eighth month is the [stove god's] Sacred Birthday. One should offer incense and flowers, and worship and make invocation to him.[109]

Most of these observances have counterparts in other texts. The *Tsao Chün pao chüan*, for example, says that the stove should be cleared and cleaned after every meal, and a stick of incense burned.[110] The observances on the first and fifteenth of the month are noted in a section titled "Stove Regulations" (*Tsao kuei*) near the beginning of the *Ching tsao ch'üan shu*, which advises that "worship and offerings" (*pai ssu*) be made, and in the vernacular *Tsao Chün ching*, where it says that in the homes of the

---

[108]According to the stove myth, the stove god is the agent of the stars of the Dipper.
[109]*Ching tsao ch'üan shu* (*Tsao Chün ching* section), p. 4b.
[110]*Tsao Chün pao chüan*, p. 8a.

virtuous "there are bright lamps (*ming teng*) at the full and new moons."[111] The seven-wick lamp representing the stars of the Northern Dipper is found in the *Ching hsin lu*.[112] Sometimes a text specifies only once-monthly observances, as in the *Tsao Wang ching ch'an ho k'o*, which is to be recited at the new moon.[113]

An additional note on the nature of the offerings and the proper state of mind while making them appears in a section titled "Auspicious Days for Making Prayers and Offerings to the Stove God" (*Ch'i ssu tsao shen chi jih*) in the *Tsao Chün ching* of the *Ching tsao ch'üan shu*:

> The entire family should make respectful ritual with concentrated minds, and peace and security may be assured. If on these days one can make a vow to do good (*li shan yuan*), to value writing and grain, release living things, and the like, these [vows] can all achieve special success. If one recites scriptures or bows in confession one will assuredly reap a reward of good fortune. Whenever a day comes for making offerings to the stove, there is no need to prepare a great many foods and fruits. One need only have a sincere heart, and offer a cup of clear tea. This may be accompanied by jujube cakes (*tsao kao*), rice-flour dumplings (*fen t'uan*), or wheat cakes.[114]

The jujube cake and dumplings are remarkably similar to popular New Year offerings, perhaps an accommodation to popular custom.

The stove god's birthday presents a special case. Two texts, the *Ching tsao p'ien* in the *Ching tsao ch'üan shu* and the vernacular *Tsao Chün ching*, complain that people tend to neglect this day. The *Ching tsao p'ien* says:

> Everyone knows enough to celebrate the Sacred Birthdays of all the various gods; only that of the Lord of the Stove is lacking. This is particularly inexplicable. In addition there are men and women who cross seas and climb mountains to burn incense and pray at temples; the only thing they do not realize is that there is a Lord of the Stove, Overseer of Destiny in their own homes, most manifest and most potent. They do not make offerings to him. How can one cast aside the near and seek out the distant in this way?[115]

[111]*Ching tsao ch'üan shu*, p. 3b; *Tsao Chün ching*, p. 6b.
[112]*Ching hsin lu*, p. 84a.
[113]*Tsao Wang ching ch'an ho k'o*, p. 1a.
[114]*Ching tsao ch'üan shu* (*Tsao Chün ching* section), p. 4b.
[115]Ibid., p. 3a.

The *Tsao Chün ching* says:

> [People] know enough to respect all the Buddhas and all the gods and saints,
> On their birthdays, on their taboo days, they give felicitations and
>   congratulations to welcome [the gods] with ritual.
> [But] on the Sacred Birthday of the Lord of the Stove, people do not make
>   offerings to him;
> He guards the Eastern Kitchen, lonely, cold, and desolate in the extreme.
> The third day of the eighth month, in autumn, is the time of his
>   Sacred Birthday.
> I say this to you, to all the world, for everyone to hear together:
> Virtuous men and faithful women offer incense fires,
> Every family, every household, lights a bright lamp.
> This increases good fortune, and also increases longevity;
> There will be no calamity or harm.[116]

It is obvious that these texts lay particular stress on the importance of showing the proper reverence toward the stove deity. Tsuda Sōkichi, who has made a study of two recent stove texts, a *Tsao Chün fu shou ching* ("The Lord of the Stove's Scripture on Good Fortune and Longevity," a text I have not seen) and the vernacular *Tsao Chün ching*, contrasts the stress on the third day of the eighth month with the absence of New Year observances. He believes that the *Tsao Chün ching* was compiled by Buddhists (the opening lines of the scripture claim that it originated with the Buddha himself and was brought to China by Hsüan-tsang in the T'ang), and the *Tsao Chün fu shou ching* by Taoists, and argues that Buddhists and Taoists wished people to abandon the New Year observances to the stove in favor of the birthday. He sees this as being primarily a ploy to encourage people to adopt Buddhist and Taoist practice and turn away from the improper popular rite.[117]

My own conclusion on the importance attached to the god's birthday is somewhat different. None of the recent texts studied here can really be said to be "Buddhist" or "Taoist"; all of them integrate teachings from different traditions. The point the *Ching tsao p'ien* and *Tsao Chün ching* seek to establish is that the god's power and status are fully as great as

---

[116]*Tsao Chün ching*, pp. 2a–b.
[117]See Tsuda's arguments on this question in "Shina no minkan-shinkō ni okeru sōjin" (cited n. 3), pp. 148–53.

those of any other deity. The inclusion of the stove myth, which stresses the divine origin of the god, is another facet of the same concern. If people celebrate the birthdays of other gods, and cross mountains and seas to worship them, then they should not neglect a god of equal importance within their own homes. The observance of the stove god's birthday is simply a matter of according him the same respect as is shown other deities; the birthday is the one day in the year that belongs exclusively to him. Buddhist or Taoist ritual is not at issue; if anything, the injunction in the *Ching tsao p'ien* not to "cast aside the near to seek out the distant" would be as much to the detriment of Buddhist and Taoist deities as to other "distant" gods. The point is to stress the divinity of the stove god, and lend greater authority to the message in the texts.

Buddhists and Taoists aside, however, Tsuda has raised a question of fundamental importance. Why is it that these texts lay so much stress on ritual forms other than the New Year rite? It is not impossible that the text compilers promoted what they regarded as proper form for its own sake as an acknowledgment of the spiritual authority of a particular body of teachings; certainly this was an element of the *Tao tsang* scriptures within the context of Taoism. At the same time, however, it is quite clear that there was something about the popular cult itself that aroused deep dissatisfaction.

A significant comment on the New Year rituals appears in the preface of the *Ching tsao ch'üan shu*. This appears in the second section of the preface, which, in contrast to the first, on the purpose of the work (discussed above), is written in simple literary Chinese for the benefit of the recipients of the text:

All the households of the world, great and small, know to send off the stove on the twenty-third or twenty-fourth of the *La*-month, and to receive the stove on New Year's Day. But they know nothing of revering the stove on ordinary days. Of what use is a single welcome and sendoff? In this book [it tells how] the stove god's special function is to scrutinize the good and evil of a household; [this book] is to remind those who have lost their way. If you believe in this book, please put it in a clean place. If the entire family is pious every moment, then if you seek anything there will inevitably be a response (*yu ch'iu pi ying*).[118]

[118]*Ching tsao ch'üan shu*, p. 2a.

The key phrase in this passage is "pious every moment" (*shih k'o ch'ien hsin*). Here, in a nutshell, is the explanation for the stove taboos and ritual prescriptions that constitute "revering the stove." They are designed to ensure that reverence and respect toward the stove god are maintained constantly throughout the year. The recipient of the text is promised that he can get anything he wishes if he is able to do this. There is nothing wrong with making observances to the stove god at the New Year, but they are not enough.

The *Ching tsao ch'üan shu* preface says nothing about the nature of the New Year observance itself, but other texts do. For example, the *Ch'u shen Tsao Chün ching* in the *Ching tsao ch'üan shu*, a brief vernacular scripture in seven-syllable verse that shows certain points of correspondence with the *pao chüan*, has the following:

> The Lords of the Stove in the Seventy-Two Palaces are numerous;
> They check and inspect, and on the twenty-fourth day of the twelfth month,
> They hurriedly set out and ascend to the Courts of Heaven.
> From this point on there will be much wealth and high status;
> The glory of wealth and high status will extend for ten thousand years.[119]

Nothing is said about the observance to be made, but the implication is that the New Year is the time that good fortune is meted out. Still more of the significance of the rite is explained in the *Tsao Chün pao chüan*:

> Also, there is the twenty-fourth day of the *La*-month;
> At the *tzu* hour [11 P.M.–1 A.M.] the Lord of the Stove ascends to the
>   Courts of Heaven.
> The merits and transgressions of the entire family, large and small,
> Are reported so that the Jade Thearch may hear of them.
> In the next year, on the first of the first month,
> At the *tzu* hour, [the Stove Lord] returns to his place, and sits in
>   the Divine Court.
> When you see him off and welcome him back you should be sincere
>   and respectful;
> You may not neglect or slight the Lord of the Stove!
> You offer ritual to the god to seek good fortune and long life;
> You do not ingratiate yourself with the stove on the level of Wang-sun.[120]

---

[119]*Ching tsao ch'üan shu* (*Tsao Chün ching* section), p. 8b.
[120]*Tsao Chün pao chüan*, p. 3b. Wang-sun is Wang-sun Chia 王孫賈, the man who questions

These two texts contain material quite different from the others. The monthly reports to Heaven are still mentioned, but in both cases fall on the twenty-fourth rather than the last day of each month.[121] The *Ching hsin lu* incorporates something quite similar; it says that the god makes his yearly report on the twenty-fifth day of the twelfth month, and the monthly reports on the twenty-third day.[122] In the *Ch'u shen Tsao Chün ching* and *Tsao Chün pao chüan*, at least, the New Year ascent to Heaven can be explained as being the twelfth of the monthly ascents, rather than something separate and unrelated, as reports on the last day of the month would have to be. Neither of these texts implies that the New Year rites are any more important than any of the other observances, and in fact the primary message of each is the importance of moral rectitude in general; both extol filial piety, help for the needy, and the like. However, they do suggest that the rite itself can, under the right conditions, bring good fortune.

Of particular significance is the reference to "ingratiating" (*mei*) in the *Tsao Chün pao chüan*. The choice of words is based on a classical allusion to the *Lun yü*, but there can be no doubt that this is a criticism of the usual attitude of those performing the popular sendoff ritual. Rather than ignoring or rejecting the New Year rites, the *Tsao Chün pao chüan* suggests that they be performed with sincerity rather than the usual attitude of ingratiation, thus attempting to implant in the New Year rites the spirit of the entire system of stove taboos and regular observances. At the same time, the New Year observance is given no more importance than any other.

A much newer text, the *Ssu-ming chih kuang*, also makes specific comments on the nature of the New Year observances. This work, first published in 1982, is a compilation of revelations and dialogues with the stove god made through a spirit medium. It is something quite different from the traditional stove texts, and cannot be said to represent the same scriptural teachings. Its principal aim seems to be to effect a revival of the stove cult, which it admits is much reduced due to the introduction of gas-burning stoves. The text concedes that many of the teachings and taboos

---

Confucius on the value of "ingratiating oneself with the stove" (*mei yü tsao* 媚於竈) in the *Lun yü*; see *Lun yü* (*Shih-san ching chu shu*) 3.7b.

[121] *Tsao Chün pao chüan*, p. 6a.

[122] *Ching hsin lu*, p. 83b.

of traditional stove texts are no longer relevant in the context of modern hygiene and social mores, but continues the tradition of the scriptural cult by insisting on the divinity of the god and the importance of constant, sincere reverence toward him. There is no mention of the god's monthly ascents. The New Year is represented as the only time the god makes his report, the explanation being that the theme of the festival as a whole is the winding up of old accounts and beginning afresh. However, the text stresses the constant nature of the god's supervision, and the necessity for constant discipline: if a fault is mended within three days' time, it is not recorded, but after three days it stands as a black mark against one's name and must be reported.

As for the New Year observances themselves, the god has the following to say in reply to a question about the sweet offerings made to him:

With regard to [the question about] eating sweet soup dumplings (*t'ien t'ang yuan*) and speaking good words [about the family], this is no more than a foolish and ignorant idea among people of the world. Immortals are not gluttons; if they eat sweet dumplings they will report the truth just the same. If the people of the world want to obtain advantages by inviting me to eat sweet dumplings only once a year, that would make things just too easy for them. If they were to worship me with sweet dumplings every day, there might be some possibility of getting favorable results.

If the people of the world want me to say good things about them, that is a simple matter. I will teach you how. When you send off the god of the stove, [prepare] three bowls of red dumplings. The whole family, young and old, should kneel before the stove and speak the truth; with the dumplings all in the bowls, you should confess and atone for every sin you have committed throughout the year, and swear that in the coming year you will mend your faults and renew yourself without fail. If I see that you have sincerely mended your faults, and have made a clean breast of all your sins, then the sweet flavors sealed up within the glutinous rice soup dumplings in the bowl will transform and remove all salty, astringent, bitter, and spicy flavors.[123] I will take the three bowls of soup dumplings back to Heaven for tasting, and if you have revealed most of the substance of your sins, the Jade Thearch will

---

[123]*Hsien* 鹹, *se* 澀, *k'u* 苦, *la* 辣; these, in contrast to sweet, are flavors symbolic of the unpleasant things the family did.

be greatly delighted, and I will take advantage of this opportunity to expunge the sins of the hosts of living beings. This alone is the most effective way. Otherwise, if you let me take back three bowls of sweet soup dumplings, and files filled with [reports of] sins committed, then even if I do eat them they will be tasteless.[124]

In terms of the ritual forms advocated in this text, there can be no doubt that this is a major break with the traditional scriptural cult. The New Year rite, including the sweet offerings, has been accepted as the principal observance to the stove god. But despite this concession, the text still stresses the need for constant sincerity and denies the effectiveness of an annual ritual performed for form's sake. Clearly the compiler of the *Ssu-ming chih kuang* felt the same dissatisfaction with the popular cult as did his counterparts before him, and to this extent the passage just cited articulates a principle common to all the texts.

CONCLUSIONS

The surviving stove texts are clearly not the scriptures of the popular stove cult, but neither are they entirely unrelated to it, for they are unmistakably a response to it, and an attempt to influence it. Historically, the earliest extant stove texts, those in the *Tao tsang*, most likely came into existence during the Sung dynasty, when the popular cult had achieved its modern form; the more recent texts seem to have proliferated in the Ch'ing period, at a time when local histories prove that the cult had spread to every part of China. The texts cannot be dismissed as irrelevant to the study of the popular cult. Their existence, purpose, and actual effect must be accounted for as much as possible within the context of popular practice.

In the preceding pages, a clear contrast has been established between the New Year rite in the popular stove cult and the ritual observances prescribed in the stove god scriptures. This contrast is revealed by different ritual forms, and a fundamental difference in attitude toward the stove god and the demands he makes upon his followers. And yet the ritual prescriptions in the texts were obviously intended to shape popular practice. Was their failure to do so really as complete as the gap between the two would suggest?

[124]*Ssu-ming chih kuang* 司命之光 (Taichung: Sheng-te pao-kung sheng-te tsa-chih shê 聖德寶宮聖德雜志社, 1982), p. 10.

On the basis of internal evidence in the texts themselves, including the earlier *Tao tsang* scriptures, it is easy to infer that they were intended to modify popular practice, and this intention is made quite explicit in some of the later works. The relatively simple language of the *Tao tsang* scriptures suggests that they were designed to be accessible to as many people as possible; in the recent texts the language is often even simpler and more colloquial, and the aim of wide dissemination is explicitly stated. It is hard to imagine that stove texts would have continued to be produced over so many centuries if they had no effect on popular belief.

Unfortunately, external evidence on the stove texts and their effect is scarce. We know that stove god and other *pao chüan* were performed by specialists summoned in times of misfortune. Although the occasion for such performances is unrelated to the observances of the popular stove cult, the stove god *pao chüan* were composed for effective oral presentation, with simple language, much repetition, and a clear narrative structure. Something of the teachings in them would have been conveyed to the audience. Here at least is evidence that the teachings of the scriptural stove cult were in fact circulated.

We also know that the texts were copied by hand (as in the case of the *Tsao Huang pao chüan*), printed, and, in Taiwan and Hong Kong at least, made readily available in temples. But it does not necessarily follow that many people acquired them, or were aware of their content. Kubo Noritada has made investigations on how such texts circulate in Taiwan and Hong Kong. He had assumed that stove texts such as the *Ching tsao ch'üan shu* and *Tsao Chün pao chüan* enjoyed wide distribution, but was surprised to find that they were not widely known, and most likely to be found in the possession of scholars.[125]

The most fundamental question is whether beliefs or practices in the texts have been successfully introduced into the popular cult. It is difficult to find definitive proof one way or the other, but some observations can be made.

First, there is the matter of the stove god's function as spirit inspector. This appeared in the esoteric tradition from at least the third century A.D., and yet cannot be established with certainty in the popular cult until the T'ang period. This might suggest that the popular belief in this attribute

[125]See Kubo, *Okinawa no shūzoku* (cited n. 1), p. 357.

of the deity might be derived from these esoteric teachings. The deliberate introduction of this idea into general belief by a clerical or literate elite makes an intriguing hypothesis. The *T'ai-shang kan ying p'ien* is clearly an attempt to convince a general audience that numerous deities, including the stove god, keep careful watch over everyone's behavior, with grave consequences for health and fortune. Such a spirit inspector at the heart of every household would have been a convenient instrument for enforcing general adherence to religious or moral teachings of any kind. The sources for this early period are too scanty to show how this might have happened, or indeed whether it happened at all; for all we know the esoteric teachings might ultimately have derived from popular belief. Still, the god's role as spirit inspector should be noted as an important point of correspondence between the popular cult and the esoteric teachings that were absorbed into the *Tao tsang* scriptures and the later textual tradition.

Another similarity between texts and actual practice is the observance of stove taboos. This is an important part of the teachings in virtually all the stove texts, and to some extent has its counterpart in popular belief. As has been noted above, stove taboos appear in Fan Ch'eng-ta's twelfth-century "Canto on Sacrificing to the Stove," suggesting that they were part of popular custom even in the Sung dynasty. In modern times the stove taboos were found by Fei Hsiao-tung in a lower Yangtze village, and by Kubo Noritada in Taiwan. Fei, who was unaware of the existence of the taboos in written form, gives only very general information, but Kubo provides a detailed list. The taboos he found include prohibitions against noise, quarreling, scolding or beating children, and acts of violence near the stove; women menstruating or in the first month after birth coming near the stove; women facing the stove with legs parted; putting unclean things on the stove or burning unclean fuel, excrement, or other fouled articles inside it; striking the stove or cutting things on top of it; and heating water that has been used to wash the feet.[126] All of this corresponds closely to the texts, and might suggest that the textual teachings have been successfully introduced into general practice. However, as in the case of the god's function as spirit inspector, the taboos are something that appear at least from the fourth century A.D. in the esoteric tradition,

---

[126]Ibid., pp. 365–67.

and they might have existed in popular belief long before the earliest surviving texts were created. Also, the pervasiveness of the taboos even now is in some doubt. Aside from Kubo and Fei, none of the many sources on the stove cult mention them. This may be because practices of this sort were too commonplace to attract the attention of casual observers as festivals or periodic observances might have done, and that therefore only someone like Kubo, who knew what to look for, would have found them. Still, in the absence of more extensive fieldwork, there is no certain evidence that popular stove taboos are commonplace throughout China.

Another possible area of influence from the texts is the nature of the food offerings. In the *Ching Ch'u sui-shih chi* and the poetry of Fan Ch'eng-ta pigs' heads and wine are mentioned, and yet in recent times vegetarian offerings prevail. The stove texts also advise exclusively vegetarian offerings, and Tsuda suggests that the change in popular practice may have been due to Taoist influence.[127] Influence from the texts is one possibility, but there were certainly other factors at work. Fan Ch'eng-ta does mention meat offerings, but contemporary accounts in the *Meng liang lu* do not, which suggests that then, as now, solely vegetarian offerings were made in some places and meat ones in others. The use of vegetarian offerings might also be a reflection of the god's status; in many places he may simply not have been important enough to receive meat offerings. Valerie Hansen cites a passage from a Southern Sung drama in which a local earth god complains that he has never received meat offerings, and has to content himself with "bean-paste dumplings and rice cakes" and the diminishment in powers this entails.[128] The preponderance of non-meat offerings to the stove god is not conclusive evidence of influence from the stove texts.

Some periodic observances to the stove prescribed in the texts are also documented in popular practice. These include the burning of incense to the god twice daily, offerings on the first and fifteenth of each month, and observances on the third day of the eighth month, the god's birthday.[129] In

---

[127]Tsuda, "Shina no minkan-shinkō ni okeru sōjin" (cited n. 3), p. 155.

[128]Hansen, *Changing Gods in Medieval China, 1127–1276* (Princeton: Princeton University Press, 1990), pp. 50–51.

[129]For the daily and twice-monthly observances, see the sources cited in note 41 above. For the stove god's birthday, see Tsuda, "Shina no minkan-shinkō ni okeru sōjin," pp. 154–55; Tun and Bodde, *Annual Customs and Festivals in Peking* (Hong Kong: Hong Kong University Press, 1965), p. 68; and Bredon and Mitrophanov, *The Moon Year* (cited n. 30), p. 75.

the case of the daily and twice-monthly offerings, the stove god is not the only recipient of these observances, and it seems unlikely that they were performed because of instructions in stove texts. The birthday celebration is an unusual case, as many of the sources indicate that it took place in temples. This is a phenomenon worth further investigation, but is not directly relevant to the influence of stove texts within domestic ritual.

The evidence against the influence of the texts on the popular cult is more convincing. Certain of the rituals prescribed in the texts never appear in accounts of popular practice, one example being the seven-wick lamp used to represent the stars of the Northern Dipper. Most telling of all, however, is the god's ascent to report at the end of each month. This was firmly established in the earlier esoteric tradition from at least the fourth century, and continued in the *T'ai-shang kan ying p'ien, Tao tsang* scriptures, and all later texts, and yet no trace of it is to be found in popular belief. Kubo found no informants in Taiwan or Hong Kong who knew anything of the monthly reports.[130] For centuries the stove texts taught that the god ascended each month, but the population at large seems to have known only of his annual report at the New Year. This is the most convincing evidence of the failure of the textual teachings to make any significant impact on popular belief, particularly within the context of the New Year observances.

The difference in the rituals prescribed in the stove texts and those actually performed at the New Year clearly illustrates the fundamentally popular character of the latter. The main purpose of the New Year observances is the propitiation of the stove god, in which bribery (the offering of foodstuffs, spirit money, and the like) and urgent and earnest, if not necessarily sincere, entreaty is paramount. Smearing sticky candy onto the god's mouth goes a step further. This act establishes a measure of control over the god, in the face of which he is deemed to be helpless. This bespeaks a certain lack of awe or respect, and it is worth noting that an attitude of contempt is reflected in some popular tales about the deity.[131]

---

[130]Kubo, *Okinawa no shūzoku*, p. 360. Po Sung-nien has a stove god image from Yunnan on which it says that the god ascends on the twenty-third day of each month, just as in the *pao chüan*. However, this image contains an unusually large amount of writing, which might suggest direct influence from the stove texts. See Po and Johnson, *Domesticated Deities and Auspicious Emblems*, pp. 50–51.

[131]Chard, "Folktales on the God of the Stove" (cited n. 40), pp. 173–78.

Overall it is the notion that a single rite can in itself be potent enough to nullify the guilt of a year's misdeeds that was most objectionable from the standpoint of the scriptural teachings.

The rituals prescribed in the texts do not appear in the New Year observance; likewise, the rituals actually practiced do not appear in the texts, except once or twice in the most cursory fashion. In particular, there is no mention of the paper image of the god in any of the stove texts. One might argue that all gods have images, and that the image as manifestation of the god himself was so taken for granted that it was never mentioned. However, the burning of the image and its subsequent renewal are the two most central points in the popular observance, and would have to be included in instructions for the rite, if such were to be formulated. Presumably the text compilers felt the use of the image to be either improper or unimportant. The image was an intimate and familiar presence in the lives of the majority of people in Ch'ing and early twentieth-century China, and, as argued above, was likely the primary factor in the spread and perpetuation of the stove cult. It is this tension between image and scripture that epitomizes the contrast between the stove cult as it really existed and as the educated compilers of the stove texts wished it to be.

Mu-lien

in Pao-chüan

The Performance Context and Religious Meaning
of the *Yu-ming Pao-ch'uan*

DAVID JOHNSON

*T*his paper has two subjects: first, the long prosimetric narratives with religious or didactic themes that are often called *pao-chüan*—how they and allied genres were performed, who their audiences were, and whether those performances are preserved in the *pao-chüan* texts we can read today. Second, a particular *pao-chüan* that tells the story of Mu-lien, the pious monk who was so devoted to his mother that he braved the terrors of the deepest pit of Hell to save her. The story was known throughout China in late imperial times and still is widely known today. The epic stage versions of it, which were important to the symbolic life of villagers throughout much of southern China, are among the greatest creations of the Chinese popular religious imagination.[1] But Mu-lien has also been

[1]See my "Actions Speak Louder Than Words: The Cultural Significance of Chinese Ritual Opera," in David Johnson, ed., *Ritual Opera, Operatic Ritual: "Mu-lien Rescues His Mother" in Chinese Popular Culture* (Berkeley: Chinese Popular Culture Project, 1989), pp. 1–45. An excellent bibliographic guide to the rapidly developing field of Mu-lien studies is Mao Keng-ju 茆耕茹, "Mu-lien tso-p'in, lun-wen pien-mu kai-lüeh (tseng-ting kao)" 目連作品, 論文編目概略 (增訂稿), in Chung-kuo i-shu yen-chiu yuan Hsi-ch'ü yen-chiu so 中國藝術研究院戲曲研究所, et al., eds., *Mu-lien hsi yen-chiu wen-chi* 目連戲研究文集 (Hofei, 1988), pp. 337–77. Titles of some important recent publications together with brief comments on the phenomenon of Mu-lien studies in the PRC can be found in my "Report on the International Conference on Chinese Southern Opera and Mulian Opera, Fukien, 2/26/91–3/5/91," *CHINOPERL Papers* 16 (1992–1993).

told in chantefable for a thousand years.[2] It was the most popular subject for the *pien-wen,* popular prosimetric narratives dating from the T'ang and Five Dynasties (if the surviving texts are any indication),[3] and in the Ch'ing dynasty it still was a popular subject for the lineal descendants of the *pien-wen,* the *pao-chüan.*[4] Studying the *pao-chüan* genre and the Mu-lien story together is therefore very appropriate. Opera and ritual, with their potent combinations of words, elaborate visual imagery, and music were without rival as summoners-up of emotions, each in its own way. But narrative song or story, presented to much smaller audiences on less formal occasions, spoke to the individual more directly. Hence *pao-chüan* versions of the Mu-lien story are likely to have much to tell us about popular piety and village religion.

In what follows I look first at the performance context of *pao-chüan* and a wide variety of similar prosimetric didactic texts. I then turn to the *Yu-ming pao-ch'uan,* a particularly impressive *pao-chüan* version of the Mu-lien story. I discuss the relationship of this text to performance and then review its contents, comparing it in detail with a T'ang *pien-wen* about Mu-lien. In conclusion I discuss the differences between the *pien-wen* and the *pao-chüan,* trace many of those differences to the influence of Mu-lien operas, and finally attempt to understand why the *pao-chüan* and the operas, despite their close kinship, are in the end so different.

Pao-chüan is not an easy term to define. Texts that call themselves *pao-chüan* can be quite different from each other in both content and intention. Some are religious works that have been venerated for centuries (such as Lo Ch'ing's *Wei-wei pu-tung T'ai-shan shen-ken chieh-kuo pao-chüan*), while others were intended mainly to entertain (such as the anonymous *Ying-t'ai pao-chüan,* which recounts the romance of Liang Shan-po and

---

[2]"Chantefable" is a narrative genre that employs a combination of prose and verse (hence the adjective "prosimetric").

[3]Victor H. Mair, *T'ang Transformation Texts* (Cambridge: Council on East Asian Studies, Harvard University, 1989), p. 86. Mair in various publications lists nine *pien-wen* or *pien-wen* fragments about Mu-lien, plus two more prosimetric narratives that he does not classify as *pien-wen* but that are very similar: S. 2614, S. 3704, P. 2319, P. 3107, P. 3485, P. 4988 verso, Peking 876, Peking 3789, Peking 4085; P. 2193, Peking 2496.

[4]See Cheng Chen-to 鄭振鐸, *Chung-kuo su-wen-hsüeh shih* 中國俗文學史 (Taipei: Shang-wu yin-shu kuan, 1967 rpt. of the 1938 ed.), vol. 2, p. 327. The most comprehensive catalogue, Li Shih-yü's *Pao-chüan tsung-lu* (see note 6), lists twenty-six different versions, and it is not complete.

Chu Ying-t'ai).[5] On the other hand, there are many texts that resemble one or another of the various sub-types of *pao-chüan*, but that are called something else, such as *ching, pao-ching, pao-ch'an, pao-ch'uan,* and so on.[6] For example, the five books of Lo Ch'ing are the foundation of *pao-chüan* studies, yet only two have the term in their titles. In another case, a text listed in Li Shih-yü's catalogue (no. 332) and Fu Hsi-hua's catalogue (p. 9) as a *pao-chüan*—*San-shih chiu-mu Mu-lien chi ch'üan-chuan*—is classified as a *t'an-tz'u* in the draft catalogue of the collection of popular performing literature at the Academia Sinica in Taiwan.[7]

Thus not only are there great differences between texts self-labelled *pao-chüan*, there also are many texts labelled or classified as something else that are almost indistinguishable from texts with the label. Therefore even if we settled on a vague and commodious definition of *pao-chüan*—something like "prosimetric narratives intended for non-elite audiences, of substantial length, and with pronounced religious or ethical themes"—we would probably find any number of texts that by our definition were *pao-chüan*, but that were labelled something else.

It may be that we have to re-think the concept of genre when it is applied to the great corpus of Chinese popular literature, especially the branch of it that was intended for performance. In classical Chinese literature genres tend to be very clearly defined, because educated men spent centuries refining the categories. Literary anthologies, collected works, and literary criticism all encouraged the development of clearly defined literary kinds, and these became part of the mental furniture of the high literate elite, who in their own writings conscientiously followed the models bequeathed to them by tradition. As a consequence, even foreign scholars

[5]Sawada Mizuho 澤田瑞穗, *Hōkan no kenkyū* 寶卷の研究, rev. ed. (Tokyo: Kokusho kankōkai, 1975), pp. 172–73.

[6]Texts with these terms in their titles can be found all through the *pao-chüan* catalogues of Sawada (cited n. 5) and of Li Shih-yü 李世瑜: *Pao-chüan tsung-lu* 寶卷綜錄 (Peking: Chunghua shu-chü, 1961). See also Fu Hsi-hua 傅惜華, *Pao chüan tsung-lu* 寶卷總錄 (Peking: Pa-li ta-hsüeh Pei-ching Han-hsüeh yen-chiu suo, 1951), p. 5, and Tseng Tzu-liang 曾子良, "Pao-chüan chih yen-chiu" 寶卷之研究 (M.A. thesis, Cheng-chih ta-hsüeh [Taiwan], 1975), p. 11.

[7]*Chung-yang yen-chiu yuan Li-shih yü-yen yen-chiu suo suo ts'ang Su-ch'ü tsung-mu mu-lu* 中央研究院歷史語言研究所所藏俗曲總目目錄, compiled by Yang Shih-feng 楊時逢 (ms., no date), p. 2. (The title is given as *Mu-lien chiu-mu san-shih te-tao* 目蓮救母三世得道, following the cover rather than the first page of the text.)

have a clear sense of the differences between (for example) *fu*, *shih*, and *tz'u* poetry.

The situation is very different in the realm of non-elite literature, perhaps especially with regard to performance genres and folk songs. This literature was seldom taken seriously by the educated and was produced by individuals who were relatively unselfconscious about genre. Moreover, it was written to be performed in one way or another, and many of the characteristic features of performance, such as music, which are essential to folk taxonomies, are absent from the written remains that we study. Of course there are certain gross generic distinctions that are fairly easy to make in Chinese popular performing literature: between ensemble performance and solo or duo performance, for example; between verse, prose, and prosimetric forms; and between musical and non-musical forms. But these distinctions do not add up to a taxonomy.

This may however be a serious problem only for bibliographers. After all, it is just the *pao-chüan* genre whose existence has been called into question; the texts still exist. We should study the origins, evolution, and internal diversification of the Chinese popular prosimetric tradition as a whole, and leave taxonomic questions to the cataloguers. This will encourage us to make connections between historical periods and across linguistic boundaries, which is essential to a proper appreciation of the true importance of popular and long-lived stories such as "Mu-lien Rescues His Mother." In addition, recognizing that virtually all works in the Chinese prosimetric tradition were originally intended for performance or were derived from such works will enable us to see more clearly the kinship not just between the different varieties of prosimetric or chantefable literature, but also between chantefable and ballads and storytelling, and between those largely solo forms and the myriad operatic genres.

PERFORMING DEVOTIONAL LITERATURE:
PAO-CHÜAN, SHAN-SHU, AND OTHERS.

We know a certain amount about how *pao-chüan* were performed, although there are all too few good first-hand descriptions.[8] I shall first review the

---

[8]After a certain amount of experimentation I have found that it is impossible to avoid the term *pao-chüan*, ambiguous and imprecise though it is. There just is no way to work a phrase like "prosimetric narrative with religious or ethical themes" into any exposition grace-

evidence I have collected regarding private performances of *pao-chüan*, and then turn to public performances of closely related genres.

Of the descriptions of private performances, one of the most suggestive is a brief account by Chu Chieh-fan of a trip he made in 1946 to the ancient pilgrimage center of Mount Hua, twenty miles or so southwest of the great bend of the Yellow River at T'ung-kuan, in eastern Shensi. One evening he heard chanting in a nearby room. He went over and saw a young woman seated on the *k'ang* (heated sleeping platform) with a book in her hands, chanting and singing in a clear, beautiful voice. The women who were gathered around her listened very intently and seriously. Chu asked to see the texts she was chanting, which all turned out to be booklets printed by commercial bookshops (*fang-chien yin-hsing te hsiao ts'e-tzu*). He gives the titles of seven, though he makes it clear that there were more: *Hsing-shih su-shuo* ("Plain talk to awaken the world"), *Su-yü ko* ("Songs in plain words"), *Chi-te mien-nan* ("Accumulating virtue and avoiding troubles"), *Yen wang le* ("The pleasures of Yama" [?]), *Huan yang pao-ch'uan* ("Precious tradition on returning to the *yang*"), *Shu chia o-tzu* ("The evil son squeezed by trees" [?]), and *Meng Chiang nü k'u ch'ang-ch'eng* ("The woman of Meng-Chiang Village weeps at the Great Wall"). He says the booklets were of many types: "ballads [*su-ch'ü*], morality books [*shan-shu*], *pao-chüan*, folksongs [*ko-yao*], proverbs, and so on."[9] This is important information, first because it tells us that the pilgrim leader was performing *pao-chüan*, but also because she was chanting other kinds of texts as well. We will see another example of this versatility in the evidence from the *Chin P'ing Mei tz'u-hua* that will be discussed shortly.

The relationship of the woman Chu calls the leader to the rest of the group is unclear, although it seems similar to that of the person called *fo t'ou* to the groups of pilgrims to the Upper T'ien-chu Monastery near Hangchow observed by Chün-fang Yü in recent years: "Pilgrims came to Hangchow in groups . . . led by group leaders (*hsiang t'ou*) who took care of practical matters. Some groups also had, in addition, a spiritual leader called *fo t'ou* (Buddhist leader) who knew how to chant scriptures, sing pilgrimage songs and go into trance, become a spokesperson for Kuan-

---

fully, no matter how academic its intended audience.

[9]Lou Tzu-k'uang 婁子匡 and Chu Chieh-fan 朱介凡, *Wu-shih nien lai te Chung-kuo su wen-hsüeh* 五十年來的中國俗文學 (Taipei: Cheng-chung shu-chü, 1963), pp. 307–8.

yin (*huo p'u-sa*, "living bodhisattva"), and practice healing among fellow pilgrims."[10] Yü adds that the pilgrims (almost all of whom were women)[11] "relaxed in the evening by visiting each other, sharing gossip and laughter, exchanging stories about Kuan-yin and singing pilgrim's songs together. The stories they told about Kuan-yin all came from [the] *Hsiang-shan pao-chüan*, but with strong local coloring."[12] The pilgrims also sang short songs about Kuan-yin called *Kuan-yin ching* ("Kuan-yin sutras"). Yü believes they may have been composed in trance by "living bodhisattvas" of earlier times, since Kuan-yin herself frequently speaks, or sings, in them.[13]

The pilgrim leader encountered by Chu Chieh-fan was not a typical *pao-chüan* performer. Rather she was the leader of a group of the faithful, and in that sense was like the leaders of sectarian congregations. But the setting of the Mount Hua performance was very similar to that of other *pao-chüan* performances, as we shall see.

Valuable descriptions of *pao-chüan* performances can be found in the late-sixteenth-century novel *Chin P'ing Mei tz'u-hua*,[14] though each scene

[10]"Miracles, Pilgrimage Sites and the Cult of Kuan-yin," paper presented to the JCCS Conference on Pilgrims and Sacred Sites in China, January, 1989, p. 27. Professor Yü has also produced a videotape, *Kuan-yin Pilgrimage* (1989), that shows a "living bodhisattva" leading a group in singing.

[11]Yü, pp. 26–27.

[12]Yü, p. 31.

[13]Yü, p. 32. It was not at all uncommon for pious women to create their own devotional songs. For example, in 1928 Tung Tso-pin reported in the journal *Min-su* 民俗 (*Folklore*) on what were popularly called *Lao-p'o ching* ("Old ladies' sutras") in Nan-yang. (I assume that the Nan-yang in Honan is meant, but have not been able to consult the original article to confirm this.) The old women of Nan-yang were devout believers in the Pure Land doctrine, but they knew nothing of the sect's history or its scriptures. Instead they composed their own "scriptures," which were in the form of short songs. "They deeply revere these 'sutras,'" writes Tung, "and transmit them orally, regarding them as secret treasures. They do not readily pass them on to others, so it is very difficult to collect them. If someone who eats meat is allowed to chant one of these 'sutras,' it is a terrible sin." (Lou and Chu, *Wu-shih nien lai te Chung-kuo su wen-hsüeh* [cited n. 9], p. 315, quoting Tung Tso-pin 董作賓, "Ching-t'u tsung te ko-yao hua" 淨土宗的砍謠化, *Min-su* 民俗 17/18 [July 25, 1928].) The ones Tung quotes are short, simple ditties, much like folksongs, and with folksongs' directness and aptness of phrase. They also resemble the *Kuan-yin ching* described and recorded by Chün-fang Yü, though they appear to be more verbally inventive. There also were "Old ladies' sutras" in Shaohsing in the 1930s, almost as short and simple as those from Nan-yang and Hangchow. (Lou and Chu, p. 314, quoting an article by Yeh Ching-ming 葉鏡銘 in *Min-su* 75. Lou and Chu quote several other, more complex kinds of women's devotional songs as well, on pp. 314–19.)

[14]See Sawada (cited n. 5), pp. 285–99, and Catherine Karlitz, *The Rhetoric of Chin P'ing Mei* (Bloomington: Indiana University Press, 1986), pp. 59–66.

appears to portray a somewhat different type of text or performance style. These passages are worth a close look, both because of the exceptional detail with which the performances are described and also because of the early date of the book. Of course, the setting is one of wealth and leisure, not to say decadence, but some of the women of Hsi-men Ch'ing's household may not have been that far removed in educational level from the pilgrims observed by Chu Chieh-fan.

Most important for our purposes are the works performed in *hui* 39 and 74. It is worth noting that these very early texts have characteristics of both the old and new style *pao-chüan* as defined by Sawada, Li Shih-yü, and others. (The new style appeared in the nineteenth century.) For example, one has a moderately complex introductory section, which is characteristic of older *pao-chüan*, but the other has no introduction, which is said to be characteristic of more recent ones. Both have a simple one- or two-*chüan* structure, said to be a feature of more recent *pao-chüan*, but both also frequently use song-forms (*ch'ü-p'ai*), which is supposed to be an older feature.[15] This shows once again that it is extremely difficult to make neat generic or sub-generic distinctions where Chinese popular performing literature is concerned.

In *hui* 74 Meng Yü-lou, one of Hsi-men's wives, is celebrating her birthday. In the evening the door of the women's quarters is closed and Yüeh-niang, another wife and the most pious among them, announces that she has asked the resident nuns to recite (*hsüan*) the "Scroll About Woman Huang" (*Huang-shih nü chüan*, a variant title of the *Huang-shih nü pao-chüan*).[16] A table—in other scenes referred to as a "sutra table" (*ching cho*)—is placed on the *k'ang*, and three nuns sit cross-legged beside it. The ladies find seats in the room, Yüeh-niang washes her hands and burns incense, and then Sister Hsüeh "opened the 'Scroll About Woman Huang' and in a strong voice began to recite."[17] The performance goes on until

---

[15]Sawada (cited n. 5), pp. 36–37, 53; Li Shih-yü, "Pao-chüan hsin-yen" 寶卷新究, *Wen-hsüeh i-ch'an tseng-k'an* 文學遺產增刊 no. 4 (Peking: Tso-chia ch'u-pan shê, 1957), pp. 169–70; and his "Chiang Che chu sheng te hsüan chüan" 江浙諸省的宣卷, ibid., no. 7 (Peking: Chung-hua ch'u-pan shê, 1959), pp. 199–200.

[16]This was a popular story in devotional literature and has recently been studied in detail by Beata Grant. The story line is more or less the same in the *Chin P'ing Mei tz'u-hua* version and the versions studied by Grant. See "The Spiritual Saga of Woman Huang: From Pollution to Purification," *Ritual Opera, Operatic Ritual* (cited n. 1).

[17]Tai Hung-sen 戴鴻森, ed., *Chin P'ing Mei tz'u hua* 金瓶梅詞話 (Peking: Jen-min wen-

the second watch (9–11 P.M.). The text as presented in the novel begins with a long introductory section combining prose, *gatha* verse (*chi*), and song-form verse, and the *pao-chüan* proper[18] also contains song-form verse, as well as seven- and ten-character verse and prose. It appears to have been a solo performance by Sister Hsüeh, unlike some of the others described in the novel.

In *hui* 39 another work that resembles extant *pao-chüan* is performed. It is not named, but from the story it has been identified as the *Wu-tsu huang-mei pao-chüan*.[19] Here also the occasion is a birthday, this time P'an Chin-lien's. Yüeh-niang suggests summoning the nuns to "tell 'tales of cause and effect' and sing Buddhist songs."[20] Terms like *pao-chüan* or *hsüan chüan* are not used; instead, the nuns are invited to *shuo yin-kuo*—tell stories about karmic cause and effect—and this term is used twice. A sutra table[21] is placed on the *k'ang*, and the nuns apparently sit beside it. The ladies gather around the *k'ang*, incense and candles are lit, and the performance begins. This time Sister Hsüeh is joined by Sister Wang, and the two have equal parts in the performance. As in the Woman Huang scroll, the story is presented in a wide variety of forms, ranging from prose to song-form verse, and the nuns are said to accompany themselves by striking a *chi tz'r*.[22] There is a break for refreshment in the middle, and then the nuns take up the story again. The performance goes on into the fourth watch (1–3 A.M.), and almost everyone leaves or falls asleep before it is over. But Yüeh-niang wants to know how the story ends, and Sister Hsüeh obliges, relating in the darkest and quietest hour of the night the miraculous birth and boyhood of the future Fifth Patriarch of the Ch'an sect.[23]

Two other performances of didactic literature are described in the *Chin P'ing Mei tz'u-hua* and are worth a brief look here, even though they are rather different from *pao-chüan* recitations. *Hui* 73 relates events that took

---

hsüeh ch'u-pan shê, 1985), p. 1076.

[18]Note that this text refers to itself as a *pao-chüan*: ibid., p. 1052.

[19]Sawada (cited n. 5), p. 291.

[20]*Chin P'ing Mei tz'u-hua*, p. 493.

[21]Called this on p. 496.

[22]I have not been able to identify this, though there was an ancient wooden percussion instrument of the same name. But see below, n. 45.

[23]*Chin P'ing Mei tz'u-hua*, p. 498.

place on the day before the recitation of the Woman Huang scroll, discussed above. Meng Yü-lou's birthday is already being celebrated, and the ladies have gathered together while Hsi-men Ch'ing is amusing himself elsewhere. Yüeh-niang washes her hands and lights incense, and they all settle down to listen to Sister Hsüeh "discourse on the dharma" (*chiang-shuo fo-fa*).[24] What follows is very much like a storyteller's performance. The text is all in prose, with only incidental verses, in the style of the *hua-pen*. (In fact the same story can be found in the late-sixteenth-century collection of vernacular short stories, *Liu-shih chia hsiao-shuo*, more commonly known as the *Ch'ing-p'ing-shan-t'ang hua-pen*.[25]) But it is just as concerned with karmic cause and effect as the chantefables of *hui* 39 and 74.

In *hui* 51 there is yet another kind of performance. This also takes place on the birthday of one of Hsi-men Ch'ing's wives. Once again, Yüeh-niang wishes to hear Sister Hsüeh "discourse on the dharma," this time by having her perform a *Diamond Sutra* "lesson" (*Chin-kang k'o-i*). The setting is the sitting room (*ming chien*) of Yüeh-niang's suite. A sutra table is set up and incense lit. Then Sister Hsüeh and Sister Wang take their seats facing each other, with an acolyte standing on either side chanting the Buddha's name. The ladies sit around them to listen.[26] After an introduction by Hsüeh, the performance proceeds, with Wang asking questions about the teachings or actions of the Buddhas, bodhisattvas, or patriarchs, and Hsüeh answering her in pithy, concentrated language. This text is overtly didactic, not to say catechistical, and has no narrative character at all.[27]

Thus *Chin P'ing Mei tz'u-hua* describes four occasions during which the women of a wealthy late-sixteenth-century household gather on the birthday of one or another of them to listen to popular devotional literature recited by nuns who specialize in such performances. (Note that the nuns, like the pilgrim leader described by Chu Chieh-fan, are able to perform several genres of pious literature.) Two of the performances are clearly of the *hsüan chüan* type, though there are some slight differences between them: the one that presents a text called a *pao-chüan* is a solo,

<hr>

[24] *Chin P'ing Mei tz'u-hua*, p. 1054.

[25] Patrick Hanan, *The Chinese Short Story: Studies in Dating, Authorship, and Composition* (Cambridge: Harvard University Press, 1973), pp. 8, 3. Hanan refers to this story as "Hung 13." See also Sawada (cited n. 5), p. 294.

[26] *Chin P'ing Mei tz'u-hua*, pp. 659–60. My thanks to David Roy for explaining "*ming chien*."

[27] Ibid., pp. 660–62; Sawada (cited n. 5), pp. 289–90.

while the one called *shuo yin-kuo* is a duet. Certainly in one case, and probably in both, a written text, characterized by a rich combination of verse forms and prose, is used as a script. Both the texts closely resemble the form that is conventionally known as *pao-chüan*. An atmosphere of reverence is created by setting up a sutra table and burning incense, by the presence of the nuns, and by their elevated position on the *k'ang*, above the listening women.

Hsi-men Ch'ing was so wealthy his wives could afford to have nuns in residence. It was of course far more common for the performers of devotional literature to be brought into a household only on special occasions, as when someone had made a vow to the gods to sponsor the recitations of *pao-chüan*. Sawada quotes a poem by Ch'en To, who lived in the late fifteenth and early sixteenth century, which describes such a performance. A "man [or men] of the Way," who wears a long cotton gown rather than a monk's robe, goes from house to house, hoping to find people who have made vows and will invite him in to hold a service. During the service, a picture of the Buddha is hung up in the main hall of the house, and the "man [or men] of the Way" "proclaims [*hsüan*] . . . the *Diamond Sutra [pao-]chüan*." Both the setting and the text remind one very much of the scene from *Chin P'ing Mei tz'u-hua* just recounted. Such performers still could be found in the 1920s. Ch'ien Chao-chi, in a 1922 report, says that in southern Kiangsu and northern Chekiang there are itinerant performers, usually dressed like monks, who beg for alms by going from door to door beating a "wooden fish" and singing *pao-chüan*.[28]

Other *pao-chüan* performers had a permanent place in the community, as we learn from an important note by Cheng Chen-to, the great pioneering collector and student of Chinese popular literature.

> Every locale in southern China still has a person who "proclaims scrolls [*hsüan chüan*]," who occupies a position of great authority. "Proclaim scrolls" means "perform *pao-chüan*." When a scroll is "proclaimed," incense is always burned and the buddhas invited. There is a strong religious atmosphere, unlike ordinary *t'an-tz'u* performances. They sing the *Hsiang-shan pao-chüan*, the *Liu Hsiang-nü pao-chüan*, and others, which are the most potent means in existence for the propagation of Buddhism. Countless women and girls have been

---

[28]Quoted in Lou and Chu, *Wu-shih nien lai te Chung-kuo su wen-hsüeh* (cited n. 9), pp. 306–7.

moved by them, and have wept, sighed, worried, and even prayed passionately for women in the *pao-chüan*.[29]

Performers could be brought in as part of birthday celebrations (as in the *Chin P'ing Mei tz'u-hua*), or to help cure illness. The *Hai-shang yeh-yu pei-lan*, which was published in 1883, states that when they

> 'proclaim scrolls' [*hsüan chüan*], I do not know what books they use, but they are one or two *chüan* long. A group of five or six people sit down together and chant them, in imitation of the chanting of sutras by monks and priests. They set up the pictures of many Buddhas and arrange sacrificial offerings in the main hall [of the house in which they are performing]. They are neither Buddhist monks nor Taoist priests and do not wear priestly garb. They mumble along from morning to night, when they have a big meal and then disperse. They claim they can bring down good fortune. . . . This practice is especially popular among prostitutes, who never fail to have the "proclaiming of scrolls" [*hsüan chüan*] when there is a birthday to be celebrated in their house, or when there is illness to be exorcised.[30]

In the late-nineteenth-century novel *Sao mi chou* ("The broom that sweeps away delusions") there is a passage (noted by Sawada) describing a similar practice: "In the cities of Chekiang, newly-impoverished wanderers have recently appeared who compose vulgar ballads in seven-character meter which they sing seated, facing each other. They call it 'proclaiming scrolls [*hsüan chüan*].' Women particularly like to listen. [The performers] are constantly invited into people's homes for birthday celebrations, or in cases of illness."[31] In the 1860s, Mao Hsiang-lin noted that in Wu (Chekiang and southern Kiangsu) people always summon a spirit-medium when someone is sick. "The practice most widespread among them is called 'proclaiming scrolls' [*hsüan chüan*]. They have 'Kuan-yin

---

[29]Cheng Chen-to 鄭振鐸, *Chung-kuo su-wen-hsüeh shih* 中國俗文學史 (Taipei: Shang-wu yin-shu-kuan, 1967 rpt. of the 1938 edition), vol. 2, p. 307. Cheng does not make it clear just where these *pao-chüan* performances took place, but on balance it seems probable that they were private rather than public.

[30]Li Chia-jui 李家瑞, "Hsüan chüan," originally published in *Chü hsüeh yüeh-k'an* 劇學月刊 4.10 (1935); reprinted in Wang Ch'iu-kuei 王秋桂, ed., *Li Chia-jui hsien-sheng t'ung-su wen-hsüeh lun-wen chi* 李家瑞先生通俗文學論文集 (Taipei: Hsüeh-sheng shu-chü, 1982), p. 51. Emended on the basis of Sawada (cited n. 5), pp. 84–85. Date from Sawada. I do not know what region is referred to in this account.

[31]Sawada, pp. 86–87. I have translated Sawada's Japanese translation of this passage.

scrolls,' 'Ten kings [of hell] scrolls,' and 'Stove god scrolls.' They are in dialect, just like the songs of blind balladeers. Those who sing accompaniments to the scrolls are all female spirit-mediums. When they 'proclaim scrolls' they always go on until late at night. When dawn breaks, they disperse."[32]

Huang Chih-kang, writing in the early 1950s, mentions another practice involving *pao-chüan* recitation that is likely to have had an exorcistic purpose, though he seems to suggest it was for entertainment. "Not too long ago [*pao-chüan*] were performed in the home of the deceased on the night before the burial, to help those who were sitting up with the coffin to stay awake."[33] The article on *hsüan chüan* in the *Great Chinese Encyclopedia* states that *hsüan chüan* specialists performed not only *pao-chüan* but also the "minor scrolls" (*hsiao chüan*) of rituals such as "reverencing the incense," "purifying the stove," and the like. Some even specialized in Buddhist masses for the dead.[34] Li Shih-yü also states that *pao-chüan* performers undertook ritual duties, such as chanting prayers for the dead.[35] Another sign that *pao-chüan* reciters were regarded as something more than entertainers is the fact that they were called "master" (*hsien-sheng*), a bit of popular deference that they shared with some shadow opera performers.[36]

While it is true that *hsüan chüan* could mean many things—it is commonly said, for example, that shadow opera players in late Ch'ing times greeted each other by asking "what scrolls are you proclaiming?"[37] and there is other evidence that shadow opera performers referred to their scripts as "scrolls"[38]—still it is likely that in most cases, *hsüan chüan* meant

[32]Mao Hsiang-lin 毛祥麟, *Tui-shan shu-wu mo-yü lu* 對山書屋墨余錄, quoted in *Li Chia-jui hsien-sheng t'ung-su wen-hsüeh lun-wen chi*, pp. 51–52, and Sawada, p. 83. Book title and certain emendations from Sawada.
[33]Huang Chih-kang 黃之岡, *Ts'ung yang-ko tao ti-fang hsi* 從秧歌到地方戲 (Shanghai: Chung-hua shu-chü, 1951), p. 104.
[34]*Chung-kuo ta pai-k'o ch'üan-shu: Hsi-ch'ü, ch'ü-i* 中國大百科全書: 戲曲, 曲藝 (Peking, 1983), p. 521b.
[35]"Chiang Che chu sheng te hsüan chüan" (cited n. 15), p. 210.
[36]*Chung-kuo ta pai-k'o ch'üan-shu: Hsi-ch'ü, ch'ü-i*, p. 521b.
[37]T'ung Ching-hsin 佟晶心, "Chung-kuo ying-hsi k'ao" 中國影戲考, *Chü-hsüeh yüeh-k'an* 劇學月刊 3.11 (November, 1934), p. 10a.
[38]Sun K'ai-ti 孫楷弟, *K'uei-lei hsi k'ao-yüan* 傀儡戲考原 (Shanghai: Shang-tsa ch'u-pan shê, 1952), p. 64, states that they were called *chüan pen* 卷本. T'ung, "Chung-kuo ying-hsi

"to proclaim—i.e., to perform—*pao-chüan*." So we can summarize what we have learned so far as follows: performing *pao-chüan* was a devotional or exorcistic act, one that was intended to lead the listeners to salvation or to bring more immediate benefits, such as the expulsion of demonic influences. The performances frequently lasted for a long time, and were often held at night. The texts presented tended to be prosimetric narratives. The performances almost always took place in the intimate setting of a family or quasi-family group (pilgrims, prostitutes), usually in private homes. And the primary audience was women.

As far as one can tell, the *pao-chüan* that were presented in these intimate domestic or quasi-domestic settings were all quite orthodox in their teachings. But according to many scholars, *pao-chüan* originated in the new popular religions of the Ming dynasty, such as the Lo and Hung-yang sects.[39] Sectarian *pao-chüan* presented in many cases a cosmology and theology that were radically different from the prevailing orthodoxies, though they had the prosimetric form and narrative techniques of their less subversive cousins.

A central feature of the regular meetings of the devotees of the new sects was the recitation of their scriptures, which often were called *pao-chüan*. According to Susan Naquin, "detailed descriptions of sutra [*pao-chüan*] recitation are rather rare," but in general, "when the group met, they bowed to the altar and to the scriptures themselves, lighting incense and offering fruit or tea. . . . Then they sat and chanted the scriptures in unison, simultaneously beating out a rhythm with the tok! tok! of the wooden-fish . . . and the ding! ding! ding! of the brass-bowl bell."[40] If Naquin's description is accurate, it is clear that in sectarian *pao-chüan* recitation there was no distinction between performer and audience. This is a sharp and probably fundamental difference from the "domestic" model I have just described.

---

k'ao" (cited previous note), p. 13 a–b, states that troupes sometimes had an old performer called the "scroll-checker" (*ch'a chüan* 察卷), whose responsibility it was to prevent off-color material from being performed.

[39]Li Shih-yü presents the most extreme version of this thesis in his "Pao-chüan hsin-yen" (cited n. 15), p. 165.

[40]"The Transmission of White Lotus Sectarianism in Late Imperial China," in David Johnson, Andrew J. Nathan, and Evelyn S. Rawski, eds., *Popular Culture in Late Imperial China* (Berkeley: University of California Press, 1984), p. 262.

We should note, though, that in another of her writings, Naquin describes what appears to be a sectarian *pao-chüan* performance that is somewhat reminiscent of the "domestic" ones we have looked at above. "Sect literature [*pao-chüan*, or *ching*] contained a variety of . . . tales of the Eternal Mother, often interwoven with traditional myths and legends. . . . These stories . . . provided sect members with a convenient proselytizing device." She then quotes a confession dated 1808: "'Sung Chin-yao and others often assembled [and] . . . listened to [their teacher] Ku Liang tell stories about buddhas and immortals. . . . When Ku Liang sat and talked, they didn't close the gate, and so people would come to listen . . . and in that way became familiar [with the teachings of the sect].'"[41] Ku Liang's storytelling sounds a bit like that of Sister Hsüeh in *hui* 73 of the *Chin P'ing Mei tz'u-hua*, or that of the pilgrim song-leader encountered by Chu Chieh-fan on Mount Hua. But of course the settings are very different. In addition the role played by *pao-chüan* in the lives of the believers in White Lotus–type sects seems to have been very different from the role they played in the lives of those who adhered to more orthodox beliefs, a difference that is reflected in performance styles.

Both sectarian and non-sectarian *pao-chüan* were presented in private or quasi-private settings. But Li Shih-yü states that after the mid-nineteenth century *pao-chüan* were also performed in more public venues, such as temples and temple fairs, as well as teahouses, inns, and restaurants.[42] Descriptions of such performances are very rare, but this may be due to the fact that the term *hsüan chüan* was usually reserved for recitations in private settings, since we have a great deal of information about the public performance of didactic or moralistic narratives that sound rather like *pao-chüan* but have different generic labels.

In 1922 Ch'ien Chao-chi wrote that in Kiangsu and Chekiang singers referred to the performance of *pao-chüan* as "*shuo yin-kuo*." They used a combination of speech and song, and accompanied themselves with a single iron cymbal. *Shuo yin-kuo* took place not in private homes, how-

---

[41]*Millenarian Rebellion in China: The Eight Trigrams Uprising of 1813* (New Haven: Yale University Press, 1976), p. 19. Sung Chin-yao was a sect leader.
[42]Li Shih-yü, "Chiang Che chu sheng te hsüan chüan" (cited n. 15), p. 201.

ever, but at fixed times in village and small town teahouses.[43] The historian Ku Chieh-kang, at that time still in his twenties, wrote a brief reply to Ch'ien's communication. In Soochow, he asserted, *hsüan chüan* and *shuo yin-kuo* are different types of performance. In the former, the principal performer recites the text, and after each sentence three or four assistants chant the Buddha's name in unison. The "wooden fish" and a small brass bowl (*ch'ing*)[44] are used in accompaniment. In *shuo yin-kuo* on the other hand, two performers sing in turn, accompanying themselves with clappers and a brass cymbal.[45] This sounds very much like the *shuo yin-kuo* performance in the *Chin P'ing Mei tz'u-hua*. Since the *Chin P'ing Mei tz'u-hua* was a product of late-sixteenth-century Shantung,[46] it would appear that *shuo yin-kuo* had existed in eastern China for more than three hundred years by the early twentieth century. (Incidentally, the dispute between Ch'ien and Ku over what *shuo yin-kuo* "really" was is a good example of the sort of definitional quibbling to which I took exception earlier. The interesting point is not whether *shuo yin-kuo* uses one or two performers, or is also called *hsüan chüan*, but how similar the various performances called *shuo yin-kuo* are, and how much they resemble many of the performances known as *hsüan chüan*.)

Another example was a kind of performer called "*Sacred Edict* lecturer." It was decreed in 1729, apparently in response to the spread of new religious ideas among the populace, that lectures explaining the so-called *Sacred Edict* (*sheng-yü*) of the K'ang-hsi Emperor, together with the Yung-cheng Emperor's commentary, should be given regularly in towns and villages across China.[47] These lectures do not appear to have been particularly successful, and the entire system had fallen into decay by the mid-nineteenth century.[48] But it gave rise to a fascinating popular variant

[43]Ch'ien Chao-chi 錢肇基, "T'ung hsün" 通訊, *Ko-yao chou-k'an* 歌謠周刊 vol. 1, p. 90, quoted in Lou and Chu, *Wu-shih nien lai te Chung-kuo su wen-hsüeh* (cited n. 9), pp. 306–7.
[44]This term is usually translated "stone chime," but according to Sawada it is the familiar brass bowl of ritual recitations. See Sawada (cited n. 5), p. 91.
[45]Perhaps the *chi tz'r* used by Sister Hsüeh (above, p. 62) was an iron or brass cymbal.
[46]Andrew Plaks, *The Four Masterworks of the Ming Novel* (Princeton: Princeton University Press, 1987), pp. 55–65.
[47]See Victor Mair, "Language and Ideology in the Written Popularizations of the *Sacred Edict*," in *Popular Culture in Late Imperial China* (cited n. 40), p. 350.
[48]Mair, pp. 353–54.

that is very reminiscent of *hsüan chüan* performances. Kuo Mo-jo, in his recollections of his boyhood in Szechwan around the turn of the century, describes the performances of *Sacred Edict* lecturers:

> *Sacred Edict* lecturers, who recited *shan-shu* about loyalty, filial piety, and fidelity, often came to our village. Most *shan-shu* were nothing but our own legends or tales. In form, the narratives were a combination of speech and song, very much like *t'an-tz'u*, though not identical to them [recall that Cheng Chen-to in the passage quoted earlier (p. 64) was also reminded of *t'an-tz'u* by the *hsüan chüan* he heard]. . . . At a street corner they would set up a high platform made of three square tables, one placed atop the other two. On the platform, incense and candles were lit as offerings to the plaque of the *Sacred Edict*. A chair was placed on the right-hand table. If two people performed together, then a chair was placed on each of the side tables. When it came time for the *Sacred Edict* lecturer to preach, he, dressed in the cap and gown of an official, would kowtow deeply four times to the plaque. Then he would stand up again and, drawing out his voice, would recite the ten maxims of the *Sacred Edict*. After that, he would get back up on the platform and begin his performance. As for style of delivery, he would recite from a text quite artlessly. The sung parts were sung with drawn-out tones, to which was added the sound of weeping at tragic moments. Some of the lecturers would accompany themselves with bells, "fish tubes," bamboo clappers, and the like to help their tunes along. This artless kind of storytelling was a form of entertainment that people in the villages liked very much. They would stand before the *Sacred Edict* platform and listen for two or three hours. The better storytellers could make their audiences weep.[49]

We can see from this fascinating account that *Sacred Edict* lectures were prosimetric narratives accompanied by simple instruments such as clappers. The stories were about "loyalty, filial piety, and fidelity," and could last several hours. The "lecturer" (or lecturers—there were two at times) lit incense and candles before beginning, and performed sitting on an elevated platform. Their recitals could make the villagers weep. All this

---

[49]"Shao-nien shih-tai" 少年時代, in *Mo-jo wen-chi* 沫若文集 (Shanghai: Hsin wen-i ch'u-pan shê, 1955; originally published in 1947 by Hai-yen shu-tien of Shanghai), vol. 6, pp. 29–30. (I have benefited from Victor Mair's translation of this passage in "Language and Ideology" [cited n. 47], pp. 354–55.) Note that K'ang-hsi's *Sacred Edict* had sixteen maxims, not ten. See below, note 53.

sounds very much like the descriptions of the *pao-chüan* performances given earlier, except for the public setting and the Confucian themes.

It should be noted that the *shan-shu* of Kuo Mo-jo's account obviously were not the *shan-shu*, usually translated "morality books," that have been studied by Sakai Tadao[50] and others, but rather were prosimetric texts that served as scripts for didactic storytellers. As it happens, we know a fair amount about this kind of *shan-shu*, because twenty traditional texts were discovered in western Hupei in the early 1980s. Among them there was one about Woman Huang, very similar in content to the Woman Huang scroll of *hui* 74 of the *Chin P'ing Mei tz'u-hua*.[51] Liu Shou-hua, who found them, remembers watching *shan-shu* performances while growing up in Hupei. According to Liu (in Beata Grant's paraphrase), "after the harvest was in, a tall platform would be erected in a clearing in the fields and decorated with candles and incense. Then a professional performer would ascend the platform and, with the help of a written text, chant the story. The atmosphere was rather somber and sad, and [the performance] would often elicit weeping and wailing from the women. . . . The most popular forms of entertainment among the rural villagers were local drama, shadow plays, and these *shan-shu* performances."[52] The similarity of these performances to the Szechwan *shan-shu* recitations described by Kuo Mo-jo is striking. Clearly this form of village entertainment-cum-indoctrination was very widespread in the early twentieth century.

The article on *shan-shu* in the *Great Chinese Encyclopedia* states that the form originated in the *Sacred Edict* lectures of the Shun-chih reign-period (1644–1661). It adds that the *Sacred Edict* lectures were replaced in late Ch'ing by another prosimetric genre called the "Ten Great Good Deeds" (*Shih ch'üan ta shan*)—honoring parents, establishing schools, and so on.[53] Later this came to be called "*shan-shu* lecturing" (*hsüan-chiang shan-shu*), "*shan-shu* storytelling" (*shuo shan-shu*), and finally just *shan-shu*. In the early period, *shan-shu* were performed only at the Lantern Festival and the Mid-Autumn Festival, but gradually they came to be presented more

---

[50]Sakai Tadao 酒井忠夫, *Chūgoku zensho no kenkyū* 中國善書の研究 (Tokyo: Kokusho kankōkai, 1960).

[51]Beata Grant, "Woman Huang" (cited n. 16), p. 253.

[52]Ibid., pp. 249–52.

[53]Could this, as Grant suggests, be the source of Kuo Mo-jo's confusion, noted in n. 49, about the number of maxims in the *Sacred Edict*?

and more frequently. The performers were professionals, each troupe having one chief singer and several others who sang responses to him. According to this article, the texts took the form of question and answer, and combined speech and singing, which reminds us of the "discourse on the dharma" of Sister Hsüeh and Sister Wang in *hui* 51 of the *Chin P'ing Mei tz'u-hua,* discussed earlier. There was no instrumental accompaniment, and performers used only very simple props, such as fans and "wake-up blocks" (like teahouse storytellers).[54] This account, though not entirely accurate as to the formal characteristics of the genre, nevertheless is very valuable because it clarifies the connection between *Sacred Edict* lectures and *shan shu* performances.

Another genre that seems to have been virtually identical to *shan-shu* and *Sacred Edict* lectures was called simply "lecturing" in at least one early twentieth-century Hunan village: "In the alleyways and at the foot of the bridge, I would often go and listen to performers reciting and singing. . . . On the fifteenth of the first month there would also be lecturing [*hsüan chiang*]. The lecturer would place candles and incense on the "platform of good and evil" [*shan-o t'ai*] and, seated [on it], would tell tales of good and evil."[55] It is quite obvious that this Hunan "lecturing" was closely related to the *Sacred Edict* lectures in Szechwan and *shan-shu* performances in Hupei we have already discussed.

Yet another type of edifying storytelling developed in southeastern Shansi in late Ch'ing times.[56] A cult known as the "Way of the Heavenly Immortal" (*T'ien hsien tao*) or the "Hall of Western Transformation" (*Hsi hua t'ang*) had as its sole activity "persuading people to become virtuous by telling stories [*chiang-yen ku-shih*] to them; they did not have congregations, festivals, or pilgrimages." Their teachings were Buddhist, with strong

---

[54]*Chung-kuo ta pai-k'o ch'üan-shu: Hsi-ch'ü, ch'ü-i* (cited n. 34), p. 340.

[55]Hsieh P'u 謝璞, "Che-li you fen-fen te 'nai-chih'" 這里有芬芬的 '奶汁', *Ch'u-feng* 1982:1, quoted in Liu Shou-hua 劉守華, "'Shan-shu'—Chung-kuo nung-ts'un ku-shih wen-hsüeh te i-ko chung-yao p'in-chung" '善書'——中國農村故事文學的一個重要品種, *Min-chien wen-i chi-k'an* 民間文藝季刊 1983.4, p. 126. I quote here from the translation by Beata Grant, "Woman Huang" (cited n. 16), p. 252, with slight changes.

[56]This paragraph is based on a brief unpublished paper by Mr. Chang Chen-nan 張振南 entitled "Shang-tang ti-ch'ü te 'Hsi hua t'ang'" 上黨地區的 '西化堂' (ms. in the author's possession). Mr. Chang gives no indication of his sources, but he has done extensive field-work and textual research on the traditional village culture of southeastern Shansi, of which he is a native and long-time resident.

admixtures of Taoist and Confucian ideas. "The *Hsi hua t'ang* had no organizational structure, but was for the most part made up of village gentry, retired merchants, and local landowners. Most were in their fifties and sixties, and came from very well-to-do families. . . . Their activities usually took place at village temple fairs and opera grounds, but sometimes also in the streets and alleys of towns. The lecturer [*chiang-yen che*] would set up an awning covered with several strips of blue cloth, under which he placed a small table, two meters high. On the table he put a teapot of water, a fan, and the texts he was going to perform. He adjusted his clothing, sat down on a tall stool, and began to lecture. He declaimed verse, he spoke and sang, he used song-forms and rhymes, and added explanations as well." Mr. Chang lists a dozen titles that were performed, the first four of which all had to do with the Mu-lien story.[57] "Because the stories that were presented were all in praise of filial sons and virtuous daughters-in-law,[58] they were greatly loved and esteemed by audiences. When older men and women who had disobedient sons or unvirtuous daughters-in-law heard the stories tell about filial sons and virtuous daughters-in-law, so completely different from their own, they could not stop the tears from streaming down and the sobs from rising in their throats. Some were so entranced by the stories that they would not even buy anything to eat."

Thus we have two basic settings for the performance of *pao-chüan* and analogous genres: one private, the other public. The first kind of performance was often called *hsüan chüan*, while the second was known by a wide variety of names, including *shuo yin-kuo*, *Sacred Edict* lectures, *shanshu* recitations, lecturing, and *hsüan chüan*. By late imperial times these performances seem to have taken place constantly, not just on certain festivals or during specific rituals. This of course makes sense, since they did not require large troupes or cost a great deal of money. Though some performances were private, they were not clandestine, except in the case of "sutra" recitation by followers of the heterodox new religions of Ming and after—but sectarian *pao-chüan* performances were probably somewhat out of the mainstream of the tradition I am describing in any case.

[57]Clearly the texts were prosimetric. At least four of the titles listed can be found in Li Shih-yü's catalogue of *pao-chüan*.
[58]Emending *sun* "grandsons" to *hsi* "daughters-in-law."

The "orthodox" *pao-chüan* performances and closely-related "lectures" described above took place in an atmosphere of considerable solemnity, as was appropriate given their purpose of persuading listeners that virtue was rewarded and evil punished, if not in this life then in the next, and that the buddhas and other divine beings took a direct and immediate interest in what people did and intervened constantly in human affairs. They taught what Hell was like, in minute detail, and, to a lesser extent, described the bliss of the Western Paradise. They were the final stage in the translation of the profound doctrines of the great religious and ethical systems—Buddhism, Taoism, "Confucianism"—into terms that ordinary people could understand and live by. Above all, we know that these performances could move people deeply. They moved them because their subject was so frequently the punishment of sins that at least some in the audience had committed, because they depicted injustices and cruelties that many had experienced, and, finally, because they gave expression to the profound yearning for salvation that both guilt and suffering can beget.

Because *pao-chüan* performances had a powerful impact on people they are of central importance in the study of popular religion in late imperial China. Audiences understood what the performer was singing or chanting, and responded to those words. Hence we can recover, within limits, something important about the religious consciousness of ordinary people by studying the scripts the *hsüan chüan* performers used. But this raises an important question: Are the *pao-chüan* available to us scripts, or anything like scripts? The second part of this paper will begin with an attempt to answer this question.

THE *YU-MING PAO-CH'UAN*

Relationship of the Yu-ming Pao-ch'uan *to Performance*

The many versions of the Mu-lien story recounted in *pao-chüan* can be divided into at least two large plot "systems," one recounting in elaborate detail Mu-lien's ancestors and their lives (*ch'ien Mu-lien*), the other narrating the two reincarnations he was required by Buddha to undergo as a consequence of accidentally freeing millions of dangerous demons from Hell while rescuing his mother (*hou Mu-lien*).[59] The texts within each system

---

[59]There are two general studies of the history of the Mu-lien story: Chao Ching-shen 趙景深,

frequently differ at significant points, and they can also vary greatly as to length and complexity. To survey all the different versions would be a very large task, one I have no intention of undertaking. Even analyzing the five *pao-chüan* about Mu-lien available to me would make this paper far too long. I will therefore focus on a single text, the one I found to be the most impressive as religious literature.

"The Precious Tradition of Mu-lien Rescuing His Mother in Hell" (*Mu-lien chiu-mu yu-ming pao-ch'uan*, to which I shall refer by the short title *Yu-ming pao-ch'uan*) is a block-printed, thread-bound book of 222 pages, with an additional five pages of prefaces and a frontispiece. Two of the prefaces are dated: one Kuang-hsü 7 (1881) and the other Kuang-hsü 25 (1899). It is listed in the catalogues of Fu Hsi-hua (p. 9) and Li Shih-yü (no. 278B). A bibliographic description and brief summary are given in Sawada.[60] The title page of the edition I used (from the collection of Professor Wu Hsiao-ling, Peking, to whom I am grateful for permission to copy this and related works) has the date Kuang-hsü 24 (1898). There is a colophon stating that one hundred copies were printed in the *wu-wu* year, presumably 1918. The *Yu-ming pao-ch'uan* was frequently reprinted; Li Shih-yü lists three editions, and the title page and colophon of Wu Hsiao-ling's copy provide evidence of two more. It is written almost entirely in a combination of ten-character verse and unpunctuated prose. Some other verse forms are encountered, especially in the first half.

What does this text have to do with the private and public performances of *pao-chüan* and analogous works discussed in the first half of this study? The copy I consulted had no added punctuation marks and showed no signs of wear, as it would if it had been used at all frequently as a script (or prop). It may well have been read aloud at one time or another but it was in the first instance probably intended for private reading. In what relation, then, do its words stand to the words used in any actual performance of

---

"Mu-lien ku-shih te yen-pien" 目連故事的演變, originally published in his *Yin-tzu chi* 銀字集 (1946), reprinted in Wang Ch'iu-kuei 王秋桂, *Chung-kuo min-chien ch'uan-shuo lun-chi* 中國民間傳說論集 (Taipei: Lien-ching ch'u-pan shih-yeh kung-ssu, 1980), pp. 219–36; and Ch'en Fang-ying 陳芳英, "Mu-lien chiu mu ku-shih chih yen-chin chi ch'i yu-kuan wen-hsüeh chih yen-chiu" 目連救母故事之演進及其有關文學之研究, M.A. thesis, National Taiwan University, 1978.

[60]Pp. 125–26. The works by Fu, Li, and Sawada are cited in notes 5 and 6.

pao-chüan about Mu-lien in late Ch'ing times? The answer to this question is important, because we cannot properly interpret the text and assess its significance without some sense of its intended and actual audiences. Nor, obviously, can we use it to think about the larger issue of *pao-chüan* performance if it does not have some credible tie with such performances.

According to Sawada and Li, printed *pao-chüan* of the nineteenth century had certain formal characteristics that set them apart from earlier ones: they tended to be of a length that could be performed in five to seven hours and to be divided into two sections, so that the performer could take a break in the middle;[61] they used very simple opening and closing formulae rather than the elaborate ones used earlier; they relied heavily on seven- or ten-character verse and made relatively light use of song-form verse (*ch'ü-p'ai*);[62] and they used the conventional thread-stitched binding rather than the folded style with thick covers that had been traditional when *pao-chüan* were regarded as scriptures.[63]

Not all nineteenth-century *pao-chüan* were printed. Some were handwritten, having been produced as an act of piety, by a performer copying a script, or even by a bookseller. Li Shih-yü says that he knows the location of 274 of the latter type.[64] They were typically written on a tough, durable paper called "horse-head paper" or "Korean paper" that could easily last many years.[65] They came into the hands of collectors and libraries after 1949, when the performance of *pao-chüan* was forbidden, or at least strongly discouraged. Before 1949 they probably were treated as professional secrets by the performers who owned them and seldom made available voluntarily to anyone but their disciples. Thus some of them may have preserved performance traditions a century or more old. These could well have been the independent creation of some long-dead master, polished and refined by later performers in the same school or family.

---

[61]Note that this accords well with the much earlier description of the *Wu-tsu huang-mei pao-chüan* recital in *hui* 39 of *Chin P'ing Mei*, which it will be recalled had a break for refreshments in the middle and ended in the fourth watch, very late at night.

[62]Sawada (cited n. 5), p. 53; Li, "Chiang Che chu sheng te hsüan chüan" (cited n. 15), pp. 200–201, 211.

[63]Sawada, pp. 37, 80–81.

[64]"Chiang Che chu sheng te hsüan chüan," pp. 202–3. On p. 205, he says that there were both manuscripts and printed texts among the "new-style" *pao-chüan* he collected, so at least some manuscript *pao-chüan* had the formal characteristics just discussed.

[65]Ibid., p. 202.

Others could have been adaptations of local operas, narrative songs, or other performance genres. Whatever their origins, it is important to recognize that manuscript *pao-chüan* existed in the late nineteenth and twentieth centuries, and we will return to them shortly.

The *Yu-ming pao-ch'uan* fits quite well Sawada's and Li's profile of *pao-chüan* printed in the nineteenth century: it was first written in 1881; it was printed from wooden blocks, not by lithography; it evidently was printed for free distribution as an act of religious piety; it is thread-bound; it has two nearly equal sections (though not formally divided into *chüan* or *ts'e*); it is long enough to take from five to seven hours to perform (I estimate that if a performer chanted our text at a fairly even pace, pausing for emphasis but not drawing out individual words in the manner of opera, it would take about six hours to read straight through); it is heavily reliant on ten-character verse; and it has rudimentary introductory and concluding passages that do not use Buddhist formulae. We can say with some confidence therefore that our text belongs to a well-defined type of *pao-chüan* that was especially common in the third quarter of the nineteenth century. The question therefore now becomes, What was the relation of that class of *pao-chüan* to *hsüan chüan* performances?

I believe that the *pao-chüan* printed by the morality-book shops (*Shan-shu chü*) in the late nineteenth century probably were closely related to *pao-chüan* that were performed. Texts seem to have always been part of *hsüan chüan* performances, either as props or as actual scripts. This suggests at the very least that audiences believed such performances were rooted in texts, and there is good reason to believe that they in fact were. *Hsüan chüan* performances of the late nineteenth century were part of a rich tradition of reciting or chanting scriptures and other religious writings, one that can be traced back to T'ang times. In the *pao-chüan* performances described in the *Chin P'ing Mei tz'u-hua*, "sutra tables" were used and in one case a nun-performer is said to open a book and begin to recite.[66] In many of the other examples given above of the public and private performance of *pao-chüan* and *pao-chüan*-like works, the use of a text is either described or clearly implied. And this makes sense, not only because of what might be termed the moral authority of the text but also

---

[66] See above, pp. 61–62.

because *pao-chüan* were filled with verse, which is difficult to extemporize, and therefore are likely to have been recited from a text (or memorized, which of course also implies reliance on a text at some point). Remember too that, according to Sawada, *hsüan chüan* performers occasionally purchased old *pao-chüan* and then modified them for performance.[67] If they were going to change them radically, why prowl through antiquarian book shops looking for them?

Just as *hsüan chüan* performances seem to have been based on texts, *pao-chüan* often were closely related to scripts. Commercial publishers sometimes sought out performers' manuscripts of *pao-chüan* they thought would be appealing, spruced them up with illustrations and good calligraphy, and sold them as their own.[68] (The 274 manuscripts known to Li Shih-yü, mentioned above, are undoubtedly of this type.) Then too, since people took *hsüan chüan* seriously, even to the point of holding performances when a family member was ill, it stands to reason that the texts sold by the morality-book shops would have followed the performance versions as closely as possible. There is even a hint in one of the prefaces of the *Yu-ming pao-ch'uan* that it might be read aloud, which of course would be a strong reason for retaining the characteristics of *hsüan chüan* performance.[69] Finally, as I pointed out earlier, printed *pao-chüan* from the mid- and late-nineteenth century frequently preserve formal features that grew out of the needs of performance: performance time of five to seven hours, a break in the middle, and so on. This suggests very strongly that the printed versions had a good deal in common with the performed versions.

The Chinese have turned oral performances into written literature since the *Book of Songs*. The history of Chinese popular literature is filled with important examples of this cultural habit: the Tun-huang *pien-wen*, Yuan drama, Ming *hua-pen*. In every such case, there has been deep controversy and puzzlement over the relationship between the written works that are all that we can study and the performances from which they are assumed to have been derived. These problems have no simple solution. A comment by Victor Mair, who has dealt with similar issues in his studies

---

[67] Sawada, p. 79.
[68] Ibid., pp. 38, 80.
[69] See p. 2b, lines 2–3 of the "Prefaces" section: "Readers [of the *Yu-ming pao-ch'uan*] appear frightened and listeners change countenance."

of *pien-wen*, offers a useful perspective. He writes that extant *pien-wen* may "represent various points of development on a continuum ranging from oral to written."[70] That is, not all *pien-wen* have the same relationship to oral performances. The same may well be said of *pao-chüan*. Some may resemble *hsüan chüan* scripts more closely than others. Hence it is best to judge each *pao-chüan* text separately, though it is reasonable to start with the assumption that most texts are unlikely to be far removed from performance. Let us therefore now turn to an examination of the *Yu-ming pao-ch'uan* text itself.

Plot

The *Yu-ming pao-ch'uan* belongs to the *ch'ien Mu-lien* plot system, which gives great attention to Mu-lien's forebears. The story begins with a rather bizarre mythological prologue set in the reign of the virtuous Emperor Wu of the Liang dynasty (first half of the sixth century). I will briefly recount it here even though I do not understand its relation to the main story, on the principle that beginnings are significant in Chinese narratives and that therefore the reader should know something about it.

Bodhidharma (Ta-mo), "the twenty-eighth patriarch of the Western Paradise," hears Shen-kuang discoursing beautifully on the sutras and the dharma, and asks him why he is doing it.[71] Shen-kuang answers that he wants to ascend to Heaven and escape Yama, the king of Hell. Bodhidharma draws a picture of a wheat cake on a piece of paper, and says that if reciting scriptures that are just ink on paper can get you to Heaven, then looking at a drawing of a wheat cake ought to satisfy your hunger. This enrages Shen-kuang, and he strikes Bodhidharma in the face with his "white beads" (*su-chu*), knocking out his two front teeth. Bodhidharma has to swallow the teeth and blood, because he is afraid that if he spits them out there will be drought for three years. He then transforms the ten beads into the lords of the ten courts of Hell and disappears. When the ten lords manifest themselves, Shen-kuang asks them who they are and why they have come. They reply that they have come to take him to Hell. "Shen-kuang

<hr>

70 *T'ang Transformation Texts* (cited n. 3), p. 119.
71 Shen-kuang was another name of Hui-k'o, the second patriarch of the Ch'an school and successor of Bodhidharma in the orthodox Ch'an lineage. Sectarians frequently adapted such established lineages to enhance their own legitimacy.

said, 'Every day I expound the sutras and the dharma; it is impossible that I cannot escape Yama.' They replied, 'You cannot'" (2b.4–5). Shen-kuang asks who *can* escape, and is told that "that monk" (i.e., Bodhidharma) can. He begs the infernal emissaries to allow him to meet Bodhidharma again and learn the methods of escaping Yama, but they just disappear. The narrative then jumps to "another time," when Shen-kuang encounters Bodhidharma and is wounded by his Knife of Discipline (*chieh tao*). Shen-kuang then "faces the wall" in meditation for nine years, after which "the Way took root in the Eastern Regions (i.e., China)" (3a.1–4).

Presumably this prologue reflects the mythology of some Great Way of Former Heaven sect, but I have not been able to confirm this.[72] The scene then shifts to the Liang dynasty and the rebellion of Hou Ching, we are introduced to Fu T'ien-tou, Mu-lien's great-grandfather, and the main story begins. More than a third of the text is devoted to recounting the lives of T'ien-tou, his son Ch'ung, and grandson Hsiang, who is Mu-lien's father, but I shall simply ignore that section here.

The Venerable Mother of the Jade Pool (*Yao-ch'ih lao-mu*)[73] foresees that Liu Ch'ing-t'i, who will become Mu-lien's mother, is loaded with sins and will have difficulty "reaching the shore" (achieving salvation), so she commands Cassia Branch, an immortal, to be reborn as Madame Liu's son. His merit and courage are so great that as Madame Liu's son he will be able to rescue her from Hell, thus becoming a model of filial devotion to all the world and inspiring people to perfect themselves and "return to the root," thereby repaying their debt to their parents and grandparents. The Venerable Mother transforms Cassia Branch into a jewel-like radish over a foot long.[74] A mysterious peddler gives the supernatural radish to Fu Hsiang, who takes it home and places it in the household shrine. Madame Liu is greatly disturbed by the crowds of people who come to

---

[72]Marjorie Topley does not mention any of these details in her article on the sects' organization and beliefs: "The Great Way of Former Heaven: A Group of Chinese Secret Religious Sects," *Bulletin of the School of Oriental and African Studies* 26.2 (1963), pp. 362–92. References to Great Way teachings can be found at various places in the text. Mu-lien himself becomes the disciple of a Great Way master; see below.

[73]This is the central figure in the pantheon of the new religions that appeared in late Ming times, more commonly called *Wu-sheng lao-mu*, "Eternal Mother."

[74]*Lo-pu* is the large white variety known in the U.S. by its Japanese name, daikon. I have not attempted to trace the source of this rather surprising motif. In some Mu-lien operas I have seen, great play is made with the phallic character of the radish.

see the wonderful object, and finally she smashes it to bits. (This is a clear foreshadowing of her later behavior.) The fragments give off such a beautiful aroma that she devours them all (more foreshadowing). This makes her pregnant, and in due course she gives birth to a son, whom they name Radish (34b–38a). (He is given the name Mu-lien many years later, when Master K'ai-shih secretly transmits to him the doctrines of the Great Way of Former Heaven at the Hui-kuang temple in Hangchow.)[75]

When Radish is still a boy, his father, Fu Hsiang, is told by a divine messenger that he is going to die soon. He exhorts his wife and son to continue to lead virtuous lives, and above all not to eat meat. They both promise, and Fu Hsiang passes away. After mourning with great piety for three years and then resuming his life of virtue, Radish realizes that he must deepen his religious understanding, and, heeding the earlier advice of his father, goes to Hangchow in search of a teacher, accompanied by the faithful family servant, I-li. His mother is left alone with three villains, Liu-the-liar, Li-the-dog, and Chin-the-hunchback.[76] Her piety irritates and disturbs these sensualists, so they resolve to make her break her vow not to eat meat. They constantly talk in her presence of how delicious the dishes are that they are eating, and soon Madame Liu is dreaming of eating chicken. Li-the-dog explains that this is Buddha's way of telling her she has fasted long enough, and she wants to believe him. Then they cook a supremely delicious dish of chicken and go on and on about how wonderful it is until Madame Liu, tempted beyond endurance, rushes in from where she has been listening, seizes the chicken in both hands, lifts it to her face to inhale its rich aroma, and devours it (38b–45b).

She swiftly loses all control, and the bones of the animals she has eaten pile up in the back garden. An elder of the district reproves her for her bad faith, and she in a rage attacks him with a hoe and kills him. She calls for wine to be heated, but a fire cannot be started in the stove, and in retaliation she orders a chamberpot emptied on it.[77] Buddha sends divine messengers,

[75]There were a number of sects known by this name. See Marjorie Topley, "The Great Way of Former Heaven."

[76]Reading *lou* 嫂 as *lou* 傻.

[77]Putting anything unclean in or near the stove was the violation of a great taboo, one that was repeated endlessly in the stove-god scriptures and morality books that circulated throughout China at this time. See Robert Chard's chapter in this book, and his "Master of the Family: The History and Development of the Chinese Cult to the Stove," Ph.D. diss.,

in the guise of a monk and a priest, to warn her, and they too are killed. Finally the defiled stove god reports her enormities to the Jade Emperor, and he despatches hungry ghosts to drag her down to Hell for punishment (46a–50a).

At that very moment Radish, now Mu-lien, is on his way home with I-li from Hangchow, where he received the Way from Master K'ai-shih; he and the hungry ghosts will arrive at the Fu house almost simultaneously. While Mu-lien is still en route, Liu-the-liar is struck dead by a divine thunderbolt. Madame Liu summons monks and priests to carry out an exorcism, but they are frightened of her and refuse to come. This so enrages her that she beats and curses Liu's corpse. Her moral disintegration is complete: now whenever she sees a Buddhist monk or Taoist priest she beats or curses them. "One day she thought to herself, 'Chin-the-hunchback and Li-the-dog are going to die [they had exhibited symptoms of serious illness], Liu-the-liar has been struck dead by a thunderbolt, Radish has not returned, and I-li has left [he had come back briefly earlier, then returned to Hangchow]. *I* have caused no harm, and there will be no one else in the house—how can there be any retribution?' Truly she was mad" (54b.4–6).

At just this moment Mu-lien arrives. She stares at him: "'So it's Radish.'" Then she says, "'Why have you come home now and given me such a fright?'" (54b.7–8). He apologizes, but immediately asks her why she has begun to eat meat. This stuns her, and she demands to know who told him. When he says it was a god, she says that the gods, who are so distant, could not possibly know such a thing. "'Obviously it was I-li who told you,' she screamed, and began to beat I-li with a club" (55a.5). Mu-lien stops her; she then takes his hand and pulls him out to the rear garden, where she lights a stick of incense and swears by Heaven and Earth that she has not eaten meat. "'If I have eaten meat, let those sunflowers burn up'" (55a.8). No sooner has she spoken than the tall sunflowers burst into flame. She collapses, and when Mu-lien revives her, "her face was the color of dirt, and she no longer looked human. She said, 'Hit those ghosts! Hit those ghosts! Radish, get your mother a cup of tea'" (55b.2–3). (This bit of dialogue, with its abrupt shift from the terrible to the trivial, is

University of California, Berkeley, 1990.

remarkably effective.) Just then the troop of hungry ghosts despatched by the Jade Emperor arrives, armed with brass hammers and iron tridents.[78] They beat the soul out of her, and take it, "alive," down to Hell.

Mu-lien sings a long lament and then makes preparations for his mother's funeral. Shortly thereafter, Li-the-dog and Chin-the-hunchback finally die of their debauchery and are buried, only to have their remains exhumed by thunderbolts and their heads eaten by dogs. Then the day for the "return of the soul" arrives.[79] Madame Liu's soul (we are told) had been shattered by the blows of the demons, and the malignant soul (*hsiung sha*) was left behind. Her true soul (*chen hun*) is sent back to fetch it by order of the Law Official of the Three Bureaus (*San-ts'ao fa-kuan*) (56a–58a).

When she arrives, guarded by demons, the door gods dare not block her way and let her pass. She goes first to the main hall, where she pays her respects, presumably to the tablets of the ancestors and the household gods, and then visits every room. She opens the chests and tries to put on her old headdress of noble rank and her shoes—but she cannot. She begins to suspect the truth, and then comes to a mirror. "She took one look and saw that her face was hideously ugly, not that of a living person. She cried out, 'Ai-yaaa—I am so sorry!'" (58a.6–7). She clings desperately to Mu-lien, who has fallen asleep during his night-long vigil, and his spiritual power is such that the demons dare not approach her. They ask the help of the guardian spirit of the Fu family—presumably one of the gods to whom she has just paid her respects—and in a gesture of great symbolic power the god of the family tears her away from her son and throws her down at the demons' feet. They snatch at her, beat her bloody with their hammers, tie her up, and take her away (56a–59b). This is the climax of the first half of the *Yu-ming pao-ch'uan*.

Mu-lien awakes. In his dream he has seen everything that has just taken place, including his mother's plea that he go to the Western Heaven to obtain from Buddha an order that will save her from the tortures of Hell. He is at a loss how to proceed, when Kuan-yin appears to him in the guise

---

[78]Reading *ch'a* 叉 for *i* 乂 in 55b.5.

[79]For this belief, see C. H. Plopper, *Chinese Religion Seen Through the Proverb* (New York: Paragon Reprint Corp., 1969, reprint of the 1935 edition), p. 90; and H. Y. Lowe, *The Adventures of Wu: The Life Cycle of a Peking Man* (Princeton: Princeton University Press, 1983, reprint of the 1940–1941 edition), vol. 2, pp. 125–26.

of an old woman and tells him how he can find the Buddha. He must journey to the west, wearing a saddle on his back and reciting the book she will give him (which is not identified), bowing every three paces and kneeling every five.[80] He sets off at once, beginning the epic journey to Heaven and Hell that is the main business of the narrative (60a–63b). The journey occupies over eighty pages, nearly 40 percent of the entire text, and I can only give a brief outline of it here.

After several adventures in the trackless wilderness, Mu-lien comes to Hungry Tiger Mountain. Suddenly a tiger pounces, and he is about to be devoured when two tiger-catching generals appear and save him. They greet him cheerfully, and he sees that they are none other than I-li (the faithful family servant) and Yu-ta, whom Mu-lien had encountered much earlier (p. 52b) in the guise of a bandit and who is in fact the Chin-kang Star sent down to earth. Then he hears a voice telling him that it is getting late and he should hurry. It is his father. Mu-lien asks where he is, why his father is there, and finally what he should do. His father replies paradoxically, "My son, it is still early," and vanishes (71b–72b).

This scene functions as a kind of half-way point in Mu-lien's progress from the everyday world to the Western Heaven. Before this point he has simply been trudging through the mountains like an ordinary traveler, and the appearance of two human characters reinforces the sense that we are still in the everyday world. And yet their presence in that place is clearly miraculous, and the appearance of Mu-lien's father strengthens the feeling that the real world has somehow been left behind. This is very skillfully done.

Mu-lien presses on through more adventures until the time comes for him to leave his corporeal self behind so that he can enter the Western Heaven. A white monkey, sent by Kuan-yin, steals Mu-lien's saddle and book as he is drinking from a stream. Mu-lien chases him until the monkey, clutching the book, leaps into the flames of a raging fire. His magic book destroyed, Mu-lien feels that his quest has failed. In despair he bows

---

[80]The bizarre business with the saddle was a part of several local opera traditions. See *Hu-nan hsi-ch'ü ch'uan-t'ung chü-mu* 湖南戲曲傳統劇目, vol. 34 (Ch'ang-sha: Hu-nan sheng hsi-ch'ü yen-chiu suo, 1982) [vol. 1 of the Ch'i chü Kao ch'iang *Mu-lien chuan*], pp. 195–96; and Wen I-hsüan 文憶萱, "Hu-nan te Mu-lien hsi" 湖南的目連戲, *Hsi-ch'ü yen-chiu* 戲曲研究 11 (1984), p. 219.

once in the direction of his old home, covers his head with his arms (a nice touch), leaps into the flames—and awakens in the throne room of the Buddha. He has reached the Western Heaven (72b–80a).

After many pleas by Mu-lien, Buddha gives him a "decree" that will enable him to enter Hell and search for his mother. After a flashback that recounts the interrogation of Madame Liu and the others in the first court of Hell (82a–85b), Mu-lien begins his tour of the Underworld, the central matter of the second half of the book. The narrative starts at Ghost Gate Pass (*kuei men kuan*), the entrance to the domain of Hell, with a detailed description of what happens to souls after death (87a–89a), and then follows Mu-lien as he goes from one court of Hell to the next. In each one, after observing the tortures of the damned and learning what sins they had committed, Mu-lien discovers that his mother has been sent on to the next court. In the fifth court he encounters Emperor Yama (*Yen-lo t'ien-tzu*), who makes a wager with him: if he fails in his quest, he must stay in Hell as Yama's subject; if he succeeds, Yama will bow down to him (95b). (In the end, when Mu-lien is made King of Hell [*Ti-tsang wang*, Ksitigarbha], Yama does indeed become his subordinate.)

Finally Mu-lien learns that his mother has been sent to the Avici Hell, which is not one of the ten courts but a place set aside for the worst of all sinners, those whose crimes on earth were so heinous that they will never be reborn in any form, but will suffer in Hell forever. When he reaches it, "he could see nothing but layer upon layer of blackness; he could not see the starry Dipper. Walls of molten iron many yards high surrounded it, and from it hung the names of every kind of sin" (102a.2–4). (Twelve categories of sin are listed, all quite orthodox, ranging from patricide to sacrilege.) Mu-lien floats over the wall on a magic cloud, but cannot make his way through the blinding smoke, and returns to the Western Heaven to ask help from the Buddha again (101b–103a).

After overcoming Buddha's objections to his continual attempts to obtain special treatment for his mother, who is after all a sinner of the blackest stripe, Mu-lien is given the Buddha's staff, which can open the gates of the Avici Hell, and a red pearl that can illuminate the darkness there, and returns to the Underworld. He brandishes his staff, the gates fly open, and with the pearl illuminating the gloom he enters the most hellish of the hells. All the demons who are imprisoned there escape, but Mu-lien ignores them—he is concerned only with finding his mother, and he soon does. They sing an emotional duet, at the end of which Mu-lien faints from excessive weeping (103b–105b).

When he revives, his mother is gone—she has been taken away to the tenth court to be reborn. This has come about by the decision of Yama and the Official of the Three Bureaus, who have decided to lighten her sentence one degree because of Mu-lien's great virtue. Mu-lien rushes off to the tenth court, but when he gets there his mother has already been sent back into the world. Mu-lien does not believe this until he looks for himself into the ledgers of life and death and reads that his mother has been reborn in P'ing-yang county, Shansi—as a white dog.[81] So he returns to the world, too (105b–106a).

As soon as he reaches home, he collects all the sutras in the house, loads them onto a carrying pole, and sets out for Shansi. When he reaches P'ing-yang he sees a sign warning of a vicious dog, and at once understands that it must be his mother. The dog's master watches in amazement as it comes up to Mu-lien and begins weeping. The man gives the dog to Mu-lien, and Mu-lien puts it in the sutra chest at one end of his carrying pole, ties the bundle of sutras to the other, and prepares to set off. This however creates a dilemma: if he carries his mother in front it will show disrespect to the sutras, but if he carries the sutras in front it will show disrespect to his mother. He solves the problem by carrying the pole crosswise on his shoulders, so that neither end is in front. One could not ask for a neater symbol of the synthesis of Buddhist and "Confucian" ideas that is so characteristic of the Mu-lien story.[82]

He returns to the Western Heaven, and begs Buddha to help his mother recover her human form (106b–109b).

> Buddha intoned some mantras, blew a puff of breath on the dog, and it was instantly transformed into a human. Mu-lien's face was wreathed in smiles.

---

[81]P'ing-yang was a county in Shansi (in the vicinity of modern Lin-fen) from Han to Sui times. The survival of such an old place name in this text is worth noting.

[82]This is a famous scene in regional opera and also is frequently enacted in funeral ceremonies. See for example scene 79 of the Ch'i Opera *Mu-lien chuan* cited two notes above, and Kenneth Dean, "Lei Yu-sheng ('Thunder is Noisy') and Mu-lien in the Theatrical and Funerary Traditions of Fukien," *Ritual Opera, Operatic Ritual* (cited n. 1), p. 62; Ch'iu K'un-liang, "Mu-lien 'Operas' in Taiwanese Funeral Rites," ibid., pp. 108–9.

Buddha asked Madame Liu, 'Do you wish to eat vegetarian food, or forbidden food?' Madame Liu had just sloughed off the animal's skin, and had not fully recovered her human consciousness. All she was aware of was her love of rich flavors, and so she answered at once, 'I'll take the forbidden food.' When Buddha heard this he gave an exclamation of dismay and with a flip of his whisk changed her back into a dog again. When Mu-lien saw what had happened he fell to the ground in tears. After weeping for a time, he approached the throne-hall of the Buddha, prostrated himself, and begged the Buddha over and over to save her.

> (109b.2–8)

This prose passage ends in the middle of the last column of p. 109b. Elsewhere in the text, whenever the final sentence of a prose passage ends in mid-column with the situation unresolved, it is followed by a passage of ten-character verse. Obviously a verse passage telling what happened next ought to begin on the first line of p. 110a. But instead that page begins in what seems to be the middle of a later scene with the Buddha speaking (in prose): "I, the Tathâgata, decree the following enfeoffments: the fruits of Mu-lien's merit fill the Nine Heavens; the seven [sic] patriarchs will all be enfeoffed." Then are listed the noble titles bestowed on Fu Hsiang, Chang Yu-ta, I-li, Mu-lien, and Madame Liu. (She is made Lion's Roar Buddha, and is to roar three times at every full and new moon, no doubt in tribute to her canine past; 110a.1–7.) Since our copy of the text is physically intact (there are no missing page numbers), the source of the problem is probably the exemplar on which it was based. I suspect that one double-sided folio, or possibly two, somehow became detached from the text that was used as the master copy when the blocks of our edition were carved, and that the lacuna was not noticed or was not felt to be important.

On the final page, in a brief allusion to the second great Mu-lien plot system, we are told that Mu-lien was reborn as the T'ang rebel Huang Ch'ao in order to recapture the eight million hungry ghosts he had let loose upon the world when he broke down the gates of the Avici Hell, and that after that he became the Ti-tsang Bodhisattva, the King of Hell.

Despite the defective ending, the *Yu-ming pao-ch'uan* is an impressive achievement. The story stays on track over three generations and through

journeys to Heaven and Hell, skillfully combining didacticism with entertainment that at certain moments rises to something like art. Before we
look at it more closely, I want to return to the question asked earlier: how
is this text related to the scripts that were used in *pao-chüan* performances?

I tried to show earlier that there is good reason to believe that many
nineteenth-century *pao-chüan* were based on *hsüan chüan* performances,
and we have already seen that the *Yu-ming pao-ch'uan* has a number of
formal characteristics—including its two-part structure and its length—
that probably reflect *hsüan chüan* performance practice in the late nineteenth century. Now that we have had a chance to look at the story itself,
this impression is strengthened. To begin with, the work is characterized
by narrative drive, smooth transitions, clear structure, simple language,
and the brilliant realization of a few intensely dramatic moments. These
are precisely the qualities that an oral narrative had to have if it was to
hold an audience's attention over a period of several hours.

Of course, our text could theoretically have been written with the intention of imitating a *pao-chüan* for an audience of educated aficionados.
If such an imitation was sufficiently exact, it would be just as useful for
our purposes as a script that had actually been performed. But it is far
more likely that such an imitation or pseudo–*pao-chüan* would have been
modified in certain ways to make it more enjoyable for educated readers.
Such modifications would be particularly visible in the work's literary style.
But it is hard to believe that the *Yu-ming pao-ch'uan* was written or edited
by anyone with literary pretensions. The language is plain and straightforward, with no literary flourishes, no allusions to classical literature or phi-
losophy, the simplest possible verse form and rhyme scheme, no self-conscious authorial intrusions—in short, none of the hallmarks of works of
imaginative literature written for a literati audience.

The text is filled with references to the doctrines and divinities of popu-
larized Buddhism, and to a lesser extent of Great Way of Former Heaven
sects, further evidence that its intended audience was not very well educated. And it is important to keep in mind that despite its narrative drive
and dramatic climaxes, the *Yu-ming pao-ch'uan* was intended to teach, not
to entertain. In part it was designed to transmit certain of the doctrines
and myths of the Great Way of Former Heaven, but the major values it
seeks to inculcate are not "sectarian" at all: the inevitability of karmic

retribution; the sin of eating meat; the alertness of the gods to human misbehavior and the frightfulness of the punishments they mete out; the grandeur of Mu-lien's devotion and more generally the power that is wielded by one who understands the Way.[83] It is also virtually a handbook on the structure and functioning of the Underworld and the progress of the soul after death. None of this is likely to have been aimed at an audience of educated gentlemen—though it could well have been intended for their wives, as well as for women (and men?) further down the hierarchy of dominance. Moreover, the work is strongly influenced by operas about Mu-lien (as we shall see), another feature one would not expect to find in an imitation *pao-chüan* written for literati readers, but that would be perfectly appropriate in a work designed for recitation to non-elite audiences.

I conclude, therefore, that the words of the *Yu-ming pao-ch'uan* are likely to be quite close to the words used in actual *hsüan chüan* performances in the late nineteenth century. Since it must be representative of at least some other works of didactic entertainment current at that time, we can learn from it the kinds of moral teachings that ordinary people, especially women, were exposed to.

Interpretation

Pao-chüan *vs.* Pien-wen

What was the *Yu-ming pao-ch'uan* trying to teach? What does it tell us about the worldview of those who created it and those others who listened to it with, we may assume, intense attention and involvement? I want to begin to answer this question by juxtaposing the *Yu-ming pao-ch'uan* with a distant ancestor, a T'ang *pien-wen* about Mu-lien.[84] This will throw into relief elements that might otherwise escape our attention, and will in ad-

---

[83]This finding accords with the research of Daniel Overmyer. See for example his "Values in Chinese Sectarian Literature: Ming and Ch'ing *Pao-chüan*," in David Johnson et al., eds., *Popular Culture in Late Imperial China* (cited n. 40), pp. 243–45. It also corresponds well with Sawada's description of a typical *pao-chüan* of the nineteenth century and after: strong emphasis on narrative and concern for inculcating a combination of conventional lay Buddhist and local gentry values—though he also excludes proselytizing for a specific sect. See Sawada, p. 37.

[84]One among many scholars who has traced the origins of the *pao-chüan* to the *pien-wen* is Hsiang Ta 向達. See his "T'ang-tai su-chiang k'ao" 唐代俗講考, quoted in Lou and Chu, *Wu-shih nien lai te Chung-kuo su wen-hsüeh* (cited n. 9), p. 305.

dition provide valuable insights into some of the ways popular religion changed between the ninth and nineteenth centuries.

W. L. Idema states that the *pien-wen* "show a striking similarity to the other chantefable forms [that use lines of seven or ten characters] despite a gap of over four centuries between the most recent *pien-wen* and the earliest preserved *tz'u-hua* text. This fact suggests a continuous tradition from T'ang to Ming"[85]—and therefore on to Ch'ing and after.[86] Buddhist monks had paid close attention to effective preaching from the beginning of the career of Buddhism in China. The section entitled "Guiding Through Song" (*Ch'ang tao*) of the early-sixth-century *Biographies of Eminent Monks* (*Kao seng chuan*) has a passage, which I used in an earlier publication, describing the attributes of a good preacher. In addition to a good voice, intelligence, and learning, he must know how to fit his discourse to his audience: "To the elite, discourse elegantly using copious allusions from secular literature. To ordinary people, filled with anxieties, describe every-day experiences in a realistic and straightforward manner. And to those living in remote villages deep in the country, denounce sins using the local dialect."[87] This sensitivity to the different capacities of different audiences, coupled with a powerful desire to persuade people of the truth of Buddhist doctrines, led naturally to a merging of preaching and storytelling.

On the basis of the surviving manuscripts, we can identify two main types of popular preaching in T'ang times, when proselytizing was at its height: exegeses of sutras (*chiang-ching-wen*) and prosimetric narratives. The latter were for the most part either *pien-wen* or *yuan, yuan-ch'i*, and *yin-yuan*, to which Mair gives the collective label *nidâna*.[88] He insists that a sharp distinction be made between texts performed by entertainers, which in practice means *pien-wen* (as defined by him), and those performed by Buddhist "evangelists," the *chiang-ching-wen*.[89] But this dis-

---

[85]"Prosimetric Literature," in William H. Nienhauser, Jr., ed., *The Indiana Companion to Traditional Chinese Literature* (Bloomington: Indiana University Press, 1986), p. 87. *Tz'u-hua* was a general term for prosimetric narratives, current from the thirteenth to the sixteenth centuries. Ibid., p. 849b.

[86]There is a good discussion of the evolution of prosimetric literature in Sun K'ai-ti 孫楷弟, *Su-chiang shuo-hua yü pai-hua hsiao-shuo* 俗講說話與白話小說 (Peking: Tso-chia ch'u-pan shê, 1956), pp. 31–41.

[87]*Kao seng chuan* 高僧傳 13 (Taishō Tripitaka 50), p. 417c.

[88]*T'ang Transformation Texts* (cited n. 3), pp. 29–32.

[89]Victor H. Mair, "Lay Students and the Making of Written Vernacular Narrative: An In-

tinction seems too rigid to me. Not only does it ignore the whole *nidâna* genre, which is virtually identical in form to *pien-wen*,[90] it fails to account adequately for *pien-wen* with Buddhist themes, such as those about Mu-lien, whose story, according to Mair himself, was the most popular *pien-wen* subject of all.[91] Even the passage from *Kao seng chuan* just quoted makes it clear that already in the sixth century Buddhist monks routinely told stories in an effort to touch people's hearts. As I have said elsewhere, the distinction between entertainment and religion that comes naturally to us did not seem that obvious to most Chinese.

It remains to be seen what the *pien-wen* and *pao-chüan* about Mu-lien have in common, but the mere fact that by late Ch'ing times the professional performance of prosimetric narratives with religious themes had an unbroken history of over a thousand years suggests that in studying a Mu-lien *pao-chüan* and its earliest known antecedent we are touching on matters of central importance to understanding traditional Chinese popular culture.

Certain plot elements are the same in both versions: the greed of Mu-lien's mother leads her to disobey an injunction to be virtuous while Mu-lien is away, and she lies to him about it on his return; her soul is imprisoned in the Avici Hell; Hell and its tortures are described in detail; Mu-lien breaks open the gates of the Avici Hell with a staff given to him by the Buddha; and Madame Liu is transformed into a dog before achieving final salvation.[92] But there are also very significant differences.

The *pien-wen* has more long speeches and descriptive set pieces than the *pao-chüan*, perhaps a sign that it was more removed from its sources in oral performance than the *Yu-ming pao-ch'uan* was. The *pao-chüan*, as mentioned already, is exceptionally effective at maintaining the forward movement of the narrative and at keeping the reader—or listener—involved, much more so than the *pien-wen*. And its descriptions are more realistic than the *pien-wen*'s, which tend to be lyrical and rhetorical.

One of the main purposes of the *pien-wen* is to promote alms-giving, and in particular the sponsoring of "purgatorian feasts" for monks on the

---

ventory of Tun-huang Manuscripts," *Chinoperl Papers* 10 (1981), p. 5; *T'ang Transformation Texts*, pp. 148–51.

[90]See number 314 in Mair's "Lay Students," and *T'ang Transformation Texts*, p. 29.

[91]Ibid., p. 86.

[92]I rely in what follows on Victor Mair's translation of S. 2614 in his *Tun-huang Popular Narratives* (Cambridge: Cambridge University Press, 1983).

fifteenth of the seventh month, at the end of their summer retreat. Madame Liu's sin is in not giving vegetarian food to monks and beggars, and a purgatorian feast is required before she can be transformed from a hungry ghost into a human being again. The *pao-chüan*, by contrast, is far more concerned with promoting vegetarianism and teaching about the wages of sin than with advancing the interests of the *sangha*.

In the *pien-wen*, the action takes place long ago, when the Buddha was still in the world.[93] Mu-lien is one of his disciples, and from the beginning of the text is placed in a setting of supernatural magnificence. After hearing the Buddha preach, "Instantaneously, Maudgalyāyana [i.e., Mu-lien] achieved sainthood /. . . . Incense smoke curled up in wreaths from a golden censer; / The six-fold treasures moved heaven and earth, / The four divine flowers were wafted on the air and scattered through the clear skies. / A thousand sorts of elegant brocades were spread on the couches and seats, / Ten thousand styles of pearled banners hung in the air."[94] Mu-lien later retreats to the depths of the mountains, where he meditates until his mind is subdued and he achieves complete enlightenment. As a result he gains the ability to move at will throughout the universe. This is a clear reflection of Indian and early Chinese traditions about Maudgalyāyana, according to which he was especially gifted with "spiritual penetrations."[95]

The Mu-lien of the *Yu-ming pao-ch'uan* is very different. It is true that he is the earthly incarnation of an immortal and is therefore endowed with extraordinary courage and moral strength. He has also been instructed in the Great Way of Former Heaven and has even been given the name Mu-lien by a Great Way master. But his mother's ghost appears to him in a dream, the standard way for humans (not those with divine spiritual penetration) to receive messages from the spiritual realm. And when she begs him to go to the Western Heaven to intercede with Buddha on her behalf he is thrown into despair, because he knows he cannot get there on his own. Only when Kuan-yin, moved by his filial devotion, provides him with a magic book to chant, a saddle to wear, and instructions to "bow every three steps and kneel every five," can he hope to reach the Western

---

[93]Ibid., p. 87.
[94]Ibid., p. 89, with some changes.
[95]Stephen F. Teiser, *The Ghost Festival in Medieval China* (Princeton: Princeton University Press, 1988), pp. 148–50.

Heaven.[96] In fact his whole long journey to the west is a process of spiritual transformation, and it is only at the very end of it that he is able to enter the realm of the Buddha. In short, the Mu-lien of the *pao-chüan* is a far more human figure than the Maudgalyāyana of the *pien-wen*.

In the *pien-wen*, except for one very brief occasion at the outset, Mu-lien's mother appears only as a spirit or ghost, a disembodied soul. This is entirely appropriate, because the *pien-wen* is not a psychological drama about the struggle between virtue and vice, as the *pao-chüan* is (in part), but a metaphysical allegory about the difficulty of rooting out attachments (in the Buddhist sense) and, by implication, about the nature of the soul. When Mu-lien finally finds his mother in the depths of Hell, she tells him that she has "learned to awaken to repentance,"[97] but when Buddha comes to rescue all the souls suffering in Hell, "the roots of her sin were deep and fast; the karmic forces difficult to eliminate," and she becomes only a hungry ghost.[98] When Mu-lien brings her a bowl of rice, she warns off the other ghosts—"'There won't be enough extra to help anybody else!'"—and begins gobbling it greedily, only to have it burst into flames in her mouth.[99] When she tries to drink water—"her avaricious heart was simply not to be restrained"—the same thing happens.[100] Only after she is transformed into a dog, eating excrement from the latrines and drinking water that drips from the eaves, are her desires finally rooted out. And even then Mu-lien has to lead her in a week-long ritual of prayer and confession before she is finally freed from the burden of her old nature.

Thus in the *pien-wen* the experiences of Mu-lien's mother, or rather of her soul, become an extended illustration of one of the fundamental propositions of Buddhist metaphysics. There is nothing like this in the *pao-chüan*, where the interest is in her descent into evil-doing and her seizure by the minions of Hell. Significantly, the flaming mouth of a hungry ghost, a central Buddhist image, is entirely absent from the *pao-chüan*. Madame Liu's fall from grace is never adequately explained in the *pao-chüan*; certainly the reader does not feel that it was due to some deeply ingrained

[96] *Yu-ming pao-ch'uan*, pp. 62b–64a.
[97] Mair, p. 111.
[98] Ibid., p. 114.
[99] Ibid., pp. 116–17.
[100] Ibid., p. 118.

spiritual deficiency. On the contrary, she is still quite pious when her evil companions deliberately seduce her into eating meat. At the very end, when she is asked by Buddha whether she would prefer to eat food that is forbidden or food that is permitted, and answers "I'll take the forbidden food!", this is explained away by pointing out that she had only just ceased to be a dog and was not in full possession of human consciousness.[101] But in the Buddhist view, human consciousness, far from ensuring the proper answer to this question, is precisely what would lead to the wrong answer. Again, at no time is it suggested that Madame Liu has achieved any kind of enlightenment; over and over it is Mu-lien's special pleading that saves her. By the same token, the magnificent universal compassion of the Buddha is reduced to little more than the granting of favors by a monarch to a well-liked petitioner who knows the right buttons to push. The metaphysical drama of the *pien-wen* has become didactic melodrama in the *pao-chüan*.

A very good idea of what T'ang dynasty *pien-wen* performers thought was important in the story of Mu-lien can be gained by looking at the places in the text where what Mair calls "markers of narrative locus" occur.[102] He makes a persuasive case that these were the places in the recitation where the performer directed the attention of the audience to a painting illustrating the action. These must have been scenes that were felt to be essential to the story. In S. 2614, the Mu-lien *pien-wen* translated by Mair, there are sixteen such crucial moments:

1. Mu-lien meditating deep in the mountains (when he gains his "spiritual penetrations") [lines 101–2 of Mair's translation];

2. Mu-lien asking a group of hungry ghosts in Hell why they are wandering about [ll. 202–3];

3. Mu-lien in audience with Yama, the ruler of Hell [ll. 249–50];

4. Mu-lien asking why the souls at the Nai-ho River (in Hell) are weeping [l. 314];

5. Mu-lien asking the General of the Five Ways (in Hell) where his mother is [l. 386];

---

[101]See above, p. 87.
[102]Victor Mair, *T'ang Transformation Texts* (cited n. 3).

6. Mu-lien setting out to search Hell [ll. 449–50];

7. The souls of sinners being made to climb the Sword Trees and Knife Hills [ll. 494–96];

8. Mu-lien encountering a demon general (who will tell him he should get help from the Buddha) [ll. 576–77];

9. Mu-lien asking Buddha's help (which will take the form of a magic metal-ringed staff) [l. 617];

10. Mu-lien outside the gates of the Avici Hell [l. 650];

11. Mu-lien in the Avici Hell [ll. 695–96];

12. Mu-lien finally reunited with his mother [l. 804];

13. Mu-lien returning to Heaven to ask the Buddha's help again [ll. 918–19];

14. Buddha and the eight classes of supernatural beings rescuing the sufferers in Hell [ll. 952–53];

15. The householder who is to give Mu-lien rice for his mother asking him why he is begging [ll. 1027–29];

16. The rice bursting into flames in his mother's mouth [l. 1096].

Eleven of these sixteen scenes are set in Hell, and two more in the Buddha's paradise. Quite clearly, depiction of the sufferings reserved for sinners, especially those who deprive the *sangha* of its accustomed offerings, is the main purpose of the *pien-wen*. And the task is carried out with great skill: the depictions of the sufferings undergone by the souls of the damned are memorably gruesome, rising at times to a kind of visionary frenzy, as in this description of the Avici Hell:

Sword-trees reached upward for a thousand fathoms with a clattering flourish as their needle-sharp points brushed together. Knife-mountains soared ten thousand rods in a chaotic jumble of interconnecting cliffs and crags. Fierce fires throbbed, seeming to leap about the entire sky with a thunderous roar. Sword-wheels whirled, seeming to brush the earth with the dust of starry brightness. Iron snakes belched fire, their scales bristling on all sides. Copper dogs breathed smoke, barking impetuously in every direction. Metal thorns descended chaotically from mid-air, piercing the chests of the men.

Awls and augers flew by every which way, gouging the backs of the women. Iron rakes flailed at their eyes, causing red blood to flow to the west. Copper pitchforks jabbed at their loins until white fat oozed to the east. Thereupon, they were made to crawl up the knife-mountains and enter the furnace coals. Their skulls were smashed to bits, their bones and flesh decomposed; tendons and skin snapped, liver and gall broke. Ground flesh spurted and splattered beyond the four gates; congealed blood drenched and drooked the pathways which run through the black clods of hell.

    (Ll. 672–88.)

The horror reaches its climax when Mu-lien finally finds his mother:

Trickles of blood flowed from the seven openings of her head.
Fierce flames issued from the inside of his mother's mouth,
At every step, metal thorns out of space entered her body;
She clanked and clattered like the sound of five hundred broken-down
    chariots, . . .
Stumbling at every step, she came forward, . . .
'A thousand times, they pluck the tongue from out of my mouth,
Hundreds of passes are made over my chest with a steel plough;
My bones, joints, tendons, and skin are everywhere broken,
They need not trouble with knives and swords since I fall to pieces by myself.
In the twinkling of an eye, I die a thousand deaths,
But, each time, they shout at me and I come back to life.'"

    (Ll. 807–10, 814, 840–44.)

This is cosmology as nightmare. Buddhist ideas about Hell had not yet become conventionalized; Hell and its tortures are imagined so vividly that it is possible to sense how new the ideas still were to ordinary people and those who preached to them. Juxtaposing the torments of the damned with the impressive depiction (already discussed) of how hard it is to overcome the attachments that can send one to Hell creates the central tension in the *pien-wen*.

By contrast, descriptions of Hell and its tortures occupy less than 20 percent of the *pao-chüan*. (They take up nearly 60 percent of the *pien-wen*, with an additional 20 percent dealing with Madame Liu's torments as a hungry ghost.) The descriptions are also very different in style from those in the *pien-wen*. The following is typical:

Mu-lien travelled through Hell searching for his mother in vain;
Depressed and enfeebled, he beat his breast and cried out to azure Heaven.
The Bureau of the Dead was utterly dark, and stretched on forever;
He could hear the legions of souls whimpering and crying from hunger
    and cold.
He did not know where he had got to;
Then he saw a cage where fires blazed fiercely and the demons were cruel.
They bound the sinners hand and foot and roasted them to charcoal;
Everyone was screaming as if their hearts were in boiling oil.
Mu-lien went on and looked about;
He saw the Hell of Tendon Pulling, where the suffering was unbearable.
The ghost-perpetrators were seized and their tendons pulled out,
    a punishment of the greatest cruelty.
The pain was so great that they trembled in every fiber, words can hardly
    express it.
Then he saw the Hell of Ice, and a cold wind pierced his vitals.
Iron tridents were used to drive the sinners off to one side.
They were stripped naked, without a thread to cover them.
The icy cold pierced them to the bone and froze them pitiably.
'To see the torments of this Hell is truly terrifying;
I exhort you to reform at once and turn toward virtue.
You must never sell counterfeit medicines, causing people's diseases
    to be neglected;
You must never make counterfeit goods to cheat people with;
You must never misuse the gods to beg for alms fraudulently;
You must never poison fish and shrimps, which angers Heaven above.
To induce people to gamble and fornicate is no trivial sin;
To incite people to quarrel and sue is also a transgression.
I exhort you to preserve your good heart, to turn away from evil and
    toward virtue;
Then even though there are the torments of Hell, you will be untouched.
I have passed through all these Courts of Hell searching carefully,
But have not seen my mother; where can she be?
The torments of Hell make people cry out in pain;
How pitiful it is that my mother should have to bear them.'
Mournfully he spoke, his vitals shattered by pain.
All he could do was seek out King Yama and ask him about the true
    state of affairs.

> Mu-lien, seeing how severe the punishments were in Hell, wondered to him-
> self how his mother could bear the suffering. Full of sorrow, he came to the
> fourth Court of Hell. The King of the Five Offices [who was in charge of the
> Court] heard him arrive and descended from his hall to welcome him. They
> exchanged courtesies, but did not go back up. Mu-lien said, 'I was told that
> my mother was in the fourth Court; how is it that I cannot find her?' The
> King of the Five Offices said, 'The sins of your mother are as weighty as a
> mountain; she is to be punished in each Court. She has been sent under
> guard to the fifth Court.'"
>
> (Pp. 92a.6–93b.2.)

The *pao-chüan*'s Hell is clearly a rather different place from the *pien-
wen*'s. The rulers of the various Courts are more like local officials than
devilish impresarios of suffering. The tortures inflicted on the damned,
though certainly horrible, are not described in the loving detail we find
in the *pien-wen*, and are accompanied by injunctions against this or that
sort of improper behavior that further lessen the impact. Hell has been
domesticated.

If terrifying descriptions of the agonies of the damned are not central to
the *pao-chüan*, what is? If we simply count pages, the story of Mu-lien's
father, grandfather, and great-grandfather takes up 30 percent of the whole
(68 pages out of 222); all the scenes in Hell, with the exception of the final
destruction of the Avici Hell, occupy about 19 percent (42 pages); Mu-
lien's journey to the Western Heaven (including his preparations for it),
17 percent (38 pages); and the seduction and death of Mu-lien's mother,
15 percent (34 pages).[103] But the emotional importance of these sections
is not proportionate to their length. We have already seen that the description of Hell is rather routine. (Significantly, the most emotionally
charged episode in Hell, Mu-lien's meeting with his mother, occurs after
he has made another journey to Heaven to get help from the Buddha, and
even then it is cut short when Mu-lien faints and his mother is hurried
away by meddlesome infernal bureaucrats.)

The big section on Mu-lien's forebears is clearly the product of the
"swelling" that the story had undergone during its long development in
oral tradition, and also does not generate any real emotional engagement

---

[103]The totals do not add up to 100 percent or 222 pages because I have not listed minor
sections.

on the part of the reader/listener. It is in a sense a very long prologue, descended from the first day's performances of multi-day operas about Mu-lien. Mu-lien's journey to the Western Heaven is very well told, and builds skillfully to an impressive climax, but for the most part is just a series of mildly entertaining encounters with wild animals and divine beings, some allegorical, some not.

This leaves the long section on Madame Liu's seduction and descent into depravity, her death at the hands of the demons despatched from Hell to seize her soul, and her final realization that she is indeed damned. This is the climax of the first half of the *pao-chüan* and seems to me by far the most emotionally charged part of the entire text as we now have it, the true heart of the story.

After Madame Liu starts eating meat the Fu household, which for generations had seen the practice of good works of all kinds, is transformed into a place of sensual indulgence and shocking violence. A local elder, distressed at Madame Liu's behavior, walks through the compound: "'The Life-saving Courtyard [where birds and fish were set free] has been changed into a killing ground; the Fragrant Orchid Hall has become a chamber of evil'" (47a.4–5). The sense of the debasing of virtue, the seduction and degradation of a good but weak woman by evil men, is extremely strong. One cannot help but feel pity for a person so badly abused; but one also is repelled at what she becomes. She hacks to death with a hoe the virtuous elder who remonstrates with her, she beats the corpse of Liu-the-liar, she swears a false oath to her own son. This is didactic melodrama at its most effective: the innocent but susceptible woman seduced by cynical villains, and, once seduced, unable to avoid complete moral collapse.[104]

Then comes retribution: the sunflowers burst into flame before her eyes and a troop of demons rushes on stage to seize her soul and take it down to Hell. This irruption of the demonic into everyday life, the jaws of Hell suddenly gaping open in the middle of the flower garden, is brilliantly handled and must have created an unforgettable impression. But Madame Liu does not understand what has happened to her until her soul is forced to return home. Gradually, in a scene that evokes both pity and terror, she comes to realize that she is dead, and is damned. When she

---

[104]I should make clear that no sexual misbehavior is involved, or even implied as far as I can tell.

cries out "I am so sorry," and clings desperately to her son, terrified of what awaits her, one recalls that many sources testify that the performers of *pao-chüan* could make their audiences weep. This extraordinary depiction of moral collapse, retribution, and remorse is in my opinion the main business of the *pao-chüan*: and none of it is in the *pien-wen*.

Certainly both the Mu-lien *pien-wen* and the *Yu-ming pao-ch'uan* had serious religious or at least moralistic purposes and both are telling "the same story." Yet they are also profoundly different. This is probably in large measure a reflection of the deep changes that Buddhism had undergone in the millennium between the ninth and nineteenth centuries. The Buddhism the *pien-wen* is popularizing is still highly doctrinal and theological, just beginning to come to terms with indigenous popular ideas and values. By making Mu-lien's mother a spirit, abstract and disembodied, throughout the story, and presenting Mu-lien himself as little different from a god, the *pien-wen* is better able to make its theological points, but at the cost of distancing its characters from the audience. As noted above, the central tension in the *pien-wen* is created by directly juxtaposing the difficulty of overcoming attachments with the penalties for failing to do so. This strikes me as a quintessentially clerical anxiety.

The *pao-chüan*, by contrast, has protagonists that are all too human (even if not depicted realistically), and clearly reflects a sensitivity to popular taste. In it, Buddhist teachings have been completely domesticated and are virtually taken for granted. On the other hand, the demonic elements that in the *pien-wen* are all safely confined to the Underworld are very much a part of this world in the *pao-chüan*, and hence far more threatening.[105] This is undoubtedly another sign of its popular provenance.[106] The *pao-chüan*'s intended message is very simple: if you honor the precepts of conventional morality and also the Buddhist prohibition against taking life you will not suffer the torments of Hell. But if you break any of the moral rules, you will pay a heavy penalty. The emphasis is entirely on how

---

[105]The depiction of Hell that is an essential part of the Mu-lien story naturally would have tended to attract additional material about ghosts and demons. One has the feeling that the Mu-lien story only gradually became entangled with the demonic and exorcistic elements that were so central to the operatic versions, and that the process had not yet begun in T'ang times; or if it had, that those elements were rigidly excluded from orthodox Buddhist versions of the story as the worst sort of paganism.

[106]The Great Way of Former Heaven material is another area of difference between the *pien-wen* and the *pao-chüan*, but there is not much of it.

to behave, and in this sense the *pao-chüan* is only a step or two removed from the *Sacred Edict*. The *pien-wen*, on the other hand, is concerned with the state of a soul, with the cravings that are the irresistible causes of action, and also with promoting the well-being of the sangha. Its point of view is at bottom that of the clergy.

Chantefable *vs.* Opera

But the differences between the *Yu-ming pao-ch'uan* and the Mu-lien *pien-wen* are not due simply to the evolution of popular Buddhism. Again and again we find that features of the *pao-chüan* version of the tale that are absent in the *pien-wen* version—the long section on Mu-lien's ancestors, the Liang dynasty setting, the supernatural radish, the oath in the flower garden, the white monkey that guides Mu-lien, the motif of balancing mother and sutras on a carrying pole, and, most important of all, Madame Liu's evildoing and damnation—are also found in Mu-lien operas. Clearly they were brought into the *pao-chüan* from them.[107] Madame Liu's false oath and her seizure by the demons is the central moment in the *pao-chüan* because it was the central moment in the operas.[108] This is extremely persuasive evidence of the immense influence of opera on popular consciousness in late imperial times.

But this *pao-chüan* is not just a simplified version of a Mu-lien opera; far from it. I began this paper with the intention of studying a non-operatic performance version of the Mu-lien story, because my earlier work had convinced me of the central importance of performance in Chinese culture and I wanted to improve my understanding of traditional performance literature.[109] But while it is true that Mu-lien operas and the *Yu-ming pao-ch'uan* have much in common, it is their differences that are most significant.[110] Even though opera and *pao-chüan* both were performance genres,

---

[107]Note that Cheng Chen-to believed that the great difference between the Mu-lien *pao-chüan* in circulation in the 1930s and the fourteenth-century edition in his collection was due to the influence of Ming and Ch'ing operas about Mu-lien. *Chung-kuo su-wen-hsüeh shih* (cited n. 4), vol. 2, p. 318.

[108]See my "Actions Speak Louder Than Words" (cited n. 1), pp. 17–19.

[109]See ibid., pp. 31–32, and "Scripted Performances in Chinese Culture: An Approach to the Analysis of Popular Literature," *Han-hsüeh yen-chiu* 漢學研究 [Taipei] 8:1 (1990), pp. 37–55.

[110]For simplicity's sake I will speak in what follows as if all Mu-lien operas are the same, but of course they are not.

their inner natures are antithetical. *Pao-chüan*'s strongest affinities are with written texts, not with what I have called scripted performances such as operas and rituals. *Pao-chüan* could move listeners to tears; but the emotion generated by the capture of Madame Liu in the *Yu-ming pao-ch'uan* is of a different order of magnitude, in fact is of a different type, than that aroused by the comparable scene in one of the great Mu-lien operas. *Pao-chüan* have much more in common with scripture than with opera, or ritual: they are discursive not mimetic, they rely almost entirely on words and very little on the non-verbal, they have more to do with private than communal experience, and in the end rely for their effect more on reason than emotion. For all they have in common, the Mu-lien *pao-chüan* and the Mu-lien operas represent two different aspects of Chinese popular religion, and of religion in general.

The basic distinction I am making here has been developed with great insight by Roy Rappaport in his work on ritual.[111] In his view, the Holy (the term he uses to refer to all those aspects of religion that involve belief and behavior) has two aspects. One, "the ultimate constituents of which are in language . . . faces language, reason, the public order, and their problems." This he calls "the sacred."[112] But the Holy also has a "nondiscursive, affective, and experiential aspect," an "ineffable, or emotional aspect." Rappaport calls this "the numinous"; it is at the heart of what William James called "the religious experience."[113] Rappaport associates the "sacred" with what he calls liturgical orders: "more or less invariant sequences of formal acts and utterances repeated in specified contexts,"[114] but with the emphasis seemingly on the utterances, on language. The "numinous," on the other hand, is evoked by acting in unison, and in public.[115]

Rappaport is concerned with ritual, and the language he is interested in is the highly specialized language of liturgies. Nevertheless, his identification of two fundamental aspects of religious behavior and belief, one rooted in language and involved with reason and the social-political order, the

[111]Especially his essay "The Obvious Aspects of Ritual," in Roy A. Rappaport, *Ecology, Meaning and Religion* (Berkeley: North Atlantic Books, 1979), pp. 173–221.
[112]Ibid., pp. 213.
[113]Ibid., pp. 211, 213.
[114]Ibid., p. 176.
[115]Ibid., pp. 194, 213.

other nondiscursive and emotional, generated by actions carried out in public and in unison, helps us understand why in the end the *Yu-ming pao-ch'uan* and Mu-lien operas are so different from each other. The *pao-chüan*, as I pointed out above, is far more dependent than opera on language alone to make its points; and those points are very heavily directed toward a certain kind of public order, both Buddhist and "Confucian." The operas, on the other hand, use both verbal and non-verbal means to communicate, and are far more "non-discursive, affective, and experiential" than the *pao-chüan*. Certainly the *Yu-ming pao-ch'uan* "faces language, reason, the public order, and their problems," while Mu-lien operas are in important ways "non-discursive, affective, and experiential."

Religious *pao-chüan* have of course frequently been called scriptures, and some even call themselves that (e.g., the *Stove Lord Scripture* [*Tsao Chün ching*]). They were designed to inculcate certain values, to proselytize, to indoctrinate. They stand therefore for the part of popular religion that was imposed by educated or semi-educated clergy, both regular and sectarian, and scholar-gentry moralists. That is why the *pao-chüan* and the *pien-wen*, for all their differences, have so much in common. Opera, on the other hand, has a deep kinship with ritual.[116] It was not, and is not, a natural vehicle for indoctrination. Scriptures did not make good scripts, or liturgies. The emotional power of opera, combined with its social-religious role, made it difficult for the elite to turn it to what they considered socially beneficial uses.

Popular religion always has two aspects: that which the people have made genuinely their own, no matter what its origin, so that they themselves pass it on with no prompting from their "betters"; and those ideas and values that are always being preached at them, and with which they are perfectly familiar, but which they never make wholly their own— because they demand too much, because they conflict with beliefs already deeply ingrained, or because they contradict people's personal experience. Those who wish to understand the first aspect of Chinese popular religion will do well to study Mu-lien operas; those whose interest is in the second, in the always uneasy relation between the rulers and the ruled, should turn to works like the *Yu-ming pao-ch'uan*.

[116]See my "Actions Speak Louder Than Words" (cited n. 1), pp. 29–32.

The Liturgies

for Sacrifices

to Ancestors

in Successive Versions

of the Family Rituals

PATRICIA EBREY

*I*n *The Social Life of the Chinese,* published in 1865, Justus Doolittle described a large ancestral hall in Foochow and the rites held there on an autumn equinox. The hall had been built near the end of the eighteenth century and was richly endowed. Ancestral tablets were displayed at its rear. In front of them was a table with a pair of candlesticks, a large censer, and two flower vases. Near it were other tables with a pig, a goat, and various utensils. In front of them was a second incense table, and on the walls of this room were two large pictures of some of the ancestors. There was also a large iron stove for burning mock money. Before the ceremony began, food was laid out, including five kinds of green vegetables, five kinds of fruit, five kinds of grain, cakes in five different shapes, some pig flesh, hair, and blood, an additional ten dishes of cooked food including meat, fish, and fowl, and ten cups each of tea and wine. During the ceremony the men lined up facing the ancestral tablets. A master of ceremonies directed them, telling them when to kneel, bow, and rise up. The sacrifice was performed by a boy of six or eight who was the eldest son of eldest sons on back to the descent group's first migrant ancestor. This boy made three libations of wine, pouring it onto straw. Three times cups of wine and bowls of vegetables were presented to the spirits. The master of ceremonies knelt to chant the text of a prayer, with all of those participating also kneeling. "During the progress of the worship they all knelt down five times, and while on their knees bowed down their heads simultaneously three times. There was no weeping, no smiling, and no talking, except by the professor of ceremonies. All was orderly, still, solemn, and reverent." When the ceremony was over, the cooked foods formed the basis of a feast for those participating.[1]

The ancestral rituals that took place in this hall bear a remarkably close resemblance to the sequences of steps described in the many versions of Chu Hsi's (1130–1200) *Family Rituals* (*Chia-li*, or *Chu Tzu chia-li*). It seems quite likely that the master of ceremonies at the sacrifice had a copy of one of the more detailed of these texts, such as Ch'iu Chün's (1420–1495) *Family Rituals with Specifications of Procedures* (*Chia-li i-chieh*). In the tradition of Confucian scholarship within which Chu Hsi compiled his liturgy and Ming authors revised it, ancestral sacrifices were not mysterious rituals, nor the creations of gods, nor conveyed to humans through revelation, nor passed down in secret. They had originally been created by human sages who understood the principles of heaven and earth, including the social and psychological needs of people. A scholar could know what the sages' rituals had been like by studying the classics, especially the *Etiquette and Ritual* (*I-li*) and *Record of Ritual* (*Li-chi*). Yet because circumstances vary, new forms might better achieve the true purposes of the rituals than old forms. Hence scholars could and should write new liturgies: every step, procedure, and distinction in the liturgies in the ca-

---

[1] *Social Life of the Chinese, with some Account of their Religious, Governmental, Educational, and Business Customs and Opinions, with Special but not Exclusive Reference to Fuhchau* (New York: Harper, 1865), I, 230–35, quotation p. 235. For a summary of other descriptions of ancestral rites by early Western observers, mostly missionaries, see James Thayer Addison, *Chinese Ancestor Worship* (Shanghai: Chung Hua Sheng Kung Hui, 1925). For ethnographic accounts of domestic ancestral rites in the twentieth century, see Francis L. K. Hsu, *Under the Ancestors' Shadow* (Stanford: Stanford University Press, 1971 [original edition 1948]), pp. 50–52, 183–92; David K. Jordan, *Gods, Ghosts, and Ancestors: The Folk Religion of a Taiwanese Village* (Berkeley: University of California Press, 1972), pp. 93–102; Emily M. Ahern, *The Cult of the Dead in a Chinese Village* (Stanford: Stanford University Press, 1973); and Stevan Harrell, *Ploughshare Village: Culture and Context in Taiwan* (Seattle: University of Washington Press, 1982), pp. 194–206. Most of the many studies of lineages treat ancestral rites as important to the identity and solidarity of the lineages, but say little about what occurs during the rites. Short descriptions are found in Daniel Harrison Kulp, *Country Life in South China: The Sociology of Familism* (New York: Teachers College, 1925), pp. 302–5, and Hsu, *Under the Ancestors' Shadow*, pp. 190–91. Fuller descriptions of both domestic and lineage ancestral rites are available for Korea. See Roger L. Janelli and Dawnhee Yin Janelli, *Ancestor Worship in Korean Society* (Stanford: Stanford University Press, 1982).

nonical *Etiquette and Ritual* and later books could be questioned as a guide-line for current performance and modified if need be. Indeed, Neo-Confucian leaders argued that such work was urgently required. During the Sung and Ming periods, Confucian scholars, teachers, and officials, committed to spreading the influence of Confucianism throughout society, wrote step-by-step guides to the performance of family rituals, hoping thereby to promote the practice of more authentic rituals by the educated and uneducated alike. Authentic rituals would foster filial piety, sincerity, and orderly families. By promoting them scholars could combat the prevalence of Buddhism and Taoism, which had infiltrated even such ancient rituals as ancestral rites and funeral ceremonies.

The people who consulted these liturgical texts need not have shared the goals or assumptions of the authors. Even well-educated readers often felt free to pick and choose, cookbook fashion, among parts of the texts, consulting certain sections when performing a particular rite, yet ignoring others entirely. Despite such haphazard use, these liturgical texts contributed significantly to shaping the performance of family rituals in China. As texts with relatively concrete and explicit meanings, they fostered continuities over time and uniformities across class and region in the ways Chinese performed weddings, funerals, and ancestral rites. People in different places could assign greater or lesser importance to specific details, but they were not free to read these books in any way they chose; the wording of the texts constrained them from, for instance, reversing the order of steps. At the same time these liturgical texts fostered class- or education-based differences in the performance of rites: those educated in the Confucian curriculum, considering themselves literati (*shih-ta-fu*) or aspiring to be recognized as such, had to perform rites in a more conspicuously Confucian manner than others.

Many of the larger issues concerning the social and intellectual context of these liturgies are discussed in my recent book, *Confucianism and Family Rituals in Imperial China: A Social History of Writing About Rites.*[2] This essay, by contrast, will focus on the content of the liturgies, specifically the liturgies for ancestral rites. From the time the *Record of Ritual* (*Li-chi*) was written, if not earlier, Chinese observers have recognized that ancestral

[2]Princeton University Press, 1991.

sacrifices convey meanings.[3] Scholars tended to emphasize the ways the rites expressed filial piety and symbolized the hierarchy of society, as higher ranks would perform more elaborate versions of the same rites. They rarely alluded to what the rites taught about the nature of death or the ancestors. Confucian scholars, like Confucius himself, were reluctant to discuss what an ancestor was or the metaphysical basis of his connections to his descendants. Their understandings on these issues were conveyed not through discursive essays but through liturgies specifying how to serve each ancestor. In the first part of this essay I try to specify the meanings conveyed by these liturgies by examining precisely what steps were specified and the patterns and contrasts they formed. In this part I concentrate on ancestral rites as imagined, not as performed. In a later section I consider the complex relationships between these liturgical texts and how people in various social groups performed ancestral rites. By way of conclusion I discuss how the availability of these texts influenced the historical evolution of ancestral rites.

LITURGIES FOR THE
SEASONAL SACRIFICES
IN THE *FAMILY RITUALS*

The *Family Rituals* was drafted by the Neo-Confucian philosopher Chu Hsi in the late twelfth century, based closely on a more detailed manual written by Ssu-ma Kuang (1019–1086) in the late eleventh century, itself based on the canonical *Etiquette and Ritual* and the T'ang government's *Ritual of the K'ai-yuan Period (K'ai-yuan li)*.[4] The *Family Rituals* provides detailed step-by step liturgies for the ceremonies associated with the ancestral cult that ordinary people could perform at home. The first of its

---

[3] See especially the chapters "Li-yün," "Li ch'i," "Chi fa," and "Chi i," translated in James Legge, *Li Chi, Book of Rites* (New Hyde Park, N.Y.: University Books, 1967 reprint of 1885 ed.), I, 364–515 and II, 201–235. See also Hsün Tzu's "Li yün," in Burton Watson, trans., *The Basic Writings of Mo Tzu, Hsün Tzu, and Han Fei Tzu* (New York: Columbia University Press, 1967), pp. 91–94, 109–11.

[4] In Ch'ing times some doubts about Chu Hsi's authorship of the *Family Rituals* were raised, most notably by Wang Mao-hung 王懋竑 (1668–1741). The most damaging evidence was that the earliest *nien-p'u* for Chu Hsi said that he wrote the book in 1170, but Chu Hsi in his own writings never mentioned it as a completed work, and in the early 1190s referred to his disappointment at never having been able to finish a book of this sort. Already in the nineteenth century two scholars had come to the defense of Chu Hsi's authorship of the *Family*

five chapters covers general principles and the next four are on cappings, weddings, funerals, and sacrifices.[5] Protocols for services to the ancestors occur in every chapter. The first chapter describes daily "looking in" on the ancestors, slightly more elaborate "visits" to be held twice a month, and offerings to be made on popular festivals. The second and third chapters describe how to report to the ancestors on the major family events of cappings, pinnings, betrothals, and weddings. The very long fourth chapter explains how to treat the recent dead and gives liturgies for eight funerary sacrifices to be performed once the dead were buried. The fifth

———————

Rituals. Ku Kuang-yü 顧廣譽 (1800–1867) and Hsia Hsin 夏炘 (1789–1871) independently wrote essays refuting Wang Mao-hung's attack on the authenticity of the *Family Rituals.* Both Hsia and Ku pointed out that the reference in Chu Hsi's chronological biography to his writing the *Family Rituals* while in mourning was misleading. Although Chu Hsi probably worked on the *Family Rituals* while in mourning for his mother, he did not produce a finished version then. The draft status of the *Family Rituals* would account for Chu Hsi's failure to mention it as a finished book. These scholars found it implausible that Chu Hsi's closest disciples and his son could have been fooled by a forgery, and pointed out how often in letters or conversations Chu Hsi discussed the practical issues of how to perform rites in his day, showing his strong interest in the subject matter of the *Family Rituals.* Chu Hsi also frequently referred to writing he was doing on particular rites in ways that correspond to the text of the *Family Rituals.* Ku Kuang-yü also cited the testimony of Ch'en Ch'un (1159–1223), who was explicit about talking to Chu Hsi in 1190 while the latter was prefect of Chang-chou about the draft of the *Family Rituals* that Chu Hsi had lost. Ch'en also reported that in 1211 he saw a copy of the *Family Rituals* at the home of Chu Hsi's youngest son Tsai, who asserted that it was the copy Chu Hsi had earlier lost. Ch'en reported that this book had five parts, one on general principles and one each on cappings, weddings, funerals, and sacrifices, and that each part was divided into chapters, and each chapter into main points and details. Ch'en later discussed minor differences between this draft and an early printed version. Twentieth-century scholars who have looked into the issue of the authorship of the *Family Rituals* have largely accepted the judgments of Hsia Hsin and Ku Kuang-yü. Ch'ien Mu, Ueyama Shumpei, Kao Ming, and Ch'en Lai agree that the weight of the evidence is very strong that the *Family Rituals* is Chu Hsi's book, although, like many of his other books, he probably had students draft some parts for him. Ch'ien Mu emphasizes, among other points, that there would have been no advantage to anyone to attribute a book to Chu Hsi shortly after his death as he was in official disfavor and his teachings labelled false teachings. Ch'en Lai gives particular weight to the clear evidence that Chu Hsi had written a liturgy for sacrifices in the early 1170s, arguing that if this part of the *Family Rituals* is genuine it is likely that the rest is as well. For full discussion of these issues and citation of the relevant sources, see my *Confucianism and Family Rituals,* pp. 102–44, 193–200.

[5] See my translation, *Chu Hsi's* Family Rituals: *A Twelfth-Century Chinese Manual for the Performance of Cappings, Weddings, Funerals, and Ancestral Rites* (Princeton: Princeton University Press, 1991). Appendix B reproduces the earliest surviving text of the *Family Rituals,* that in the 1343 *Chu Tzu ch'eng-shu.* Another easily accessible version of the *Family Rituals* is in vol. 142 of the Commercial Press (Taipei) reprint of the *Ssu-k'u ch'üan-shu.*

chapter, entirely on ancestral sacrifices, has the liturgies for the seasonal sacrifices to the four most recent generations of ancestors, special sacrifices on their death days, sacrifices to first ancestors and early ancestors, and sacrifices at graves.

Implicit in Chu Hsi's description of the steps in the seasonal ancestral rites are a variety of ideas about the relations of the living and the dead and about differentiation among the living. One descendant by virtue of his kinship position has a closer, more privileged, relationship with the ancestors and serves to mediate between them and other descendants. This individual must pay obeisance to the ancestors, showing that everyone serves someone and filial piety is a necessity rooted in the order of things. The ancestors can send blessings to their descendants, especially blessings of health, happiness, and progeny. Certain ways to serve the ancestors are particularly efficacious. The people and objects should be prepared by washing. Words addressed to the ancestors should be written and read aloud by someone other than the chief sacrificer. Food is an especially appropriate offering. Its use suggests that the relationship of the dead to their descendants is comparable to other relationships that involve feeding, such as the care of young children and the elderly, or even women's provision of food to men. Thus it is emotionally complex, involving love and duty, the dependence of the one receiving the food sometimes coupled with the submission of the one presenting it. The dead who are not true ancestors, having no surviving patrilineal descendants, will be fed, but not by the same people who feed the true ancestors, and always after the true ancestors. Concerning the living, the staging of the ancestral rites shows that men and women play complementary roles, but men always take the lead. This is true both of those making offerings and those receiving them. It also shows that generational seniority takes precedence over differentiation by gender; the wife of the great-great-grandfather is served before the great-grandfather.

These and other ideas were conveyed not through theoretical or discursive comments, but by the patterns of actions prescribed. To demonstrate this, let me outline the sequence of steps in the most important of the ancestral rites, the seasonal sacrifices to the ancestors.

Prerequisites

A family wishing to hold these rites first had to know which ancestor or ancestors it should serve and who should preside at the service. The *Family Rituals* employs the descent line heir (*tsung-tzu*) system. Sacrifices to any given ancestor were to be presided over by his eldest son, who would be succeeded by his own eldest son, who would then perform sacrifices to both his father and grandfather, and so on for up to four generations. In cases where a married couple did not leave an heir, rites would be performed for them at the shrine of the man's grandfather, where their tablets would be treated as associated tablets. The depth of the rites performed would thus vary from one to four generations from household to household, and households headed by younger sons would not perform rites at all. To put this another way, in many households an eldest brother would serve as presiding man for the rites to his own father (who had been a younger son) and the audience would consist of all the descendants of his father (i.e., his sons, unmarried daughters, his younger brothers, and their sons and unmarried daughters) and the wives of the men. In the much less common case of an eldest brother whose ancestors for three generations back had also all been eldest sons, the presiding man would be considered the descent line heir of the great-great-grandfather and the audience would consist of all men descended from this fourth generation ancestor, plus their wives and unmarried daughters. The younger son whose father, grandfather, and great-grandfather had all been younger sons would have to go to different households to participate in separate ceremonies for each of his own ancestors.

Once the ancestors to receive offerings were identified, the family needed wooden ancestral tablets inscribed with their names. These should have been made shortly after the person died, or at least by the time he or she was buried. The family also needed an ancestral shrine (or more literally "offering hall" *tz'u-t'ang*) to house the tablets. The size of the shrine could vary, but it was to have an inner area that could be closed off with a door or curtain. Within the inner area would be space for an incense stand, a table or tables that could hold all the tablets, normally kept in boxes, plus cups for wine and tea and bowls for fruit. When the tablets were laid out, they would be arranged in order of seniority, the earliest ancestor at the extreme west, his wife next to him, then his eldest son, then the latter's wife, and so on. The inner part of the ancestral shrine would also have to be big enough for three people to stand. The outer area, ideally conceived as the courtyard in front of the shrine, should be large enough for immediate family members to stand in rows. Some ceremonies were held inside the ancestral shrine and some just outside its door. All the major ones, however, were held in the largest room of the house. This main hall also had to have an inner and outer area. Preferably the inner area would be a raised hall and the outer one its adjacent courtyard so that those approaching the ancestral altar would walk up a few steps. One could make do, however, by drawing steps with chalk on the floor or ground to divide a large space into an imagined inner/higher section and an outer/lower section.

In addition to the presiding man, the family had to identify in advance several other people who would play significant roles in the rites. These were the presiding woman (normally the presiding man's wife), a liturgist, the oldest of the presiding man's brothers, another relative, and several attendants. If tablets for any collateral relatives were kept at the family's shrine, the presiding man and woman would not handle the service to them. More junior relatives would have to be identified to perform these acts. The family also had to have available a variety of common objects, such as plates, cups, chopsticks, ewers, baskets, incense burners, wash basins, towels, tables, and so on.

In the liturgy, the ritual is presented as a series of steps, here numbered and organized into the preparatory phase, the sacrifice proper, and the exit phase.

Preparatory Phase

1. *Divination.* Near the end of the preceding month a date for the sacrifice is selected by a divination performed in front of the ancestral shrine. Male descendants and attendants observe the divination, which is performed by the presiding man tossing crescent-shaped blocks. In advance he selects three possible dates. He proposes the first date, and if the blocks indicate that it is auspicious the divination is complete. If not he proposes the second date. If that also is not auspicious, he settles on the third date, not checking on its acceptability. The liturgist then opens the door of the ancestral shrine and all present bow in the direction of the tablets in their

boxes. The presiding man enters the inner area, burns incense, and bows again. The liturgist, who follows him, kneels to read a report to the ancestors giving the date for the sacrifice. After the presiding man and the liturgist descend, those present turn so that the male descendants and the attendants look across the room at each other rather than at the ancestors. The liturgist, representing the descendants, charges the attendants with the responsibility of preparing for the sacrifice by the appointed day.

2. *Purification*. Three days before the sacrifice purification begins. It involves the men moving out of the women's quarters, and both the men and the women bathing and putting on clean clothes and refraining from anything unclean or ill-omened from then until after the ritual.

3. *Preparation of the spaces and objects*. The day before the sacrifice, the men, women, and attendants each have specific tasks to accomplish by way of preparation. For instance, the men sweep the hall and supervise the slaughter of the animals, the women arrange the incense stands, and the reeds and sand needed for libations of wine, and see to the cooking and arrangements of food. "At each place should be six kinds of fruit, three kinds each of vegetables and dried meat, a plate each of meat, fish, steamed buns, and cakes, a bowl each of soup and rice, a skewer each of liver, and two skewers each of meat."

4. *Final preparation*. At daybreak, both the men and women dress formally, wash their hands, and perform separate tasks involving the laying out of food, dishes, and wine. The food is warmed up until very hot and put in boxes.

The Sacrifice Proper

5. *Getting the ancestral tablets*. When it is fully bright, all family members line up in front of the ancestral shrine in order (that is the men on one side, the women on the other, each in rows according to generation, with the oldest in each generation toward the center). The presiding man and presiding woman are in distinct central forward positions. The presiding man ascends the steps, lights incense, then addresses all the ancestors and ancestresses separately by title. He reports that the sacrifice is to take place and that he is moving them to the larger room. He washes his hands before putting the tablets in a basket. The presiding woman then washes her hands and takes the tablets for the ancestresses, followed if necessary

by a junior handling tablets for collateral lines. The tablets are then arranged on the tables in the main room where their places were earlier set.

6. *The spirits are greeted.* This is accomplished by everyone bowing to them.

7. *The spirits are invoked.* This involves the presiding man and three attendants who hold wine and wine utensils for him. The presiding man begins by burning incense. After a while he kneels and with the help of the attendants pours wine on the reeds and sand. He then prostrates himself, rises, bows, and comes down to his place.

8. *The food is presented.* The presiding man and woman, assisted by attendants, go up to set out many small dishes of food in front of each place, starting with the most senior ancestor, then his wife. They go together, the man putting out one kind of dish, then the woman putting out another, repeating this many times.

9. *The first offering.* Starting again with the most senior ancestor and ancestress, the presiding man makes a further libation of wine and his eldest brother puts out grilled meat. The liturgist kneels and reads a prayer from the presiding man to the ancestors. This procedure is repeated at each of the pairs of seats.

10. *The second offering.* The presiding woman adds more grilled meat to each seat.

11. *The third offering.* A brother, son, other relative, or guest adds more grilled meat to each seat.

12. *The spirits are urged to eat.* This is accomplished by the presiding man pouring a cup of wine for each of the ancestors and ancestresses and the presiding woman arranging their spoons and chopsticks.

13. *The door is closed.* This is to allow the spirits to eat in private.

14. *The door is opened.* The liturgist does this after coughing three times as warning. The presiding man and woman then serve the ancestors tea.

15. *The food is removed.* The presiding man, the liturgist, and the attendants all participate. More wine is sacrificed on the reeds. The liturgist addresses the presiding man in the words of the ancestors, conveying blessings of fertility. The presiding man prostrates himself, rises, bows twice, and kneels to begin receiving the food. After drinking wine he prostrates himself again. The liturgist announces that the meal is over, and everyone bows twice, with the exception of the presiding man.

The Exit Phase

16. *Everyone bows to take leave of the spirits.*

17. *The tablets are put back by the presiding man and woman, assisted by another relative when there are collateral relatives' tablets.*

18. *The presiding woman supervises clearing away the dishes.*

19. *In separate quarters the men and women have family feasts.*

In listing these steps I have simplified the *Family Rituals,* which is quite explicit about the directions each person faces, where objects should be placed, and so on. Let me quote the section called "Invoke the spirits" to illustrate its specificity.

> The presiding man goes up [the steps toward the tablets] and inserts his plaque while he lights incense. He then takes out his plaque, steps back a little, and stands there. One attendant opens the wine and takes a cloth to wipe the mouth of the wine bottle, then fills the decanter with it. Another attendant takes the cup and saucer on the table at the eastern steps and stands to the presiding man's left. A third attendant takes the decanter and stands to the presiding man's right. The presiding man inserts the plaque and kneels. The one holding the cup and saucer also kneels and hands them to the presiding man. Then the one with the decanter also kneels and pours wine into the cup. The presiding man, taking the saucer in his left hand and the cup in his right, pours the wine onto the reeds. He passes the cup and saucer to the attendant, then takes out his plaque. After he prostrates himself, he rises, bows twice, comes down the steps, and resumes his place.

As described in this liturgy, a performance of the seasonal ancestral rites would take perhaps an hour or two. Prayers, for instance, were not long. Below is the prayer that the liturgist reads, kneeling, at the first offering.

> On the day of the new moon of this month of this year, such year cycle, I, filial great-great-grandson A, of such office, presume to report clearly to your honor, our late great-great-grandfather, of such office, and our late great-great-grandmother, of such title, such surname: The succession of atmospheric forces flows and changes. The time now is the middle of spring. When we think back with gratitude on the seasonal service, we cannot overcome our long-term longings. We presume to take this pure offering of a

soft-haired animal [i.e., lamb or goat], a vessel of millet, and sweet wine, and respectfully present them as our seasonal service. Please enjoy them along with the associated spirits, such-type relative, of such office, and such-type relative, of such title, such surname.

A slightly altered version of this prayer would be repeated at each of the other pairs of tablets. The ancestors' response was not long either.

The worship service is over. We had an excellent repast. We wish our such-type relative to receive fully the five blessings, preserve his agnates, and benefit his family.[6]

SEASONAL SACRIFICES WITHIN THE LARGER SCHEME OF SERVICE TO THE DEAD

It would have been extraordinarily difficult for a Chinese in any period from the Sung through the Ch'ing to read the section in the *Family Rituals* that specified how to perform the seasonal sacrifices without interpreting it in terms of its similarities and differences to other sorts of rituals, as imagined or as performed. The *Family Rituals* itself provides the basis for such comparisons, giving as it does the protocols for many other forms of service to ancestors. Seasonal rites have a particular place in two larger cycles of rites: the multi-year cycle focusing on each dead person, and the yearly cycle of major and minor rites performed in a household to the dead of several sorts.

Any given performance of the seasonal sacrifices, seen in these larger cycles, indicates the stage of the relationship between the living and the dead. After death but before full ancestorhood the living descendants have to wail in their presence and are unsuited to handling their tablets. In the prime of ancestorhood, the relationship of the dead with their descendants can be direct and joyful. The food they receive is abundant, it is all fully edible, and it is indeed eaten by their descendants shortly after the ancestors have taken their fill. The ancestors have not yet passed to the stage where their *hun* soul loses much of its individuality and can appropriately be offered uncooked food.

Seasonal sacrifices are only performed to those who might be considered

---

[6]The five blessings were long life, wealth, health, virtue, and a complete life span.

in the prime of ancestorhood. Each step in the rites indicates ways in which such ancestors are both like and unlike the recent dead and the distant dead. What might be termed a "death course" (by analogy to "life course") starts when a person dies and continues, in shifting stages, for decades. In the first phase, from the time a man died until his burial, he would be represented not by an ancestral tablet but by a piece of cloth.[7] His descendants, led by his eldest son the chief mourner, would wail and bow before this object, something they would not do before a full ancestor. People other than his own descendants (servants or a liturgist) would set out meat, other food, and wine at least twice a day before the soul cloth. The soul cloth would be buried with the body, and from then on the dead would be represented by a wooden tablet inscribed with his name and title as well as the name and kinship relationship of the descendant chiefly responsible for serving him. During this second phase a series of funerary sacrifices would be performed, the first on the day of the burial. The chief mourner, a liturgist, and attendants would perform the acts in front of the wooden tablet. The other mourners, arranged by degree of mourning but divided by gender, would form the audience. The audience, thus, was not defined or arranged in the same way as for seasonal sacrifices. During the next couple of weeks four more similar sacrifices would be held, the last of which would be done in the ancestral hall in the presence of all the ancestors residing there (that is, the tablets of the recently deceased's father, grandfather, and so on, depending on how many were eldest sons). These tablets would be handled by a liturgist and female attendants, rather than the descendants still in mourning, with the descent line heir of the most remote ancestor (not necessarily the chief mourner) presiding over the sacrifice, as he would from this point on.

On the first and second anniversaries of this man's death, sacrifices would be held to mark transitions in the obligations of mourners. With the permanent installation of his tablet on the second anniversary, the dead became a full ancestor. If he had been an eldest son, his tablet would be moved to the ancestral shrine, possibly forcing the rearrangement of

---

[7]The sequence would largely be the same for the wife of this man, with the exception that if she died before him she would not gain a regular place on the ancestral altar until he had died. Moreover, her tablet would be taken out for his death day anniversary, but not his for her death day anniversary.

the old tablets and the retirement of his great-great-grandfather's tablet if it had been housed there. If the dead man had been a younger son, his tablet would be installed in a newly created shrine. A couple of months after the second anniversary, the final funerary sacrifice would be held, marking the end of mourning for the children and widow of the deceased.

During the period of prime ancestorhood, service to ancestors included daily "looking in," twice-monthly visits, periodic offerings, and occasional reports and death-day sacrifices, all less elaborate than the four seasonal sacrifices. All of these forms of interaction resembled in broad outline the visit of a junior to a senior: the junior enters, greets the elder with a bow, conducts the business, and bows to take leave. All also resembled in similar broad terms the ways people approached gods: a person bows, burns incense, makes a report, query, or plea, sometimes accompanied by food and drink, and bows again. Additional elements are added as the service becomes less routine and more special. The twice-monthly visits involved offerings of fruit, wine, and tea. On holidays the food associated with the holiday would also be added. Reports of trips varied according to the circumstances. For instance, when the presiding man expected to be away ten days or longer, before departing he was to open the outer door of the shrine, bow twice, burn incense, report his plan, and bow twice again. When he would be away a month or longer, he was to open the inner door, bow twice while still in the outer area, ascend the stairs, burn incense, report his plan, bow twice, go down the stairs, face the shrine again, and bow twice more.

The twice-monthly visits added to this basic structure the opening of the tablet cases and the presentation of food and drink in front of the tablets. These additions brought with them further similarities to the seasonal sacrifices, such as a preparatory stage involving abstinence and the cleaning of utensils, hand washings, place settings, and the participation of women. In both visits and sacrifices everyone attending would bow, those making the libation of wine would kneel, and the presiding man alone would prostrate himself. The contrasts between the full-scale sacrifice and the visit were in part differences in degree. For the visit, purification would last only one night, and the text does not say everyone had to observe it. Only one sort of food, fruit, would be offered. A single joint libation would be made to all the ancestors and ancestresses. Besides these differences in degree, there were differences that affected the nature of the ritual itself. No liturgist participated in the visit, nor were any prayers spoken or read. The ancestors were never left alone to eat and they made no reply. To put a construction on these differences, the visit was something the living did, whether or not the ancestors were participating. The seasonal sacrifices, by contrast, symbolically posited actual communication.

Ancestors in their prime were distinguished by generation. The man thought of as the great-grandfather of the family's new baby on his death became the ancestor in the father generation, later moving to grandfather, and so on. Although emotional ties must always have been strongest to the most recent dead, the most senior generation of ancestors had to be treated with greatest deference and were always served first. The more junior ancestors, however, received more individual attention. In his first generation as an ancestor the deceased would receive an individual sacrifice in the fall. Moreover, death day anniversaries, some commentators suggested, should only be continued so long as there was a living member of the household who had personally served the deceased. These two individual sacrifices would be similar in structure to the seasonal sacrifices, though the quantities of food would be reduced to one-tenth and two-tenths, respectively, and the food would not form the basis of a family feast. Because descendants participated frequently in the individualized death-day services, they would have sensed that in the seasonal sacrifices ancestors were being grouped together into a hierarchical structure.

When his eldest son died, the ancestor would be promoted, passing from "father" to "grandfather" among the ancestors at this altar. Each time the ancestor was promoted, part of his tablet would have to be repainted, showing that he was no longer served by his son so-and-so, but by his grandson so-and-so. After his promotion to great-great-grandfather among the ancestors he could be promoted only to the vague category of early ancestors who indefinitely receive an undifferentiated offering in the spring. This sacrifice again bore many similarities to the seasonal sacrifices, but would involve uncooked offerings (blood, hair, heart, lungs, intestines) in addition to cooked ones and would not be followed by a family feast. Even as a part of the rather indistinct category of early ancestors, the dead could also continue to receive annual sacrifices at his grave in the third month.

The purposes of the various people assisting the presiding man in the seasonal sacrifices become apparent when different types of service to ancestors are compared. Every ceremony required at least two active participants, one of whom was the presiding man. For all ceremonies that required touching the ancestral tablets he had to be assisted by a woman (usually his wife) to handle the tablets for female ancestors. For any ceremony involving the reading of a prayer, a liturgist was required, who always read it from a kneeling position. For any ceremony involving the pouring of liquids (wine, water, or tea), attendants had to assist. The normal assumption seems to have been that servants filled this role best. Perhaps it was to the glory of the ancestor to have servants attend him, as it would be to the living.

The food and drink offered to the ancestors at the seasonal sacrifices also become more meaningful when compared to those offered on other occasions. The major differences are first between simple offerings of fruit, or fruit and a festival food, and varied meal-like offerings including rice and soup as well as several dishes. Of those including the full range of items, three groups are distinguishable. At the pre-ancestor stage, for the funerary sacrifices, it is assumed that most people will make meatless offerings. This may reflect the fact that the mourners are not to eat meat, but perhaps also (certainly unconsciously on Chu Hsi's part) the prevalence of Buddhist vegetarian funerary feasts. Sacrifices to ancestors in the prime of ancestorhood involve grains, meat, and vegetables, varying only in quantity (several times more for the seasonal sacrifices than for death-days, for instance). At the diffuse ancestor stage, some uncooked meat appears. At both the pre-ancestor stage and diffuse ancestor stages, the *Family Rituals* does not mention the descendants consuming the food.[8]

OTHER FRAMES OF REFERENCE

Some frames of reference are not provided in the *Family Rituals* itself, but would depend on the reader's knowledge of other liturgies and other forms

---

[8]For an analysis of the "semantics" of food in funerary rituals in modern Taiwan, see Stuart E. Thompson, "Death, Food, and Fertility," in *Death Ritual in Late Imperial and Modern China*, eds. James L. Watson and Evelyn S. Rawski (Berkeley: University of California Press, 1988).

of ritual. The *Family Rituals* provides liturgies only for the general population (never clearly defined). It thus posits that whatever the structure of a given household in this population, whatever its members feel toward each other, whatever they remember of their ancestors, they perform the rites the same way, thus reducing those differences at least temporarily to irrelevancies. It is thus significant that these rites were not appropriate for *every* other household. Chu Hsi and those who consulted his book were well aware that the emperor and other clearly specified members of the political elite were supposed to perform ancestral rites in ways that demonstrated their superiority. Nevertheless, the liturgies for ancestral rites in the *Family Rituals* conform in their broad outlines to the ancestral rites performed by the emperor as well as other sacrifices of the state cult modeled directly or indirectly on the ritual classics.

These rites, described in detail in successive imperial manuals such as the *Ritual of the K'ai-yuan Period*, the early-twelfth-century *New Forms for the Five Categories of Rites of the Cheng-ho Period* (*Cheng-ho wu-li hsin-i*), and the *Collected Rituals of the Ming* (*Ming chi-li*), invariably called for a period of purification, careful preparation of the people, objects, and spaces to be used, a chief sacrificer who had a privileged relationship to the spirits receiving the sacrifice, a liturgist who chanted the prayers, and so on. These imperial codes regularly included liturgies for officials' domestic ancestral sacrifices in ways that corresponded to imperial ancestral rites but on a reduced scale, thus expressing and reproducing the political hierarchy. The higher the rank of the officiant, the more elaborate each step should be.[9] Since Chu Hsi drew on this tradition (through his use of Ssu-ma Kuang's *Letters and Etiquette* [*Ssu-ma shih shu-i*], itself drawing from the *Ritual of the K'ai-yuan Period*), not surprisingly the liturgy in the *Family Rituals* fits easily into this larger framework, coming fairly close to prescriptions for the lowest officials. The major exception to this generalization is that in the *Family Rituals*, Chu Hsi followed Ch'eng I (1033–1107) in rejecting the long-established principle of differentiating the number of

---

[9]For a discussion of the structure of rites in the state cult, see A. R. Zito, "City Gods, Filiality, and Hegemony in Late Imperial China," *Modern China* 13.3 (1987), 333–71. One significant difference between domestic ancestral sacrifices and these state cult sacrifices is that in the latter the foods offered were often burned or buried rather than eaten by the participants.

generations of ancestors each rank can worship; instead officials of all ranks, educated men, and illiterate commoners are all told to sacrifice to four generations of ancestors.[10]

There are also homologies between the way sacrifices to ancestors are described in the *Family Rituals* and the way people commonly approached gods, either in small domestic shrines or in temples.[11] These included burning incense, making small offerings of food and drink, making reports and requests, performing divinations, and so on. The divination performed to select a day for the seasonal sacrifices was performed with the help of a liturgist, echoing imperial practice and the text of the *Etiquette and Ritual.* Yet it was done not with yarrow stalks, as in the *Etiquette and Ritual* and the *K'ai-yuan Ritual*, but with wooden divining blocks, which by Sung times were a well-entrenched feature of temple-based religion. The presiding man thus was asking his ancestors a question through the same medium he might use if visiting a local temple to Kuan-yin or Wen-ch'ang to ask about the birth of sons or success in the examinations.

LITURGIES FOR SEASONAL SACRIFICES
IN MING REVISIONS
OF THE *FAMILY RITUALS*

Beginning in the early fifteenth century, many authors took to revising the *Family Rituals* to make it more convenient to consult or better suited to local needs. They did not present these products as original creations, but as abbreviated, updated, expanded, or otherwise improved versions of Chu Hsi's text. Several dozen such books were written in Ming times; of these I have been able to locate and read eighteen.[12] During the course of the Ming these veered in two directions: toward the ever larger and

[10]See Patricia B. Ebrey, "Education Through Ritual: Efforts to Formulate Family Rituals During the Sung Period," in *Neo-Confucian Education: The Formative Stage*, Wm. Theodore de Bary and John W. Chaffee, eds. (Berkeley: University of California Press, 1989), pp. 277–306.

[11] For discussions of similarities and contrasts between rites to ancestors and rites to gods in modern Taiwan, see Stephan Feuchtwang, "Domestic and Communal Worship in Taiwan," and Arthur P. Wolf, "Gods, Ghosts, and Ancestors," in *Religion and Ritual in Chinese Society*, Arthur P. Wolf, ed. (Stanford: Stanford University Press, 1974), pp. 105–30, 131–82.

[12]See the Appendix to my *Confucianism and Family Rituals* for a list of forty-nine Ming versions.

more scholarly on the one hand, and toward the briefer, simpler, and more accommodating on the other. The more scholarly were sometimes expensively produced books, but could also be economically produced, as the simpler ones were, with crowded pages and blocks used long after they had gotten blurry. Only a few of the authors of the simpler versions were prominent in literary or philosophical circles. More common were local magistrates or teachers writing for what they saw as the needs of the communities they guided.

All of these revised versions alter in some way the liturgy for ancestral rites, bringing it more into line with what was commonly done or what the authors thought could in fact be done. Below is a list of the more significant changes.[13]

1. *Rearrangement of the positions of the tablets.* Almost no one, it seems, was satisfied with Chu Hsi's arrangement of ancestral tablets, in which the westernmost position was the most honorable. Many authors recommended the plan of the Cheng communal family, which added a tablet for the first ancestor in the center, then had ancestors on the west, the most senior toward the middle, and the ancestresses on the east. This plan emphasized gender distinctions and downplayed couples. Even more popular was the plan given by Ch'iu Chün and adopted in the *Ming hui-tien,* in which couples stayed together but the two more senior generations were in the center, flanked by the two more junior generations. Ch'iu reversed the order of each couple, putting the wives to the west of their husbands, so that a daughter-in-law would never be next to her father-in-law—she would either be next to her son, grandson, or her husband's

---

[13]Most of these eighteen versions exist only in single copies, kept in various rare book collections. Thirteen of them I found only in China, where it was not possible to make copies, only to take notes. As my notes are not always adequate to answer the questions posed in this paper, here I primarily cite five versions found in the U.S. or Japan for which I have copies. These include the three earliest and most influential ones: Feng Shan's 馮善 *Chia-li chi-shuo* 家禮集說 (ca. 1400–1434) (Ts'ui-ch'ing t'ang, 1589); T'ang To's 湯鐸 *Chia-li hui-t'ung (Wen-kung)* 家禮會通 (文公) (Nan-ching: Ch'ih-chung-t'ang, 1450 ed.); and Ch'iu Chün's 丘濬 *Chia-li i-chieh* 家禮儀節 (1618 ed.), all three of which exist in multiple copies, plus two late Ming ones based on Ch'iu Chün's book, Chu T'ing-li's 朱廷立 *Chia-li chieh-yao* 家禮節要 (preface 1536) and an anonymous revision of uncertain date, published under Ch'iu Chün's name as though it were his book. When these last two books largely repeat Ch'iu Chün's specifications, I have not cited them. I also cite an anonymous commentary to the *Hsing-li ta-ch'üan (Hsin-k'o)* 性理大全 (新刻) (sixteenth-century edition at the University of Chicago library).

grandfather, making quite explicit the need for the ordering of the dead to correspond to the ordering of the living.[14] Compare Chu Hsi's and Ch'iu Chün's plans as shown below.

Chu Hsi's arrangement of ancestral tablets

FFFF   FFFM   FFF   FFM   FF   FM   F   M

Ch'iu Chün's arrangement

M   F   FFM   FFF   FFFM   FFFF   FM   FF

F = Father   M = Mother

2. *Substituting paper tablets for wooden ones for economy or to allow younger sons to conduct rites without making duplicate tablets.*[15]

3. *Holding the seasonal sacrifices on the solstices and equinoxes or popular festivals.* Commented versions of the *Family Rituals* noted that Ssu-ma Kuang had said it was all right to follow the practice of using the solstices and equinoxes, already established by the T'ang, and that Chu Hsi, in a conversation with disciples, had concurred with Ssu-ma Kuang on this point.[16] Some Ming versions of the *Family Rituals* simply called for holding the rites on these days, with no discussion of divination. Ch'iu Chün gave both alternatives and recommended reporting to the ancestral altar the date of the rites, even when solar dates were used.[17] T'ang To went so far as to suggest that the sacrifices could be held on popular festivals so long as there was one in each season. He proposed five sacrifices a year: on New Year, then Ch'ing-ming for the spring, Double Five for the summer, Mid-Autumn for the fall, and the winter solstice for the winter.[18]

4. *A single prayer addressed to all ancestors to shorten and simplify the ceremony.*[19]

5. *A master of ceremonies to call out the steps of the rites.* T'ang To added a script for the performance of sacrifices. An assistant would keep everyone on schedule by calling out the steps to be performed, such as "Invoke the spirits," "Urge the spirits to eat," or "Bow prostrate."[20] Ch'iu Chün gave

---

[14]*Chia-li i-chieh* 1 t'u 40b–43b.
[15]*Hsing-li ta-ch'üan* 21:12b; *Chia-li hui-t'ung* 9:7b.
[16]*Hsing-li ta-ch'üan* 21:11b–12a.
[17]*Chia-li i-chieh* 7:2b.
[18]*Chia-li hui-t'ung* 9:7a.
[19]*Chia-li chi-shuo* 154b–155a; *Chia-li hui-t'ung* 9:16b–17b; *Chia-li i-chieh* 7:12b–13b.
[20]*Chia-li hui-t'ung*, ch. 9.

an even more detailed script; for instance during the seasonal sacrifices, when it was time to set out the spirit tablets, he had someone say, "Wash hands," "Open the cases," "Take out the tablets," "Go to the front of the incense stand," "Kneel," "Burn incense," "Report," and "Carry the tablets to their places."[21] To speak the parts, Ch'iu called for employing two "masters of ceremonies" (*li-sheng*) for the seasonal sacrifices (and one for most other ceremonies). "Rituals are often complicated, so that without people to lead, call out, and assist, it is impossible to do everything precisely."[22]

6. *Holding rites for collateral lines together with the rites for the main line and excluding women from the rites.* As explained above, in Chu Hsi's scheme a descendant of younger sons might have to go to four separate households to participate in the rites to all four of his direct ancestors. It seems unlikely that many people went to this much trouble; probably most such descendants only participated in the rites to their most immediate ancestors. In Chu Hsi's time and even more in the next few centuries some people were performing ancestral rites on a quite different basis, as a joint activity of a descent group. The early-sixteenth-century writer whose commentary is included in the annotated versions of the *Great Compendium on Nature and Principle* (*Hsing-li ta-ch'üan*) explained why women should be excluded in such cases: "At the sacrifices at an altar for four generations of parents, the descendants will all be closely related, so for men and women to assemble in the same hall will not cause embarrassment. At sacrifices to first and early ancestors, the descendants will be distantly related and moreover numerous. Therefore women do not join the ranks. This is nothing other than natural principles."[23]

7. *Burning paper money.* This practice, associated especially with Buddhist and Taoist services for the dead, was popular in the Sung. Some Sung scholars seem to have rejected it on the grounds that it was Buddhist, while others said it was no different in principle than the burial of objects in tombs as token offerings to the dead, explicitly called for in the classics. Many authors of Ming revised versions argued that it was innocuous.[24]

8. *Omitting opening and closing the door.* Wang Yüan, author of one of

[21]*Chia-li i-chieh* 7:6a–b.
[22]*Chia-li i-chieh* 2:1b.
[23]*Hsing-li ta-ch'üan* 21:17b.
[24]*Chia-li chi-shuo* 156a–b; *Chia-li hui-t'ung* 9:7b, 19a.

the earliest revised versions of the *Family Rituals* (one not extant) is quoted in a later revised version as arguing for this simplification of ancestral rites on the grounds that "The ancient ritual had an impersonator; one closed the door for the impersonator to eat the nine course meal. Today in sacrifices impersonators are not used, so this step can be omitted. . . . The complexity of the current ritual makes it difficult for people to practice, so it must be cut before they will begin to practice it."[25]

9. *Displaying portraits of the ancestors during the sacrifice.*[26]

10. *Omitting the slaughter of sacrificial animals as an unnecessary canonical flourish.*[27]

11. *Having only women serve the tea.*[28]

12. *Presenting food offerings in multiples of five.*[29]

One should also note the features of Chu Hsi's *Family Rituals* that authors of revised versions did not change. None of them omitted purification, invoking the spirits, pouring libations of wine to them, the triple offering with a woman making the second offering, the use of written prayers, or offering a varied meal including cooked meat, grain, and vegetables. In other words, the basic structure and sequence of steps were maintained by all authors, as were the texts of prayers. Another feature they did not change was the exclusion of Buddhist ideas or practices. Even the most accommodating of late Ming versions maintained a firm line against the intrusion of Buddhist merit ceremonies.

Nor did any of the revised versions alter the emphasis on differentiation among family members. It is common in anthropology to treat ancestral rites as rites of solidarity concerned especially with reproducing the bonds among the kinsmen defined by links to a common ancestor. Certainly the rites described here could have that effect. Yet in all liturgies the distinctions among family members are much stressed and the focus of the ritual is on the interaction of the presiding man and the tablets, not on the other members of the family, who are treated more like an audience. To the extent that solidarity is sought it is an organic solidarity based on dif-

---

[25]*Chia-li hui-t'ung* 9:1a–2a.
[26]*Chia-li hui-t'ung* 1:10a.
[27]*Hsing-li ta-ch'üan* 21:13b; *Chia-li hui-t'ung* 9:13b.
[28]*Chia-li chieh-yao* 72a.
[29]*Chia-li i-chieh* 7:5a–b.

ferentiation, not one based on people temporarily stepping out of their ordinary social roles.[30]

If we reimagine the seasonal sacrifices incorporating the more common revisions, they clearly look different. A ceremony punctuated by the shouted orders of two alternating masters of ceremony would not be experienced in the same way as one in which the main participants either acted silently or kept telling each other what to do. But ceremonies still involved written prayers, assorted food encoding changes in the relations of the living and dead, distinctions by generation, age, and gender, and a special place for the ritually senior descendant and his wife. The seasonal sacrifices still fit in much the same place within the larger scheme of service to the dead, distinct from service to pre-ancestor dead or diffuse ancestors, more elaborate than the visits, reports, and offerings also presented to ancestors in their prime.

The biggest difference between Chu Hsi's version and later revisions is that the later liturgies have fewer allusions to canonical sources and the practices of the emperor and more to the everyday ways people used to approach their gods. Burning paper money, calling out the steps of the rites, representing the ancestors by likenesses and not simply written names all brought ancestral sacrifices closer to temple-based worship. Ancestors became a little more like gods, and hence the relationship of descendants to their ancestors resembled more closely the relationship of parishioners to local gods or of the faithful to Kuan-yin and other common deities.

A considerably greater alteration in meaning took place when sacrifices were held as descent group rather than descent line rites. Relationships between the living and the dead became collective rather than dyadic; a group of descendants made offerings to a group of ancestors. Distinctions between elder and younger sons were not as prominent, since their tablets ended up in the same place. Women were excluded from the ceremony altogether, so gender differentiation was represented in a fundamentally different way: men had a unique relationship to distant ancestors.

---

[30]It is true, of course, that a man who might in ordinary life be the family head, deferring to no one in the household, had to prostrate himself before his ancestors, but this was no more than what he would do before officials or other superiors. And the descent line heir was not necessarily the family head. He could be, as in the case described by Doolittle, a young boy. On the symbolic effects of stripping people of their social roles in rituals, see Victor Turner, *The Ritual Process: Structure and Anti-Structure* (Ithaca: Cornell University Press, 1969).

Let us briefly return to the ceremony described by Doolittle. It was for a descent group of considerable size, and the ceremony was for the "early ancestors," not those in what I have called here the prime of ancestorhood (whether more recent ones were also included is unclear from Doolittle's account). Nevertheless the date chosen was one specified in many revised versions of the *Family Rituals* for a seasonal sacrifice, and the types of food were quite close to what Ch'iu Chün gave, who also mentioned types of food in multiples of five. Pouring wine on straw, three offerings, prayers chanted by a specialist, numerous bowings and prostrations were all features found in both the original *Family Rituals* and all revised versions. Having a master of ceremonies who called out the steps was introduced by Ch'iu Chün and copied by most of those after him. Hanging portraits in the hall was allowed in some revisions, as was excluding women from rites for early ancestors. The social context in which this ritual occurred— the richly appointed hall of a large descent group—differed significantly from that envisioned by Chu Hsi or Ch'iu Chün. Yet the symbolism of the food, the wine, the choice of chief sacrificer, the arrangement of the space, and so on all conveyed notions quite similar to those conveyed in domestic ancestral rites.

LITURGIES AND RITUALS

So far, I have examined the meanings encoded in Confucian liturgies for ancestral rites; in other words, the meanings in the rites as imagined by Confucian authors. These meanings would be more forcefully conveyed, and conveyed to more people, if they were embodied in performance and not simply implicit in books. But these liturgies are neither ethnographic descriptions of what their authors did, nor sacred texts that priests followed as closely as possible when performing a rite in order to make it efficacious. Their relationship to the performance of rituals is rather different.

Certainly the *Family Rituals* was not intended to describe what people commonly did at the time it was written. Sung scholars complained that common people often let Buddhist and Taoist influences contaminate their ancestral service, holding sacrifices on Buddhist or Taoist festival days or even entrusting the service to monks to perform. Nor were the family practices of Confucian scholars all uniform. They differed over the days used for rites, the objects used to represent ancestors, the numbers

of ancestors served, and the person chosen to officiate.[31] Chu Hsi, like
Han Ch'i (1008–1075), Ch'eng I, Chang Tsai (1020–1077), Ssu-ma Kuang,
Chang Shih (1133–1180), Lü Tsu-ch'ien (1137–1181), and others before him, tried to revive some practices described in the classics that seemed
of particular moral significance, vehemently rejected customary practices
of Buddhist origins, and was willing to accept customs he judged harmless as an expedient to encourage wider practice of Confucian rites.

Some of the items in Chu Hsi's liturgy for ancestral rites were rooted in
traditions going back to the classics and were very much part of ordinary
behavior. Offering ancestors food is called for in the classics and was questioned by virtually no one in Chu Hsi's time. Extensive participation of
women in both sacrifices and the less formal service to ancestors appears
to reflect common practice at least among the upper class. Some items
were features specified in the classics that had fallen out of common practice but which Chu Hsi wished to revive. Divining for the day for the
ceremonies, for instance, is mentioned nowhere as a common practice
and was apparently included as a canonical flourish or in deference to
Ssu-ma Kuang's earlier retention of it in his *Letters and Etiquette*. The use
of a liturgist may also fall into this category. Some items in Chu Hsi's
liturgy were common but non-canonical customs that Chu Hsi saw as

---

[31]Both practices and proposals varied. The family of Tu Yen 杜衍 (978–1057) was said to
make the four seasonal rites at the equinoxes and solstices, use mats instead of tables and
chairs, not burn paper money, and have the younger men in the family serve as assistants
instead of servants. Chang Tsai reported that he made a single offering to his ancestors at
the beginning and mid-point of each month and at New Year, and triple offerings at the
seasonal sacrifices on the solstices and equinoxes. At Ch'ing-ming and the festival of the
first day of the tenth month he made a single offering and visited the graves. For death day
anniversaries, Chang Tsai would take out all the tablets and offer wine and food but not
burn paper money. Both Chang Tsai and Ssu-ma Kuang followed the common upper class
practice of making offerings to three generations of ancestors. Ch'eng I, however, argued
that everyone should be able to make sacrifices back four generations. Both Chang Tsai and
Ch'eng I objected to the use of ancestral portraits, which Ssu-ma Kuang accepted. Ch'eng I
proposed reviving the classical use of wooden tablets and drew diagrams of what they were
to look like, and even specified their dimensions. Ssu-ma Kuang had the family head officiate at ancestral rites, whereas both Chang Tsai and Ch'eng I were insistent that the descent
line heir should officiate. (*Ch'üeh-sao pien* 卻掃編, by Hsü Tu 徐度 [Ts'ung-shu chi-ch'eng
ed.], 2, p. 115. *Chang Tsai chi* 張載集, by Chang Tsai 張載 [Peking: Chung-hua shu-chü,
1978], pp. 289–90, 315, 365–66. *Erh Ch'eng chi* 二程集, by Ch'eng Hao 程顥 and Ch'eng I
程頤 [Peking: Chung-hua shu-chü, 1981], i-shu 15, pp. 167, 163; wen-chi 10, pp. 627–28.
Ssu-ma shih shu-i 司馬氏書儀, 10 ch., by Ssu-ma Kuang 司馬光 [Ts'ung-shu chi-ch'eng
ed.], ch. 10.)

harmless. Chu Hsi's arrangement of tablets from the west reflects the custom in his family and what he thought was the common practice. Finally, a few items reflect innovations Ch'eng I had proposed. Extending sacrifices to four generations of ancestors and eliminating portraits were done out of deference to Ch'eng I.

After the *Family Rituals* was published, it provided a widely available, step-by-step description of how to perform ancestral rites. Certainly educated men who were committed to Chu Hsi's vision of Confucianism would have been the most likely to study the book carefully and model their rituals on it. Yet not all of them followed it in a strictly literal fashion. From the time the *Family Rituals* was first published, scholars took a flexible approach to following its prescriptions. Chu Hsi's disciple Ch'en Ch'un stressed that it was not necessary to follow the text literally: details could be altered once the main meaning was grasped.[32] Another disciple, Yang Fu, wrote a lengthy commentary in which he stressed that the extant book had never been finished and contained inconsistencies; on these grounds he often suggested emendations. Yang Fu's commentary along with two others of late Sung or Yüan date were regularly published with the *Family Rituals* in the Ming, and this commented version was included in the 1415 imperial collectanea of Neo-Confucian writings, the *Great Collection on Nature and Principle*. By early Ming times the claim that one followed the *Family Rituals* was widely recognized as a claim to literati (*shih-ta-fu*) status. With even the imperially authorized version advocating emendations, most literati were satisfied to follow the "basic meaning" of the text. In practice this sometimes meant little more than that one eschewed Buddhist practices.

The influence of the *Family Rituals* on wider social groups took different forms. Chu Hsi tried to write an educational text, a liturgy designed for the less educated who needed to be told what to do more than they needed analyses of classical precedents.[33] The text is written in plain language, with extensive use of concrete terms and almost no obscure allusions. In revised versions, terms for objects that might not be widely understood

---

[32]*Pei-ch'i ta-ch'üan chi* 北溪大全集, by Ch'en Ch'un 陳淳 (1153–1217) (Ssu-k'u ch'üan-shu ed.), 14: 3a–4a, 6a–b.
[33]See ch. 5 of my *Confucianism and Family Rituals* (cited n. 2).

were regularly glossed. The authors of revised versions, in their prefaces, frequently stated that they had compiled a version to help get their neighbors, relatives, students, or the residents of their county or prefecture to perform more orthodox family rituals. By the late Ming authors were writing quite abbreviated texts, showing that they were making real efforts to reach this audience. Moreover, by late Ming times, teachers and other Confucian scholars were often serving as masters of ceremonies, making it possible for well-to-do families to model their ceremonies on these books without having to read them; all they had to do was engage a master of ceremonies.[34]

Just because the less educated were frequently told to follow the instructions in these books does not, of course, imply that they did so. But given the circulation of these books, ordinary people are likely to have learned that the *Family Rituals* provided the standard for correct Confucian rituals and that following it carried prestige. Even when people did not consult any version of it, such knowledge could have had a subtle influence on what they did; they would have seen their own performance as a local variant of some knowable standard, a standard recorded in books.

The profusion of versions of the *Family Rituals* shows the need people of various levels of education felt for liturgies. Even if they did things not authorized in liturgies, they still wanted to have liturgies to consult. They bought revised versions of the *Family Rituals* in sufficient numbers that booksellers kept producing new ones and reprinting old ones. Even those who did not acquire a full-length liturgy for family rituals might have a reference book that included checklists of the key steps in family rituals in addition to long lists of the terms of address and reference for all sorts of relatives and other matters of etiquette. By Ch'ing times, if not earlier, the names for steps in the rites seem to have been widely recognized, and simple check lists could help people perform them in the right order.

Judging from the sorts of revised versions of the *Family Rituals* that were published and circulated, buyers sought liturgies that were simultaneously orthodox, universal, and comfortable. Liturgies that purported

<hr>

[34]On masters of ceremony, see Doolittle, *Social Life of the Chinese*, pp. 250–52 (cited n. 1); Susan Naquin, "Funerals in North China: Uniformity and Variation," in *Death Ritual in Late Imperial and Modern China*, edited by James L. Watson and Evelyn S. Rawski (Berkeley: University of California Press, 1988), pp. 64–66.

to be updated versions of Chu Hsi's *Family Rituals* dominated the market, undoubtedly because this text was the approved one. Even though family rituals were performed at home, in distinctly local contexts, people did not want handbooks explicitly presented as guides to the performance of rituals as done in southern Fukien or western Shantung with emphasis on local idiosyncrasies; rather they wanted ones that presented the rituals in them as correct for everyone. Authors, in their prefaces, might say that they were responding to local needs, writing a ritual manual because people in their area were superstitious or afraid of ghosts. Still they would write a general liturgy, one that drew on universal models, not one that in any way celebrated distinctive local customs. Liturgies may have been local in the sense that they were written by a local person and never circulated very widely. But they were not local by intent: I have never discovered a liturgy which decries the influence of the classics, Chu Hsi, or imperial ritual texts or argues that the residents of a defined place—eastern Kwangtung or northern Szechwan, for instance—should preserve their distinctive local customs to protect the cultural integrity of their locality.

What people took to be universal models, of course, often departed rather far from Chu Hsi's text in ways that probably reflected local practice. Book-buyers apparently sought liturgies that would guide them through the steps of the rituals they wanted to perform; they did not want liturgies that would instruct them to perform rituals in unfamiliar ways. To put this another way, they wanted books that would label as orthodox what was commonly done by those around them. There is no sign that they saw any magical potency in adherence to the most ancient of texts.

The circulation of these liturgies no doubt contributed to the remarkable similarity in the ways Chinese served their ancestors in different periods and in different places. By late imperial times, if not earlier, nearly every home had an ancestral altar with wooden or paper tablets inscribed with the names of ancestors. Food and drink were presented at regular intervals, including death day anniversaries, and at major rites all the members of the family would assemble and make obeisances.[35]

The circulation of Confucian liturgies does not deserve all the credit for these similarities. It is clear from the history of the *Family Rituals* that

---

[35] See the sources cited in note 1.

there were sources for the continuity of ritual practice outside of liturgies. Ming authors of revised versions urged accepting practices that were already common in Sung times (such as burning paper money and using portraits) but that had not been included in the *Family Rituals*. Apparently these practices had survived without being authorized in any standard text. Thus even in a highly literate society in which people knew there were books and theories about ritual, and sought out these books, written liturgies were at best only one of the agents involved in reproducing ritual forms. Liturgies probably played a large role in the perpetuation of identically worded prayers, and may well have fostered the perpetuation of a basic structure of the sacrifices, such as the triple offering. Yet practices could be perpetuated without being authorized in books of any sort, perhaps by the same sorts of social processes by which the cult of the kitchen god spread, discussed in Robert Chard's chapter in this volume.

CONCLUSIONS

The wide availability of competing liturgies played a significant but not totally determining role in shaping the ways ancestral rites came to be practiced in late imperial China. In conclusion, I would like to consider in a rather speculative and comparative way the difference these texts made. Rituals are often said to convey dramatically basic principles of cosmic order that not only legitimate those in authority but do so by making these principles part of what is assumed to be the nature of things.[36] In China ancestral rites are often said to convey notions fundamental to Chinese culture and society, such as the interdependence of the living and the dead and the necessity of filial piety and long-term planning. Yet the rites, as rituals, seem rather weak vehicles for communicating such powerful ideas. Could ancestral rites act to make basic cultural premises part of what people take for granted when the rituals themselves did not take people very far out of their ordinary lives and when moreover the didactic content was obvious, when even the unschooled could see that

[36]For some well-written discussions of anthropological approaches to ritual, see Clifford Geertz, *Local Knowledge: Further Essays in Interpretive Anthropology* (New York: Basic Books, 1983), pp. 19–35; Maurice Bloch, *From Blessing to Violence: History and Ideology in the Circumcision Ritual of the Merina of Madagascar* (Cambridge: Cambridge University Press, 1986), esp. pp. 1–11; and Stanley Jeyaraja Tambiah, *Culture, Thought, and Social Action: An Anthropological Perspective* (Cambridge, Mass.: Harvard University Press, 1985), pp. 123–66.

the rituals carried moral messages about submission and hierarchy? Ancestral rites were solemn, not ecstatic ceremonies. No one did anything they could not or would not do in non-ritual contexts. Little emphasis was placed on the violent killing of the animals or comparable allusions to death and its transformation. There were no improbable juxtapositions suggesting the communication of ideas people could not put into words. Were ancestral sacrifices powerful enough ceremonies to compel understandings of the social or cosmic orders?

Everywhere, perhaps, rituals tend to ossify, to develop toward empty formalism. According to Tambiah, "All the substantive features which nourish the formalism of ritual also conspire to empty it of meaning over time. Cosmological ideas, because they reflect the epistemological and ontological understandings of a particular age in which they originated, and because they are subject to the constraints of remaining accurate and invariant, are condemned to become dated over time and increasingly unable to speak to the minds and hearts of succeeding generations facing change and upheaval."[37] In these circumstances, old rituals may still be used, but to express social and political differentiation more than to communicate fundamental, deeply-held cosmological truths.

In the Chinese case, there may well have been some ossification of this sort. In Shang and early Chou times, the ancestral rites performed by rulers seem to have been very powerful ceremonies, creating and expressing fundamental beliefs about men, death, ghosts, and the cosmos. As newer cosmological ideas, especially newer ideas about the souls and the fate of the dead, emerged from late Chou times on, a certain amount of what was done during ancestral rites may have lost meaning for most participants. As Jack Goody points out, we see empty formalism in much of our own rituals, but expect other people's to convey the most important principles of their culture.[38] Perhaps we should be ready to grant Chinese rituals their share of empty formalism and to admit the possibility that they may have had little effect on anyone's thinking or emotional responses.

Yet it would be wrong to overestimate the degree of ossification in Chinese ancestral rites. Ancestral rites were not unchanging. Many specific steps

[37]Tambiah, *Culture, Thought, and Social Action*, p. 165.
[38]"Against Ritual" in *Secular Ritual*, Sally F. Moore and Barbara G. Myerhoff, eds. (Amsterdam: Van Gorcum, 1977).

and procedures described in the classics fell out of common practice, even among those who read the classics, such as divining with yarrow stalks for the timing of many rites. Ritual procedures of non-canonical origins—ones more closely tied to newer cosmological conceptions and social realities—were fitted into the syntax of the Confucian ritual sequence, much as dialect words can be absorbed into a basic language structure. Thus burning incense and paper money were fitted into ancestral rites. Written liturgies, from Sung times on, incorporated and thereby legitimated these adaptations. If ancestral rites as commonly practiced were completely ossified, Christian missionaries would not have found the Chinese so reluctant to give them up. These rites had emotional force even for people with relatively little to gain by confirmation of the hierarchy of society.

The cognitive and ideological power in Chinese ancestral rites came, I would argue, not from specific ceremonies, no matter how important, but from the cumulative effect of the larger patterns of rites. To put this another way, particular performances gained their potency by their power to remind those participating of all of the other performances in some way homologous. As discussed earlier, each time a cup of wine was placed before a tablet the act echoed in major and minor ways other ceremonies. The ways the act differed from these other acts served to place the relationship between the living worshipper and the dead ancestor into a larger model encompassing the "death course" of the ancestor, the hierarchy of the ancestors, the political hierarchy of the society, and the pantheon of those deserving offerings of wine.

The Janellis have suggested that in Korea domestic ancestral rites were emotionally powerful and had much to do with the relationship people had with their near ancestors, but that descent group rites were social ceremonies concerned more with group solidarity.[39] In China as well, the ancestral rituals of lineage or descent groups may have been relatively ossified in this sense, weakly charged emotionally, but conveying messages about social and political hierarchy. At the domestic level, where the identity of the dead was easier to keep in mind, the same symbolic forms may have carried more powerful cosmological messages.

Distinguishing domestic and descent group ancestral rites brings us to another general issue regarding Chinese ancestral rites. Anthropologists

---

[39]*Korean Ancestor Worship* (cited n. 1), esp. pp. 122–23.

have traditionally linked rituals to the social groups that perform them. Thus ancestral rites are seen as inseparable from the households, patrilines, and descent groups that carried them out, and changes or variations in the one should be reflected in changes in the other. This is in part because rituals convey the basic principles through which people interpret their social and physical environment and thus create the social structures tied to these rites. In China, however, the fit between forms of ancestral rites and the groups performing them seems often to have been no more than approximate.[40] Changes in the social composition of groups performing rites did not necessarily bring about corresponding changes in the rites. Small descent lines and very large descent groups conducted rites that followed the same sequence of steps. And variation in the way rituals were performed did not necessarily produce variations in participants' perceptions of the world, since rituals were never the only force forming their concepts and categories. For instance, it seems unlikely that variations in the arrangements of ancestral tablets (sometimes gender distinctions coming before generational ones, so that men were on one side and women on the other, at other times couples kept together) closely correlated with differences in social organization. Nor, to give another example, is there evidence that descent groups which had the descent line heir preside at rites were otherwise much different from those that had the man most senior in generation and age officiate.

China, of course, is not the only place where the symbolic forms of rituals have persisted in changing social contexts. Maurice Bloch, for instance, has shown how the symbolic content of initiation rituals in Madagascar proved remarkably constant even when the social and political uses to which they were put and the composition of the groups participating underwent major changes.[41] Whatever the sociological logic fostering survivals of symbolic forms, in the Chinese case we must also recognize the importance both of texts as the medium for transmitting knowledge of the rituals and of Confucianism as the set of ideas guiding the composition of these texts. The history of the *Family Rituals* shows that in a highly

---

[40]Most of the anthropological analyses of Chinese ancestral rites listed in note 1 are concerned with the social aspects of the rituals, such as who participated, who officiated, and who was served. It is perhaps because these seem to vary in illogical ways that they have attracted so much attention.

[41]*From Blessing to Violence*, pp. 165–67.

literate society like China's, where texts were consulted in planning rites, ritual actions could be preserved or modified because of processes tied to texts. As most scholars recognize, writing changes the ways in which traditions are adapted to circumstances. Books can survive for centuries, much of their meaning intact. They can become sacred objects, to be studied and put into practice even if inconvenient.[42] In the Chinese case, Confucian authors had great respect for classical texts but did not carry this respect to the point of forcing adherence, even among themselves. Scholars were urged to keep in mind that rituals should vary with circumstances and that every new liturgy would eventually have to be modified. Thus every procedure in the established liturgies could be revised. This de-mystified view of ritual is, in comparative terms, relatively rare. Sally F. Moore and Barbara G. Meyerhoff, for instance, state that ritual "banishes from consideration the basic questions raised by the made-upness of culture" and that the ultimate danger for rituals is the discovery that they are arbitrary inventions of mortals.[43]

Because they recognized that rituals were man-made, Confucian scholars often consciously analyzed the symbolism in them and tried to make them convey acceptable messages. As seen above, Ch'iu Chün wanted to alter the arrangement of ancestral tablets to reflect acceptable male-female proximity among living household members: no woman's tablet should be next to her father-in-law's. Ch'iu Chün, like most Confucian analysts, had no sense that ritual might work more powerfully when it did something other than simply mirror the approved social order. He did not see that rituals could work by a logic different from the logic of sentences. Thus, the innovations Confucian scholars proposed were not necessarily the same sorts of ones that might have appeared "naturally" in a society with a different intellectual tradition. The meanings of features of the rites were evaluated according to values articulated outside the rituals themselves; purposeful adjustments were made by leading writers (such as Ch'eng I, Chu Hsi, and Ch'iu Chün); and these had greater authority than more "natural" developments because of the cultural value placed on adherence to written versions and culture-wide standards.

[42]See Jack Goody, *The Logic of Writing and the Organization of Society* (Cambridge: Cambridge University Press, 1986).
[43]*Secular Ritual*, pp. 16–18.

The Cult of the

Wu-t'ung / Wu-hsien

in History and Fiction

The Religious Roots of the *Journey to the South*

URSULA-ANGELIKA CEDZICH

*S*inologists have recently shown an increased interest in the lives and ideas of the vast majority of the Chinese populace, those lacking formal Confucian education. This has led them to study aspects of Chinese culture that reflect the mentality of the ordinary Chinese people better than does the classical textual tradition—notably religion, iconography, opera, and, of course, popular literature. In this context stands a group of four Ming novels that had until recently been relatively unknown among Western scholars of Chinese literature.

These short novels are commonly known as the *Tung-yu chi* (*Journey to the East*), which narrates the adventures of the Eight Immortals,[1] the *Nan-*

To the memory of Anna Seidel.

This article is a completely revised version of my paper presented at the Conference on the Rituals and Scriptures of Chinese Popular Religion in Bodega Bay, California, in January 1990. I should like to thank Ann Tait and Phyllis Brooks, who read through earlier drafts, and Richard von Glahn, who made some valuable sources available to me. I am particularly grateful to David Johnson, whose criticism and detailed comments helped to improve the final version considerably.

[1] The earliest edition of the *Tung-yu chi* 東遊記, attributed to Wu Yuan-t'ai 吳元泰 and printed by Yü Hsiang-tou 余像斗 around the turn of the seventeenth century, is preserved in the Naikaku Bunko 內閣文庫 in Tokyo. This illustrated woodblock print, which is divided into two *chüan* 卷 each comprising twenty-eight sections (*tse* 則), includes a short preface by Yü Hsiang-tou and bears the full title *Hsin-k'an pa-hsien ch'u-ch'u tung-yu chi* 新刊八仙出處東遊記. See Sun K'ai-ti 孫楷第, *Jih-pen Tung-ching so-chien hsiao-shuo shu-mu* 日本東京所見小說書目 (Peking: Jen-min wen-hsüeh ch'u-pan shê, 1981), pp. 84–85.

yu chi (*Journey to the South*), the subject of this study, the *Hsi-yu chi* (*Journey to the West*),[2] and the *Pei-yu chi* (*Journey to the North*), which describes the career of Chen-wu, the Emperor of the North, and was recently translated by Gary Seaman.[3] Together they form a collection entitled *Ssu-yu chi* or *Four Journeys*. The earliest extant editions of this collection date from the Ch'ing dynasty,[4] although presumably it was originally put together not long after the completion of its component parts, in the late sixteenth or early seventeenth centuries.[5]

The *Four Journeys* might have aroused no interest at all among scholars of classical literature had it not included the *Hsi-yu chi*, whose role in the formation of the famous novel of the same name (best known in the hundred-chapter edition attributed to Wu Ch'eng-en) had, of course, to be taken into account.[6] For the same reason any scholarly attention paid to the other three parts of the *Ssu-yu chi* was usually restricted to the question of

[2]The earliest editions of *Hsi-yu chi* attributed to Yang Chih-ho 楊致和, who probably was a Fukienese publisher active toward the end of the sixteenth century, are transmitted in the *Ssu-yu chi* 四遊記 editions of 1811 and 1830. See notes 4 and 6 below.

[3]Gary Seaman, *Journey to the North: An Ethnohistorical Analysis and Annotated Translation of the Chinese Folk Novel* Pei-yu chi (Berkeley and Los Angeles: University of California Press, 1987). See also Gary Seaman, "The Divine Authorship of *Pei-yu chi* [*Journey to the North*]," *Journal of Asian Studies* 45:3 (May 1986), pp. 483–95. Seaman also presented a paper on the aspects of Chinese funeral drama integrated in the *Nan-yu chi* 南遊記 (*Journey to the South*) at the 40th Annual Meeting of the Association of Asian Studies, 1988, in San Francisco.

[4]The earliest extant reprint of the *Ssu-yu chi* 四遊記, an illustrated version, dates from 1811; a slightly later edition of 1830 is obviously a facsimile reprint, based on four different prints, which presumably reproduces earlier editions from the Ming ; a third Ch'ing edition printed at the Hsiao p'eng-lai hsien-kuan 小蓬萊仙館 publishing house dates probably from around the same time. See Sun K'ai-ti, *Chung-kuo t'ung-su hsiao-shuo shu-mu* 中國通俗小說書目 (Peking: Chung-kuo ta tz'u tien pien-tsuan ch'u, 1933), 5, p. 234, and 9, p. 322; Liu Ts'un-yan 柳存仁, "*Ssu-yu chi* te Ming k'o-pen 四遊記的明刻本," *Ssu-yu chi* 四遊記 (Taipei: Ho-lo t'u-shu ch'u-pan shê, 1980), p. 415; and Ch'en Hsin 陳新 (ed.), *T'ang San-tsang hsi-yu shih-e chuan; Hsi-yu chi chuan* 唐三藏西遊釋厄傳; 西遊記傳 (Peking: Jen-min wen-hsüeh ch'u-pan shê, 1984), p. 327.

[5]The suggestion that Yü Hsiang-tou himself, the putative author of the *Nan-yu chi* and the *Pei-yu chi*, compiled the first edition of the the *Ssu-yu chi* by adding his own works to the earlier novels, *Tung-yu chi* and *Hsi-yu chi* (see Ch'en Hsin, *T'ang San-tsang hsi-yu shih-e chuan; Hsi-yu chi chuan*, p. 315), still has to be tested. Only a thorough examination of the various *Ssu-yu chi* editions could prove or disprove this point.

[6]For a detailed and convincing discussion of the role of the *Hsi-yu chi* version attributed to Yang Chih-ho and the *T'ang San-tsang hsi-yu shih-e chuan* 唐三藏西遊釋厄傳 ascribed to Chu Ting-ch'en 朱鼎臣 in the textual history of the hundred-chapter version of the *Hsi-yu chi*, see Glen Dudbridge, "The Hundred-chapter *Hsi-yu chi* and Its Early Versions," *Asia Major*, n.s. 14:2 (1969), pp. 141–91.

the extent to which the origin and transmission of these novels could be related to the textual history of the *Hsi-yu chi*. The *Tung-yu chi*, the *Nan-yu chi*, and the *Pei-yu chi* were regarded as insignificant products of inferior literary quality, characterized by unpolished style and crude structure. In addition, the contents of the *Pei-yu chi* and the *Nan-yu chi* appeared uninteresting because they could not be related directly to any of the better-known tales of Chinese popular literature, and the backgrounds of their stories—particularly in the case of the *Nan-yu chi*—were largely ignored.

However, this last mentioned novel, the *Nan-yu chi*, or *Journey to the South*, merits close attention, not primarily from a literary point of view, but because of its etiology, which leads us into the thick of popular religious practice.

The *Nan-yu chi* came to my attention in connection with my study of the history of a cult which, in the course of its development, underwent the most puzzling changes. Rooted in the worship of archaic nature demons called Shan-hsiao, this cult, under the influence of Buddhism, subsequently renamed its objects Wu-t'ung. Following the Sung court's recognition of the Wu-t'ung sanctuary in Wu-yuan (Kiangsi) in 1109, the cult split into two separate lines of tradition: the gods of the newly canonized cult in Wu-yuan, under the name Wu-hsien or Five Manifestations, soon rose to regional (and, under the first emperor of the Ming dynasty, even national) importance, while the old Wu-t'ung, supported by a following of shamans and mediums, continued to be worshipped all over South China. Unlike the Five Manifestations, however, the Wu-t'ung remained proscribed as the objects of an illegitimate cult (*yin-ssu*).

The same cult underwent an astonishing transformation within the Taoist tradition. In the course of the fight of the Taoist clergy against both the Wu-t'ung and the Wu-hsien, they developed one of their heavenly generals, Marshal Ma (Ma yuan-shuai), into both a powerful antagonist and an orthodox image of those "demonic gods." This process resulted in a complete fusion of both sides, and in the integration of the once-rejected spirits into the Taoist pantheon.

Reading the *Nan-yu chi*, I recognized that the novel was inspired throughout by the complex history of the Wu-t'ung and Wu-hsien.[7] Indeed, the

[7] I drew attention to the Wu-t'ung cult and outlined its history in my article "*Wu-t'ung*: Zur

Journey to the South cannot be understood without understanding the complex history of these cults. Hua-kuang, the divine protagonist of the novel, impersonates all the various spirits and gods who were at various times the cult's objects. In the course of his career, Hua-kuang is reincarnated three times in order to be punished for his offenses against the celestial bureaucracy. Because he rescues his third mother, a cannibalistic demon, from the tortures of Hell, he is finally forgiven his transgressions and admitted to the Buddho-Taoist pantheon of popular gods. Yet the *Journey to the South* is not simply another paradigm of filial piety, nor did it originate as a mere copy of the famous Mu-lien story cycle. As we will see, Hua-kuang's lives and adventures tell a far more important story—that is the story of the cult he was part of. This significant point could easily be missed by modern literary critics unaware of the religious background of the novel, but it was immediately apparent to contemporary readers of the *Journey to the South,* familiar with the religious traditions of their time. What is more, in the *Nan-yu chi* these people not only recognized their beliefs but found them cast into a coherent and respectable mold.

The *Journey to the South* can be satisfactorily explained only by turning to the cult history that forms its background. In this article I will trace some of the basic ideas underlying the story of Hua-kuang to their origins in an ancient religious tradition. We shall see that the author or compiler of the *Nan-yu chi* drew on a multitude of materials, accessible to him not only in written sources that are now largely lost, but also in the living society around him. Particularly interesting is the way the author integrated all these traditional elements and themes into his account of one of the most problematic cults in all of Chinese popular religion. I will also look carefully at the cultural background of the author of the *Nan-yu chi* as well as at the social group for whom the novel was written. Finally, we shall see that popular traditions, from which the *Journey to the South*

---

bewegten Geschichte eines Kultes," *Religion und Philosophie in Ostasien. Festschrift für Hans Steininger zum 65. Geburtstag,* edited by G. Naundorf, K.-H. Pohl, and H.-H. Schmidt (Würzburg: Königshausen und Neumann, 1985), pp. 33–60. For a useful compilation and discussion of source material relating to the Wu-t'ung tradition, see Wu Shou-chüan 吳守娟, *Wu-t'ung shen ch'uan-shuo* 五通神傳說 (Tung-hai University M.A. thesis, 1987). Rich documentation on the history of the cult is also provided by Richard von Glahn, "The Enchantment of Wealth: The God Wutong in the Social History of Jiangnan," *Harvard Journal of Asiatic Studies* 51:2 (1991), pp. 651–714, a study on the Wu-t'ungs' role as gods of wealth.

clearly originated, may themselves have been influenced in due course by the publication of the novel. First, however, let us turn to the text itself.

THE TEXT AND ITS AUTHOR

The problems concerning the origin, the authorship, and the transmission of the *Nan-yu chi* in its various editions are still far from being solved and merit a study in their own right. Only a thorough search for possible antecedents of the *Journey to the South* and a careful comparison of the different editions from the Ming up to the present could clarify the numerous questions involving this text. However, such an investigation would go far beyond the scope of this study, and I will restrict myself to the most important data about the text and its putative author or compiler.

Though usually transmitted as a part of the *Ssu-yu chi*, various versions of the *Journey of the South* also exist today as separate publications, often distributed by temples.[8] In all these modern versions, the text is divided into eighteen chapters (*hui*) of variable length. The narrative itself is written in colloquial style, interspersed with many dialogue passages, which could mean that at least part of the contents had previously circulated in the form of opera scripts.

The earliest extant edition of the *Nan-yu chi*, an illustrated woodblock print, is in the British Museum in London, which also has similar reprints of the *Pei-yu chi* and the *Tung-yu chi*.[9] According to the photo reprint of this edition of the *Nan-yu chi* recently published in Taiwan, the text bears the alternative titles *Hua-kuang t'ien-wang nan-yu chih-chuan* (*The Journey to the South of the Heavenly King Hua-kuang*) and *Ch'üan-hsiang Wu-hsien ling-kuan ta-ti Hua-kuang t'ien-wang chuan* (*Fully Illustrated Hagiography of the Heavenly King Hua-kuang, the Great Emperor and Divine Agent of the Five Manifestations*).[10] The book comprises four volumes (*chüan*) which

---

[8]In Taiwan, for instance, there circulates an undated edition commissioned by the Wu-hsien temple in Chi-lung 基隆. It is entitled *Wu-hsien ta-ti Hua-kuang t'ien-wang chuan* 五顯大帝華光天王傳 (*Hagiography of the Heavenly King Hua-kuang, the Great Emperor of the Five Manifestations*).

[9]These reprints were first described by Liu Hsiu-yeh 劉修業, *Ku-tien hsiao-shuo hsi-ch'ü ts'ung-k'ao* 古典小說戲曲叢考 (Peking: Tso-chia ch'u-pan shê, 1958), pp. 87–88.

[10]*Hua-kuang t'ien-wang nan-yu chih-chuan* 華光天王南遊志傳 (series: Ming-Ch'ing shan-pen hsiao-shuo ts'ung-k'an ch'u-pien 明清善本小說叢刊初編, Taipei: T'ien-i ch'u-pan shê,

are subdivided into eighteen sections. The blocks for the text were carved by a certain Li P'u in the Ch'ang-yuan-t'ang bookstore.[11] A colophon at the end of the last *chüan* refers to a *hsin-wei* year as the date of the print. Liu Ts'un-yan, who dates the very similar *Pei-yu chi* print to 1602,[12] concludes that this *hsin-wei* year must correspond to either 1571 or 1631. The latter date appears more probable since both the *Pei-yu chi* and the *Nan-yu chi* prints seem to be recuts of the original editions, whose publication most likely dates to the 1570s or early 1580s.[13] Both the prints of the *Nan-yu chi* and the *Pei-yu chi* give Yü Hsiang-tou as the author or compiler,[14] and most subsequent editions of the novel repeat this information.

Yü Hsiang-tou, born in the middle of the sixteenth century,[15] has an interesting background. During the late sixteenth and the early seventeenth centuries he was the head of two printing shops, the Shuang-feng-t'ang[16] and the San-t'ai-kuan, in Chien-yang (northern Fukien). Under the Northern Sung dynasty, his ancestors established printing businesses

---

1985). All references to the *Nan-yu chi* in the following pages will be made to this photo reprint.

[11]The Taiwanese photo reprint of the British Museum version of the *Nan-yu chi* does not reproduce the cover page, which gives the name of Li P'u 李鋪. A microfilm of the British Library print of the *Nan-yu chi* in my possession, no. PS8920698/OMP. 8362, is my source here.

[12]Liu Ts'un-yan, "*Ssu-yu chi* te Ming k'o-pen" (cited n. 4), p. 429. The British Library reprint of the *Pei-yu chi* was photo reprinted in the same series as the *Nan-yu chi*: *Pei-yu chi Hsüan-ti ch'u-shen chuan* 北遊記玄帝出神傳 (Taipei: T'ien-i ch'u-pan shê, 1985).

[13]A *Hua-kuang chuan* 華光傳 and a *Pei-yu chuan* 北遊傳, which must be identical with our novels, are already mentioned in an introductory note following the preface of 1586 to the Wan-li (1573–1620) edition of the *Hsü-pien San-kuo chih hou-chuan* 續編三國志後傳. See Sun K'ai-ti, *Jih-pen Tung-ching so-chien hsiao-shuo shu-mu* (cited n. 1), pp. 47–49.

[14]Both editions state that Yü Hsiang-tou had composed or compiled (*pien* 編) the respective novels. Yü's byname (*tzu* 字) is given as Yang-chih 仰止; his Taoist-sounding style (*hao* 號), San-t'ai shan-jen or San-t'ai kuan shan-jen 三台 [館] 山人, is obviously derived from the name of one of his printing and editing shops, i.e., the San-t'ai kuan.

[15]Yü's exact dates are unknown. Kuan Kuei-ch'üan, who studied an 1896 manuscript copy of the Yü lineage record (*Shu-lin Yü-shih tsung-p'u* 書林余氏宗譜) kept in the Fukien Provincial Library, concludes that Yü Hsiang-tou was born around 1550. See Kuan Kuei-ch'üan 官桂銓, "Ming hsiao-shuo chia Yü Hsiang-tou chi Yü-shih k'o hsiao-shuo hsi-ch'ü 明小說家余象斗及余氏刻小說戲曲," *Wen-hsüeh i-ch'an tseng-k'an* 文學遺產增刊, 15 (1983), p. 129.

[16]Shuang-feng 峰雙 was the style of Yü Hsiang-tou's father, Yü Meng-ho 余孟和. See Hsiao Tung-fa 肖東發, "Chien-yang Yü-shih k'o-shu k'ao-lüeh (shang) 建陽余氏刻書考略 (上)," *Wen-hsien* 文獻 21 (1984), p. 239, and Kuan Kuei-ch'üan, "Ming hsiao-shuo chia Yü Hsiang-tou chi Yü-shih k'o hsiao-shuo hsi-ch'ü," p. 126.

in this region that soon became renowned all over China. Most important were the publishing houses of Yü Jen-chung and Yü Chih-an during the Southern Sung and the Yuan. Both Yü Jen-chung (fl. 1181–1197) and Yü Chih-an (fl. 1304–1345) published, among other books, a number of excellent editions of the Confucian classics.[17]

During the Wan-li period of the Ming dynasty (1573–1620), the Yü publishers, following the general trend of the time, specialized in printing popular (mostly illustrated) editions of fiction and historical novels. The numerous surviving books issued either by Yü Hsiang-tou himself or by one of his immediate predecessors or successors show that this branch of the Yü family enterprise had become one of the most profitable and flourishing printing firms in Fukien at that time.[18] Moreover, as there was a high public demand for printed versions of popular narrative complexes alive in oral tradition and the performing arts such as opera, some of the Yü publishers even set out to compose potentially profitable novels of their own. In 1606, for example, Yü Hsiang-tou printed a book titled *Lieh-kuo chih-chuan* which is credited to Yü Shao-yü, evidently a great uncle of his.[19] Yü Hsiang-tou himself is believed to have written books like the *Huang Ming chu-ssu kung-an chuan* and the *Hsi-Han chih-chuan*,[20] in addition to the *Pei-yu chi* and the *Nan-yu chi*. He also seems to have been responsible for a number of changes, including the addition of the tale of the subjugation of T'ien-hu and Wang Ch'ing, to an edition of the *Shui-hu chuan* printed in his Shuang-feng-t'ang workshop.[21] Another family member, Yü Ying-ao, a nephew of Yü Hsiang-tou, was credited with authorship of the *T'ang-kuo chih-chuan* and the *Ta-Sung chung-hsing Yüeh-*

---

[17]For a list of the various works published by Yü Jen-chung 余仁仲 and Yü Chih-an 余志安 see Hsiao Tung-fa, "Chien-yang Yü-shih k'o-shu k'ao-lüeh (shang)," pp. 234–36. Hsiao Tung-fa does a good job in clearing up the confusion between these two publishers, which has led bibliographers to date some of their editions incorrectly.

[18]For a whole range of texts printed at the Yü family printing shops see, e.g., Sun K'ai-ti, *Jih-pen Tung-ching so-chien hsiao-shuo shu-mu* (cited n. 1), pp. 31–46. A critical and, above all, unprejudiced evaluation of the numerous contributions of the Yü publishers to the trade of printing and editing during the Ming is found in Hsiao Tung-fa, "Chien-yang Yü-shih k'o-shu k'ao-lüeh (hsia 下)," *Wen-hsien* 23 (1985), pp. 237–50.

[19]See Sun K'ai-ti, *Jih-pen Tung-ching so chien hsiao-shuo shu-mu*, p. 98, and Kuan Kuei-ch'üan, "Ming hsiao-shuo chia Yü Hsiang-tou chi Yü-shih k'o hsiao-shuo hsi-ch'ü," p. 129.

[20]Ibid., p. 125.

[21]See Sun K'ai-ti, *Jih-pen Tung-ching so-chien hsiao-shuo shu-mu*, pp. 97–106.

wang chuan, which were actually compiled by Hsiung Ta-mu, also a publisher and author active in Fukien during the Chia-ching period of the Ming dynasty (1522–1566).[22]

Many of the book-printers in sixteenth- and seventeenth-century Fukien also tried their hand at writing, primarily in order to enhance business. Their literary products were not necessarily high literature, and they dealt with their materials in a fairly free-wheeling manner. Often theater scripts or similar models were simply rewritten in novel form and published under the editor's name. Sometimes a clever entrepreneur would even appropriate one author's work and republish it under a different author's name, as happened with Hsiung Ta-mu's novels which, reprinted by the San-t'ai-kuan, were ascribed to Yü Hsiang-tou's nephew Yü Ying-ao.

Yü Hsiang-tou's reputation among all these book-printers was not particularly high. As he himself testified, he was one of those reproached with merely copying the works of others.[23] On the other hand, Yü Hsiang-tou was certainly not as uncultivated as some of his critics tried to make him appear. As the head of a successful, well-established publishing house, he belonged to the well-to-do upper middle class of sixteenth-century urban society. Although he did not obtain an examination degree, he obviously did not lack a certain degree of erudition. The Yü lineage records contain the interesting information that Yü Hsiang-tou's grandfather, Yü Chi-an (1492–1562), founded a Buddhist temple, the Ch'ing-hsiu ssu, on his lands in order to provide his descendants with a place for their studies.[24] Of course, we are not told in this source who the teachers were in this private school, or what exactly they taught. But the mention of the *Odes* and the *Documents* (*Shih Shu*) indicates an emphasis on the Confucian classics.[25] From this we may conclude that Yü Hsiang-tou was acquainted with a considerable portion of Chinese literature and that his educational background enabled him to become a creative writer himself.

[22]Ibid., pp. 31–46; and Kuan Kuei-ch'üan, "Ming hsiao-shuo chia Yü Hsiang-tou chi Yü-shih k'o hsiao-shuo hsi-ch'ü," p. 126.

[23]See Yü Hsiang-tou's introductory note to his edition of the *Tung-yu chi* (*Hsin-k'an pa-hsien ch'u-ch'u tung-yu chi*) quoted in Sun K'ai-ti, *Jih-pen Tung-ching so-chien hsiao-shuo shu-mu*, pp. 84–85.

[24]See Kuan Kuei-ch'üan, "Ming-Ch'ing hsiao-shuo chia Yü Hsiang-tou chi Yü-shih k'o hsiao-shuo hsi-ch'ü," p. 127.

[25]Ibid.

However, Yü Hsiang-tou's role in the creation of the *Nan-yu chi* and the *Pei-yu chi* is by no means certain. Liu Ts'un-yan believes that Yü only revised and republished earlier versions of the novels.[26] On the other hand, Gary Seaman has recently proposed looking for the origin of the *Pei-yu chi* in revelations of spirit-mediums.[27] It seems to me that Liu is more nearly correct than Seaman. Certainly Yü was responsible for putting the novels into their present form, since they both include poems explicitly identified as the works of "Mr. Yü" (Yü-shih).[28] At the same time, it is highly improbable that the complex stories of the two novels were entirely the product of Yü's creative imagination. Therefore, he probably drew heavily on earlier sources. What do we know of them? In particular, can we identify earlier literary versions of the *Nan-yu chi* story on which Yü might have relied? The only work we know of that might have served as a direct model is an opera script titled *Hua-kuang hsien sheng* (*Hua-kuang Manifests His Holiness*). It is mentioned in Shen Te-fu's *Wan-li yeh-huo pien*, but unfortunately it has not been preserved and nothing is known about its contents.[29]

Looking further for other, possibly earlier, versions of the *Nan-yu chi* story, we find a comparable tale in the *San-chiao yuan-liu sou-shen ta-ch'üan*.[30] This is a brief passage of uncertain date,[31] relating the career not

[26]"*Ssu-yu chi* te Ming k'o-pen" (cited n. 4), pp. 427–28.

[27]*Journey to the North*, pp. 11–23. It should be mentioned in this context that Ch'en Chung's 陳伀 commentary to the Taoist scripture on the Dark Emperor, *T'ai-shang shuo Hsüan-t'ien ta-sheng Chen-wu pen-chuan shen-chou miao-ching* 太上說玄天大聖眞武本傳神咒妙經 (HY 753), relies heavily on a *Hsüan-ti shih-lu* 玄帝實錄 (*Veritable Records of the Dark Emperor*), which was said to have been revealed by the Perfected Tung Su-huang 董素皇 and Chang Ya 張亞 (alias Tzu-t'ung ling-ying ti-chün 梓潼靈應帝君) to the Taoist master Chang Ming-tao 張明道 at Hsiang-yang 襄陽 (Hupei) during spirit-writing seances beginning in 1184; cf. HY 753, 1.4b–5a, 5.12b–15a, 6.27b–28a. A close comparison with such material could perhaps help to clarify the question of the *Pei-yu chi*'s revelation.

[28]For the poems see *Hua-kuang t'ien-wang nan-yu chih-chuan*, *chüan* 1, section 1.4b, *chüan* 2, section 6.21a–b and *Pei-yu chi hsüan-ti ch'u-shen chuan*, *chüan* 1, section 4.16a.

[29]Shen Te-fu 沈德符, *Wan-li yeh-huo pien* 萬歷野獲編 (ed. of 1827), 25.30b.

[30]*Hui-t'u san-chiao yuan-liu sou-shen ta-ch'üan* 繪圖三教源流搜神大全 (ed. of Yeh Te-hui 葉德輝, 1909, reprinted Taipei: Lien-ching ch'u-pan shih-yeh kung-ssu, 1980), 5.8a–9a.

[31]The *San-chiao yuan-liu sou-shen ta-ch'üan* is an enlarged and augmented edition of the Yuan work *Sou-shen kuang-chi* 搜神廣記. It cannot be earlier than the late sixteenth century, since it quotes a poem from the hundred-chapter edition of the *Hsi-yu chi*; compare ibid. 7.22a with *Hsi-yu chi* (Peking: Jen-min wen-hsüeh ch'u-pan shê, 1981), 10.127. An edition of the original Yuan work entitled *Hsin-pien lien-hsiang sou-shen kuang-chi* 新編連相搜神廣記 and attributed to Ch'in Tzu-chin 秦子晉 was recently reproduced in the series *Chung-kuo*

of Hua-kuang but of Marshal Ma, a deity who, from the twelfth century on, figures in southern Chinese Taoist rituals and is closely connected with the Wu-hsien and the Wu-t'ung demons. This text bears such a striking resemblance to our novel that it almost summarizes its action. Like Hua-kuang in the *Nan-yu chi*, Marshal Ma is reborn three times, becomes involved in the same quarrels with the celestial authorities, wins the same battles, rescues his mother from purgatory, and is finally pardoned for his sins because of his filial love toward her.

Yet there are a few significant differences, including the fact that Marshal Ma in his crucial last incarnation becomes the son of the Mother of Demons, Kuei-tzu mu. (In the *Nan-yu chi*, Hua-kuang becomes the son of Chi-chih-t'o, the monster who had devoured and taken on the form of the pious Lady Hsiao of Wu-yuan.) The short account in the *San-chiao yuan-liu sou-shen ta-ch'üan* also gives no hint of a relationship between Marshal Ma and the cult of the Five Manifestations, whereas the connection between Hua-kuang and the cult is an important feature of the *Nan-yu chi*. These differences suggest that, rather than one having originated from the other, the *Nan-yu chi* and the legend of Marshal Ma were both derived from an earlier common source, now lost. This source may have been the above-mentioned Hua-kuang play, but since the contents of this *tsa-chü* remain unknown, we have no means to prove this hypothesis.

We do however have evidence that by the sixteenth century Hua-kuang had long since become a popular figure in both drama and fiction. He appears, for example, in a play on the famous theme of Hsüan-tsang's journey to the West: a *tsa-chü* in twenty-four acts entitled *Hsi-yu chi*. This printed script, which was rediscovered in Japan in the early 1920s,[32] was attributed to the Yuan playwright Wu Ch'ang-ling,[33] but most probably

---

min-chien hsin-yang tzu-liao hui-pien 中國民間信仰資料彙編, edited by Wang Ch'iu-kuei 王秋桂 and Li Feng-mao 李豐楙 (Taipei: Hsüeh-sheng shu-chü, 1989).

[32]The text of this play was first published in Japan in successive issues of the journal *Shibun* 斯文 9:1 (1927)–10:3 (1928). The circumstances of the discovery are described in a postface to the published script by Shionoya On 鹽谷溫.

[33]The attribution of the *Hsi-yu chi tsa-chü* 雜劇 to Wu Ch'ang-ling 吳昌齡 occurs in a preface (dated 1614) to the play script, reproduced in *Shibun* 10:3 (1928), appendix. Wu Ch'ang-ling, who was probably active in the late thirteenth century, is credited with a play titled *Hsi-t'ien ch'ü-ching* 西天取經 in the fourteenth-century catalogue of drama *Lu-kuei pu* 錄鬼簿. See *T'ien-i ko lan-pen ko-hsieh pen cheng hsü Lu-kuei pu* 天一閣藍本格寫本正續錄鬼簿 (facsimile ed., Peking: Chung-hua shu-chü, 1960), 1.17b–18a.

dates from a considerably later period.[34] In Scene 8 of this play, Kuan-yin appoints ten heavenly protectors for Tripitaka on his dangerous journey to the foreign countries in the western regions. Hua-kuang is one of these divine guardians. The arias in which he describes himself include a number of features that recur in the *Journey to the South*, such as the symbols of power that characterize him as a deity of fire. We also find in the arias allusions to narrative details elaborated in the *Nan-yu chi*, such as the brawl Hua-kuang provokes in the heavenly palace of the Jade Emperor.[35] Hua-kuang also shows up in the *Shui-hu chuan*, where he is typically associated with two magic treasures, a three-cornered golden brick and a golden lance; these tokens are also found in the *Nan-yu chi*.[36] And the *Feng-shen yen-i* contains the motif of the deity Ma Shan's creation from the wick of a lamp, which resembles Hua-kuang's birth from the light of a lamp in front of the Tathāgata Buddha in the *Journey to the South*.[37]

Yet all these sources provide no more than a few isolated details proving that Hua-kuang and his transformations already had inspired the imagination of playwrights and novelists. None of them can be regarded as a direct model for Yü Hsiang-tou's *Journey to the South*. The true source of all these literary elaborations of the Hua Kuang story, including the *Nan-yu chi*, lies in the vast realm of oral narrative art, which in turn drew its ideas directly from the long tradition of the cult of Hua-kuang. Before we turn to the fascinating history of this cult, a summary of Hua-kuang's story as presented in Yü Hsiang-tou's *Journey to the South* is in order.

[34]The ascription to Wu Ch'ang-ling was convincingly refuted by Sun K'ai-ti, who argued that the play was in reality the work of Yang Ching-yen 楊景言 (alternatively Yang Ching-hsien 楊景賢), a Mongol born under the Yuan, who lived until the early 1400s. See Sun K'ai-ti, "Wu Ch'ang-ling yü tsa-chü *Hsi-yu chi* 吳昌齡與雜劇西遊記," first edition 1939, reprinted in *Tsang-chou chi* 滄州集 (Peking: Chung-hua shu-chü, 1965), pp. 366–98. Sun K'ai-ti's thesis has again been questioned by Glen Dudbridge, who surmises that the play might even have been created as late as the sixteenth century; cf. G. Dudbridge, *The Hsi-yu chi: A Study of Antecedents to the Sixteenth-Century Chinese Novel* Hsi-yu chi (Cambridge: Cambridge University Press, 1970), pp. 75–89. In the appendix to this book, pp. 193–200, Dudbridge also gives a summary of the contents of the twenty-four scenes of this *Hsi-yu chi tsa-chü*.

[35]See *Shibun*, 9:5 (1927), appendix.

[36]*Jung-yü-t'ang pen Shui-hu chuan* 容與堂本水湖傳 (repr. Shanghai: Shanghai ku-chi ch'u-pan shê, 1988), 13.178 and 37.534.

[37]*Hsiu-hsiang p'ing-tien Feng-shen pang ch'üan chuan* 繡像評點封神榜全傳 (Ssu-hsüeh ts'ao-t'ang 四雪草堂, 1695 ed., reprinted 1883), *chüan* 12, chapter 63.21a and *Hua-kuang t'ien-wang nan-yu chih chuan, chüan* 1, section 1.7b.

THE STORY OF HUA-KUANG IN THE *NAN-YU CHI*.

Hua-kuang, or Flowery Radiance, the protagonist of the *Nan-yu chi*, was originally the halo of light from a lamp in front of the Tathāgata which intensified as the lamp heard the Buddha's preaching. Eventually this radiance was transformed by the Tathāgata into the deity Miao chi-hsiang. Miao chi-hsiang's nature is therefore pure fire. He is the essence, the spirituality, and the origin of fire. No wonder that this deity had a fiery temper that got him into serious trouble more than once.

At the very beginning of his blessed existence as a disciple of the Buddha, Miao chi-hsiang, in a fit of rage, burns the malicious Single Fire Demon (Tu-huo kuei) to death. For this act of heartlessness he has to be punished—and so, endowed with five supernatural powers, he is incarnated in the womb of the Goddess of Horse-Ear Mountain (Ma-erh shan niang-niang).[38] Lady Horse-Ear is the widow of the Great King of Horse-Ear Mountain (Ma-ehr shan ta-wang) who had been killed by the Iron-shod Dragon King of the Eastern Sea (Tung-hai t'ieh-chi lung-wang) in a rivalry over their magic treasures. Lady Horse-Ear calls her son (the reincarnated Miao chi-hsiang) Three-Eyed Spiritual Radiance (San-yen ling-kuang), because he is born with three eyes. Only three days after his birth Three-Eyed Spiritual Radiance avenges his father's murder and defeats the arrogant dragon king.

Soon afterwards, San-yen ling-kuang's young existence comes to a premature end, as he steals the golden lance of the Great Emperor of Purple Vacuity of the North Pole (Pei-chi tzu-wei ta-ti) and is crushed by him.[39] But the Heavenly Worthy of Wondrous Joy (Miao-lo t'ien-tsun) takes pity on the dim little radiance roaming around in space—Hua-kuang's remains—and causes him to be born again, this time as a son of the deity Heavenly King Flaming Devil (Yen-mo t'ien-wang) and his wife.

Hua-kuang becomes the disciple of the Heavenly Worthy of Wondrous

---

[38]Ma-erh shan 馬耳山 and Ma-pan-t'ou 馬半頭 are the Chinese translations of Skr. Aśvakarṇa, the name of one of the seven concentric mountain ranges around Mount Sumeru. See, e.g.: *Tsa A-han ching* 雜阿含經 (T 99) [translated in the mid-fifth century], 16.114a; *Ch'i-shih ching* 起世經 (T 24) [translated in the second half of the sixth century], 1.312a; *Ch'i-shih yin-pen ching* 起世因本經 (T 25) [translated at the end of the sixth, beginning of the seventh century], 1.367a.

[39]*Hua-kuang t'ien-wang nan-yu chih-chuan, chüan* 1, section 1.1a–12a.

Joy and is instructed in the arts of warfare. Proving his newly-acquired abilities in the techniques of deceit, he is rewarded by his master with a three-cornered golden brick, a magic treasure that enables him to transform himself at will. Ending his apprenticeship, he wins renown by subduing the evil spirits of water and fire, and is appointed Great Marshal of the Troops and Horses of the Ministry of Fire (Huo-pu ping-ma ta yuan-shuai).[40]

However, at an official banquet held in the heavenly palace, Hua-kuang clashes with the Crown Prince Golden Spear (Chin-ch'iang t'ai-tzu), heir to the Jade Emperor's throne, and thus incurs the Emperor's wrath.[41] Pursued by the celestial armies he flees to the north, where he is stopped and subjugated by the Dark Emperor (Hsüan-ti). After appointing Hua-kuang to be his thirty-sixth general and exacting the promise that Hua-kuang would renounce heresy and return to the correct way (*kai-hsieh kuei-cheng*), the Dark Emperor lets him go free. Following the compassionate advice of this sovereign, Hua-kuang then escapes by burning down the Gate of Precious Virtue of the Southern Heaven (Nan-t'ien pao-te kuan).[42]

Descending now into the world of mortals, Hua-kuang presents himself as a savior of mankind. He subdues the demons Ch'ien-li yen and Shun-feng erh, whose insatiable demands for human sacrifices had weighed heavily on the inhabitants of the Country of a Thousand Fields (Ch'ien-t'ien kuo). For this virtuous deed Hua-kuang is rewarded by the king of the country with an official cult and a temple. Unfortunately, the new temple is erected at the site of the defunct sanctuary of another popular god, General Fire Whirl (Huo-p'iao chiang). This deity takes revenge for the demolition of his shrine by kidnaping the royal princess while she is offering incense in Hua-kuang's new temple. Hua-kuang is first suspected of the crime, but he soon succeeds in saving the princess and convicting the true evildoer.[43]

In the meantime, the Jade Emperor has found out Hua-kuang's whereabouts and sent his celestial armies after him. Hua-kuang barely escapes capture by entering, once more, the womb of a woman; he is reborn,

---

[40]Ibid., section 2.12a–17b.
[41]Ibid., *chüan* 2, section 4.1a–6a.
[42]Ibid., section 5.6a–12b.
[43]Ibid., section 6.12b–21a.

together with four brothers, into the Hsiao family of Wu-yuan.[44] There he immediately gets involved in a chain of dramatic confusions. His mother is in reality a horrible man-eating demon, called Chi-chih-t'o, who had devoured the real Lady Hsiao while she was praying for a child before the Buddhist altar in her garden.[45] This monster who, without anybody in the family realizing it, continues to eat people from the neighborhood, is eventually caught by a dragon divinity and incarcerated in the infernal regions of Mount Feng-tu. Hua-kuang, who has no idea about the real circumstances of his birth or his mother's true nature, presumes that she has been abducted and killed, and tries to find her.

Disguising himself as the Heavenly Worthy of Grand Unity who Saves from Suffering (T'ai-i chiu-k'u t'ien-tsun), he performs a ritual (*tao-ch'ang*) for the orphaned souls of the dead[46] and interrogates them about his mother's whereabouts—to no avail.[47] This blasphemous impersonation, however, earns him once more the persecution of the Emperor of Heaven. But the now indifferent Hua-kuang rejects all authority and breaks every rule in his desperate search for his mother. Exercising his supernatural powers and resorting to violence and deceit, he pursues his aim.

He defeats the celestial Marshal Sung Wu-chi and captures the fierce fire crows of the Holy Mother of Hundredfold Increase (Pai-chia sheng-mu).[48] Pursuing the dragon who carried his mother away, he assaults the Bodhisattvas Wen-chu and P'u-hsien (Mañjuśri and Samantabhadra) and dares to oppose even Kuan-yin and the Buddha.[49] In a battle with the powerful Na-cha, who was sent by the Jade Emperor himself to subdue him, Hua-kuang loses his precious three-cornered golden brick.[50] He then

[44]Ibid., section 8.22b–33a.
[45]Ibid., section 7.21b–22b.
[46]The description in the text indicates that Hua-kuang's ritual corresponded to the widespread rites for the hungry ghosts (餓鬼) celebrated by Buddhists and Taoists alike and called "Release of the Burning Mouths" (*fang yen-k'ou* 放燄口) or "Universal Salvation" (*p'u-tu* 普度) respectively. For the description of a modern Taoist ritual of Universal Salvation see, e.g., Duane Pang, "The *Pu-tu* Ritual: A Celebration of the Chinese Community of Honolulu," in Michael Saso and David Chapell, eds., *Buddhist and Taoist Studies* I (Honolulu: The University Press of Hawaii, 1977), pp. 95–122.
[47]*Hua-kuang t'ien-wang nan-yu chih-chuan*, *chüan* 2, section 8.32b–33a.
[48]Ibid., *chüan* 3, section 9.1a–10a.
[49]Ibid., section 10.10a–18a.
[50]Ibid., section 11.18a–26a.

tricks the Holy Mother Jade Bracelet (Yü-huan sheng-mu) out of her treasured golden pagoda, hoping to make another three-cornered brick out of it. This entails a skirmish with the Holy Mother's daughter, the unconquerable Iron Fan Princess (T'ieh-shan kung-chu). With the help of a miraculous drug Hua-kuang defeats the beautiful princess and takes her as his wife.[51] Soon afterwards, as he resumes the search for his mother, he is suspected a second time of accosting a mortal woman, but again is able to prove his innocence by revealing the true malefactor: a white snake demon.[52]

Stumbling from one hazardous adventure to the next, Hua-kuang is obsessed by the single thought of finding his mother. Not even when he finally meets the unfortunate real Lady Hsiao in the Administration of the Shadows (*yin-ssu*) and learns about the true identity of the creature from whose womb he was born is he willing to give up his campaign to free the abominable monster. He assures Lady Hsiao that he will obtain her rebirth into a prestigious family,[53] but then again adopts the appearance of the Heavenly Worthy of Grand Unity who Saves from Suffering, works his way through to Mount Feng-tu, and finally liberates the man-eating ghoul, Chi-chih-t'o, his monstrous mother.[54]

Committing a final fraud which also results in his last battle, Hua-kuang takes on the form of the divine monkey, the Great Sage Equal to Heaven (Chi-t'ien ta-sheng), and steals the peaches of immortality from the garden of the Queen Mother of the West (Hsi wang-mu). He feeds the fruit to Chi-chih-t'o, and thus redeems her from her cannibalism.[55] Because of this outstanding proof of filial devotion, the Jade Emperor forgives all of Hua-kuang's previous sins.[56] Nevertheless, Hua-kuang still has to be drastically reminded of his promise to the Buddha: only after suffering the loss of a leg is he willing to convert to Buddhism, after which he is made Great Emperor of Superior Morality among the Buddhas and Divine Agent of the Five Manifestations (Fo-chung shang-shan Wu-hsien ling-kuan ta-ti).[57]

---

[51]Ibid., *chüan* 3, section 12.26a to *chüan* 4, section 13.1b.
[52]Ibid., section 13.2a–9a.
[53]Ibid., section 15.10a–12b.
[54]Ibid., section 17.15a–18b.
[55]Ibid., 18b–25a.
[56]Ibid., 25a.
[57]Ibid., section 18.25a–28a.

So far the story of the *Nan-yu chi*. Nobody will deny that this tale presents us with a puzzling main character. First of all, is Hua-kuang a Buddhist or a Taoist deity? Somehow he seems to transcend these familiar categories—or rather to belong to both of them—although the novel obviously emphasizes Hua-kuang's Buddhist affiliation. Thus, we are told that Hua-kuang was created by the Buddha himself from the halo of light of a lamp in front of him. Hua-kuang is also often helped by Buddhist mentors through the critical stages of his career, before he—willy-nilly—finally takes his refuge in the Buddha. Other elements in the story, such as the scenes at the Jade Emperor's court, or Hua-kuang's posing as the Heavenly Worthy of Grand Unity who Saves from Suffering, clearly reveal Taoist inspiration. Hua-kuang's supernatural powers and exorcistic qualities could be those of a Taoist as well as a Buddhist deity. However, many themes and motifs in the *Nan-yu chi* cannot be derived from either the Buddhist or Taoist traditions, among them Hua-kuang's slightly suspect relationship with women, his rebirth together with his four brothers in Wu-yuan, a well-known city in Kiangsi, and his mysterious loss of a leg at the end of the tale. Are these features merely entertaining embellishments intended to make the novel more appealing to a popular audience? I hope to show that they were more.

THE CULT BEHIND HUA-KUANG'S STORY

Early History

The story of the *Journey to the South* presents a number of themes with ethical and religious messages already familiar to us from Chinese literature, particularly devotional literature and popular drama and fiction. Expiation of guilt through repeated reincarnations is a motif that frequently recurs in Buddhist scriptures as well as in popular religious texts. The ultimate model of the truly devoted son who descends to the underworld in order to save his mother is, of course, Mu-lien. And Hua-kuang's insubordination or his constant disguises and repeated deceptions may well remind us of Monkey, the hero of the *Journey to the West*.

Yet Hua-kuang's character and adventures appear far too well-defined to be dismissed as poor copies of better-known tales. In fact, the various themes of the *Nan-yu chi*, even the seemingly familiar ones, fall into place only when we examine their significance in relation to Hua-kuang's cult. Since it also stands to reason that the meaning of the *Nan-yu chi* as a whole depends on a clear understanding of its main figure, we must ask: Who is Hua-kuang? What are his origins and what is his cultic background?

Pursuing the question, we must keep in mind one particular feature of the novel. Since the author wants to let Hua-kuang—as well as his cult—appear in a positive light, he endeavors to obscure rather than clarify his antecedents. Nevertheless, once we know where to look, we can see that the novel cannot conceal Hua-kuang's connection with a cult that emanated from one of the most ancient and most condemned forms of demon worship. This cult and its history can be reconstructed from a variety of sources, both secular and religious, leading us back to mythological times.

Hua-kuang's ultimate ancestors belong to a vast and varied category of archaic nature demons. Defined as transformations of the powerful old essences of rocks and trees (*mu-shih chih ching*) in the mountains, these spirits were believed, like foxes, to be capable of changing into every possible form. But although they were variously described as dragons,[58] bulls,[59] birds,[60] monkeys,[61] humans,[62] or half-human, half-animal monsters, their most distinguishing feature was that they had only one leg.

In ancient sources these mountain spectres appear as Wang-liang,[63] or as the mythic monopod K'uei.[64] This last curious and multi-faceted being is introduced in the *Shu-ching* as the music minister of the sage ruler Shun.[65] The *Chuang-tzu* presents the K'uei as a foolish one-legged animal that won-

---

[58]See, e.g., the description of the K'uei 夔, a variant of these spirits, in *Shuo-wen chieh-tz'u* 說文解字 (Peking: Chung-hua shu-chü, 1979), 112b, and the quotation from Ko Hung's *Pao-p'u-tzu nei-p'ien* below.

[59]See, e.g., *Shan-hai ching chien-shu* 山海經箋疏 (Ssu-pu pei-yao ed.), 14.6b, regarding the K'uei.

[60]See, e.g., Jen Fang 任方 (460–508), *Shu-i chi* 述異記 (Lung-wei pi-shu ed.), 2.17b.

[61]See, e.g., Wei Chao's commentary on the *Kuo-yü* quoted below.

[62]As, for example, in the *Shen-i ching* 神異經, a collection of *mirabilia* ascribed to Tung-fang Shuo 東方朔 but probably dating from the post-Han period (Han-wei ts'ung-shu ed.), 9b.

[63]The Wang-liang 罔兩 (alternatively 魍魉 or 蛧蜽) are mentioned among the spirits depicted on the legendary bronze tripods of the Hsia 夏 dynasty in the *Ch'un-chiu Tso-chuan* (*cheng-i*) 春秋左傳 (正義), (Shih-san ching chu-shu 十三經注疏, Peking: Chung-hua shu-chü, 1983), 21.11b. A thorough study of the Wang-liang and related spirits is found in Kiang Chao-yuan, *Le voyage dans la Chine ancienne* (Vientiane: Editions Vithagana, 1975).

[64]On the K'uei see also Marcel Granet, *Danses et légendes dans la Chine ancienne* (Paris: Presses Universitaires de France, 1959), vol. II, pp. 505–516.

[65]*Shang-shu cheng-i* 尚書正義 (Shih-san ching chu-shu ed.), 3.18b–19a.

ders how the millipede, despite his many legs, moves so much more easily
than itself, whose single leg already causes it trouble.[66] The *Han-fei tzu*
regards K'uei as a historical person and denies his one-legged appearance,[67]
whereas the *Shan-hai ching* states that a K'uei spirit was a kind of blue,
one-legged bull without horns, and relates that the Yellow Emperor once
used the skin of a K'uei for a drum whose resonance struck the world
under heaven with awe.[68] According to the *Shuo-wen chieh-tzu* a K'uei
spirit resembled a one-legged dragon, but had horns, hands, and a human face.[69] The *Kuo-yü* quotes Confucius with the following words: "According to what I have heard, the phantoms of trees and rocks are called
K'uei or Wang-liang . . . ," and Wei Chao's (204–273) commentary adds:

> "Trees and rocks" means mountains. It is said that the K'uei have only one
> leg. The people of Yüeh call these phantoms Mountain Sao (Shan-sao) or
> Mountain Hsiao (Shan-hsiao). They [also] exist in Fu-yang [south of present
> Hangchow]. They have human faces, the bodies of monkeys, and are able to
> speak human language. Other names [of these spirits] are Unipeds (Tu-tsu),
> Wang-liang, and Mountain Essences (Shan-ching). By imitating the voices
> of men [such spirits] can confuse people.[70]

This passage makes clear that the Wang-liang or K'uei mountain spirits
of the written tradition were known to the people under a number of different names, probably regional. Wei Chao mentions the terms Shan-
hsiao, Shan-sao, Shan-ching, or Tu-tsu; other sources report names like
Shan-hui (Mountain Hui),[71] Shan-tu (Mountain Tu),[72] or Mu-k'o (Tree
Dwellers)[73] for such spirits. Ko Hung (284–343) provides a particularly
interesting description of them:

> Mountain Essences (Shan-ching) have the shape of babies. They have only
> one leg with its heel reversed. They take pleasure in doing harm. Should a

---

[66]*Chuang-tzu chi-shih* 莊子集釋 (Peking: Chung-hua shu-chü, 1982), 6B.591 ff.

[67]*Han-fei tzu chiao chu* 韓非子校注, Wai-ch'u shuo 外儲說, *tso-hsia* 左下, *shuo* 說 2 (Kiangsu
jen-min ch'u-pan shê, 1982), pp. 415–16.

[68]*Shan-hai ching chien-shu* 14.6b.

[69]*Shuo-wen chieh-tz'u* 說文解字 (Peking: Chung-hua shu-chü, 1979), 112b.

[70]*Kuo-yü* 國語 (Shanghai: Shanghai ku-chi ch'u-pan shê, 1978), 5, *Lu-yü* 魯語 2.201.

[71]See, e.g., *Shan-hai ching chien-shu* 3.6b.

[72]See, e.g., *Shan-hai ching chien-shu* 10.2b, in the commentary of Kuo P'u 郭璞 (276–322).

[73]See, e.g., the quotation of Jen Fang's *Shu-i chi* in *T'ai-p'ing yü-lan* 太平御覽 (Ssu-pu

traveler in the mountains hear in the dark someone speak loudly with a human voice, then he has to do with one of the name of Ch'i; if he is acquainted with this name and shouts it out, it dares not do him any harm. There also [are spirits] named Jih-jou who can be [frightened off when] called by their names. Furthermore there exist certain Mountain Ching like drums, of a carnation color, and with one leg, which are known by the name of Hui. Others, named Chin-lei, have human forms, are nine feet long and wear fur coats and hats of bamboo. Others are the so-called Fei-fei, resembling five-colored dragons with red horns. No such being has the courage to do any outrage when, as soon as it is seen, its name is shouted at it.[74]

The most common designations for demons of this category were Mountain Hsiao (Shan-hsiao), and Mountain Sao (Shan-sao). As de Groot has observed, the many ways of writing Hsiao and Shan-hsiao suggest that these were approximations of a colloquial word denoting the demons.[75] A third-century source confirms that the sounds *hsiao* or *sao* imitated the typical cry of the demons.[76]

Shan-hsiao spirits were malicious and terrorized the people living in or traveling through mountain areas. Six Dynasties sources show them leading wanderers astray in the mountains,[77] throwing rocks,[78] sending diseases,[79] or burning houses,[80] unless placated with bloody sacrifices.[81] Ko Hung warns of dangers and even death awaiting those seeking the solitude of the mountains:

---

ts'ung-k'an ed.), 884.7a–b.

[74] See, e.g., *Pao-p'u-tzu nei-p'ien* 抱朴子內篇 (edition of Sun Hsing-yen 孫星衍 in Ssu-pu pei-yao), 17.4a. Translation with slight modifications according to J. J. M. de Groot, *The Religious System of China* (Leiden, 1910; repr. Taipei: Ch'eng-wen shu-chü, 1976), vol. V, p. 501.

[75] J. J. M. de Groot, *The Religious System of China*, vol. V, p. 498. The most common rendering of *Shan-hsiao* is 山魈 but there exist a number of variant forms such as: 山蕭, 山繰, 山猱. See, e.g., Tuan Ch'eng-shih 段成式 (9th century), *Yu-yang tsa-tsu* 酉陽雜俎 (Peking: Chung-hua shu-chü, 1981), *ch'ien-chi* 前集, 15.144.

[76] *Shen-i ching* 神異經 (Han-wei ts'ung-shu ed.), 9b.

[77] See, e.g., *Pao-p'u-tzu nei-p'ien* 17.1a.

[78] See, e.g., the quotation of the fifth-century *Yu-ming lu* 幽明錄 in Li Shih-chen 李時珍 (1518–1593), *Pen-ts'ao kang-mu* 本草綱目 (Peking: Jen-min wei-sheng ch'u-pan shê, 1981), 51.2922.

[79] See, e.g., *Shen-i ching* 9b.

[80] See, e.g., the quotation of the *Shu-i chi* in *T'ai-p'ing yü-lan* (cited n. 73), 884.7a–b.

[81] See, e.g., *Pao-p'u-tzu nei-p'ien* 4.11a.

If a man should enter the mountains unarmed with expedients, he is certain to suffer injury or death. He will, for example, be rendered ill, or he will be wounded or stabbed, scared and disquieted, or he will see lights and shadows, or smell strange odors. Sometimes those beings will cause big trees to snap in the absence of any wind, or rocks to tumble down with no palpable reason, men being thus hit and killed. Sometimes they will bewilder men, and cause them to run about, deprived of reason, and tumble down into abysses. Sometimes again they will send tigers upon men, or wolves, or venomous snakes. Therefore, nobody should go into the mountains without a valid reason.[82]

In fact, people feared these diabolic spirits so much that they not only tried to propitiate them with offerings, but, from early times on, also developed means to drive them away. K'uei spirits are mentioned in Chang Heng's (78–139) *Rhapsody of the Eastern Capital* among the demons expelled through the No exorcism performed at the Han court toward the end of the year;[83] while their popular alter egos, the Shan-hsiao demons, could be frightened off by the loud reports of burning bamboo.[84] The sixth-century *Ching Ch'u sui-shih chi* relates that the first ritual performed by families on the morning of the first day of the new year consisted of burning pieces of bamboo in the yard in front of the house in order to expel these demons.[85]

The Evolution of the Wu-t'ung Spirits

Belief in one-legged nature goblins of the Shan-hsiao family was persistent. Throughout the centuries, they continued to spread fear among the people and inspired various methods of expulsion and propitiation, until finally representatives of the higher religions took steps against this entrenched popular belief. However, the later history of the Shan-hsiao spirits shows that these attempts succeeded neither in eradicating nor in completely transforming the demons and their cult. All efforts to distentangle

---

[82]*Pao-p'u-tzu nei-p'ien* 17.1a.

[83]Chang Heng 張衡, "Tung-ching fu 東京賦," *Liu-ch'en chu Wen-hsüan* 六臣注文選 (Ch'in-ting ssu-k'u ch'üan-shu ed.), 3.29b–31b. Cf. also Derk Bodde, *Festivals in Classical China* (Princeton: Princeton University Press, 1975), pp. 75–138.

[84]*Shen-i ching*, 9b.

[85]Tsung Lin 宗懍 (fl. 554), *Ching Ch'u sui-shih chi* 荊楚歲事記 (Ch'in-ting ssu-k'u ch'üan-shu ed.), 1.1b.

The one-legged, bull-shaped K'uei.
Illustration from Wu Jen-ch'en, Shan-hai
ching kuang-chu *(1786).*

the fears that enshrouded these archaic nature goblins with an aura of mystery and fascination only made their cult more complex. As new forms of worship evolved, they did not replace the old cultic traditions, but co-existed with them. Some of the ideas imposed from above that were intended to supplant the old "superstitions" were absorbed in the end, but did not change the core of the original beliefs.

The first major impact of one of the high religions of China on the ancient popular tradition can be seen in the application of the Buddhist term *wu-t'ung* to the Shan-hsiao demons. The term originally designated the Five Supernatural Powers (*pañcābhijñā*) obtained through meditation, asceticism, drugs, and other methods. The monumental Madhyamika treatise *Ta chih-tu lun* defines these five powers as 1) the power to be anywhere or to do anything at will (*ju-i t'ung*), 2) the power to see anything anywhere in the form-realm (*t'ien-yen t'ung*), 3) the ability to hear any sound anywhere (*t'ien-erh t'ung*), 4) the ability to know the thoughts of all other minds (*t'a-hsin t'ung*), and 5) knowledge of all former existences of oneself and others (*su-ming t'ung*).[86]

By the twelfth century at the latest, however, the term *wu-t'ung* was used widely as another label for Shan-hsiao spirits. Hung Mai (1123–1202) states in his *I-chien chih* that the spirits called Wu-t'ung in the regions of Che-tung, Che-hsi, and Chiang-tung (roughly corresponding to present-day Chekiang, southern Anhui, and northeastern Kiangsi) and Mu-hsia san-lang or Mu-k'o in Chiang-hsi and Min (the rest of modern Kiangsi, and Fukien) were in reality none other than the K'uei, the Wang-liang, or the Shan-hsiao of old, and comparable to the fox demons of northern China. In many villages these spirits typically had no shrines, but were venerated collectively in rocks or trees.[87] According to the same source, another conflation had obviously occurred between the Wu-t'ung and a type of spirit called Wu-lang.[88]

---

[86]*Ta chih-tu lun* 大智度論 (T 1509) [translated by Kumarajiva in 406], 5.97c–98b; see also Etienne Lamotte, *Le Traité de la Grande Vertu de Sagesse de Nāgārjuna* (Louvain, Publications Universitaires, 1966), vol. I, pp. 328–33.
[87]*I-chien chih* 夷堅志 (Peking: Chung-hua shu-chü, 1981), *ting* 丁, 19.7.695.
[88]Ibid., *chih-kuei* 支癸 3.1.1238.

Hung Mai's identification of the Shan-hsiao with the Wu-t'ung is confirmed by the official Hsiang An-shih (1146–1208) in his *Family Instructions*. He remarks that a local history of Li-yang county (northern Hunan) describes shamanistic practitioners worshipping and invoking the Wu-t'ung under the alternative names Yün-hsiao wu-lang or Shan-hsiao wu-lang as the five sons of the god T'ai-i. Since the first appearance of this deity in a literary source goes back to Ch'ü Yuan's *Nine Songs*,[89] both the local history and Hsiang An-shih agree that the cult of the Shan-hsiao/Wu-t'ung derived from the cult of Tung-huang T'ai-i, celebrated in this famous work.[90] Finally, Taoist sources from the twelfth and thirteenth centuries usually mention the Shan-hsiao and Wu-t'ung together, thus indicating that according to Taoist definition both kinds of spirits belonged in the same demonological category.[91]

This identification certainly did not occur suddenly, but was the result of a slow assimilation in which the Buddhists apparently played a decisive part. The process is, of course, nowhere described and has to be reconstructed from hints scattered throughout the literature. Let us first have a closer look at the Buddhist conception of *wu-t'ung*.

The Buddhist Five Supernatural Powers could be acquired by Buddhist and non-Buddhist methods. Thus in Buddhist literature not only a thoroughly canonical deity like the Bodhisattva Wu-t'ung (Wu-t'ung p'u-sa), who flew to the Western Paradise and received the famous picture of Amitabha surrounded by fifty Bodhisattvas, each sitting on a lotus flower on an immense tree,[92] possessed the Five Powers, but also a great many heretical teachers, sorcerers, and even demons. All these powerful beings

---

[89]Chu Hsi 朱熹, *Ch'u-tz'u chi-chu* 楚辭集注 (Shanghai: Shanghai ku-chi ch'u-pan shê, 1979), 2.29–31; cf. also David Hawkes, *The Songs of the South* (Penguin Books, 1985), pp. 101–2.

[90]Hsiang An-shih 項安世, *Hsiang-shih chia-shuo* 項氏家說 (Ch'in-ting ssu-k'u ch'üan-shu ed.), 8.1b.

[91]See, e.g., "Shang-ch'ing yü-shu wu-lei chen-wen 上清玉樞五雷眞文," *Tao-fa hui-yuan* (HY 1210), 59.1a, 4a; "Kao-shang ching-hsiao san-wu hun-ho tu-t'ien ta-lei lang-shu 高上景霄三五混合都天大雷琅書," ibid. 104.5a; "T'ai-shang san-wu shao-yang t'ieh-mien huo-ch'e wu-lei ta-fa 太上三五邵陽鐵面火車五雷大法," ibid. 122.16b; "Shang-ch'ing t'ien-p'eng fu-mo ta-fa 上清天蓬伏魔大法," ibid. 166.22a–b; "T'ai-shang t'ien-t'an yü-ko 太上天壇玉格," ibid. 250.15b.

[92]Tao-hsüan 道宣, *Chi shen-chou san-pao kan-t'ung lu* 集神州三寶感通錄 (T 2106) (A.D. 664), 2.421a–b.

are commonly labelled Genii with the Five Supernatural Powers (Wu-t'ung hsien-jen). But these powers, especially if attained through unorthodox means, were relative, and could not by themselves protect their possessor from death and rebirth unless he submitted completely to the Buddhist Law. Therefore we find countless parables telling of the conversion of originally heretical Wu-t'ung spirits to Buddhism. One tradition has it, for example, that the Five Hundred Arhats (*wu-pai lo-han*) had been such Wu-t'ung genii who lived in the Himalaya before they became disciples of the Buddha.[93] This was the sense that Chinese monks gave the term when they began to use it. The famous T'ang monk Tao-hsüan (596–667) is the first to mention Wu-t'ung spirits in connection with the conversion of a mountain spirit (*shan-shen*) residing at the site of a Buddhist temple.[94]

The T'ang dynasty witnessed the rise of the famous Chinese schools of Buddhism and the establishment of a large number of new monasteries and temples throughout the empire. Buddhist monks penetrated deep into the remote and mountainous areas of southern China, where they encountered an entrenched tradition of shamanistic cults. Trying to deal with the conflicting religious beliefs centered upon the worship of ghosts and nature spirits, these monks made efforts to explain in terms of their own system the demonic phenomena inspiring fear among the people. Thus the term *wu-t'ung* may first have been employed to qualify the dreadful powers of indigenous spirits such as the old Mountain Hsiao in an attempt to demystify the "demon cults" of the people. By reducing the miraculous potencies of these objects of popular fear and worship to their own canonical concept of the Five Supernatural (but relative) Powers, the Buddhists probably hoped to break the spell the spirits held over their followers.

In the tenth century the Ch'an master Yen-shou (904–975) arrived at a new interpretation of the Five Supernatural Powers. After defining the Powers of the Way (*tao-t'ung*), the Spirit (*shen-t'ung*), Dependence (*i-t'ung*), and Retribution (*pao-t'ung*), Yen-shou ranks fifth the Demonic Power (*yao-t'ung*) which enables old foxes and the essences of rocks and trees to take forms that would permit them to possess human beings.[95] Essences of

---

[93]*A-yü wang chuan* 阿育王傳 (T 2042) (translated between 281–306), 5.116a.
[94]Tao Hsüan, *Tao-hsüan lü-shih kan-t'ung lu* 道宣律師感通錄 (T 2107), 439c.
[95]Yen-shou 延壽 (904–975), *Tsung-ching lu* 宗鏡錄 (T 2016), 15.494b.

rocks and trees were the old Shan-hsiao spirits, and so this explanation implies a close association of the Buddhist concept of *wu-t'ung* with the popular beliefs in Mountain Hsiao and the related foxes.

Later Chinese authors have advanced the opinion that spirits named Wu-t'ung were already worshipped under the T'ang dynasty. Unfortunately, the historical value of the sources usually quoted in support of this thesis is questionable. Thus it is certain that the *Lung-ch'eng lu*, which relates a typical Wu-t'ung anecdote from Lung-ch'eng (Kwangsi), is not the work of Liu Tsung-yuan (773–819),[96] and there is also no solid evidence that the following lines were really composed by Shih Chien-wu (fl. 806–820), who allegedly was disturbed by Wu-t'ung spirits while staying overnight at a Buddhist monastery:

> Originally the Wu-t'ung were servant spirits of Buddhism,
> Dressed in green they lack one leg.[97]

The earliest transmitted contemporary source testifying to a Wu-t'ung cult is no earlier than about 1035.[98] Yet there is some evidence that the term *wu-t'ung* was already used as a name for the objects of a cult by the time Yen-shou redefined the Five Supernatural Powers in his *Tsung-ching lu*. Some local gazetteers indicate the existence of Wu-t'ung shrines in Chekiang, Kiangsu, Fukien, and Kiangsi as early as the tenth century.[99]

---

[96]*Ho-tung hsien-sheng Lung-ch'eng lu* 河東先生龍城錄 (Pai-ch'uan hsüeh-hai ed.), 1.7a–b. The ascription of this work to Liu Tsung-yuan 柳宗元 is convincingly refuted by Yü Chia-hsi 余嘉錫, *Ssu-k'u t'i-yao pien-cheng* 四庫提要辨証 (Peking: Chung-hua shu-chü, 1980), 19.1170–1171.

[97]The earliest ascription of this poem to Shih Chien-wu 施肩吾 is found in Yeh T'ing-kuei's 葉廷珪 (*chin-shih* 1115) *Hai-lu sui-shih* 海錄碎事 (Ssu-k'u ch'üan-shu chen-pen ed.), 13.25a. Wu Shou-chüan points out that "demonic Wu-t'ung" are juxtaposed to the ox-head lictor, A-fang, of the Buddhist hell in an inscription composed by Cheng Yü 鄭愚 in the ninth century; see Wu, *Wu-t'ung shen ch'uan-shuo* (cited n. 7), p. 28. However, read in its context this rather enigmatic passage should probably be understood in the following way: "Their minds harbor evil thoughts and their mouths lie; they take advantage of the dullness [of others] and intimidate the blind and the deaf; [but] the ox[-headed] A-fang with his demonic Five Supernatural Powers spots and arrests them, [as] he sees [everything] in the West and the East. . . . (心作惡、口脫空、欺木石、嚇盲聾、牛阿房、鬼五通、專覷捕、見西東 . . .)" See Cheng Yü, "Ta-Wei Hsü-yu shih ming 大溈盧祐師銘," *T'ang-shih chi-shih* 唐詩紀事 (Ssu-pu ts'ung-k'an ed.), 66.13b–14a.

[98]See p. 165 below.

[99]The *Chia-ting Ch'ih-ch'eng chih* 嘉定赤城志 (1223; Sung-yuan ti-fang chih ts'ung-shu ed.)

Whether these claims are historical or not, it is clear that the cult of spirits called Wu-t'ung began to take specific form near Buddhist temples and monasteries. It would seem that belief in the old Shan-hsiao mountain spirits was inveterate enough that the monks could not simply extirpate them, but had to "baptize" them into the brand of popular Buddhism they spread among the people. Buddhism thus came to exercise an influence on the transformation and evolution of the old nature goblins' cult that went far beyond merely renaming them Wu-t'ung.

Hung Mai tells of the prophetic powers of a Wu-t'ung spirit named An-lo shen (God of Peace and Happiness) who was worshipped in a pagoda at the Yün-chü monastery in Chien-ch'ang (Kiangsi).[100] A legend recorded in 1233 relates this cult directly to the founding of that famous Ch'an monastery. It says that five mountain deities (shan-shen) donated land to the eighth-century monk Tao-yung, who built a Ch'an sanctuary on it. The shan-shen took lodging in an old tree near the temple and were granted the name An-lo kung (Dukes of Peace and Happiness) by the grateful monk.[101]

Here we see another important theme in the history of the Wu-t'ung

---

31.4b–5a, relates that a Wu-t'ung shrine whose object(s) of worship were granted the official title Pao-te wang 保德王 existed in T'ai-chou 台州 already during the time of the kingdom of Wu-Yüeh 吳越 (908–978); the shrine was rebuilt in 994 and, in 1123, received the official designation "Yu-cheng miao 佑正廟." The *Su-chou fu-chih* 蘇州府志 (1379; Taipei: Ch'eng-wen ch'u-pan shê, 1983), 15.24a, refers to the *Hsiang-fu t'u-ching* 祥符圖經 of 1011 in connection with an early Wu-t'ung sanctuary in the city of Soochow. According to the *Hsien-ch'un P'i-ling chih* 咸淳毗陵志 (1268; Sung-yuan ti-fang chih ts'ung-shu ed.), 14.5b, the prefect of P'i-ling (mod. Ch'ang-chou 常州 in Kiangsu) erected a shrine dedicated to the Wu-t'ung in 906 in order to avert fires from the commandery. In Foochow 福州, a sanctuary to the Wu-t'ung was said to have been built in the early tenth century by the first ruler of the kingdom of Min 閩. See *Ch'un-hsi San-shan chih* 淳熙三山志 (1182; Berkeley East Asian Library microfilm of an undated late Ming collation by Hsü Po 徐燉 of a manuscript copy originally in the possession of Hsieh Chao-chih 謝肇淛 [*chin-shih* 1592]), 8.13b–14a. According to an inscription in the Wu-hsien miao of Te-hsing 德興, quoted in Wang Hsiang-chih's 王象之 *Yü-ti chi-sheng* 輿地紀勝 (1221; edition of 1849), 23.14a, this shrine had been founded in 651. Similarly, according to local tradition, the main temple of the Wu-hsien gods in Wu-yuan was founded as a sanctuary dedicated to the Wu-t'ung spirits in 886. See the quotations from the *Tsu-tien ling-ying chi* 祖殿靈應集 (Collected Records of the Miraculous Responses of the Ancestral Shrine [of Wu-yuan]), in *Hsin-pien lien-hsiang sou-shen kuang-chi* (cited n. 31), *ch'ien-chi* 前集, 25a–26a and *Hui-chou fu-chih* 徽州府志 (1502; Ming-tai fang-chih hsüan ed.), 5.42b–43a.

[100] *I-chien chih* (cited n. 87), *chih-kuei* 支癸, 10.4.1295–1296.

[101] *Hsin-pien lien-hsiang sou-shen kuang-chi, ch'ien-chi,* 25b–26a.

cult. Chinese monks often seem to have assumed that the term *wu-t'ung* referred to a group (or groups) of five deities rather than to an indefinite number of spirits. Hence another name for the multifaceted spirits: Five Saints, or Wu-sheng.

The identity of Wu-sheng and Wu-t'ung is confirmed by many later authors from the sixteenth century on;[102] it is also stated in earlier sources, though in a less general way. In the thirteenth century the appellation Wu-sheng seems to have chiefly referred to the orthodox forms of the spirits. Thus, the scholar Hu Sheng (1198–1281) protests against any confusion of the respectable Wu-hsien deities, whom he also calls Five Saints (Wu-sheng), with the ordinary, generic Wu-t'ung.[103] A Wu-sheng temple that existed already in the twelfth century in Hangchow is identified a century later as a shrine of the orthodox Five Manifestations (Wu-hsien). And a Yuan hagiographical work in its section on the Wu-sheng deals only with the Five Manifestations and the five mountain gods of the Yün-chü monastery mentioned above.[104]

But the Five Saints were already known before the twelfth and thirteenth centuries; as early as the eleventh century they were worshipped in a Buddhist temple in Soochow.[105] We also notice that their name is in general relatively often mentioned in connection with Buddhist temples. A late thirteenth-century Taoist source, for example, relates that a shrine to the Five Saints who Protect the Dharma (Hu-fa Wu-sheng) was erected in a Kuan-yin temple in Feng-ch'eng (Kiangsi).[106] A thirteenth-century local history of Hangchow reports the transformation of a sanctuary of the Five Saints Dressed in White (Pai-i Wu-sheng) into a small independent monastery in 1247.[107] And according to a fourteenth-century local

---

[102]See, e.g., the accounts by T'ien Ju-ch'eng 田汝成 (*chin-shih* 1526) and Lu Ts'an 陸粲 (1494–1551) translated below, pp. 194–95 and 197–99.

[103]Cf. the quotation of Hu Sheng's local gazetteer *Hsing-yuan chih* 星源志 (1269) in *Hsin-pien lien-hsiang sou-shen kuang chi, ch'ien-chi*, 26a–b. For the Wu-hsien deities in contrast to the ordinary Wu-t'ung, see below.

[104]Ibid., 24b–26b.

[105]*Wu-chün t'u-ching hsü-chi* 吳郡圖經續記 (1084; Sung-Yuan ti-fang chih ts'ung-shu ed.), 2.13a–b.

[106]Postscript of 1296 to Yang Chih-yuan's 楊智遠 (fl. 1082) "Mei-hsien shih-shih 梅仙事實," *Mei-hsien kuan chi* 梅仙觀記 (HY 600), 9b.

[107]Ch'ien Shuo-yu 潛說友 (from 1270 on prefect of Lin-an), *Hsien-ch'un Lin-an chih* 咸淳臨安志 (ed. of 1830, Sung-Yuan ti-fang chih ts'ung-shu ed.), 82.8b.

gazetteer there was a hall dedicated to the Wu-sheng among the buildings attached to the Liang-kuang ssu in Chen-chiang (Kiangsu).[108]

All this suggests that the names Wu-t'ung and Wu-sheng both derived in fact from the Buddhist environment. Although I so far lack first-hand evidence, I believe that from the beginning both terms denoted the same kind of spirits—the ancient Shan-hsiao. Apparently the Buddhists not only renamed and reexplained the archaic southern Chinese mountain demons, but also resorted to additional methods in their attempt to channel the ecstatic cult tradition of the Shan-hsiao spirits along the lines of Buddhist orthodoxy. As Wu-t'ung the Shan-hsiao were adopted into the system, organized in groups labelled Five Saints, and thus transformed into divine protectors of the Buddha's Law and Buddhist monasteries (Hu-fa shen and Ch'ieh-lan shen).[109] The need to distinguish between Wu-t'ung and Wu-sheng arose only after the Buddhist Wu-t'ung had been readopted by the old shamanistic cult tradition of the Shan-hsiao demons. In the sixteenth century and after, however, this distinction no longer existed, since the borders between the separate cult traditions had become increasingly blurred. I shall return to this later.

The conversion of demons or non-Buddhist deities to the way of the Buddha is a well-known theme in Buddhist canonical literature. In particular, the texts of the esoteric schools of Buddhism present hosts of ferocious demon kings and numerous gods of the old Hindu pantheon who had submitted their exorcistic and protective powers to the ritual tradition of Buddhism. Similar cases of integration can be observed in China. The conversion of indigenous gods and, connected with this, the reformation of popular cults were major objects of Buddhist proselytizers in China. Reports concerning the foundation of Buddhist monasteries and temples abound with stories of the submission of local deities to the Buddhist Law. The salvation of the serpent mountain god of Lu-shan by the famous Parthian monk An Shih-kao (fl. 148–170) and the adoption of

---

[108]*Chih-shun Chen-chiang chih* 至順鎮江志 (1332; Sung-Yuan ti-fang chih ts'ung-shu ed.), 9.5b.

[109]See, e.g., the *Min-tu chi* 閩都記 of 1612 (reprint of 1831), 31.9a, which designates the descendants of the Wu-t'ung spirits, the Wu-hsien 五顯, explicitly as the Ch'ieh-lan shen 伽藍神 of a Buddhist temple near Ku-t'ien 古田 (Fukien).

Kuan Yü as the divine protector of the Yü-ch'üan monastery in Hu-pei may serve here as two examples.[110]

Despite all their efforts, Buddhists succeeded no more than Taoists and Confucianists would in completely converting or superseding the popular cults. Rather, the impact of Buddhism had a stimulating effect on the evolution of popular religious traditions. The full extent to which Buddhism helped to form and propagate the ritual practice of popular religion will be recounted later, when we examine the rise to official honors of the Wu-hsien, another offshoot of this ancient cult. First, however, we have to ask how the Buddhist attempt to transform the Shan-hsiao into Wu-t'ung was received by the public.

Popular Beliefs in the Generic Wu-t'ung

The reshaped Buddhist cult of the Wu-t'ung soon escaped from temples and monasteries, and during the eleventh and twelfth centuries the spirits came to be worshipped throughout southern and central China.[111] Around 1035, the literatus Li Kou composed an inscription for a private Wu-t'ung shrine close to the city of Chien-ch'ang (Kiangsi) in which he praised the "deities whose name was neither found in traditional literature nor en-listed in the official register of sacrifices (*ssu-tien*), and whom upright and noble people would usually ignore," for having saved his family from an epidemic. He compares the "deities" to the plague-spreading ghosts of the untended dead (*li*), but makes no mention of either their relationship with the Shan-hsiao or their Buddhist connection.[112]

---

[110]For An Shih-kao's 安世高 salvation of the serpent god of Lu-shan 廬山 see *Kao-seng chuan* 高僧傳 (T 2059), compiled around 530 by Hui-chiao 慧皎 (497–554), 1.323b–c. For a translation and explanation of this passage see Hisayuki Miyakawa, "Local Cults around Mount Lu at the Time of Sun En's Rebellion," in Holmes Welch and Anna Seidel, eds., *Facets of Taoism: Essays in Chinese Religion* (New Haven and London: Yale University Press, 1979), pp. 94–96. For Kuan Yü's 關羽 role as a guardian deity of the Yü-ch'üan 玉泉 monastery see Tung T'ing 董侹, "Ching-nan chieh-tu-shih Chiang-ling yin P'ei kung ch'ung-hsiu Yü-ch'üan Kuan-miao chi 荊南節度使江陵尹裴公重修玉泉關廟記," (dated 802) *Ch'in-ting ch'üan T'ang-wen* 欽定全唐文, 684.14b–15b.

[111]According to Wu Tseng's 吳曾 *Neng-kai chai man-lu* 能改齋漫錄 (postfaced by Wu Tseng's son in 1157; Shou-shan ko ts'ung-shu ed.), 18.21a–b, Wu-t'ung spirits had already revealed their diabolical character in K'ai-feng between 1056 and 1064.

[112]"Shao-shih shen-tz'u chi 邵氏神祠記," *Li Kou chi* 李覯集 (Peking: Chung-hua shu-chü, 1981), 24.267–68.

However, from numerous anecdotes in Hung Mai's *I-chien chih* it becomes clear that, in the popular sphere, the Wu-t'ung spirits had by the twelfth century reassumed the characteristics of their ancestors. Like the Shan-hsiao, the Wu-t'ung had only one leg and were characterized by their extreme ambiguity. On the one hand, they could shower their followers with (often stolen) riches, or even rescue them from a plague. On the other hand, they were mischievous and always ready to play tricks on people.

According to one episode in the *I-chien chih*, a one-legged being frequently stole food from the kitchen of the household of an official in Kuei-chi (Chekiang). The houseowner was considering moving to a different place in order to avoid further harm when he found out that his neighbor worshipped a spirit whose picture, set up on a domestic altar, showed nothing but a huge leg. A local patrician and ordained Taoist priest identified the spirit as a one-legged (*tu-chiao*) Wu-t'ung of the Hsiao category and finally ended the demon's apparitions in the kitchen.[113]

Above all, however, Wu-t'ung spirits were utterly disreputable and also feared because they were said to force women to comply with their sexual demands. This trait seems to have been no particular characteristic of the Shan-hsiao, but became the main feature of the popular Wu-t'ung and was, as Hung Mai confirms, directly related to various forms of psychosomatic disorders in women said to derive from demonic possession by Wu-t'ung incubi. Moreover, the specific powers of mediums serving the Wu-t'ung were also believed to be the results of sexual relationships with the spirits:

> [Wu-t'ung demons] particularly like to debauch [women]. [Approaching their victims] they change into handsome noblemen or into any form a woman would dream of. Sometimes also they just show their original form and appear as monkeys, shaggy dogs, or frogs. Although their appearances vary, their bodies are always nimble and muscular and feel cold like ice or steel to the touch. . . .
>
> Some [possessed] women turn into mediums whom people then call "immortals." Others who try to oppose [the demons' approaches] and therefore fall ill are said to have contracted "immortals' disease (*hsien-ping*)." Some [women] fall down as if dead and remain up to a month in a state of catalepsy [after the demons take possession of them]. Revived, they claim that they

---

[113]*I-chien chih* (cited n. 87), *chih-ching* 支景, 2.5.890.

have had sexual intercourse with a noble man in a magnificent palace. Some are abducted and reappear only after days. Others go crazy after such an encounter and forever remain mentally deranged.

Not all of the women defiled [by Wu-t'ung] are virtuous. [In fact,] the spirits themselves claim they can only approach women destined [to meet this fate] on account of their deeds in previous lives.[114]

If Wu-t'ung spirits began liaisons with married women they would not allow the husbands to have sex with their wives any more. In the *I-chien chih* we are told of a husband who frequently found himself thrown out of the bed or locked out of the chamber when he woke up, while the demon had spent the night with his wife.[115] Wu-t'ung spirits were also held responsible for pregnancies and monster births. Hung Mai reports that women allegedly involved with Wu-t'ung gave birth to monkeys, pigs, or lumps of flesh.[116]

Later, in the late sixteenth and early seventeenth centuries, the Wu-t'ung came to be closely associated with the cult of the gods of wealth and achieved a notorious reputation for demanding sexual favors in return for the bestowal of riches.[117] However, the themes of sex and wealth were already linked in the twelfth century. Thus, according to another anecdote in the *I-chien chih*, a destitute migrant who resettled with his family in Shu-chou (Anhui) suddenly became rich because he worshipped a one-legged Wu-t'ung. During the nocturnal rites he held for the spirit at a small domestic shrine, his entire family sat naked in the dark. But the demon demanded more: he involved all the women of the household in sexual relationships, and some of them even gave birth to the spirit's offspring. When the bride of the family's eldest son finally refused to participate in these lascivious practices, the Wu-t'ung visited diseases upon the family and literally scattered the household's money in all directions.[118]

Yet despite this broad relapse into demonism and medium cults, the purified Buddhist Wu-t'ung did not disappear. On the contrary, these divine figures, worshipped in groups of five in Buddhist temples, inspired one of the most successful cults in the flourishing cities of southern China.

---

[114]Ibid., *ting* 丁, 19.7.696.
[115]Ibid.
[116]Ibid., 696–97.
[117]See the article by Richard von Glahn mentioned in note 7 above, p. 698.
[118]*I-chien chih, chih-kuei* 支癸, 3.1.1238–39.

The Rise of the Wu-hsien Gods

Rapid economic growth and the spread of urbanization in South China from the tenth century on brought about fundamental changes not only in the social structure of local communities, but also in the sphere of popular religion. Temple gods and their cults became a means of expressing the identity and enhancing the prestige of cities and towns, where commoners, local gentry, and county magistrates joined together in their efforts to gain recognition for the divine embodiments of their pride. The central government, anxious to ensure the cooperation of powerful localities, adapted its policies. As Valerie Hansen has demonstrated, the late eleventh and early twelfth centuries show a sudden increase in the number of popular cults recognized by the state and in official titles granted to local deities. Around the same time, the procedures regulating the inclusion of popular cults in the official register of sacrifices and the stipulations concerning the further promotions of deities were standardized.[119]

These circumstances also precipitated a crucial turn in the history of the cult of the Wu-t'ung: in 1109, the Wu-t'ung temple of the city of Wu-yuan in Hui-chou (Kiangsi) obtained official recognition and was renamed Ling-shun miao. Fourteen years later, the deities of the temple were granted two-character names of honor and were promoted to the rank of count (*hou*). In 1174, they received entirely new names and were made dukes (*kung*),[120] and in 1202, on the occasion of a donation of five fans inscribed by the emperor himself, the temple gods were proclaimed kings (*wang*).[121] Another city, Te-hsing in Jao-chou (Kiangsi), which fiercely competed with Wu-yuan to gain recognition for its own Wu-t'ung temple,[122] had finally to renounce its claim and acknowledge the primacy of the temple in Wu-yuan.[123]

[119]Valerie Hansen, *Changing Gods in Medieval China, 1127–1276* (Princeton: Princeton University Press, 1990), chapter 4.

[120]*Sung hui-yao chi-kao* 宋會要輯稿 (facsimile of Hsü Sung's 徐松 edition of 1809, Taipei: Hsin wen-feng ch'u-pan shê, 1962), *li* 20.157b–158b.

[121]Ibid., and the quotation from Hu Sheng's 胡升 (1198–1281) *Hsing-yuan chih* 星源志 (1269) in *Hsin-pien lien-hsiang sou-shen kuang-chi, chien-chi* (cited n. 31), 26a–b.

[122]See, e.g., the quotation from Hu Sheng's *Hsing-yuan chih* in ibid.

[123]According to the *Yü-ti chi-sheng* (cited n. 99) 32.14a, the Te-hsing temple, though officially named Ling-shun miao, was still remembered by its original name, Wu-t'ung miao, among the people. The same temple was also known as Wu-hsien miao from the late twelfth century on. (See *I-chien chih, san-chih* 三志, *chi* 己, 10.4.1378.) The *Sung hui-yao chi-kao, li* 20.158a, states that in 1145, when two new characters were added to each of the honorary

Yet, while this meteoric rise to prominence of the deities in the Wu-yuan temple took place, the Wu-t'ung spirits in general had fallen under state proscription in 1111 and their shrines in the capital had been destroyed.[124] How was this possible?

Partly, the answer can be found in the bureaucratic procedures regulating the registration of cults at the Court of Imperial Sacrifice (T'ai-ch'ang ssu). Petitions asking for state recognition of a cult were usually submitted by the official representatives of a given place. These local magistrates supported their request by a detailed report on the deities of the temple under their jurisdiction. Similar cults in other counties or prefectures naturally fell beyond their responsibility. In turn, if the central government approved a request, recognition was given only to the distinct tradition of the temple whose supporters had submitted the petition.[125] This temple could establish affiliations with an unlimited number of branch temples (*hsing-tz'u*) and thereby spread its cult far beyond the borders of its original location, but the branch temples derived their legitimacy exclusively from the approved temple and the local tradition it represented.

Local influence played, in other words, a preeminent role in the state's system of dealing with popular religious affairs, as well as in the developments following the official recognition of a cult. Any attempt to gain recognition for a cult like that of the Wu-t'ung had to be initiated by the representatives of a specific place. But there was no single place that could speak up for the Wu-t'ung spirits as a whole since their cult thrived throughout the southern regions of the country. Besides, it is hardly imaginable that any of the ordinary medium cults of the ambiguous generic Wu-t'ung would ever have been approved by the state.

---

names of Wu-yuan's five deities, the government also "ordered another temple in Hsin-chou 信州 (Kiangsi) to adopt the same names for its gods." Although Te-hsing at that time belonged to Jao-chou 饒州 rather than to Hsin-chou, this passage could nevertheless refer to Te-hsing's temple, as Wu-yuan is also made erroneously a part of Ning-kuo 寧國 (Anhui) in this source. Other evidence for Wu-yuan's victory over Te-hsing in the rivalry for the cult is found in *I-chien chih, san-chih, chi,* 10.6.1379 and *Meng-liang lu* 夢梁錄 (1275; Hsüeh-chin t'ao-yuan ed.), 14.12a–b. According to the first source, a shrine to the Five Saints (Wu-sheng) in Hangchow was in 1177 still regarded as a branch temple of Te-hsing's Wu-hsien temple, and about a hundred years later the same shrine is listed in the second source as a branch temple of Wu-yuan's Wu-hsien temple.

[124]*Sung hui-yao chi-kao, li* 20.14b–15a.

[125]Cf. Valerie Hansen, *Changing Gods in Medieval China, 1127–1276*, pp. 91–104.

When Wu-yuan, Te-hsing,[126] and, possibly, some other localities[127] launched initiatives to enroll their respective Wu-t'ung shrines in the official register of sacrifices, in all these cases local tradition had already made a distinction between their deities and the Wu-t'ung spirits worshipped and feared elsewhere in southern China.[128] And precisely here lies the real answer to the question why the central government took such a radically different attitude towards the generic Wu-t'ung on the one hand and Wu-yuan's Wu-t'ung cult on the other. The supporters of Wu-yuan's Wu-t'ung had purged their deities of all dubious associations and presented them in a respectable and acceptable form. This can be clearly seen in the history of the cult in Wu-yuan.

[126]Apart from Hu Sheng's mention of the rivalry beween Wu-yuan and Te-hsing for recognition of their respective Wu-t'ung shrines as the legitimate place of origin of the cult (see note 122 above), we lack any concrete evidence of the initial steps undertaken by Te-hsing to gain official sanction for its deities. A late source, the *Ku-chin t'u-shu chi-ch'eng* 古今圖書集成, *Chih-fang tien* 職方典 (facsimile of the Kuang-hsü T'ung-wen shu-chü ed., Peking: Chung-hua shu-chü, 1934), 859.45c, reports that the temple gods of Te-hsing were granted the title Wu-t'ung hou 侯 in 669 and promoted to dukes (kung 公) between 937 and 943, but it is questionable whether this corresponds to historical truth. That the city did make attempts to achieve further promotion of the deities during the late twelfth century is confirmed by an episode in the *I-chien chih* (cited n. 87) *san-chih, chi*, 10.6.1379–80. According to this account Te-hsing submitted a request to the provincial Fiscal Commission (*yün-ssu* 運司), whereupon the vice-magistrate of neighboring Shang-jao 上饒 County came to inspect the shrine. There the official remembered that once, in a dream in his childhood, he had entered a temple where he saw the magnificently adorned icons of five divine kings. He therefore wrote a favorable report on the temple in Te-hsing and recounted his own strange experience in connection with the deities; subsequently Te-hsing's Five Manifestations were promoted.

[127]See, e.g., the *Chia-ting Ch'ih-ch'eng chih* (cited n. 99), 31.4b–5a, which relates that the deities of a local Wu-t'ung shrine were granted the official title Pao-te wang 保德王 between 908 and 978; in 1130 the shrine received a new plaque and was renamed Yu-cheng miao 佑正廟.

[128]According to local tradition in Te-hsing, for example, in 651 a certain Chang Meng 張蒙 was led to a lode of silver-bearing ore by a divine youth while hunting a white deer nearby. The grateful people built a temple called Wu-t'ung miao beside the place; *Yü-ti chi-sheng* (cited n. 99), 23.14a. The *Jao-chou fu-chih* 饒州府志 (1872; repr. Taipei: Ch'eng-wen shu-chü, 1975), 4.18 and 4.29, gives a modified version of this story: according to this source the event took place under the Sui dynasty and there were five divine beings who showed Chang Meng the silver. The text adds that the deities once more appeared under the Sung dynasty and drew the attention of the citizens of Te-hsing to springs of water with high concentrations of copper and iron sulphates, useful in the refining of copper and silver. These legends illustrate well the prestige localities derived from popular cults. Based upon the mineral resources of silver and the sulphate springs, Te-hsing county, founded in the tenth century, experienced an economic upsurge during the Sung. This prosperity was directly attributed to five gods. Accordingly, the deities could be conceived in a positive way that lacked all ambiguous features characteristic of the generic Wu-t'ung.

According to the records of Wu-yuan's Wu-t'ung temple, five divine beings dressed in yellow appeared in 886 to Wang Yü, an inhabitant of the city of Wu-yuan. They asked for a cult to be dedicated to them and, in return, promised to protect the city. The citizens of Wu-yuan built a temple for the deities, which was named Wu-t'ung Temple.[129] Except for the name of the temple, nothing in this founding legend is reminiscent of the one-legged goblins whose awesome powers and sensual appetites elsewhere impressed and frightened the people. Wu-yuan's Wu-t'ung appeared as five dignified and benevolent lords, associated with the five elements of the classical Chinese cosmology, and, seemingly, had no relationship to the dubious, generic Wu-t'ung.[130]

This does not mean, however, that awareness of this relationship was completely lost. On the contrary, echoes of contemporary beliefs in the generic Wu-t'ung lingered on both among skeptics of the educated class and the common people. Chu Hsi (1130–1200), Wu-yuan's most renowned scion, was urged by his family to pay his respects in the Wu-t'ung Temple, but he criticized and ridiculed the worship of the Wu-t'ung, only regretting that he could take no steps against the latter because of their official status. He obviously made no distinction between the demonic Wu-t'ung and Wu-yuan's five patron deities.[131]

There also existed different traditions concerning the origin of the gods of the Wu-t'ung temple. The imperial decree of enfeoffment seems to have referred to a popular tradition according to which these gods were the deified spirits of five brothers who had for a millennium manifested their divine powers in the region of Chiang-tung.[132] Chu Mu (fl. 1225–1264), in his *Fang-yü sheng-lan,* gives the additional information that these

---

[129]See the passages quoted from the *Tsu-tien ling-ying chi* 祖殿靈應集 (Wu-yuan temple records) in *Hsin-pien lien-hsiang sou-shen kuang-chi, ch'ien-chi* (cited n. 31), 24b–25b, and *Hui-chou fu-chih* (cited n. 99), 5.42b. In connection with the branch temple of Wu-yuan's Wu-t'ung temple, the Ling-shun miao 靈順廟, located near the prefectural city of Hui-chou, the *Hui-chou fu-chih* refers to an inscription which dates the epiphany of the Five Manifestations as far back as 627 (5.37a–b). The same source, moreover, quotes a passage from Hu Sheng's *Hsing-yuan chih* of 1269 according to which the five deities originally descended at the beginning of the K'ai-yuan 開元 period (713–741) in the township of Ch'ang-lin 長林 near Wu-yuan city, and not, as stated in the temple records, into the garden of Wang Yü 王瑜 in the city of Wu-yuan itself (5.44a).

[130]See the quotation from Hu Sheng's *Hsing-yuan chih* cited above, n. 121.

[131]*Chu-tzu yü-lei* 朱子語類 (Kyoto: Chubun shuppansha, 1970), 3.18a.

[132]See *Yü-ti chi-sheng* (cited n. 99), 20.18a, and *Hui-chou fu-chih* (cited n. 99), 5.37a–b.

five brothers, in their human lives, had belonged to a family named Hsiao.[133] This tradition draws on the still older identification of the Wu-t'ung with the archaic Shan-hsiao (Mountain Hsiao), as the character denoting the family name was also used as a variant for the word *hsiao* in Shan-hsiao.[134] The significance of the Hsiao brothers tradition, which implies the identity of Shan-hsiao, Wu-t'ung, and Wu-yuan's reshaped temple gods, is pointed out by later writers such as Lu Ts'an (1494–1551),[135] and also recurs as a motif in the *Nan-yu chi*: as mentioned earlier, in his third incarnation, Hua-kuang, the hero of the novel, is reborn along with four brothers into a family named Hsiao in Wu-yuan.[136]

Nevertheless, the official Wu-yuan tradition, which held that the deities had revealed themselves to Wang Yü and thus avoided any allusions to either the Shan-hsiao or the Wu-t'ung, prevailed as the standard version of the origin of the cult and determined its further development in Wu-yuan and beyond.

With the imperial grant of a new temple plaque in 1109 and the successive promotions of Wu-yuan's deities in the following years, the Wu-t'ung cult split into two separate traditions. In 1111 the ordinary Wu-t'ung spirits, worshipped throughout the southern portion of the empire (including K'ai-feng), were declared objects of an illicit cult (*yin-ssu*) and henceforth often severely persecuted by local authorities. Meanwhile the cult of Wu-yuan's deities developed into one of the most prominent cults of southern China.

In 1174 the five gods of the Ling-shun miao in Wu-yuan were granted new official titles: Hsien-ying kung, Hsien-lo kung, Hsien-yu kung, Hsien-ling kung, and Hsien-ning kung.[137] Since all these titles began with the character *hsien* (manifestation), the deities soon became known among the people as the Wu-hsien, or Five Manifestations.[138] Under this new name the five gods were soon worshipped in numerous branch temples in every major city in the lower Yangtze valley. In the thirteenth century,

[133]Chu Mu 祝穆, *Fang-yü sheng-lan* 方輿勝覽 (Ch'in-ting ssu-k'u ch'üan-shu ed.), 16.8b.
[134]See, e.g., *Yu-yang tsa-tsu, ch'ien-chi* (cited n. 75), 15.144.
[135]See the translation of Lu Ts'an's 陸粲 account of the Wu-t'ung, pp. 197–99 below.
[136]See pp. 149–50 above and p. 203 below.
[137]*Sung hui-yao chi-kao* (cited n. 120), *li*, 20.157b–158b.
[138]That this appellation had already become popular by the late twelfth century is attested in *I-chien chih* (cited n. 87), *san-chih, chi*, 10.6.1378–79.

Wu-hsien temples affiliated with the main temple in Wu-yuan existed in Soochow, Hangchow,[139] Yen-chou,[140] Ning-po,[141] T'ai-chou,[142] Ch'ang-chou,[143] Yü-feng,[144] Chen-chiang,[145] Tan-yang,[146] Chü-jung,[147] Foochow,[148] and even in such remote places of southern China as Ts'ang-wu in Kwangsi.[149] By the fourteenth and fifteenth centuries, the cult of Wu-yuan's five deities had spread as far to the west and to the north as Szechwan and Peking.[150]

There also existed a link between the Wu-hsien of Wu-yuan and the Buddhist tradition. Wang Yü, who according to the legendary account summarized above had initiated the construction of a shrine to the five deities in 886, was styled Shuang-shan.[151] The *Hui-chou fu-chih* of 1502 states that a man named Wang Shuang-shan donated the land for the founda-

[139]On the branch temples in Soochow and Hangchow see below.
[140]In Chekiang; the temple was founded in 1201. See *Ching-ting Yen-chou hsü-chih* 景定嚴州續志 (1260–1264; Ts'ung-shu chi-ch'eng ed.), 4.46.
[141]In Chekiang; the temple was founded between 1205 and 1208 by an official upon his return from Hui-chou 徽州 to his native place in Ning-po. See *Yen-yu Ssu-ming chih* 延祐四明志 (1320; Sung-Yuan ti-fang chih ts'ung-shu ed.), 15.12b.
[142]In Chekiang; the shrine was built in 1221. See *Chia-ting Ch'ih-ch'eng chih* (cited n. 99), 31.7b.
[143]In Kiangsu; see *Hsien-ch'un P'i-ling chih* (cited n. 99), 14.5b.
[144]Mod. Chia-ting 嘉定 (Kiangsu) near Shanghai; the temple was founded on the grounds of the Buddhist temple Hsin-an ssu 新安寺 by a native of Yü-feng 玉峰, who obviously brought ashes from the incense burner of Wu-yuan's main temple. See *Yü-feng chih* 玉峰志 (1252; Sung-Yuan ti-fang chih ts'ung-shu ed.), 3.20a–b.
[145]In Kiangsu; two Wu-hsien temples existed there in the thirteenth century: one, allegedly founded during the T'ang, may have been an older Wu-t'ung shrine which became a branch temple of the Wu-hsien temple in Wu-yuan in 1241; the other one was founded between 1241 and 1252. See *Chih-shun Chen-chiang chih* (cited n. 108), 8.8b–9a.
[146]In Kiangsu; this temple was erected by a local patrician named Ts'ai Feng 蔡逢 in 1248. See ibid., 8.18b.
[147]In Kiangsu; a pre-existing sanctuary (dedicated to the generic Wu-t'ung?) became affiliated with Wu-yuan's Wu-hsien temple between 1241 and 1252. See Chang Ning 張寧 (*chin-shih* 1454), "Chü-jung hsien Wu-hsien ling-kuan miao-pei 句容縣五顯靈官廟碑," *Fang-chou chi* 方洲集 (Ch'in-ting ssu-k'u ch'üan-shu ed.), 18.7a–8a.
[148]This Wu-t'ung shrine, founded during the tenth century, was later located inside a tower of the old city wall of Foochow 福州. It was converted into an affiliate of Wu-yuan's Wu-hsien temple at an uncertain date, presumably during the Sung dynasty. See *Ch'un-hsi San-shan chih* (cited n. 99), 8.13b, and *Min-tu chi* (cited n. 109), 3.11b.
[149]See Ch'en Ju 陳汝, "Ts'ang-chou ch'ung-hsiu Wu-hsien miao chi 蒼州重修五顯廟記," (1368), *Yung-lo ta-tien* 永樂大典 (Peking: Chung-hua shu-chü, 1960), 2343.4a.
[150]See below p. 192 and n. 229.
[151]*Hui-chou fu-chih* (cited n. 99), 5.43b.

tion of the Chih-lin yuan, a Ch'an Buddhist monastery west of the city of Wu-yuan, in 875.[152] Now this Chih-lin yuan was the institution to which Wu-yuan's Wu-t'ung shrine was originally attached.[153] Although we cannot be certain that Wang Shuang-shan, the sponsor of the Chih-lin yuan, and Wang Yü, the alleged founder of the Wu-t'ung Temple, were the same person, it does seem likely, and hence Wu-yuan's distinct Wu-t'ung tradition probably originated in the Chih-lin yuan.

This connection may be another reason why Wu-yuan's five gods, instead of being declared objects of an illicit cult along with the generic Wu-t'ung, were sanctioned by the state. Nowhere in contemporary sources does there appear any mention that the state proscription of the ordinary Wu-t'ung spirits also extended to those Wu-t'ung who as the Five Saints (Wu-sheng) served as guardians of Buddhist monasteries. The Five Manifestations (Wu-hsien) of Wu-yuan thus may have ultimately derived their respectability from their Buddhist affiliation.

The close relationship between the Chih-lin yuan and the Ling-shun Temple and its Wu-hsien cult also is evident from later imperial favors granted to these sanctuaries. When the ancestral temple of the Five Manifestations in Wu-yuan was rebuilt on the initiative of the influential Wang family and officially renamed Wan-shou ling-shun wu p'u-sa miao in 1314, the Chih-lin ssu also received a new temple plaque and was henceforth called Wan-shou ssu.[154]

Buddhism also influenced the ritual practice of the cult. According to the Wu-yuan temple records, the five gods appeared in a dream to the magistrate Ling-hu Tso between 984 and 987, revealing to him a method to rid the county of a dreadful plague. Since this revelation took place on the Buddha's birthday, the eighth day of the fourth month, the people of Wu-yuan henceforth commemorated their deliverance from the pestilence by annual festivals held on this date.[155] Whatever the historical authenticity of this account, it is a telling example of the deep interpenetration of the cultic practices of Buddhism and popular religion: the traditional celebra-

---

[152]Ibid., 10.58b.
[153]Ch'eng Chü-fu 程鉅夫 (1249–1318), "Wu-yuan shan Wan-shou ling-shun wu p'u-sa miao chi 婺源山萬壽靈順五菩薩廟記," *Hsüeh-lou chi* 雪樓集 (Ch'in-ting ssu-k'u ch'üan-shu ed.), 13.19a.
[154]Ibid.
[155]*Hui-chou fu-chih*, 5.43a.

tions commemorating the Buddha's birth set the framework for the veneration of the local gods, while the emphasis of the festival shifted from the Buddha to the Five Manifestations.

In the course of the twelfth and thirteenth centuries, Wu-yuan's Wu-hsien festival developed into one of China's great temple fairs. Every year during the fourth month pilgrims from all over the country and even from overseas flocked to the city to visit the temple and watch the colorful processions.[156] Merchants, peddlers, and all sorts of performers probably also profited from the occasion, and added to the splendor of the event. In 1211 a young man from Hangchow, Chou Hsiung, died during the festive commotion, and a new cult arose: the unfortunate Chou was incorporated into the divine retinue of the Five Manifestations and, in 1235, received his first official title.[157] Similar accidents may have prompted the authorities to ban the festival temporarily in the mid-thirteenth century.[158]

With the establishment of subsidiary Wu-hsien temples in Chekiang, Kiangsu, and other southern Chinese provinces, Wu-yuan's Wu-hsien festival was also adopted by several cities. Beginning around 1241, the deities'

[156]See, e.g., the quotation from Hu Sheng's *Hsing-yuan chih* cited above, n. 121.

[157]See the highly interesting inscription for Chou Hsiung's 周雄 shrine in his native Hsin-ch'eng 新城 (Hangchow) composed by Fang Hui 方回 (1227–1307) in 1300: "Fu-te miao pei 輔德廟碑," *T'ung-chiang hsü-chi* 桐江續集 (Ch'in-ting ssu-k'u ch'üan-shu ed.), 36.26a–29a. Fang Hui reports that Te-hsing 德興, the city competing with Wu-yuan for the recognition of its own Wu-t'ung shrine, was the first to petition for the canonization of Chou Hsiung. The request was approved in 1235, and Chou Hsiung was granted the title I-ying chiang-chün 翊應將君. In 1238 the government allowed the shrine in Chou's native place, Hsin-ch'eng, to use the same titles as the temple in Te-hsing. In 1244 the prefecture of Hui-chou 徽州 (to which Wu-yuan county belonged) requested the deity's promotion, and Chou Hsiung received the title I-ying hou 侯. In 1259 Chou Hsiung's descendants began to rebuild the temple of their divine ancestor in Hsin-ch'eng in the style of Wu-yuan's Ling-shun miao. The construction was completed after more than twenty years. This example shows well the role of different competing localities in the process leading to the official recognition of a cult. Although Chou Hsiung was a native of Hsin-ch'eng and died in Wu-yuan, the first shrine to obtain sanction from the central government was located in Te-hsing. This shrine remained the main temple of Chou Hsiung's cult, despite the fact that Chou's descendants promoted his worship greatly in his native Hsin-ch'eng. Note also that, as Hui-chou's intercession in 1244 makes clear, requests for the promotion of deities did not need to come from the place of the ancestral temple but could be submitted by other localities as well.

[158]See Huang Chen 黃震 (1213–1280), "Shen chu-ssu ch'i-chin she-hui chuang 申諸司乞禁社會狀," *Huang-shih jih-ch'ao* 黃氏日抄 (Ch'in-ting ssu-k'u ch'üan-shu ed.), 74.27a. During the Yuan, however, the festival again attracted crowds from all over the region. See Fang Hui, "Jao-chou lu chih-chung Wang-kung mu chih-ming 饒州路 治中汪公墓誌銘," *T'ung-chiang chi* 桐江集 (Taipei: Kuo-li chung-yang t'u-shu kuan, 1970), *pu-i*, 40.

images from Soochow's two major Wu-hsien sanctuaries, the Shang-shan an and the Ju-i an, were paraded through the streets to the city's Northern Temple (Pei-ssu) every year between the fourth and eighth days of the fourth lunar month. The pomp of the processions and the performances that accompanied the celebrations made this festival one of Soochow's most popular annual events.[159]

In Hangchow, the seat of the Southern Sung emperors since 1138, a shrine dedicated to the Five Saints (Wu-sheng) existed already in the mid-twelfth century.[160] This temple was famous for its murals by the celebrated painter Su Han-ch'en (fl. 1119–1163).[161] A century later, the number of temples affiliated with Wu-yuan's Ling-shun miao in Hangchow and its hinterland had increased to ten.[162] Hangchow honored the Five Manifestations twice a year: on the Buddha's birthday, and again in the ninth month, on the day considered the deities' own birthday.[163] These celebrations were joined by the city's guilds and various worshipping associations who vied with each other to display the most luxurious offerings.[164]

The close affinity to Buddhism that promoted the cult's growth in its native place, Wu-yuan, was equally evident in Soochow and Hangchow. Early in the thirteenth century a Buddhist monk brought wooden sculptures of the Five Manifestations from Wu-yuan and installed them in the "Temple of the Wish-Fulfilling [Jewel]" (Ju-i an), a small Buddhist monastery in Soochow established in 1203 at the site of a Buddhist pagoda from the early twelfth century.[165] Another set of wooden statues arrived

[159]*Su-chou fu-chih* 蘇州府志 (1379; Taipei: Ch'eng-wen ch'u-pan shê, 1983), 15.24a–b.
[160]*I-chien chih* (cited n. 87), *san-chih, chi,* 10.6.1379.
[161]See Chou Mi 周密 (1232–1298), *Wu-lin chiu-shih* 武林舊事 (Chih pu-tsu chai ts'ung-shu ed.), 5.17a. The same temple and its murals are mentioned again in the sixteenth century by T'ien Ju-ch'eng 田汝成 (*chin-shih* 1526), *Hsi-hu yu-lan chih* 西湖遊覽志 (Taipei: Shih-chieh shu-chü, 1963), 8.91.
[162]See *Hsien-ch'un Lin-an chih* (cited n. 107), 73.14a–b, 74.12a, 76.17a–18a, 78.10a–b, 82.8b.
[163]See *Meng-liang lu* (cited n. 123), 19.8b. This text gives the twenty-ninth day of the ninth lunar month as the birthday of the Wu-hsien gods. However, since all other sources agree on the twenty-eighth of the ninth lunar month, the *Meng-liang lu* may be in error here.
[164]Ibid., 19.8b.
[165]See *Su-chou fu-chih* (cited n. 159), 15.24a, and the inscription composed by Liu Hsüan 劉鉉 around the middle of the fifteenth century: "Ch'ung-chien Wu-hsien wang tz'u chi 重建五顯王祠記," *Wu-hsien chih* 吳縣志 (1642), 21.17b. This passage, along with Ku Ju-pao's 顧儒寶 inscription for Soochow's Shang-shan an 上善庵, also from the *Wu-hsien chih*, was kindly made available to me by Richard von Glahn, who copied it by hand from the original edition found in Japan. Von Glahn notes the date 1439 for Liu Hsüan's inscription; however,

from Wu-yuan in 1209 and was first set up in a Taoist institution, the Kuang-hsiao kuan, before it found permanent accommodation in the Buddhist-sponsored "Temple of Superior Goodness" (Shang-shan an), whose main building was constructed in 1240.[166] Significantly, six of the ten Wu-hsien temples in the Hangchow area were also directly attached to Buddhist monasteries.[167]

In some places, older Wu-t'ung or Wu-sheng sanctuaries existed prior to the assimilation with Wu-yuan's specific Wu-hsien tradition. Hangchow's oldest Wu-sheng shrine, for instance, seems to have been originally unrelated to Wu-yuan's Ling-shun miao. Hung Mai, a native of Po-yang in Jao prefecture, apparently wanted to give weight to his home prefecture's claims on the cult and maintained in an episode of his *I-chien chih* that the Hangchow shrine was a branch temple of Te-hsing's Wu-hsien Temple.[168] Only in the thirteenth century was this Wu-sheng shrine recognized as one of the capital's numerous branch temples of the main temple in Wu-yuan.[169] Another example is the Wu-t'ung shrine in the city of Foochow. According to the *Ch'un-hsi San-shan chih* of 1182, the origin of this sanctuary was as early as the tenth century. Between 1004 and 1008 a temple building (Wu-t'ung miao) was constructed, which was enlarged and refurbished in 1040 with the help of a Buddhist monk.[170] A considerably later source, the *Min-tu chi* of 1612, identifies the deities worshipped in this ancient shrine as the Wu-hsien gods.[171] In Ch'ang-chou (Kiangsu) a temple, by 1268 commonly known as the Temple of the Five Manifestation Kings (Wu-hsien wang miao), was purportedly founded as early as 906 by the prefect Chang Ch'ung, who hoped thereby to stop the fires afflicting the prefecture.[172] Similarly, the origin of a branch temple of the Five Manifestations in Chen-chiang (Kiangsu), like the main temple in

---

this seems to be somewhat in conflict with other statements made in the text. Thus, Liu Hsüan remarks that by then eighty years had passed since the beginning of the Hung-wu period (1368–1398), which would bring us to a date around 1448. The date of 1439 may be due to a slip of the pen.

[166] *Su-chou fu-chih*, 15.24a.

[167] *Hsien-ch'un Lin-an chih* (cited n. 107), 73.14a–b, 74.12a, 76.17b–18a, 78.10a–b, 82.8b.

[168] Te-hsing was located in Jao prefecture. *I-chien chih* (cited n. 87), *san-chih, chi*, 10.6.1379.

[169] *Hsien-ch'un Lin-an chih*, 73.14a–b; *Meng-liang lu* (cited n. 123), 14.12a–b.

[170] *Ch'un-hsi San-shan chih* (cited n. 99), 8.13b–15a.

[171] *Min-tu-chi* (cited n. 109), 3.11b.

[172] *Hsien-ch'un P'i-ling chih* (cited n. 99), 14.5b.

Wu-yuan called Ling-shun miao, was traced back to the T'ang, to a time before the cult of Wu-yuan's five deities began to spread.[173] And another shrine in a village east of the city of Chü-jung (Kiangsu) was already old when it became affiliated with Wu-yuan's Wu-hsien temple, evidently sometime between 1241 and 1252.[174] The last three sources do not identify the earlier names of the temples and the deities worshipped there, but all of them clearly assume that their cult traditions had continued in (more or less) unbroken lines from early times on up to their assimilation with Wu-yuan's cult of the Five Manifestations. Although, in general, one has to be cautious with the dates of temple foundings claimed in later sources, as they are often intentionally pushed back in time to enhance the prestige of a tradition,[175] it is not unlikely in these three cases that the temples, like those in Hangchow and Foochow, housed earlier Buddhist or popular types of Wu-t'ung or Wu-sheng spirits prior to their affiliation with Wu-yuan's Wu-hsien cult.

Buddhist influence on the fast-spreading cult of the Five Manifestations is revealed in still other ways. Thus pagodas or similar multi-storied structures, typical of Buddhist architecture and often the sites of minor Buddhist guardian deities, also were characteristic of sanctuaries dedicated to the Wu-hsien. As early as 1082, for instance, years before Wu-yuan's local gods were officially recognized, a pavilion (*ko*) was erected to the left of the city's shrine, which at that time was still called Wu-t'ung miao.[176] Soochow's Ju-i an was rebuilt at a different site in 1225; the new building was a two-storied pavilion with a place of worship for the Five Manifestations below and a room for the transmission of Buddhist scriptures above.[177]

These lofty edifices attached to shrines of the Five Manifestations could be dismissed as a minor feature had they not gained a specific significance: they came to symbolize the central deity of the Five Manifestations, Huakuang. During the thirteenth and fourteenth centuries towers, pavilions,

[173]*Chih-shun Chen-chiang chih* (cited n. 108), 8.8b–9a.
[174]See "Chü-jung hsien Wu-hsien ling-kuan miao-pei," *Fang-chou chi* (cited n. 147), 18.7a–8a.
[175]This is almost certainly the case with the early dates claimed for the first apparition of the Wu-hsien gods by the rival cities of Wu-yuan and Te-hsing; see pp. 170–71, above.
[176]*Hui-chou fu-chih* (cited n. 99), 10.71b.
[177]"Ch'ung-chien Wu-hsien wang tz'u-chi," *Wu-hsien chih* (cited n. 165), 21.17b–18a.

or pagodas dedicated to Hua-kuang sprang up at the Wu-hsien temples in Soochow,[178] Hangchow,[179] Wu-yuan,[180] Hai-yen (Chekiang),[181] and other places.[182]

Hua-kuang's roots are thoroughly Buddhist, though different opinions concerning his identity existed already in canonical Buddhist literature and Six Dynasties Chinese translations of such texts. A Hua-kuang (Padmabrabha) appears in the *Lotus Sutra*, where he is said to be the incarnation of Śāriputra as the Buddha of a blissful era in the distant future.[183] Other sources, such as various versions of the lists of Buddhas of the past, present, and future, speak of Hua-kuang as the first of the one thousand Buddhas of the great *kalpa* of the past.[184] The esoteric Tantric tradition, whose influence permeated Buddhist ritual practice throughout the Sung and later, seems to have entrusted Hua-kuang with more specific functions. According to an explanation attributed to the

---

[178]The first edifice dedicated to Hua-kuang at Soochow's Shang-shan an 上善庵 was erected in 1254. Between 1264 and 1293 a Hua-kuang Pavilion 華光閣 was built in front of the temple, and between 1295 and 1296 another Hua-kuang ko was erected behind the shrine. See *Su-chou fu-chih* (cited n. 159), 15.24a, and Ku Ju-pao 顧儒寶, "Wan-shou tz'u chi 萬壽 祠記," (ca. 1514), *Wu-hsien chih* (cited n. 165), 21.19b–21a. In Wu-chiang 吳江 near Soochow, a Hua-kuang Pavilion was erected in the precincts of the Ch'an monastery Chieh-tai ssu 接待寺 in 1283. See *Wu-chiang hsien chih* 吳江縣志 (1747; Chung-kuo fang-chih ts'ung-shu ed., Taipei: Ch'eng-wen ch'u-pan shê), 11.53b.

[179]In 1270, the new prefect of Lin-an 臨安, Ch'ien Shuo-yu 潛說友, a strong supporter of the cult of the Five Manifestations in the capital, sponsored the erection of a Hua-kuang Tower (華光樓) at the city's Ling-shun miao 靈順廟, on the grounds of the Buddhist Jung-kuo ssu 榮國寺. See *Hsien-ch'un Lin-an chih* (cited n. 107), 73.4a–b and 78.10a–b.

[180]A Hua-kuang lou existed at the Ling-shun miao in Wu-yuan at the latest during the first half of the fourteenth century. See *Hui-chou fu-chih* (cited n. 99), 10.33b. Whether or not this pagoda was identical with the pavilion built in 1082 (see p. 178 above) is not clear. In 1397, when the whole temple complex of the Ling-shun miao was restored, the Hua-kuang Tower too was reconstructed according to old plans. Ibid., 5.43b.

[181]Between 1241 and 1252 a pavilion dedicated to Hua-kuang and the Five Manifestations was built on the grounds of the Buddhist Te-tsang ssu 德藏寺 in Hai-yen 海鹽. This sanctuary and a well nearby attracted large crowds of pilgrims because of the healing powers ascribed to the water of the well. The site therefore became a profitable source of income for the Buddhist monks resident at the temple. See Lu Ying-lung 魯應龍, *Hsien-ch'uang kua-i chih* 閑牕括異志 (Yen-i chih-lin ed.), 3a–b.

[182]For example, in 1276, a Hua-kuang Tower was added to the branch temple of the Five Manifestations in Ts'ang-chou (Kuang-hsi). See "Ts'ang-chou ch'ung-hsiu Wu-hsien miao-chi" (cited n. 149), 2343.4b.

[183]*Miao-fa lien-hua ching* 妙法蓮華經 (T 262) (translated by Kumarajiva in 406), 2.11b–c.

[184]See, e.g., *San-chieh san-ch'ien fo yuan-ch'i* 三劫三千佛緣起 (T 446) (translation ascribed to Kalayasas 畺良耶舍, active in Nanking in the first half of the fifth century), 364c.

famous Taoist master Po Yü-ch'an in a text of the thirteenth century, Hua-kuang figured among the divine attendants of Śākyamuni, who, in the guise of the redoubtable *vajra* bearer Ucchuṣma (Hui-chi chin-kang), subdued Brahmā, the ruler of the Hindu pantheon. Po complains that spirits like the Great Sage Hua-kuang were already being adopted by pseudo-Taoist practitioners into their rituals.[185] A little later, in the supplement to a Taoist hagiography of the exorcistic god Wen Ch'iung composed by Huang Kung-chin in 1274, the Bodhisattva Hua-kuang appears as the fourth[186] and most powerful of the Five Manifestations who, taking possession of an upper-class lady's spirits, dares to oppose a Taoist priest in the most self-confident and insolent manner.[187]

The re-identification of the traditional Buddhist figure of Hua-kuang as one of the Five Manifestations undoubtedly represents another attempt on the part of the Buddhists to gain complete control over a cult that despite all previous efforts at integration had essentially remained a popular one. Yet why, among all the Buddhist divinities, it was Hua-kuang who came to be identified with the Five Manifestations is still a mystery. The rich lore evolving around the worship of relics and tutelary gods at Buddhist pagodas may hold a clue, but this remains to be seen.

Taoist Accommodation

State recognition and Buddhist support made the cult of the Wu-hsien deities respectable in the southern Chinese cities, but to gain acceptance by the Taoists was quite another matter.

Different hagiographical traditions did not blind the Taoists to the fact that Wu-hsien and Wu-t'ung were essentially the same. According to Taoist demonology, both Wu-t'ung and Wu-hsien belonged in the same category

---

[185]*Hai-ch'iung Po chen-jen yü-lu* 海瓊白眞人語錄 (HY 1296), 1.11a–b. On this text, which was compiled by Po Yü-ch'an's 白玉蟾 disciples in the mid-thirteenth century, see Judith M. Boltz, *A Survey of Taoist Literature* (Berkeley: Institute of East Asian Studies, 1987), pp. 177–78.

[186]The number refers to the fourth of the five honorary titles bestowed on the deities as well as to the fourth of the five images of the gods set up in their temples.

[187]"Wen t'ai-pao chuan pu-i 溫太保傳補遺," *Ti-ch'i shang-chiang Wen t'ai-pao chuan* 地祇上將溫太保傳 (HY 779), 2a; Huang Kung-chin's 黃公瑾 1274 postface to this text is preserved in *Tao-fa hui-yuan* (HY 1210), 253.9a–10a.

The Wu-hsien deities.
From the Tao-tzu mo-pao,
a patternbook attributed to Wu Tao-tzu
but probably dating from the Yuan or later.

as the detested Shan-hsiao, which were ruthlessly persecuted.[188] The Taoist ritual manuals of the twelfth and thirteenth centuries abound in methods of protection against Shan-hsiao/Wu-t'ung and methods of curing the different diseases (mostly demonic possession) caused by them.[189] The new cult of the Five Manifestations was, in the eyes of the Taoists, no less demonic, but more difficult to combat.

A thirteenth-century Taoist text describes an encounter between a Taoist master and Hua-kuang, the fourth deity (or more precisely the fourth of the five statues representing the five gods) in the Wu-hsien temple in Ch'ih-chou (Anhui), who had taken possession of a woman's soul, causing her death. Called to account by the Taoist, Hua-kuang retorts: "I was created through the condensation of the breaths of the mountains and rivers, the breaths of the Five Peaks and the Four Streams. I am not comparable to ordinary gods. All you can do against me, Taoist, is to put an end to my cult here in Ch'ih-chou [but you cannot exterminate me]."[190]

However, in fighting the cult a more serious obstacle than Hua-kuang's bodily indestructibility was the fact that the Five Manifestations were approved by the central government. This is the point of an anecdote in the *I-chien chih* that relates how the Five Manifestations tried to force a man in Yang-chou (Kiangsu) to leave his house to them as a temple. When the householder called a Taoist for help, the gods declared: "We have heard that you called an exorcist to punish us. But we are legitimate deities and enjoy our sacrifices with the approval of the state; we would not fear even the Heavenly Master of the Han [i.e., Chang Tao-ling]."[191]

Moreover, the cult's official status and its enormous popularity had begun to attract some members of the Taoist clergy. I have already men-

---

[188]See, e.g., Yuan Miao-tsung 元妙宗, *T'ai-shang chu-kuo chiu-min tsung-chen pi-yao* 太上助國救民總眞祕要 (HY 1217; preface dated 1116), 1.3b, where the Shan-hsiao are explained as the incorrect (stale) essences of the five elements who, arrogating to themselves the titles of sages or saints, have illicit sexual relations with women. Thus in this text the typical characteristics of the Wu-t'ung are attributed to the Shan-hsiao.

[189]See, e.g., ibid., 1.3b and 9.9b–10a, and "Shang-ch'ing yü-shu wu-lei chen-wen 上清玉樞五雷眞文," *Tao-fa hui-yuan* 道法會元 (HY 1210), 59–60.

[190]"Wen t'ai-pao chuan pu-i" (cited n. 187), 1b–2b.

[191]*I-chien chih* (cited n. 87), chih-wu 支戊, 6.10.1098–1100. It should be mentioned that the story nevertheless ends with the exorcism of the impudent "gods" (who turn out to be mere impostors, not the real Five Manifestations) with the image of a Buddhist deity that comes to life to help the householder.

tioned that statues of the Wu-hsien gods were set up in a Soochow Taoist temple in 1209.[192] Po Yü-ch'an, the early-thirteenth-century authority on Taoist liturgy, complained that on the local level, where shamans, mediums, Buddhist priests, and Taoist practitioners competed with each other, Hua-kuang and other deities from the Tantric tradition were adopted into "pseudo" Taoist rituals.[193] And the *T'ien-t'an yü-ko* (*Jade Code of the Celestial Altar*), an annotated Taoist code dating from the late twelfth or early thirteenth century,[194] explicitly warned Taoist practitioners against sacrificing to the Wu-t'ung, praying to them for their divine help, presiding over their temples, or holding mass processions or Taoist rituals in honor of them.[195] But in the long run, neither prohibitions, nor exorcism, nor the destruction of temples could protect the Taoist tradition against the influence of this popular cult. More refined strategies were needed to meet the challenge.

Taoist demonology allowed no categorical distinction between Wu-t'ung and Wu-hsien, but it was possible to differentiate between various grades of Wu-t'ung. The *Feng-tu hei-lü i-ko* (*Statutes of the Black Code of [the Infernal Regions of] Feng-tu*), another Taoist code, dating from around the mid-thirteenth century,[196] presents a tripartite subdivision of the category of

[192]See above, pp. 176–77.

[193]*Hai-ch'iung Po chen-jen yü-lu* (cited n. 185), 1.11a–b.

[194]This code of the Shen-hsiao 神霄 scriptural tradition is contained in *chüan* 249–50 of the *Tao-fa hui-yuan* (HY 1210) and bears the full title: *T'ai-shang t'ien-t'an yü-ko* 太上天壇玉格. The exact date of this text including its commentary (*cheng-i* 正義) is unknown, but since it is referred to in an explanation attributed to Po Yü-ch'an in *Hai-ch'iung Po chen-jen yü-lu*, 2.10b, we know that it existed before that work was compiled in the middle of the thirteenth century.

[195]*T'ai-shang t'ien-t'an yü-ko*, 250.2b and 3b (commentary).

[196]This code is transmitted as *T'ai-hsüan feng-tu hei-lü i-ko* 泰玄酆都黑律儀格 in *chüan* 267–68 of the *Tao-fa hui-yuan*. A note at the beginnning of the text states that it was compiled by Cheng Chih-wei 鄭知微 and annotated by Lu Yeh 盧埜. The exact dates of Cheng Chih-wei and Lu Yeh are unknown, but both of them played a role in the codification of various practices of the Shen-hsiao tradition, among others the methods and laws of the *Black Code of Feng-tu* (*Feng-tu hei-lü* 酆都黑律) contained in *chüan* 264–68 of the *Tao-fa hui-yuan*. Lu Yeh, a disciple of Cheng Chih-wei, continued the Shen-hsiao tradition in the third generation after Lin Ling-su 林靈素 (1076–1120). He was the master of Liu Yü 劉玉 who, in 1258, wrote an account of the methods centered on the divine figure of Wen Ch'iung 溫瓊 ("Ti-ch'i fa 地祇法," *Tao-fa hui-yuan* 253.1a–3b) for Huang Kung-chin's 黃公瑾 collation of this deity's hagiography, *Ti-ch'i shang-chiang Wen t'ai-pao chuan* 地祇上將溫太保傳 (HY 779) (cf. note 187 above). Liu Yü's biography, composed by his disciple Huang Kung-chin, is also contained in the *Tao-fa hui yuan*, 253.10a–12a. The *Black Code of Feng-tu* is at several instances in the text itself (cf., e.g., *Tao-fa hui-yuan*, 265.1b) said to be stricter than the *T'ai-shang t'ien-t'an yü-ko*, and therefore clearly postdates the latter.

Wu-t'ung. According to this text, Wu-t'ung of the highest order are pure concentrations of the breaths of the five elements, while Wu-t'ung of the second order are created through the condensation of the breaths of mountains and rivers, like Hua-kuang, the chief "deity" of this class, who presumptuously derived his appellation from the Buddha's halo. Taoists are warned against revering unpredictable spirits like Hua-kuang, even though they had already received appointments from the Jade Emperor of the Divine Empyrean (Shen-hsiao Yü-ti). The lowest order of Wu-t'ung are defined as concentrations of the stale breaths of weeds and trees. These spirits bring misfortune upon the people in order to extort bloody sacrifices, and have to be subjugated or exterminated.[197] This classification adapted the Taoists' conception of Wu-t'ung to the different traditions of the cult without invalidating their basic demonological taxonomy. Both Wu-t'ung and Wu-hsien still belonged to the same category, and yet there was a difference between those low spirits who had to be persecuted by all means, and those who merely needed to be avoided.

The same passage contains yet another important clue. The reference to Hua-kuang's appointment in the celestial administration of the Jade Emperor points already to the eventual integration of the Wu-t'ung/Wu-hsien into the Taoist pantheon. This integration, however, did not occur all at once, but involved another amazing process of assimilation. In the course of the twelfth and thirteenth centuries, a new Marshal (*yuan-shuai*) of the Taoist pantheon rose to prominence as he battled demons such as the Shan-hsiao/Wu-t'ung. The Divine Agent (*ling-kuan*), Ma Sheng, appears first in a Taoist context in an early-twelfth-century compilation of exorcistic rites of the T'ien-hsin school,[198] but his roots are much older—and they are Buddhist. Ma Sheng is a Chinese translation of the name of Aśvajit,[199] one of the five disciples of Śākyamuni,[200] and the teacher of

---

[197] *T'ai-hsüan feng-tu hei-lü i-ko*, 267.14b–15b.

[198] *T'ai-shang chu-kuo chiu-min tsung-chen pi-yao* (cited n. 188), 7.37b.

[199] See, e.g., Hsüan-tsang 玄奘 (ca. 596–664), *Ta T'ang hsi-yü-chi* 大唐西域記 (T 2087), 9.920c. Other translations of Aśvajit's name are T'iao-ma 調馬, Ma-shih 馬師, or Ma-hsing 馬星. The name is transliterated as O-pi 額鞸, A-shih-p'o-shih 阿濕婆恃, etc.

[200] See, e.g., *Chung-pen ch'i-ching* 中本起經 (T 196; translated in the early third century), 1.147c; *Fo pen-hsing chi-ching* 佛本行集經 (T 190) (translated in the first half of the fifth century), 25.768c.

Śāriputra.[201] Ma Sheng presumably became known to the specialists of popular religion and to the Taoist clergy through the rituals of Buddhist practitioners, and was integrated into both shamanistic rituals and Taoist liturgy.[202]

The Taoists re-explained the deity in terms of their cosmology. They derived Ma Sheng's family name from the character *ma,* corresponding to the South, and explained his personal name by his identification with the sixth star of the Southern Dipper (Nan-tou), which was named Sheng.[203] By that means, Ma Sheng became a stellar deity in the southern sky with special control over the element of fire, who was sent to cleanse the world of demonic influences.

Marshal Ma's iconography reflects the influence of the Tantric Buddhist tradition. He is described as having three eyes and often six arms, as well as three heads.[204] His first attendant is General Ma Ch'ung, a huge white snake (Pai-she ta-chiang).[205] Among his accessories are a golden lance and a three-cornered golden brick, a fire-wheel and a gourd with five hundred fire crows inside, all of which were also drawn by Taoist priests to summon him.[206]

This deity figures prominently in a series of exorcistic rituals of the thirteenth or early fourteenth centuries that are found in the enormous late-fourteenth-century compendium *Tao-fa hui-yuan.*[207] In some of these

[201]See, e.g., *Fo shuo shih-erh yu ching* 佛說十二遊經 (T 195; translated at the end of the fourth century), 147a.

[202]Ma Sheng's role in popular religious tradition is confirmed in *T'ai-shang chu-kuo chiu-min tsung-chen pi-yao* (HY 1217), 7.36b; see also *Hui-t'u san-chiao yuan-liu sou-shen ta-ch'üan* (late sixteenth century ?) 5.9a, which states that the deity was still invoked by the shamans (wu-chia 巫家).

[203]See, e.g., "Cheng-i hung-shen ling-kuan huo-hsi ta-hsien k'ao-chao pi-fa 正一吽神靈官火犀大仙考召祕法," *Tao-fa hui-yuan* 道法會元 (HY 1210), 222.1a–b.

[204]See, e.g., "Ling-kuan Ch'en Ma Chu san-shuai k'ao-chao ta-fa 靈官陳馬朱三帥考召大法," *Tao-fa hui-yuan* (HY 1210), 229.2a. For the multiplicity of arms, heads, and eyes as a characteristic of Tantric Buddhist deities see, e.g., Marie-Thérèse de Mallmann, *Introduction à l'iconographie du Tantrisme bouddhique* (Paris: Centre National de la Recherche Scientifique, 1975), pp. 1–41. I shall describe the influence of the Tantric tradition on the iconography of Marshal Ma in a separate article.

[205]See, e.g., "Cheng-i hung-shen ling-kuan huo-hsi ta-hsien k'ao-chao pi-fa," *Tao-fa hui-yuan,* 222.2a.

[206]See, e.g., ibid., 222.9b–17b.

[207]These rituals make up *chüan* 222–26 and 229–31 of the *Tao-fa hui-yuan* (HY 1210).

ritual texts we already find indications that Ma Sheng—whose main duty was to exterminate the Shan-hsiao/Wu-t'ung—was beginning to take on the qualities of his antagonists.[208] In fact, this Taoist god of fire developed into an orthodox analogue of the Wu-t'ung. As the demonic Wu-t'ung could only be overcome by an equal force, Ma Sheng was also endowed with the Five Supernatural Powers (*wu-t'ung*). Hence the aforementioned late-twelfth- or early-thirteenth-century code, *T'ien-t'an yü-ko*, has the following advice for Taoist exorcists:

> To all demonic gods there exist proper counterparts who easily can subdue those spectres. [If you want to expel] the phantoms of trees such as the Mu-hsia san-lang, sacrifice to the Great Deity Mu-lang (Mu-lang ta-shen)! [If you wish to subdue] Shan-hsiao/Wu-t'ung, appeal to the Five Supernatural Powers of the Divine Agent (Ling-kuan wu-t'ung)![209]

Around the mid-thirteenth century, the Divine Agent, Marshal Ma, also figures in the classification scheme of Wu-t'ung spirits contained in the *Feng-tu hei-lü i-ko*. There, he is included along with Hua-kuang and his group of Wu-hsien within the second order of Wu-t'ung. But as he is said to be the "most efficacious" (*chih-ling*) among the spirits of this class, his Five Supernatural Powers are clearly placed over Hua-kuang's *wu-t'ung*.[210] Thus, Ma Sheng emerged as the Taoist version of *wu-t'ung*: a pure incarnation of the Five Supernatural Powers, emanating from the cosmic energies of a stellar constellation, and untainted by the murky origins of the ordinary Wu-t'ung demons.

The final step of this development still comes as a surprise: Ma Sheng, Hua-kuang, the Five Manifestations, and the Wu-t'ung became one and the same. They merged to form one Taoist deity who could take on five different appearances or one single form.

Three short undated texts in the Taoist Canon and in its supplement, the *Hsü Tao-tsang ching* of 1607, document this complete fusion of Marshal Ma with his former foes. Two of them are scriptures (*ching*) to be recited by a Taoist priest or by the lay believers themselves at domestic

[208]See, e.g., "Cheng-i hung-shen ling-kuan huo-hsi ta-hsien k'ao-chao pi-fa" (cited n. 203), 222.4a, where Ma Sheng is already given the epithet "Hua-kuang Wu-t'ung."
[209]*T'ai-shang t'ien-t'an yü-ko* (cited n. 194), 250.15b.
[210]*T'ai-hsüan feng-tu hei-lü i-ko* (cited n. 196), 267.14b.

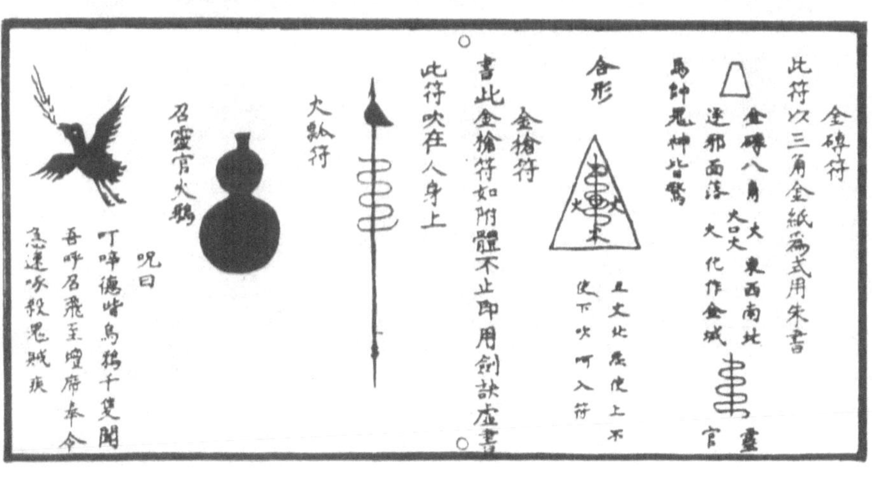

Marshal Ma and the symbols of his power.
Talismans for summoning the deity,
from the Tao-fa hui-yuan, *ch. 222, 226, 229.*

altars,[211] while the third one describes a small ritual of setting out lanterns to the deities.[212] In none of these sources is Ma Sheng referred to by his name (although he is easily identified by his iconography).[213] The Five Manifestations, on the other hand, are listed in two of the texts, the lantern ritual and one of the scriptures, by their official titles, conferred on them under the Southern Sung.[214] In addition, they had each received the title Great Marshal (ta yuan-shuai) of Heaven.[215]

The text of the lantern ritual refers to some of the Five Manifestations' attendants at their original cult center in Wu-yuan.[216] No such allusion to the native place of the gods is made in the two scriptures which describe the descent of the gods in more general terms: the deities are dispatched by the Heavenly Worthy of the Primordial Origin (Yuan-shih t'ien-tsun) to protect distressed humankind from the afflictions of a decadent age, like wars, diseases, natural catastrophes—and demons such as the Shan-hsiao.[217] Depending on the situation, these saviors of the people take on different appearances, sometimes as the Five Manifestations in the form of five Heavenly Marshals, sometimes as the Bodhisattva Hua-kuang, and sometimes in still other guises.[218] Hua-kuang and the Wu-hsien have, in other words, become high-ranking members of the Taoist hierarchy of

[211]These two scriptures are the *Ta-hui ching-tz'u miao-lo t'ien-tsun shuo fu-te Wu-sheng ching* 大惠靜慈妙樂天尊說福德五聖經 (HY 1183) and the *T'ai-shang tung-hsüan ling-pao Wu-hsien kuan Hua-kuang pen-hsing miao-ching* 太上洞玄靈寶五顯觀華光本行妙經 (HY 1436); the latter is contained in the *Hsü Tao-tsang ching* 續道藏經.

[212]*Wu-hsien ling-kuan ta-ti teng-i* 五顯靈觀大帝燈儀 (HY 206).

[213]See ibid., 4b; *Ta-hui ching-tz'u miao-lo t'ien-tsun shuo fu-te Wu-sheng ching* (HY 1183), 1b, 3b; and *T'ai-shang tung-hsüan ling-pao Wu-hsien kuan Hua-kuang pen-hsing miao-ching* (HY 1436), 6a, which all refer to symbols typical of Ma Sheng such as, for example, his three-cornered golden brick, his golden lance, his fire wheel, the white snake, etc.

[214]*Wu-hsien ling-kuan ta-ti teng-i* (HY 206), 1a, gives the titles conferred on the Five Manifestations in 1213; *Ta-hui ching-tz'u miao-lo t'ien-tsun shuo fu-te Wu-sheng ching* (HY 1183), 4a–5a, lists the titles granted to the deities in 1257.

[215]These Taoist titles are the same in both *Wu-hsien ling-kuan ta-ti teng-i* (HY 206), 1a, and *Ta-hui ching-tz'u miao-lo t'ien-tsun shuo fu-te Wu-sheng ching* (HY 1183), 4a–5a.

[216]See *Wu-hsien ling-kuan ta-ti teng-i* (HY 206), 1a, where, among other acolytes, Chou Hsiung (I-ying Chou chiang-chün 翊應周將軍) and Ling-hu Tso (Ling-hu ssu-ch'eng 令狐寺丞) are invoked along with the Five Manifestations. For Chou Hsiung and Ling-hu Tso see also pp. 174–75 above.

[217]See, e.g., *T'ai-shang tung-hsüan ling-pao Wu-hsien kuan Hua-kuang pen-hsing miao-ching* (HY 1436), 6b–7a.

[218]See, e.g., *T'ai-shang tung-hsüan ling-pao Wu-hsien kuan Hua-kuang pen-hsing miao ching* (HY 1436), 4a, where the deities are also said to appear in the guise of Fan-wang 梵王 (Brahmā), Chi-hsiang ju-lai 吉祥如來, and Jih-lu t'ien-chu 日露天主.

celestial beings. The result of their rise to prominence within the Taoist tradition is that Ma Sheng no longer seems to dominate them. In fact, instead of assimilating the popular gods to himself, Ma Sheng is now almost absorbed by them.

If the Taoist codes of the thirteenth century still rejected Hua-kuang and the Five Manifestations, what could have made the Taoists change their mind about them? What made the cult so important that the Taoists finally accepted it without restrictions and included rituals in honor of the Wu-hsien in the representative liturgies of the 1445 edition of the Taoist Canon? When did they carry out this complete rehabilitation?

The first instance of a high-ranking Taoist authority openly approving of the Wu-hsien cult occurred some time in the early fourteenth century, when Chang Yü-ts'ai (d. 1316), the thirty-eighth Heavenly Master of the dominant southern Chinese Cheng-i lineage,[219] bestowed honorary titles and a sword on two deified former caretakers of the ancestral temple of the Five Manifestations in Wu-yuan.[220] But this recognition did not refer directly to the Five Manifestations and seems to foreshadow rather than to reflect the ultimate integration of the deities into the Taoist pantheon documented in the three texts described above.

As mentioned before, none of these texts is dated, but their popular character (in addition to a number of other features)[221] suggests that all were composed at a rather late date, sometime between the late thirteenth and the fourteenth centuries. Both of the scriptures, for example, were

---

[219]For Chang Yü-ts'ai 張與材 see *Han t'ien-shih shih chia* 漢天師世家 (HY 1451) 3.13b–18a. The Heavenly Masters at Lung-hu shan 龍虎山 (Kiangsi) were since 1280 in charge of all Taoist traditions of the South; see ibid., 3.10b.

[220]See the quotation of the *Tsu-tien ling-ying chi* 祖殿靈應集 in *Hui-chou fu-chih* (cited n. 99), 5.44a. Both Hu Fa-shih 胡發世, a devoted supporter of the Wu-hsien cult, and his son Hu Te-sheng 胡德勝, renowned for his unfailing prophesies, were shortly after their deaths enshrined in the Ling-shun miao 靈順廟 and incorporated in the retinue of the Five Manifestations.

[221]For example, in both *Ta-hui ching-tz'u miao-lo t'ien-tsun shuo fu-te Wu-sheng ching* (HY 1183), 1b, and *T'ai-shang tung-hsüan ling-pao Wu-hsien kuan Hua-kuang pen-hsing miao ching* (HY 1436), 6a, 7a, Shun-feng erh 順風耳 and Ch'ien-li yen 千里眼 are named as attendants of the Five Manifestations. These deities do not appear in a Taoist context before the Ming. They do figure, however, in *T'ai-shang lao-chün shuo T'ien-fei chiu-k'u ling-yen ching* 太上老君說天妃救苦靈驗經 (HY 649), 5a, a scripture documenting the Taoist canonization of Ma-tsu 媽祖 which dates from between 1409 and 1414. For more information on this text, see Judith Magee Boltz, "In Homage to T'ien-fei," *Journal of the American Oriental Society* 106.1 (1986), pp. 211–32; Boltz also provides a full translation of this scripture.

intended for wide circulation. People were encouraged to distribute copies
of them, possibly even in printed form, as a particularly meritorious deed.[222]
Simple liturgical texts like these, to be used during household rituals,
were particularly popular during the early decades of the Ming. The lantern ritual belongs to a group of similar works which also seem to have
been revised and edited under the Ming.[223]

Indeed, it was under the reign of the first emperor of the Ming that the
Wu-hsien gods reached the height of their glory. Chu Yuan-chang elevated
the cult to national rank. In 1389, a magnificent temple, the Wu-hsien
ling-shun tz'u, was completed near Nanking, where henceforth state offerings were performed twice a year on the deities' days of honor.[224] Sung
Na (1311–1390) composed the text for a stele that was erected at the temple
building. This inscription refers to Wu-yuan as the place of origin of the
Five Manifestations. The deities are related to the energies of the five
elements, but no mention is made of their connection with the dubious
Wu-t'ung.[225]

The integration of the Five Manifestations into the Taoist liturgy most
probably must be viewed in connection with these events. The Taoists,
who saw themselves as guarantors of dynastic power,[226] could hardly oppose
an imperial cult. The high privileges accorded to the Five Manifestations
by Ming T'ai-tsu left the Taoists no choice but to honor the gods with

[222]See *Ta-hui ching-tz'u miao-lo t'ien-tsun shuo fu-te Wu-sheng ching* (HY 1183), 7b, and *T'ai-shang tung-hsüan ling-pao Wu-hsien kuan Hua-kuang pen-hsing miao-ching* (HY 1436), 9a.

[223]These rituals make up the numbers HY 197–214 in the Taoist Canon. They seem to have constituted only part of more elaborate rituals held on behalf of single households or small groups of believers. Among the deities addressed in these lantern rituals are, besides various stellar divinities, the earth god, the stove god, and also the plague gods. Structure and form of all the texts are similar and show, for instance, close resemblance to *Hung-en ling-chi chen-chün ch'i cheng-hsing teng-i* 洪恩靈濟眞君七政星燈儀 (HY 475), a lantern ritual in honor of the divine brothers Hsü Chih-cheng 徐知證 and Hsü Chih-o 徐知諤, whose cult gained imperial recognition under the Ming emperor Ch'eng-tsu (r. 1403–1425). The latter ritual and a number of similar liturgical texts focusing on the deified brothers were probably composed after the granting of new honorific titles to the deities in 1418. For further infor-mation, see Judith M. Boltz, *A Survey of Taoist Literature*, pp. 52–53.

[224]See, e.g., *Ta Ming hui-tien* 大明會典 (Ch'in-ting ssu-k'u ch'üan-shu ed.), 85.1b.

[225]Sung Na 宋訥, "Ch'ih-chien Wu-hsien ling-shun tz'u chi 敕建五顯靈順祠記," *Hsi-yin chi* 西隱集 (Ssu-k'u ch'üan-shu chen-pen ed.), 5.30a–32a.

[226]On this subject see Anna Seidel, "Imperial Treasures and Taoist Sacraments: Taoist Roots in the Apocrypha," *Tantric and Taoist Studies in Honour of R.A. Stein*, edited by Michel Strickmann (Bruxelles: Institut Belge des Hautes Études Chinoises, 1983), vol. 2, pp. 291–371.

Marshal Ma.
Illustration from
the San-chiao yuan-liu sou-shen ta-ch'üan.

appropriate positions in their pantheon. Under these circumstances, Marshal Ma was no longer needed as an orthodox substitute for the Wu-hsien but became one of the manifold incarnations of the five deities. On the other hand, since earlier Taoist authorities had irrevocably defined the Wu-hsien as a kind of Wu-t'ung, the adoption of the imperially-sponsored gods into the Taoist tradition implied that the Wu-t'ung had to be recognized as well. The Taoist opposition to the nature spirits of the common people had to revert to the oldest form of the demons. This explains why, in the text of the lantern ritual, the Five Manifestations are also openly addressed as Wu-t'ung,[227] whereas the demonic opponents of the Wu-hsien, alias Marshal Ma, are now no longer called Shan-hsiao/Wu-t'ung but simply Shan-hsiao.[228]

Wu-hsien and Wu-t'ung in the Fifteenth and Sixteenth Centuries

Direct imperial patronage of the Five Manifestations did not last long. With the move of the capital to Peking in 1421, the active interest of the dynastic house in the cult seems to have waned significantly. While the Board of Rites continued to supervise the semiannual offerings at the temple outside Nanking, no official temple was erected for the deities in the northern capital. Yet, despite the dwindling significance of the Five Manifestations in the official sphere, their cult retained a respected position in urban religious life. By this time, Wu-hsien temples were also found in north and west China.[229] The traditional temples in the south were re-

---

[227] *Wu-hsien ling-kuan ta-ti teng-i* (HY 206), 1b.

[228] *Ta-hui ching-tz'u miao-lo t'ien-tsun shuo fu-te Wu-sheng ching* (HY 1183), 2a, and *T'ai-shang tung-hsüan ling-pao Wu-hsien kuan Hua-kuang pen-hsing miao-ching* (HY 1436), 6b.

[229] In Peking, for example, a Wu-hsien sanctuary, obviously attached to a Ch'an 禪 monastery, was founded during the Yung-lo period (1404–1425). See Shen Pang 沈榜, *Wan-shu tsa-chi* 宛署雜記 (1593; Peking: Pei-ching ku-chi ch'u-pan shê, 1983), 19.233. Since at least the early fourteenth century, a Wu-hsien temple also existed in Ch'eng-tu 成都 (Szechwan); cf. *Ch'un-yang ti-chün shen-hua miao-t'ung chi* 純陽帝君神化妙通記 (HY 305), 5.10a. The last-mentioned source, a large repository of hagiographical material on Lü Yen 呂嵒 (*tzu* Tung-pin 洞賓), was compiled sometime after 1310 by the Ch'üan-chen 全眞 Taoist Miao Shan-shih 苗善時 (fl. 1288–1324). For further details on this text see Judith M. Boltz, *A Survey of Taoist Literature*, p. 67. It is worth mentioning that in Szechwan, southeast of the city of Ta-tsu 大足 on Mount Shih-men 石門, there is also a niche containing the statue of a one-legged, protective spirit among the numerous Buddhist and Taoist stone sculptures of a temple complex called 'Grotto of the Divine Palace' (Sheng-fu tung 聖府洞). This figure, its face showing the features of an animal or demon and its single leg standing on a fire wheel, is identified in a late inscription dating from 1738 as the "One-legged Great Emperor

peatedly enlarged and restored in the course of the fifteenth century,[230] and the annual festivals in honor of the five gods, with Hua-kuang most prominent among them, continued to attract large crowds in some of the cities.[231]

All along, the illicit cult of the generic Wu-t'ung had never ceased to exist. In the shadow of the prominent Five Manifestations, the belief in the one-legged goblins lived on in the countryside and in urban areas as well. Now, as excitement about the spectacular ascent of the Wu-hsien gods began to subside, the ecstatic cult of the Wu-t'ung with its shamans and mediums regained influence and flourished, particularly in the cities. Hangchow and Soochow emerged as the centers of the revived Wu-t'ung cult in the fifteenth and sixteenth centuries.

Hangchow, renowned for its distinguished Wu-hsien tradition, had always

---

Wu-t'ung" (Tu-chiao Wu-t'ung ta-ti 獨脚五通大帝). The (partly eroded) inscription mentions the image among the old sculptures (dating from the Northern Sung) evidently being restored in 1738, and modern Chinese scholars all seem to agree that the statue indeed dates from the Northern Sung—although their descriptions of the figure itself disagree considerably. See Liu Ch'ang-chiu et al., *Ta-tsu shih-k'o yen-chiu* 大足石刻研究 (Ch'eng-tu: Ssu-ch'uan sheng she-hui k'o-hsueh yuan ch'u-pan shê, 1985), pp. 337, 340, 545, as well as p. 12 for a (deplorably unclear) photograph of the statue; furthermore, Wang Chia yu 工家祐, *Tao-chiao lun-hao* 道教論稿 (Ch'eng-tu: Pa-shu shu-tien, 1987), p. 88. If this is true, we would have here a rare and early example of a one-legged Buddhist Wu-t'ung prior to the spread of the Wu-hsien cult to Szechwan.

[230]See, e.g., "Ch'ung chien Wu-hsien wang tz'u chi," *Wu-hsien chih* (cited n. 165), 21.17a–19a. This inscription was composed on the occasion of the renovation of Soochow's Ju-i an around the middle of the fifteenth century. Soochow's Shang-shan an was refurbished around 1514. See "Wan-shou tz'u chi" (cited n. 178), *Wu-hsien chih*, 21.19a–21a. One of Hangchow's Wu-hsien shrines was enlarged between 1436 and 1449. The temple burned down and was rebuilt again sometime later in the fifteenth century. See *Hsi-hu yu-lan chih* (cited n. 161), 17.232. Another Wu-hsien temple located in Chü-jung 句容 (Kiangsu) was re-erected in 1434. See "Chü-jung hsien Wu-hsien ling-kuan miao-pei," *Fang-chou chi* (cited n. 147), 18.7a–8a. Also, the Ling-shun hsing-kung 靈順行宮 in Sung-chiang 松江 (near Shanghai) was enlarged between 1450 and 1457. The temple was destroyed by a fire between 1465 and 1487, but was re-erected slightly later. See *Sung-chiang fu-chih* 松江府志 (1818), 17.10b, quoting the *Sung-chiang fu-chih* of 1512.

[231]In 1494, for example, the 'Hua-kuang Assembly' (Hua-kuang hui 華光會) of Hangchow attracted so many people that a bridge collapsed under their weight. Thereafter the festival was banned by the local authorities. See *Jen-ho hsien-chih* 仁和縣志 (printed ed. of 1687, in the collection of the Shanghai Library), 29.24b–25b. (Richard von Glahn kindly provided me with a handwritten copy of this passage.) The *Sung-chiang fu-chih* of 1818 (5.9a and 17.10b) cites contemporary gazetteers which show that in the sixteenth century Hua-kuang Assemblies were held in the city every year on the Buddha's birthday, the eighth day of the fourth month.

been a seat of worship of the generic Wu-t'ung as well. As the causes of diseases or as potential bringers of wealth, the spirits had been feared and revered by the people of the city since the Sung.[232] In the sixteenth century, Hangchow's alleys were studded with small Wu-t'ung shrines which received more religious attention than the established temples of the Five Manifestations. Moreover, people worshipping at these small altars cared little about the differences between recognized and unrecognized religious practices, and called the objects of their devotion indiscriminately Wu-t'ung, Wu-sheng, or even Wu-hsien.[233] In popular belief, the borders between the two cult traditions blurred; only members of the gentry class remained concerned about a clear distinction between the imperially sanctioned cult of the Five Manifestations and the illicit worship of the Wu-t'ung. The scholar-official T'ien Ju-ch'eng (*chin-shih* 1526), for example, tried to justify the existence of the state-endorsed temples of the Five Manifestations, as against the countless unauthorized shrines of the Wu-t'ung, by repeating the arguments already put forward in the thirteenth century:[234] the same emperor who recognized and promoted the local deities of Wu-yuan had outlawed the Wu-t'ung as the objects of an illicit cult in 1111. Therefore, to him as well as others of his class, it was clear that Wu-t'ung and Wu-hsien could not be the same, regardless of what the Taoists said and the people believed.[235] T'ien talks about the Wu-t'ung cult with the utmost disgust:

> The people of Hangchow believe above all in the Wu-t'ung gods, whom they also call Five Saints (Wu-sheng). Nothing reliable can be said about the

[232]For example, one episode in the *I-chien chih* (cited n. 87) *san-chih, jen* 壬, 3.1.1484, tells of Wu-t'ung spirits afflicting the household of Han Yen-ku 韓彥古 (d. 1192) with diseases. Another anecdote recounts how the Wu-t'ung—appearing here also in a group of five—stripped a greedy Hangchow brewer of almost all his possessions, although he had originally hoped to gain greater wealth with the help of the deities. *I-chien chih*, supplement, 7.6.1612–13.

[233]See *Hsi-hu yu-lan chih* (cited n. 161), 17.232, and Lu Ts'an 陸粲 (1494–1551), *Keng-ssu pien* 庚巳編 (Ts'ung-shu chi-ch'eng ed.), 5.91.

[234]See the quotation from Hu Sheng's *Hsing-yuan chih* cited above, n. 121.

[235]*Hsi-hu yu-lan chih* 17.232. A similar effort to distinguish between Wu-hsien and Wu-t'ung was, for example, made by Feng Meng-lung 馮夢龍 (1574–1645) in his *Ching-shih t'ung-yen* 警世通言 (Taipei: Shih-chieh shu-chü, 1958), 27.1b. Feng Meng-lung there recounts the anecdote of a young scholar living next door to one of Hangchow's Wu-hsien temples who was lured into licentious practices by two turtle demons posing as the immortals Lü Tung-pin and Ho Hsien-ku. Only through the intercession of Hua-kuang, alias Wu-hsien ling-

origins or names of these spirits, but tradition has it that they like small shrines measuring no more than three or four feet in height and breadth. The five gods, and sometimes also their consorts, share these abodes. The spirits are worshipped in such shrines under trees or in courtyards all over the city, but the cult is particularly flourishing near Hsi-ling Bridge. It is also said that the Wu-t'ung are capable of enticing women into sexual liaisons, conveying wealth, and bringing both fortune and misfortune upon people. People outdo each other in venerating these spirits; this goes so far that they do not dare to utter their name, trembling for fear of inadvertently violating a taboo. This is really one of the most ridiculous customs of Hangchow. . . . I have never believed in heretic gods, but above all I detest the Wu-t'ung. Whenever I see one of their temples, I destroy it. I have already demolished several dozen such shrines, chopped up the statues of these demons and burnt them or immersed them or thrown them into toilets.[236]

Official and private campaigns against the Wu-t'ung were frequently waged during the fifteenth and sixteenth centuries. One particularly interesting example—which also illustrates the intricate relationship between the cult traditions of the Wu-t'ung and the Wu-hsien—is found in an inscription for a Shrine of the Five Manifestations near Chü-jung city written by the scholar Chang Ning (*chin shih* 1454). Chang relates that between 1241 and 1250 an official branch-temple of Wu-yüan's Ling-shun miao replaced an unofficial Wu-t'ung sanctuary that had an ancient cult tradition of its own. After the recognized temple was destroyed during the fighting at the end of the Yuan dynasty, the Wu-hsien cult was moved to the house of a villager. But in 1435 sixty-four members of the local gentry tried to outlaw this private sanctuary because it had turned into the center of a spirit-medium cult (that is, the features of the original Wu-t'ung cult had reappeared in the worship of the Wu-hsien gods). An interrogation of the descendants of the former caretakers of the Ling-shun miao,

---

kuan, could the fraudulent spirits finally be unmasked and punished, and the youth's health be restored. Hua-kuang is thus presented as an antagonist of precisely the lascivious habits that were said to be characteristic of the Wu-t'ung. The story evokes the Taoist Wu-t'ung fighter Marshal Ma, whose qualities, as we have seen, were later transferred to Hua-kuang and the Five Manifestations. It also parallels Hua-kuang's depiction as a subduer of lewd spirits in the *Nan-yu chi*, for which see pp. 204, 206 below.

[236]T'ien Ju-ch'eng 田汝成 (*chin-shih* 1526), *Hsi-hu yu-lan chih-yü* 西湖遊覽志餘 (Shanghai: Chung-hua shu-chü, 1958), 26.476–77.

however, confirmed the original relationship of the privately maintained spirit-medium cult with Wu-yuan's Five Manifestations. Therefore in 1436 the authorities returned the old temple grounds to the people and initiated fundraising for the reconstruction of the Wu-hsien temple.[237]

Campaigns against the Wu-t'ung medium cult also occured in Soochow. In 1445 the prefect, Li Ts'ung-chih, tried to eradicate the so-called "Tea Banquets" (*ch'a-yen*) people held in homage to the Wu-t'ung;[238] another attempt to suppress the cult in the city was launched by the prefect Ts'ao Feng in 1494,[239] but in the early sixteenth century the cult there was thriving as never before, and rumor had it that both prefects had fallen victim to the spirits' revenge.[240] Soochow's largest Wu-t'ung shrine was located fifteen *li* southwest of the city on Mount Leng-ch'ieh, popularly called Mount Shang-fang. Though not related to Wu-yuan's cult of the Five Manifestations, it was founded between 1265 and 1274 on the premises of an ancient Buddhist temple, the Leng-ch'ieh ssu, whose famous seven-storied pagoda still is one of the major attractions of Soochow,[241] and became the center of Soochow's cult to the generic Wu-t'ung from the fifteenth through the nineteenth centuries. Later sources testify that illicit mediumistic practices centering on these spirits were actively supported by the Bud-

[237]"Chü-jung hsien Wu-hsien ling-kuan miao-pei," *Fang-chou chi* (cited n. 147), 18.7a–8a. Chang defends the Wu-hsien against the accusation of taking possession of people. In his opinion either "other spirits" (*i-ch'i* 異氣) merely pretending to be the Five Manifestations had spoken through the mouths of the mediums, or the suspicion of the patricians was completely unfounded.

[238]*Ku-su chih* 姑蘇志 (1506; Chung-kuo shih-hsüeh ts'ung-shu ed., Taipei: Hsüeh-sheng shu-chü, 1965), 3.40b, 40.27b, and Yang Hsün-chi 楊循吉, *Su-chou fu tsuan-hsiu shih-lüeh* 蘇州府纂修識略 (1506; Yang Nan-feng hsien-sheng ch'üan-chi 楊南峰先生全集 ed.), 3.9a. (I am grateful to Richard von Glahn for making this source available to me.)

[239]See *Keng-ssu pien* (cited n. 233), 5.98; Han Pang-ch'i 韓邦奇 (1479–1555), "Chia-i ta-fu tu-ch'a yuan yu fu-tu yü-shih Hsi-yeh Ts'ao kung mu-chih ming 嘉議大夫都察院右副都御史西野曹公墓誌銘," *Yuan-lo chi* 苑洛集 (Ch'in-ting ssu-k'u ch'üan-shu ed.), 4.12b–13a.

[240]See Yang Hsün-chi, *Su-chou fu tsuan-hsiu shih-lüeh* (1506), 3.9a, and Ch'u Jen-huo 褚人穫, *Chien-hu pa-chi* 堅瓠八集 (Pi-chi hsiao-shuo ta-kuan, hsü-pien ed.), 4.9a–b, quoting the lost Ming work *T'iao-teng chi-i* 挑燈集異.

[241]See *Ku-su chih*, 9.5a; 27.25a; 29.35b–36a; *Ku-chin t'u-shu chi-ch'eng, Chih-fang tien* (cited n. 126), 677.30c. The pagoda of the Leng-ch'ieh ssu 楞伽寺, founded in 608, was rebuilt in 978, and once more restored between 1636 and 1640, but its tenth-century structure remains virtually unchanged. The brick building represents one of the few examples of early Sung Buddhist architecture in Soochow. See Wang Te-ch'ing 王德慶, "Su-chou Leng-ch'ieh ssu t'a 蘇州楞伽寺塔," *Wen-wu* 文物 10 (1983), pp. 83–85.

dhist monks resident at the temple. The arrest of monks in connection with the persecution of the worship of the Wu-t'ung at Mount Leng-ch'ieh is mentioned in a text about Chiang-nan's governor T'ang Pin (1627–1687), who in 1686 led a devastating campaign against the cult center.[242] In 1839 Yü-ch'ien (1793–1841), the Manchu governor of Chiang-nan, considering the punishment of shamans, mediums, and a few monks inadequate to eradicate the cult, even proposed the complete destruction of the Leng-ch'ieh ssu and the Pao-chi yuan, a monastery on the south-eastern slope of the mountain that was also involved in the worship of the Wu-t'ung.[243]

Soochow's popular cult to the Wu-t'ung in the sixteenth century was stigmatized by Lu Ts'an (1494–1551) in his *Keng-ssu pien*:

The demonic spirits venerated by the people of Wu are called Five Saints (Wu-sheng), or Divine Dukes Five Manifestations (Wu-hsien ling-kung). In the villages they are called Five Gentlemen (Wu-lang). Like the Shan-hsiao and Mu-k'o these spirits belong in the category of old mountain essences. According to the *I-chien chih* they are also named One-legged Wu-t'ung (Tu-chiao Wu-t'ung) and therefore I think they must be identical with what the classical tradition describes as K'uei, the One-legged (K'uei i-tsu). In other

[242]Tung Han 董含 (*chin-shih* 1655), "Ko yin-tz'u 革淫祠," *Ch'un-hsiang ch'ui-pi* 蓴鄉贅筆 (Shuo-ling ed.), 3.25b. T'ang Pin's 湯斌 request for an imperial ordinance banning worship of the Wu-t'ung forever, which includes a detailed report on the religious activities on Mount Leng-ch'ieh 楞伽山, is found in "Hui yin-tz'u i cheng jen-hsin shu 毀淫祠以正人心疏," *T'ang-tzu i-shu* 湯子遺書 (Ch'in-ting ssu-k'u ch'üan-shu ed.), 2.55b–58b.

[243]Yü-ch'ien 裕謙, "Ch'ing hui Shang-fang shan wu-t'ung yin-tz'u shu-kao 請毀上方山五通淫祠疏稿," *Yü Ching-chieh kung i-shu* 裕靖節公遺書 (Taipei: Ch'eng-wen ch'u-pan shê, 1969), 3.1a–3b. See also Yü-ch'ien's earlier proscription of the cult dating from 1835, "Chin wu-t'ung yin-tz'u ping shih-wu hsieh-shuo shih 禁五通淫祠並師巫邪說示," ibid., 3.29a–33a, and his suggestion that the Pao-chi yuan 寶積院 be transformed into a Confucian sanctuary for paragons of chastity and filial piety, which was submitted in the third month of 1839, only five months before his request to destroy the temples: "Ch'ih-i Pao-chi ch'an-yuan kai-chien chieh-hsiao tz'u 飭議寶積禪院改建節孝祠," ibid. 6.14a–16a. It is not clear whether Yü-ch'ien's proposal was in fact approved and acted on. Yet today no trace of the Pao-chi yuan is left at the mountain, while the Leng-ch'ieh ssu 楞伽寺 was in part rebuilt during the final years of the Ch'ing. See Wang Te-ch'ing, "Su-chou Leng-ch'ieh shan t'a 蘇州楞伽寺塔," *Wen-wu*, 10 (1983), p. 83. In any case, it is worth mentioning that the Wu-t'ung and their mother are still being worshipped in two side-rooms off the main hall of today's Leng-ch'ieh ssu. Neither altars nor icons are found there; instead in each room a large bed is set up, one for the mother, the other one—covered with five quilts—for her five sons. Personal communication from Richard von Glahn.

regions the same spirits are worshipped as Hsiao Dukes (Hsiao kung); this name is directly derived from the term Shan-hsiao.[244]

These five goblins are given the titles of count or duke. Their females are titled ladies (*Fu-jen*), and their dam is called Grand Lady (*T'ai fu-jen*) or Grand Dowager (*T'ai-ma*). The people fear these spirits very much. Each household keeps an altar dedicated to them, with statues resembling kings and imperial consorts. The poor worship the gods on painted tablets called "holy tablets" (*sheng-pan*). [The Wu-t'ung] receive their sacrifices together with Kuan-yin and the City and Earth gods (*Ch'eng-huang T'u-ti chih shen*). Also worshipped is Ma Hsia, who is said to be the gods' retainer. At all offerings, animal sacrifices are presented, music is played, and the shamans (*wu-che*) sing ballads (*ko-tz'u*) telling of the gods' manifestations. [People] say the gods rejoice at hearing these songs. [These celebrations] are called "Tea Banquets" (*ch'a-yen*), or, if they include particularly sumptuous offerings, "Paper [Money] Burnings" (*shao-chih*). Even the members of the gentry class participate in these offerings. Ordinary people, however, exhaust their fortunes, and must often take loans, lest their offerings should fall behind those of the wealthy.

In every matter the gods are beseeched for their help, and whenever people want to convey wishes, "Tea Banquets" are held in order to obtain [the demons'] blessing. Each time there happens to be a favorable result, the gods are credited with it; whenever anything turns out badly, the devotees accuse themselves of not having been sincere enough. Never would anyone dare to reproach the gods. If somebody falls ill, the oracle of the shamans invariably says that the person has incurred the wrath of the Five Saints. Often [the shamans try to] prevent the sick from taking medicine, and those who believe them forsake medical help and resign themselves to death. Then there are those women who are versed in techniques such as "controlling fright" (*shou-ching*) and "visualizing spirits" (*chien-kuei*) which they claim they have been secretly taught by the Five Saints. These women have illicit sexual relations with the goblins.

It is said that these sprites have their den at Mount Leng-ch'ieh west of the city. The people living there report that torches often emerge from the lake and disappear again. They also say that sometimes five noblemen can be seen who, accompanied by their consorts and retinue, enter old tombs where

---

[244]For this allusion to the relationship between the Five Manifestations and the archaic Shan-hsiao see also p. 172 above.

they hold merry feasts and get extremely drunk. These parties usually continue far into the night before they break up.

Mostly these demons take advantage [of situations] of weakness or difficulty in order to haunt [the people]. Then they shift furniture, break down doors, steal valuables, or even set fire to houses. As the *Yu-yang tsa-tsu* states: the Shan-hsiao are capable of burning human dwellings.[245] [These demons], by nature, also like to lure women into illicit sexual relationships. [Those women] mostly die young. When [the victims are] possessed [by the demon], they fall down as if drunk. When they regain consciousness, they say that they have seen a magnificently dressed nobleman surrounded by an impressive guard in a royal palace. His consorts and more than a hundred ladies-in-waiting were sitting on both sides, all of them marvellously made up and beautiful, and the hall was pervaded by the exuberant sounds of flutes and drums. When [the spirit] had sex [with the women], they had a feeling as if a plank, cold as water, was lying down on them. Sometimes the husbands of such women do not dare to sleep with [their wives] any more. Those who still insist on sharing a bed with their spouses find themselves thrown to the floor by the sprite. The deceitfulness and lust of these demons is beyond description.[246]

These descriptions of illicit religious activities focusing on the Wu-t'ung in sixteenth-century Hangchow and Soochow demonstrate the remarkable continuity of this popular cult tradition from the Sung through the late Ming. In fact, none of the features characterizing the cult of the demonic imps in Hung Mai's anecdotes from the twelfth century are missing in these sixteenth-century accounts. The spirits' ability to enrich their devotees on the one hand and their mischievousness on the other were, as we have seen, already familiar themes in Sung popular belief. Above all, however, the feared sexual inclinations of the Wu-t'ung, involving both the demonic possession of women and the existence of medium cults, are still found at the core of the Wu-t'ung cult in the sixteenth century.

Evidently neither Buddhism, nor the state, nor Taoism had succeeded in eradicating these entrenched popular beliefs, and the respectable cult of the Five Manifestations had not eclipsed religious worship of the ambiguous Wu-t'ung. Moreover, Lu Ts'an's account as well as other reports

[245]Cf. *Yu-yang tsa-tsu* 酉陽雜俎, *ch'ien-chi* 前集, 15.144.
[246]*Keng-ssu pien* (cited n. 233), 5.91–93.

show that even members of the upper class were involved in the worship of the Wu-t'ung.[247] Although it is not clear from such statements how frequently the elite participated in Wu-t'ung offerings, it is unquestionable that the gentry shared at least some basic beliefs with the common people. Lu Ts'an's description reveals not the slightest doubts about the existence of the demons and their predilections for women, and the same can be said about most other accounts of the Wu-t'ung cult written by highly educated persons. Yet these beliefs took quite different forms. On a low social level, the concept of sexual intercourse with the spirits could corroborate the status of female mediums, while the same motif served as an explanation for serious psychosomatic disorders of upper-class women. This disparity is illustrated by the following two examples.

One dates from a considerably earlier period, but seems to support perfectly Lu Ts'an's remarks about the medium cult of the Wu-t'ung in Soochow. It is Hung Mai's somewhat ironic story about a low-class female shaman named Ssu-niang in twelfth-century Hangchow. This woman was regularly possessed by a spirit called a Wu-lang who, speaking through her mouth, made unfailing predictions in all doubtful matters. Owing to the Wu-lang's inspiration, Ssu-niang soon became a well-known medium whose fame eventually also reached upper-class circles. One day, she was invited to the house of Han Shih-liang, the brother of Han Shih-chung (1089–1151), to demonstrate her prophetic gift. Unfortunately, however, on just this occasion the Wu-lang did not respond and thus completely compromised the woman. Only several days later did the spirit resume communication with his medium and excuse himself: "The other day," he explained, "I was refused entrance by the door gods; therefore I couldn't come in."[248]

The second example is found in Lu Ts'an's *Keng-ssu pien*. It recounts the story of a female descendant of Li Po-sheng, a high-ranking official under Chu Yuan-chang's rival Chang Shih-ch'eng (1321–1367). On her

---

[247]Apart from Lu Ts'an's testimony, translated above, another statement concerning the participation of members of the upper class in the unrecognized form of the cult is found in Kuei Chuang's 歸莊 (1613–1673) highly ambivalent inscription for a Wu-sheng shrine in his native K'un-shan 崑山 (Kiangsu): "Ch'ung-chien Wu-sheng miao men-yin 重建五聖廟門引," *Kuei Chuang chi* 歸莊集 (Peking: Chung-hua shu-chü, 1962), 10.511–13.
[248]*I-chien chih* (cited n. 87), *chia* 甲, 11.13.97.

wedding day this woman was possessed by a Wu-sheng spirit. Lu Ts'an describes the incident in the following words:

> She suddenly jumped out of her litter and, dancing and singing as if she were mad, referred to herself as a Wu-sheng. The family anxiously prepared offerings, [but] the young wife ran out of the wedding chamber, singing hymns in praise [of the Wu-t'ung] like a shaman. On the family altar stood several offering-cups filled with wine, [but] the woman whirled across them without overturning one of them. [Later] she sometimes even cut herself with knives, [but] always remained uninjured. This woman still comes to my house from time to time, [but] her mind is completely deranged.[249]

These accounts clearly show the diverging views of low-class people and members of the higher classes concerning the relationship between women and Wu-t'ung incubi: what one side welcomed as divine inspiration was conceived by the other in the negative terms of mental disorder caused by demonic possession.

Higher-class members of society could not openly revere the Wu-t'ung. Even if they (or members of their families) did try to appease the spirits with private sacrifices, they had to denounce these practices publicly. At best, they could affirm the Five Manifestations, the civilized form of the cult. Then, however, it was important to draw a strict line of division between Wu-hsien and Wu-t'ung, as did the Hangchow patrician T'ien Ju-ch'eng. On the other hand, any avowal of the close relationship between Wu-t'ung and Wu-hsien by members of the higher social strata was necessarily expressed as a condemnation of both forms of the cult. This radical stance was taken, for example, by Lu Ts'an in his venomous account of the Wu-t'ung and, later, by T'ang Pin (1627–1687), who, as governor of Chiang-nan, led a rigorous campaign against the cult center in 1668 and submitted a detailed report to the throne on the religious activities at Mount Leng-ch'ieh.[250]

At the lower end of the social hierarchy, these matters were viewed differently. The supporters of the medium cult sought to bridge the gap between Wu-t'ung and Wu-hsien. By appropriating the iconographical

---

[249]*Keng-ssu pien,* 5.96.
[250]T'ang Pin, "Hui yin-tz'u i cheng jen-hsin shu," (cited n. 242), 2.57a.

features of the Wu-hsien for the Wu-t'ung and by adopting orthodox figures like the Taoist Marshal Ma the declared followers of the Wu-t'ung spirits tried to shield their cult from persecution—as the people in the outskirts of Chü-jung escaped prohibition of their cult by proving that it once had been located in an officially recognized branch-temple of Wu-yuan's Ling-shun miao.

In other words, the diverging attitudes characterizing the intricate relationship between the two forms of the cult were not only often diametrically opposed but sometimes even resulted in plain misunderstandings. The unity of the cult emphasized by at least a part of the Wu-t'ung following in order to justify their activities was completely unacceptable to middle- and upper-class citizens who were concerned with not getting openly involved in the disreputable practices of spirit mediums. Therefore, we face the seemingly paradoxical situation that the Wu-hsien and Wu-t'ung were the same (for the lower classes), and yet different (for the upper class).

On the other hand, the discrepant forces working behind these tendencies of separation and integration kept both traditions alive and bound them together. The constant interplay between the traditions produced ideas that were shared by different social strata, though also evaluated in different ways. As the lore and iconography of the Wu-hsien were assimilated by the following of the Wu-t'ung, certain features of Wu-t'ung beliefs also influenced the ideas people held about the Wu-hsien, although these Wu-t'ung reminiscences had to be given new, extenuating interpretations in order to maintain the respectability of the Five Manifestations.

The ecstatic tradition of the Wu-t'ung was influential enough to attract the attention of people of disparate social levels, all the more so as nobody, regardless of high or low birth, really doubted the demonic powers of these gods. But the standards of public morals set by a small cultured elite permitted no positive affirmation of these beliefs and the cultic practices connected with them. We know of them only through utterly negative descriptions. Hua-kuang, the Five Manifestations, and Marshal Ma, whose personalities had been shaped and civilized through Buddhist concepts and Taoist explanations, suited the general sense of propriety and were accepted—as long as they were not associated with the Wu-t'ung whose immoral properties were a threat to the sense of bourgeois decency.

The urban culture of sixteenth-century southern China clearly shows that the distinction betweeen Wu-t'ung and Wu-hsien cannot be defined by the fact that different social strata adhered exclusively to one or the other form of the cult. Rather we find that Wu-t'ung and Wu-hsien marked two sides of one coin: the ecstatic tradition of the Wu-t'ung represented the unofficial side of the cult, which was not allowed public expression, whereas the generally accepted figures of Hua-kuang and the Five Manifestations had already entered the realm of romance and opera.

TRACES OF THE CULT TRADITION IN THE *NAN-YU CHI*

At the beginning of this study I asserted that the *Nan-yu chi* cannot be understood apart from the Wu-t'ung/Wu-hsien cult. Now that we have a better idea of the complex history of the cult, let us see in what guise or disguise it appears in the novel and in the figure of the novel's hero, Hua-kuang.

To begin with the most problematic issue, namely the dubious origins of the cult: how, if at all, are the Shan-hsiao and the Wu-t'ung, Hua-kuang's one-legged ancestors, introduced?

We find that both do appear in the novel, although their identity is completely blurred. The Shan-hsiao are alluded to in the episode describing Hua-kuang's rebirth in Wu-yuan in a family named Hsiao. This account is clearly modelled on the unofficial tradition that Wu-yuan's gods were five brothers whose family name was Hsiao. Although we have seen that this legend expressed the old belief in the identity of the Shan-hsiao with the Wu-t'ung and Wu-hsien,[251] the *Nan-yu chi* does not elaborate on that theme. Were it not for the parallel account transmitted in popular lore, this indirect allusion in the novel would altogether have escaped our notice.

The term *wu-t'ung*, on the other hand, is used early on to indicate Hua-kuang's main characteristic. Just before his first incarnation as the son of the late King of Horse-Ear Mountain, Hua-kuang (alias Miao chi-hsiang) receives the Five Supernatural Powers from the Tathāgata. The Buddha's words on this occasion are:

> Herewith, I endow you with the Five Supernatural Powers (*wu-t'ung*).
> First, you will have Power in Heaven (*t'ung-t'ien*)—you will be able to
>   wander through the heavenly regions without hindrance.

[251]P. 172 above.

> Secondly, you will have Power on Earth (*t'ung-ti*)—you will break through earth without hindrance.
>
> Thirdly, you will have Power in Air (*t'ung-feng*)—you will be invisible as air.
>
> Fourthly, you will have Power in Water (*t'ung-shui*)—nothing will obstruct you in water, and
>
> Fifthly, you will have Power in Fire (*t'ung-huo*)—you will remain unscathed by fire.[252]

Obviously, this is simply a popularization of the canonical Buddhist explanation of the *wu-t'ung*,[253] which is here combined with the Buddhist Five Elements. If we read immediately afterwards that these Five Supernatural Powers materialize in the form of five fire balls (*wu t'uan huo*) as Hua-kuang enters the womb of Lady Horse-Ear,[254] we realize that the *wu-t'ung* are indeed Hua-kuang's very essence. On the other hand, any direct allusion to the mischievous Wu-t'ung goblins is consistently avoided throughout the novel.

Some of the peculiarities of the Wu-t'ung demons, however, had to be explained, or rather explained away, all the more so because they apparently still tainted Hua-kuang's character. There is first of all the notorious fondness for women which Hua-kuang inherited from the Wu-t'ung. This delicate subject is taken up twice in the novel, and in both cases it turns out that Hua-kuang had been wrongfully suspected.

In section six a demon named General Fire Whirl (Huo-p'iao chiang) broods vengefully because the King of the Country of a Thousand Fields (Ch'ien-t'ien kuo wang) has torn down his shrine and erected instead a temple to Hua-kuang. Therefore, when the king's daughter comes to offer incense in the new temple and falls in love with the statue of Hua-kuang, Fire Whirl avails himself of the opportunity to cause trouble for Hua-kuang. Fire Whirl abducts the girl and tries to force her to have sex with him. Of course, everything points to Hua-kuang as the abductor, and he is formally accused of the crime. But fortunately our hero succeeds in freeing the princess and subduing Fire Whirl, and thereby exonerates himself.[255]

---

[252]*Hua-kuang t'ien-wang nan-yu chih-chuan, chüan* 1, section 1.8b.
[253]See p. 158 above.
[254]*Hua-kuang t'ien-wang nan-yu chih-chuan, chüan* 1, section 1.9a.
[255]Ibid., *chüan* 2, section 6.15b–21b.

Hua-kuang subduing the white snake.
Illustration from the Ming edition
of the Nan-yu chi *in the British Library.*

What is interesting is that this episode reads like a revision of the thir-teenth-century Taoist text mentioned briefly earlier, which actually did accuse Hua-kuang of such an act.[256] On the occasion of his taking office, the vice governor of Ch'ih-chou (Anhui) paid a formal visit to the local Wu-hsien temple. There it happened that his concubine was struck by the beauty of the statue of the fourth deity (Hua-kuang), fainted, and sank dead to the ground. When all attempts to revive her had failed, a Taoist, Ts'ao K'o-fu, was called to perform a ritual of investigation. Soon the corpse rose, and the possessing spirit, identifying himself as Hua-kuang, explained that the woman's amorous feelings for him had enabled him to seize her souls. Then Ts'ao K'o-fu, with the aid of the divine general Wen Ch'iung,[257] destroyed Hua-kuang's cult in Ch'ih-chou. When he cut off the head of Hua-kuang's statue, blood flowed from the image of clay.[258]

In the *Journey to the South* Hua-kuang turns out to be innocent in a second instance as well. In section thirteen of the novel an evil Taoist, calling himself the Great Immortal of Falling Stones (Lo-shih ta-hsien),[259] takes on the appearance of Hua-kuang and gains access to the bedroom of a girl, Huang Pai-chiao. When the real Hua-kuang overwhelms the impostor spirit in the girl's chamber, the true identity of the Taoist is revealed: a demon in the form of a huge white snake coils on the bed. The monster submits, and Hua-kuang, hiding it in his golden lance, makes it into one of his subservient spirits.[260] This is Hua-kuang's attendant, General White Snake (Pai-she ta-chiang), known from the Taoist ritual manuals mentioned earlier.[261]

The motif of one-leggedness, another unmistakable feature of the Wu-t'ung, also appears in an episode of the *Nan-yu chi*. In the last section of the novel the Buddha is concerned that Hua-kuang has still not converted to Buddhism, despite all his promises. He dispatches his Arhats to fetch

---

[256]Cf. p. 182 above.

[257]A study of this deity, who like Hua-kuang, the Five Manifestations, and many other temple gods also played a role in both popular religion and Taoism, was recently published by Paul Katz, "Wen Ch'iung—The God of Many Faces," *Han-hsüeh yen-chiu* 漢學研究 8:1 (1990), pp. 183–219.

[258]"Wen t'ai-pao chuan pu-i," *Ti-ch'i shang-chiang Wen t'ai-pao chuan* (cited n. 187), 1b–2b.

[259]*Hua-kuang t'ien-wang nan-yu chih-chuan*, chüan 4, section 13.2a.

[260]Ibid., *chüan* 4, section 13.6a–8b.

[261]Cf. p. 185 above.

The lion carrying Hua-kuang's leg
to the Buddha.
Illustration from the Ming edition
of the Nan-yu chi *in the British Library.*

the recalcitrant disciple. Since they think it highly improbable that Hua-kuang will comply, the Arhats resort to a ruse. They descend into the world as illusionists and, performing a great many tricks, like cutting off their legs and their arms, immediately attract Hua-kuang's attention. Fascinated, Hua-kuang wants to imitate them and ends up really cutting off his own right leg. Instantly, a little lion, magically produced by the disguised Arhats, appears, grabs the leg, and carries it off to the Buddha. Hua-kuang has no alternative but to jump on his fire and wind wheels, follow the lion—and convert to Buddhism—in order to regain his physical integrity.[262]

Thus, the improper qualities of the Wu-t'ung demons—their name, their sexual misconduct, and their one-leggedness—are indeed mentioned in the novel, but never to the detriment of Hua-kuang. He is convincingly exonerated from immoral conduct, his loss of a leg is plausibly explained, and the term *wu-t'ung* itself is used only in the Buddhist sense of command over the Five Elements. All suspect qualities are given harmless or humorous explanations.

By contrast, the *Journey to the South* is quite explicit about Hua-kuang's relationship with the cult of the Five Manifestations. The text refers to the exact place of origin of the cult and lists the honorary names of the five deities. But, instead of the local legend of the origin of the Wu-hsien cult in Wu-yuan, the novel offers its own version of the descent of the gods.

As we have seen, Wu-yuan's tradition held that the five gods appeared to Wang Yü in 886 and asked him to dedicate a shrine to them.[263] The story in the *Nan-yu chi* has nothing in common with this tradition. In the novel, Hua-kuang's third incarnation takes place in Wu-yuan. His Five Supernatural Powers forming a dim halo of light, he enters the womb of the ogress impersonating Lady Hsiao. On the twenty-eighth of the ninth lunar month, the Lady gives birth to a lump of flesh that looks like the stomach of a cow. The father is desperate and tries in vain to get rid of the inauspicious object. Finally he is persuaded by a Buddhist monk (in reality Hua-kuang's teacher, the Buddha of the Royal Shine of the Fire Flame) to cut the lump open, whereupon he finds five sons enclosed in it. The children are named Hsien-tsung, Hsien-ming, Hsien-cheng, Hsien-chih,

---

[262] *Hua-kuang t'ien-wang nan-yu chih-chuan, chüan* 4, section 18.25a–28a.
[263] P. 171 above.

Hua-kuang and his brothers.
Illustration from the Ming edition
of the Nan-yu chi
in the British Library.

and Hsien-te.[264] They grow up within a few days, and four of the brothers leave home in order to become monks. Only one of them, Hsien-te, or Hua-kuang,[265] stays with the parents.[266]

This is the only allusion to the Wu-hsien cult of Wu-yuan in the *Journey to the South*. The Wu-hsien gods, at least four of the five, disappear soon after their birth and receive no more attention. As the narrative proceeds with the imprisonment of Hua-kuang's mother and his desperate search for her, the scene of the story shifts away from Wu-yuan. Wu-yuan and the local cult of the Five Manifestations are thus reduced to a single episode in Hua-kuang's human existence.

In the *Nan-yu chi* Hua-kuang in fact represents all five deities. When, after having redeemed his mother from her unsavory appetite for human flesh, he finally submits to the Buddha, he is invested as the Great Emperor of Superior Morality among the Buddhas and Divine Agent of the Five Manifestations (Fo-chung shang-shan Wu-hsien ling-kuan ta-ti).[267] Thus Hua-kuang has become the "One Manifestation" of the Five Manifestations, the incarnation of the Wu-hsien gods.

The relative marginality of the Five Manifestations in the *Nan-yu chi* also seems to reflect the actual historical situation of the cult at the time the novel was composed. As we have seen in the preceding section, the deities, who once enjoyed the patronage of the first emperor of the Ming, largely lost their preeminent role in the official sphere during the fifteenth and sixteenth centuries,[268] while the continuing popularity of the Five Manifestations among the people appears to have mainly been a reflection of the popularity of Hua-kuang.

Incorporating in a sense both the Wu-t'ung and the Wu-hsien, Hua-kuang's personality in the novel comes close to the composite Taoist deity that was created by the fusion of all these gods and demons with their

[264]These are the names bestowed by the Sung court on Wu-yuan's deities on the occasion of their promotion to kings in 1202; cf. *Hui-chou fu-chih* (cited n. 99), 5.43a.

[265]The fact that Hua-kuang is identified here with the fifth name instead of the fourth (Hsien-chih) shows that it had already become unclear which of the five deities precisely he represented. Hua-kuang was already conceived as the embodiment of all five of the Wu-hsien; see below.

[266]*Hua-kuang t'ien-wang nan-yu chih-chuan*, chüan 2, section 8.22b–27a.

[267]Ibid., *chüan* 4, section 18.28a.

[268]P. 192 above.

fierce subduer Marshal Ma, described earlier. Indeed, in the *Nan-yu chi* this Taoist general becomes Hua-kuang's innermost identity. His first incarnation, as the son of the Goddess of Horse-Ear Mountain (*Ma*-erh shan), and his appointment as the Great Marshal of the Troops and Horses (Ping-*ma* ta yuan-shuai) during his second existence are hints.[269] A much clearer indication of Hua-kuang's identity with Marshal Ma is found in Hua-kuang's fiery nature. Note the Taoist description of Marshal Ma: "Now, as for the Divine Agent (*ling-kuan*) whose family name is Ma, and whose personal name is Sheng, the ritual masters of today know only [this deity's] name without ever scrutinizing [the circumstances of] his creation. . . . [This spirit] is nothing other than the essence of the fire of the south, the king of fire, the prime breath of fire."[270]

Hua-kuang has many other characteristics in the novel that are also associated with the Taoist Marshal Ma: his three eyes, the golden lance which, in the novel, he stole from the Emperor of the North Pole, the three-cornered golden brick he received from his master, the wheels of fire and wind, the five hundred fire crows of the Holy Mother of Hundred-fold Increase (Pai-chia sheng-mu),[271] and the white snake. All these iconographic elements are already present in the Taoist ritual manuals of the thirteenth to fourteenth centuries as symbols and personifications of the powers of Marshal Ma. When the Shan-hsiao/Wu-t'ung had taken possession of the souls of a person (most commonly a woman), these symbols or spirits were visualized, invoked, and drawn as talismans by the Taoist practitioner during rituals intended to empower Ma Sheng to subdue and burn the possessing demons.

Taoist liturgy seems to have inspired not only the iconography of Hua-kuang in the novel, but also parts of the narrative itself. Thus, the theme of Hua-kuang's taking on the appearance of the Heavenly Worthy who Saves from Suffering (T'ai-i chiu-k'u t'ien-tsun) in order to gain access to

---

[269]The *Pei-yu chi* is more explicit about Hua-kuang's identity with Marshal Ma. Right before his battle with the Emperor of the North, Hua-kuang introduces himself as Ma Sheng 馬勝, whom people call the Divine Agent Ma [fond of] Flowers (=Women) and Wine (Hua-chiu Ma ling-kuan 花酒馬靈官). See *Pei-yu chi Hsüan-ti ch'u-shen chuan*, *chüan* 3, section 15.16a. Cp. above, pp. 148–49.

[270]"Cheng-i hung-shen ling-kuan huo-hsi ta-hsien k'ao-chao pi-fa" (cited n. 203), *Tao-fa hui-yuan* (HY 1210), 222.1a.

[271]*Hua-kuang t'ien-wang nan-yu chih-chuan*, *chüan* 3, section 9.4b–7a.

the Netherworld where his mother is being punished for her sins calls to mind the Taoist services for the dead during which Taoist priests transformed themselves in their meditation into T'ai-i chiu-k'u t'ien-tsun in order to rescue the souls of the deceased from Hell.[272] Modern Taoist and Buddhist liturgies have elaborated these segments of mourning rituals, nowadays generally called Smashing the Fortress [of Hell] (*Ta ch'eng*), into highly dramatic performances[273] which often stage the well-known story of Mu-lien's descent into the world of the dead in order to free his mother from the torments of Hell.[274] The similarity between these liturgical motifs and Hua-kuang's attempts in the *Nan-yu chi* to free his demonic mother from the sufferings of Hell are indeed striking.

Further direct parallels can be found in Taoist exorcistic rituals centered on Marshal Ma, Hua-kuang's alter ego. According to the ritual texts, which date from the thirteenth and fourteenth centuries, the ritual master transformed himself into Ma Sheng[275] and directed the lost souls together with the demon who had ravished them into the body of a medium (*t'ung-*

[272]See, e.g., John Lagerwey, *Taoist Ritual in Chinese Society and History* (New York: Macmillan Publishing Company, 1987), p. 229. Lagerwey gives a translation of a passage from Chin Yün-chung's 金允中 (fl. 1225) monumental ritual collection describing the visualizations a Taoist master was supposed to perform as he transformed himself into Chiu-k'u t'ien-tsun 救苦天尊 in order to open the gates of Hell and release the suffering souls of the dead. Cf. *Shang-ch'ing ling-pao ta-fa* 上清靈寶大法 (HY 1213), 35.7a–b.

[273]The roots of this dramatization of ritual reach back to at least the thirteenth century. At that time such theatrical performances within funeral rituals were still disputed among the Taoists. See, e.g., John Lagerwey, *Taoist Ritual*, p. 217, where we find the following translation from Chin Yün-chung's *Shang-ch'ing ling-pao ta-fa* (HY 1213), 34.7a–b: "In recent times people have invented rituals with [theatrical] speeches in order to make the spectacle pleasing. . . . Such rituals should be done silently rather than openly. . . . The one of High Merit ought simply to concentrate his thoughts and, with utmost sincerity, implore the Great Way and pray for the favorable response of the Emperor on High. Then there need be no fear that Hell will not open up."

[274]The integration of operatic sequences staging themes from the Mu-lien story-cycle into Taoist funerary rites has recently been studied by several experts on Taoist liturgy. See, e.g., John Lagerwey, *Taoist Ritual*, pp. 216–37. Further studies are Kenneth Dean, "Lei Yu-sheng ("Thunder is Noisy") and Mu-lien in the Theatrical and Funerary Traditions of Fukien"; Ch'iu K'un-liang, "Mu-lien 'Operas' in Taiwanese Funeral Rituals"; Kristofer Schipper, "Mu-lien Plays in Taoist Liturgical Context"; and Gary Seaman, "Mu-lien Dramas in Puli, Taiwan." All these articles have been published in: David Johnson, ed., *Ritual Opera, Operatic Ritual: "Mu-lien Rescues his Mother" in Chinese Popular Culture* (Berkeley: Chinese Popular Culture Project, 1989).

[275]See, e.g., "Chin-pi yuan-kuang huo-hsi ta-hsien cheng-i ling-kuan Ma yuan-shuai pi-fa 金臂圓光火犀大仙正一靈官馬元帥祕法," *Tao-fa hui-yuan* (HY 1210), 224.3a–4b.

tzu).[276] The medium's body was then transformed into a prison (*yü*) or, in other words, into the infernal regions of Hell inside which the demon became firmly imprisoned.[277] At this point Marshal Ma, incarnated in the Taoist priest, began to interrogate the demon, who had to reveal his name (through the mouth of the medium)[278] and set the ravished souls free, or be exterminated by the fire of Ma Sheng.[279] These rituals are echoed unmistakably by some of the themes in the *Nan-yu chi*. Hua-kuang's heroic role as a demon-slayer who saves women from evil spirits and his adventurous descents into the realms of the dead in order to rescue two of his mothers—the "real" one who was eaten by the demon, as well as the man-eating ogress herself—reflect Buddhist and Taoist funerary rites and also the exorcistic functions of Marshal Ma as he liberated the souls possessed by Shan-hsiao/Wu-t'ung during healing Taoist rituals.

CONCLUSIONS

Despite these remarkable parallels, we must not forget that the *Journey to the South* is a popular novel and not a Taoist text. Its purpose was certainly not the propagation of Taoist ritual traditions. Rather it aimed at entertaining a broad readership with exciting stories about a figure familiar to everyone throughout southern China and beyond. Yü Hsiang-tou, when he compiled and published this novel, was certainly aware of Hua-kuang's popularity and the marketability of his story.

However, the preceding pages show that Hua-kuang was more than a prized hero of popular art and a profitable source of income for a publisher. Hua-kuang represented a religious tradition which had evolved over many centuries from ancient popular beliefs in powerful nature demons into one of the most influential cults of premodern China. Telling the story of Hua-kuang, Yü Hsiang-tou drew on a great variety of elements from this complex religious background. Needless to say, he did not attempt to present Hua-kuang's religious tradition in a straightforward historical account. Yet, in one way or another, the *Journey to the South* deals

---

[276]See, e.g., "Cheng-i hung-shen ling-kuan huo-hsi ta-hsien k'ao-chao pi-fa" (cited n. 203), *Tao-fa hui-yuan*, 222.25b–28b.

[277]See, e.g., ibid., 222.33b–34b.

[278]See, e.g., ibid., 222.34b–35a.

[279]See, e.g., ibid., 222.30a–b.

with all aspects of the cult, including the highly delicate subject of its ambiguous origins. Thus not only does the novel leave no doubt about Hua-kuang's relationship with the Five Supernatural Powers (*wu-t'ung*), it even hints at Hua-kuang's connection with the old Shan-hsiao mountain goblins. The Wu-hsien gods also appear in the story, forming another aspect of Hua-kuang's variegated personality.

Various Buddhist and Taoist influences on Hua-kuang's cult also become apparent in the novel, expressed most conspicuously in the character of the hero himself. Hua-kuang is introduced as the Buddhist deity Miao chi-hsiang (a traditional appelation of Mañjuśri) and, at the same time, is also identified with the Taoist Marshal Ma. Furthermore, we have seen that the *Nan-yu chi* contains reflections of Buddhist and Taoist liturgical practice. Hua-kuang's transformation into the Heavenly Worthy who Saves from Suffering in order to gain access to the purgatory of Mount Feng-tu has parallels in Taoist mortuary rites. The same theme also bears a striking similarity to the operatic plays related to Mu-lien that are often inserted in Buddhist and Taoist services for the dead. Moreover, Hua-kuang's role as a powerful exorcist who rescues women from demonic possession using his various magic weapons directly reflects the functions of Marshal Ma and his symbols of power in Taoist exorcistic rites.

We can assume that the majority of the novel's readers were familiar with many of the aspects of Hua-kuang's cult from which the traditions and themes in the *Nan-yu chi* were derived. Therefore, at first glance, the novel simply appears to reflect current popular practices and beliefs clustered around Hua-kuang and his cult. However, looking further, we find more.

Many features of the cultic Hua-kuang that are alluded to in the novel are modified, re-explained, and recombined in a way that clearly endeavors to show him in a positive light. Thus, Hua-kuang's relationship with his dubious ancestors, the Wu-t'ung, is explained in terms of the original meaning of the Buddhist concept of Five Supernatural Powers, whereas the demonic qualities of the Wu-t'ung spirits themselves are projected onto Hua-kuang's opponents in the novel, such as General Fire Whirl, the white snake, and, above all, Hua-kuang's cannibalistic mother. Hua-kuang himself, despite his impetuous nature, is presented as a paragon of filial piety almost comparable to the saintly monk Mu-lien.

Instead of directly reflecting the multiple traditions characterizing Hua-kuang's religious background, the *Nan-yu chi*'s view of the cult is adapted to the general ethical values which ruled public life. Modifying the dubious or ambiguous aspects of the tradition, the novel provides a surprisingly consistent image of the cult. By drawing on Taoist and Buddhist traditions as well as the fundamental Chinese virtue of filial piety, the author of the *Nan-yu chi* constructed a generally acceptable framework for the cult, transforming its complex historical background into a continuous narration. The *Journey to the South* represents, in other words, the expurgated, homogeneous, and respectable story of a cult that appears firmly anchored in the generally acknowledged realm of popular religion.

It is uncertain whether this reinterpretation was a conscious attempt on the part of the author to legitimize the status of a cult that had constantly been undermined by its murky origins. Nor do we know to what extent the novel expresses the beliefs of either the author or his intended audience. Yü Hsiang-tou may simply have been a transmitter of a sanitized version of the Hua-kuang/Wu-hsien cult that had been developing independently for a long time. If on the other hand he was aware of the darker side of the cult he may simply have suppressed it in order to avoid any offense to the prescribed rules of public propriety. Hua-kuang's relationship with the Wu-t'ung was so problematic that it could only be referred to obliquely. Any positive and direct allusion to the stigmatized medium cult of the Wu-t'ung in the novel would undoubtedly have incensed those who regarded themselves as the custodians of public morals—that is, the educated members of the upper class.

The fact that the *Nan-yu chi* takes the idiosyncrasies of the higher classes into account indicates that the origin of the novel cannot be located within the immediate environment of the Wu-t'ung medium cult. This tradition was transmitted in the form of ballads and stories, now lost, that originated directly from medium seances and were recited by shamans during the "Tea Banquets" in honor of the Wu-t'ung. We can be sure that the ballads and stories of this almost exclusively oral tradition hardly resembled the well-contrived contents of the *Journey to the South*. Wu-t'ung worshippers of the lower social levels, whose religious beliefs and practices were directed by shamans and mediums, were satisfied with their own views of the objects of their cult. They hardly cared whether or not their gods were disreputable

in the eyes of others, and did not need the careful reinterpretations offered in the *Nan-yu chi*. Besides, no text that can be traced without doubt
to this milieu has survived.

However, we cannot conclude from this that the *Nan-yu chi* was aimed
at a highly educated readership. The novel's purely colloquial style rather
suggests an intended audience between the largely illiterate followers of
the medium cult on the one hand, and the members of higher social groups
on the other. But this middling group is difficult to identify precisely. All
we can say is that the *Journey to the South*, despite its plain vernacular style,
required a comparatively high degree of literacy on the part of its readers.
Moral or religious tracts written in simple classical Chinese were certainly
easier for the greater part of middle-class people to comprehend than this
novel, which not only displays a rich vocabulary but also abounds with
allusions to Buddhist and Taoist concepts and rites. The readership en-
visaged by Yü Hsiang-tou may therefore have corresponded to people of
his own social level: merchants, shopkeepers, and other independent commoners whose financial means allowed them to aquire a certain degree of
education. The modified views on the cult expressed in the novel were
probably also approved by these well-to-do citizens of the middle class.

The close link of the *Nan-yu chi* with its religious background raises
one final question. Did narrative adaptations of religious themes as found
in novels or theater scripts have any retroactive effects on the tradition
from which they originally derived? Or, more concretely, can we recognize any reflections of Hua-kuang's story as told in the *Nan-yu chi* in the
living cult tradition?

Naturally, this question must be treated with caution, for we lack any
precise knowledge about the the oral narrative tradition before it was taken
down in writing and, therefore, cannot tell exactly which conceits of the
story were already known and which originated in the novel itself. Nevertheless, a few observations can be made which may deserve consideration.
The 1684 local gazetteer of Ning-hua county (western Fukien) reports,
for example, that Hua-kuang, also called Miao chi-hsiang Tathāgata, was
the focal object of worship in the Wu-t'ung temple outside the northern
gate of Ning-hua city. The account adds that Hua-kuang was directly
compared by the people to the saintly monk Mu-lien because of the outstanding proof of filial piety he gave by redeeming his mother from her

sins.[280] We cannot fail to notice the close resemblance of this popular tradition with the plot of the story told in the *Nan-yu chi*.

Furthermore, later sources also bear evidence to Hua-kuang's prominence in the cult traditions of the neighboring province of Kwangtung. A nineteenth-century text, for example, informs us that Hua-kuang was invoked by regional shamans during the eighth and ninth lunar months as a divine protector from fire.[281] This association reminds us of Hua-kuang's specific relationship with the element of fire in the *Journey to the South*, which, as we have seen, ultimately derived from his identification with the Taoist Marshal Ma.

Finally, it is possible that Hua-kuang's preeminent role in the theatrical traditions of the southern Chinese provinces is related to dramatic versions of his story based on narratives such as the *Nan-yu chi*. Hua-kuang was not only elevated to the rank of a patron deity of the Cantonese Yüeh Opera,[282] but even today figures in numerous dramas, marionette plays, and shadow plays. To single out but two striking examples: a modern inventory of Yüeh operas lists a play entitled *Hua-kuang nao ti-fu* (*Hua-kuang Causes Trouble in the Underworld*) which appears to date from about the middle of this century. The contents of this opera deal with Hua-kuang's incarnation in the womb of the monstrous Chi-chih-t'o, Chi-chih-t'o's imprisonment in the purgatory of Feng-tu, Hua-kuang's search for her, and, finally, his success in liberating her from her underworldly prison.[283] In other words, the action of this play parallels exactly the plot of the *Nan-yu chi*.

The second example is a late-nineteenth- or early-twentieth-century Taiwanese shadow play whose tradition probably goes back to Fukien. This play, which is preserved in the collection of Kristofer Schipper, comprises sixteen short acts describing Hua-kuang's battle with Li Na-cha and his victory over the Iron Fan Princess (T'ieh-shan kung-chu), whom he finally

---

[280]*Ning-hua hsien-chih* 寧化縣志 (1684), 7.9b.

[281]Ling Yang-tsao 凌揚藻 (1760–1845), *Li-shao pien* 蠡勺編 (Ling-nan i-shu ed.), 29.11b–12a, quoting the *Yüeh hsiao-chi* 粵小記 of 1832.

[282]See, e.g., Tanaka Issei 田仲一成, *Chūgoku saishi engeki kenkyū* 中國祭祀演劇研究 (Tokyo: Tōyō Bunka Kenkyūjo, 1981), p. 547.

[283]Anonymous, *Yüeh-chü chü-mu kang-yao* 粵劇劇目綱要 (Canton: Chung-kuo hsi-chü chia hsieh-hui, 1961, repr. Hongkong, 1982), vol. 2, p. 351.

wins as his wife.[284] These episodes are covered in sections eleven and twelve of the *Nan-yu chi*. Furthermore, some of the dialogue in the shadow play appears to have been taken directly from the *Journey to the South*.[285] All this suggests that the sixteenth-century novel exercised a long-lasting influence on the theatrical traditions of Kwangtung and Fukien.

To sum up, the case of the *Nan-yu chi* shows that popular novels cannot be separated from the realities of their socio-religious environment and judged from a primarily literary point of view. Works like the *Journey to the South* are more than just the bizarre fantasies of profit-minded hacks. They represent creative syntheses of popular ideas and beliefs rooted in ancient religious traditions which eventually are integrated into the framework of continuous narrations. Moreover, the modifications and reinterpretations evident in Hua-kuang's story in the *Nan-yu chi* reveal that the expression of religious ideas in the written word was dictated by the principles of a general (Confucian) moral code often at odds with the original beliefs of the living cult tradition. But these tensions and contradictions also offer precious insights into the complexity of the Chinese popular mentality which, as a whole, was formed by the constant interaction of both the cultural heritage of the higher classes and the creative traditions of the ordinary people.

[284]See Kristofer Schipper, "Une collection des manuscrits de pièces de théâtre d'ombres chinoises," *Occasional Papers of the European Association of Chinese Studies*, 2 (Paris, 1970), p. 69: Nr. 194 [AS. ML. I-1-188]. I am grateful to K. Schipper for making a copy of this shadow play available to me.
[285]See, e.g., *Hua-kuang t'ien-wang nan-yu chih-chuan*, *chüan* 3, section 11.23b–24a with the play script [AS. ML. I-1-188], p. 15; *Hua-kuang t'ien-wang nan-yu chih-chuan*, *chüan* 3, section 11.24a–b with ibid. p. 18; and *Hua-kuang t'ien-wang nan-yu chih-chuan*, *chüan* 3, section 11.25a with ibid. p. 23.

Language Adaptation
in Taoist Liturgical Texts

CHINFA LIEN

*T*his paper is primarily concerned with Taoist liturgical texts intended for Min-speaking audiences. The texts to be examined are not found in the Tao-tsang, but rather in the Chuang-lin collection of Taiwanese Taoist texts.[1] I intend to show how imported non-Min texts were adjusted to the Min-speaking setting through a regular four-step process of contact, interaction, selection, and hybridization. The resulting hybrid texts can be identified by the many types of Min elements they contain.

Since writing is a visible record of speech, a proper understanding of the spoken language that lies behind texts is an important basis for their study. However, it is a mistake to assume that written language is subsidiary to or derivative from spoken language. As Vachek rightly argues, spoken and written language have complementary functions and each has a life of its own.[2] In this paper I rely on two distinctions: that between literary

I am indebted to David Johnson and William S.-Y. Wang for initiating this project, and offering advice and guidance. I am especially grateful to Johnson for trenchant comments which led me to reconsider and clarify my arguments. Thanks are also due to Allen Chun, Bernard Faure, Mei Tzulin, Michael R. Saso, Zhongwei Shen, Wang Chiukuei and the participants in the Conference on the Rituals and Scriptures of Chinese Popular Religion for extremely helpful suggestions on earlier versions of this paper.
[1]Michael R. Saso 蘇海涵, ed., *Chuang-lin hsü Tao-tsang* 莊林續道藏 [A collection of Taoist Manuals], 25 volumes (Taipei: Ch'eng-wen ch'u-pan shê, 1975).
[2]Josef Vachek, *Written Language Revisited* (Amsterdam/Philadelphia: John Benjamins Publishing Company, 1989).

and colloquial forms of language, and that between Min and non-Min linguistic elements. The distinction between literary and colloquial forms should not be confused with the distinction between written and spoken language. For example, both literary and colloquial elements can occur in spoken language, and also in written language.

Within the colloquial we must distinguish between Min and non-Min forms. It is insufficient to refer simply to "vernacular" elements in liturgical texts;[3] it is essential to specify whether the colloquial elements are indigenous Min elements, or derive from the spoken language of some other region.

There are norms in both literary and written colloquial Chinese. For example, most vernacular stories are written in a prestige colloquial that originated in North China during the Sung dynasty. But there are some texts that use less prestigious local colloquials.

Many texts in the Chuang-lin collection were originally written in the prestige colloquial and then adapted to the Min-speaking environment by incorporating Min colloquial elements. This shows very clearly how texts were affected by the need to communicate with an audience. Not all texts in the collection show the same degree of Min influence. Those with the most Min colloquial elements probably were aimed at audiences with the lowest levels of education, and hence had less prestige than texts with fewer Min elements.

This paper is organized as follows: the first section discusses the concept of colloquial and literary strata and the distinction between Min and non-Min, the second discusses the principles of writing southern Min dialect words in Chinese characters, the third uses linguistic criteria such as lexicon, grammar, prosody, and sandhi phenomena to identify Southern Min elements in the Chuang-lin texts, the fourth proposes the concept of hybridization to explain the linguistic adaptation of the Taoist texts in the Chuang-lin collection, the fifth shows how orthodox Taoist texts differ from their counterparts that have been adapted for a Min-

---

[3] Kristofer Schipper 施博爾, "Vernacular and Classical Ritual in Taoism," *Journal of Asian Studies* 45 (1985), pp. 21–57. In this article no attempt is made to distinguish between colloquials written in different dialects.

speaking audience, the sixth presents four case studies of hybrid texts, and the seventh provides an overview of the distribution of colloquial and literary elements in the texts.

COLLOQUIAL AND LITERARY, MIN AND NON-MIN

Colloquialism is a relative notion; that is, it may change through time and across dialects. Let us first consider the time dimension. Even if a written language does not faithfully reflect the current spoken language, it must be a derivative of earlier colloquial forms, because every written language was originally based on a spoken language. Expressions that once were colloquial may over the course of time become literary. Similarly, a linguistic form which has become literary in one dialect may remain colloquial in another dialect. For example, when meaning "walk" 行 is a bound morpheme that never occurs alone except in frozen literary compounds like jen-hsing tao 人行道 "sidewalk" and pu-hsing 步行 "walk," the meaning "walk" now being supplied in colloquial Mandarin by the word tsou 走.[4] In contrast, 行 is commonly used with the meaning "walk" in Southern Min colloquial. 走 was a colloquial word meaning "run" in Old Chinese. While still denoting "run" in Southern Min, in Mandarin it now means "walk," the meaning "run" surviving only in such stock expressions

[4]The transliteration of Peking Mandarin is given in the Wade-Giles system with no indication of tone. The sound values of Southern Min dialect are based on traditional church romanization (Douglas 1899) except that for typographical reasons diacritical marks are avoided. A nasalized vowel is indicated by a capital N that follows it and for the mid back vowels the symbol /o./ as distinct from the less open /o/ is used. Southern Min derives its seven-tone system from the four-tone system in Middle Chinese codified in the rhyme book *Ch'ieh-yun* 切韻 (A.D. 601), due to a merger of Tone II words with voiced obstruent initials with Tone III words with voiced initials. Here the modern tones are represented by numerals 1 (even tone, p'ing-sheng 平聲), 2 (ascending tone, shang-sheng 上聲), 3 (departing tone, ch'ü-sheng 去聲) and 4 (entering tone, ju-sheng 入聲) coupled with "a" (yin 陰) and "b" (yang 陽) which denote upper and lower subtone, as in /tok 4a/ 督 "to oversee" and /tok 4b/ 毒 "poisonous" where 4a and 4b mean yin-ju 陰入 and yang-ju 陽入 respectively. All the tones are given in citation tones rather than sandhi tones. (See Carstairs Douglas, *Chinese-English Dictionary of the Vernacular or Spoken Language of Amoy, with the Principal Variations of the Chang-chew* 漳州 *and Chin-chew* 晉州 *Dialects* [London: Publishing Office of the Presbyterian Church of England, 1899].)

For discussion of sandhi tones in Southern Min see William S.-Y. Wang 王士元, "Phonological Features of Tone," *International Journal of American Linguistics*, 33 (1967), pp. 93–105.

as tsou-ma-k'an-hua 走馬看花 "looking at flowers from horseback" and pen-tsou 奔走 "rush about." Thus the Southern Min colloquial expression tsau chap-hun ching 走十分鐘 "run for ten minutes" would have to be rendered as p'ao shih-fen chung 跑十分鐘 in Mandarin. These points are true of both spoken and written colloquial.

Sometimes a colloquial form in one dialect may become literary when incorporated into another dialect. Thus the literary stratum in a dialect may include imported colloquial elements as well as literary elements, as will be shown in part five. Some Taiwanese marionette or shadow play scripts preserve earlier Mandarin words or even sentences that are no longer in use in modern Mandarin. Even though they are not intelligible to Min-speaking audiences they still survive because the scripts are used in ritual performances.

An important point that should not be overlooked is that both the literary and colloquial forms in the Taoist texts under investigation make sense only when pronounced in dialect. This is obvious enough in the case of the colloquial expressions, but is also true of the literary elements. An educated native Taiwanese reads the literary texts or sections in a much earlier prestige pronunciation rather than the current standard spoken language. It would be unthinkable for a funeral ritual, for example, to be performed in Mandarin Chinese for a Min-speaking audience. Yet many wrongly believe that Taoist texts written in the koine or the standard language are dialect-neutral.[5]

There are several reasons for this. One is that practically all such texts were written in an earlier standard Mandarin and therefore the educated class raised in that tradition finds them devoid of dialectal flavor. Another is that no dialect other than Mandarin has a lasting written literature in wide circulation in the Han Chinese sphere. This lack of competing written literatures partly accounts for the apparent neutrality of Taoist texts in Mandarin. A third is that sometimes the dialect elements are very old and no longer recognizable as such. From a purely linguistic point of view,

---

[5]The koine was in fact a variety of Old Mandarin based on Northern Chinese which gradually took shape during the T'ang and Sung period. It can be found in religious texts and various genres of popular literature. See Jerry Norman, *Chinese* (Cambridge: Cambridge University Press, 1988), pp. 111–12.

however, Mandarin is just one dialect among many, unintelligible to an illiterate Min-speaking monolingual.

In the implanted Taoist texts dealt with here a distinction between literary and colloquial Min should be made and is attestable. Take the hybrid expression m 3b thang 1a ki 1a-go 3b 不通飢餓 (p. 4805)[6] meaning "should not go hungry" where m 3b thang 1a is colloquial whereas the dissyllabic word ki 1a-go 3b is literary. (Both ki 1a and go 3b are glossed as literary in Douglas.) The colloquial counterpart of ki 1a-go 3b "hungry" is iau 1a commonly written as 枵. As shown above, colloquialism is a relative concept. In Min go 3b 餓 is a literary form while in modern Mandarin o 餓 is a free and colloquial form and the morpheme chi 飢 is a fossilized form that only occurs in stock expressions. This distinction is also manifested in grammatical particles such as auxiliaries. Sometimes a text uses both the colloquial auxiliary tioh 4b 著 and the literary one su 1a 須, as in

hing 1b-tong 3b ku 2a-chi 2a tioh 4b soe 3a-ji 3b
行動舉止著細二 (p. 4818);

toan 1a-ching 3a nng 3b-ji 3b su 1a kin 2a-ki 3b
端正二字須謹記 (p. 4818).

Colloquial Min represents a linguistic system which is older than that of literary Min, since the colloquial stratum is indigenous to the Min dialect whereas the literary stratum is taken from the T'ang and Sung standard language.

To call the language of Taiwanese Taoist liturgy "vernacular" without specifying the dialect inevitably leads people to assume that it has something in common with the Mandarin of the most widespread written popular literature. This is a serious mistake. There is no such thing as a trans-dialectal vernacular, a vernacular that can be divorced from the local patois. Chinese has many vernacular languages, varying from region to region, generally subordinated to modern or older standard languages. Hence the simple distinction between "vernacular" and "classical" texts that has been made by some specialists does not do justice to linguistic realities. At the very least, it is necessary (in the case of the Taiwanese Taoist texts) to distinguish between Min and non-Min vernaculars. (As will be shown

---

[6]All citations in this form refer to the *Chuang-lin hsü Tao-tsang* (cited n. 1).

in section four, there are linguistic criteria that can be used to distinguish Min lexical and grammatic elements from non-Min ones in our texts.) Thus, in this paper I do not use the vernacular-classical dichotomy, but employ instead the two dichotomies mentioned above—literary/colloquial and Min/non-Min—to label linguistic strata or elements in the Taoist texts with which I am concerned. This is the only way to do full justice to their linguistic complexities.

Utterances in a given language are by definition perfectly comprehensible to native speakers of that language, but to others only if they are bilingual. With written language the case obviously is different. There comprehensibility has to do with the difficulty of the text and the educational level of the reader. Written language is by definition incomprehensible to the illiterate. For those who can read, comprehensibility is closely linked to a text's literariness: the more literary, the harder it is to understand. Classical texts are more difficult than colloquial texts to grasp since their language is highly codified and detached from daily use. But colloquial elements in a text are also difficult for a reader to understand if they are not either from the standard dialect (if there is one) or the reader's own dialect. Thus an educated Min speaker will find it extremely difficult to understand colloquial Cantonese expressions, particularly if they are written in demotic characters. Indeed, he would need some practice before he could readily understand texts written in Min colloquial, such as the goa 1a-a 2a-chhek 4a 歌仔冊 "ballad-books," in which practically all local pronunciations are written in demotic characters. But in the end he could understand them simply by reading the lines aloud, thus getting at the sounds behind the borrowed characters, whereas he could never do this with comparable Cantonese texts.

PRINCIPLES OF WRITING
SOUTHERN MIN DIALECTS
IN CHINESE CHARACTERS

There are basically two strategies for using Chinese characters to write Southern Min, or any dialect: phonetic borrowing and semantic borrowing. The first strategy is to borrow the sound of a character without regard for its meaning:

Phonetic loanwords

sound	gloss	character	page of Chuang-lin hsü Tao-tsang
tat 4b	to be worth	達	4830
beh 4a	want	卜	4838

The second strategy is to retain the meaning of the character while giving it a different, local, pronunciation:

Semantic loanwords

gloss	character	sound	page
able, competent	賢	gau 1b	4829
child	子[7]	kiaN 2a	4830

Semantic borrowing is not uncommon. The kunyomi 訓讀 of Sino-Japanese, in which Chinese characters are given a Japanese pronunciation, as when shan 山 is pronounced /yama/ rather than /san/, is an example of semantic borrowing.

The representation of dialects in Chinese characters probably operates on these two axes because in Chinese writing both semantic and phonetic information are encoded in the same graph.[8] In the first strategy, phonetic information is exploited at the expense of semantic information; in the second, the situation is reversed. The exploitation of these two strategies seems to be universal in Chinese colloquial literatures and is not limited to Taoist texts.[9] In decoding colloquial texts these two ways of representing dialect words in Chinese characters have to be constantly kept in mind. A

[7]It is often claimed that the correct character for "child" is 囝 kiaN 2a. This claim is based on the gloss in *Chi-yun* 集韻, a rhyme book of the Sung period, where under the lexical item 囝 it says that 閩人呼兒曰囝 "Min people call "children" kiaN 2a" (p. 389). However, I think 囝 should also be regarded as an earlier semantic loanword, since the character is coined on the same principle, that is, it also contains the semantic radical 子 whose pronunciation tsu 2a is totally unrelated to kiaN 2a. Tu Ting et al. 丁度等, eds., *Chi-yun* 集韻 (Shang-hai ku-chi ch'u-pan shê, 1985).
[8]William S.-Y. Wang, "Language in China: A Chapter in the History of Linguistics," *Journal of Chinese Linguistics* 17 (1989), pp. 183–222.
[9]As will be shown in section 3, there is some measure of agreement in the use of vulgar or

grasp of these two strategies coupled with an intimate knowledge of the dialect and sensitivity to the clues furnished by rhyming patterns, sandhi phenomena, dialect-specific native words, and the like will allow one to arrive at a quite satisfactory reconstruction of the sound values of such texts.[10]

LINGUISTIC CRITERIA
FOR IDENTIFYING MIN ELEMENTS
IN TAOIST TEXTS

Mutually unintelligible Chinese dialects differ not only in pronunciation but also in lexicon and grammar. In this section we will use lexicon, demotic words, grammar, prosody, and sandhi phenomena to identify Southern Min elements in Taoist texts from the Chuang-lin collection.

Lexicon

In the following table each Min word is paired with a synonymous non-Min loan word also used by Min speakers. They are coexistent forms constituting a semantic field in a multi-layered linguistic system. That is,

---

demotic words in local rhyme books (Lin Fan), scripts of plays (Anonymous1) and the booklets of Ballads (Anonymous2/3). The relevant source materials are:

Lin Fan chü-shih 林梵居士, *Tseng-pu shih-wu-yin* 增補十五音 [An enlarged edition of Sip-go.-im] (Taichung: Jui-ch'en shu-chü, 1987).

Anonymous1, *Li-ching-chi hsi-wen* 荔鏡紀戲文 [Scripts of the play "The Lichee Mirror"] (Taipei: T'ien-i ch'u-pan shê, 1983), 2 volumes.

Anonymous2, "Tsap 4b-geh 4b hoe 1a-thai 1a piN 3b-kiaN 2a koa 1a" 十月花胎病子歌 ["Ballad of the Ten Months of Pregnancy"] (Hsinchu: Chu-lin shu-chü, 1986).

Anonymous3, "Khoan 3a-se 3a liau 2a-kai 2a koa 1a" 勸世子解歌 ["Ballad of Morality"] (Hsin-chu: Chu-lin shu-chü, 1986).

[10]The identification of authentic etyma is based on consideration of the development of the phonological system. In some cases they are also attested in written documents. In particular, the determination of etymological correctness of a word is based on the correlation of its modern sound values and reconstructed values in segmentals (i.e. initials and finals) and suprasegmentals or tones. This approach is safe from the whims of laymen's random judgment.

Phonological consideration is also important in cases like 若 naN 3b "if" (4810) and 爾 li 2a "you" (4809). The two graphs out of context would be taken as belonging to the literary stratum, but given the right context they are in fact colloquial expressions. Script is more conservative than speech. As the sound-graph relation becomes more and more obscure, the old graph is replaced by a phonologically more transparent graph; for example, "if" is sometimes rendered as 那 (4824), which is evidently a phonetic loan.

a sememe or a minimum semantic unit is realized as a pair of coexistent
forms—Min and borrowed. The page number indicates the place in the
Chuang-lin hsü Tao-tsang where the Min word was found. For the Min
word script variants are given in parentheses.

Min	*loan*	*gloss*	*page*
ang ɪa-bo.2a 翁某	hu ɪa-chhe ɪa 夫妻	man and wife	4833
tsa ɪa-po. ɪa 叱埔	lam ɪb-jin ɪb 男人	man	4808–9
tsa ɪa-bo. 2a 叱么 / 查某	lu 2a-jin ɪb 女人	woman	4809
kan 2a 簡	pi 3b 婢	slave	4811
lang ɪb 人 (儂)[11]	jin ɪb 人	person	4833
kiaN 2a 子 (囝)	ji ɪb, tsu 2a 兒, 子	child, son	4828

The Min words have a homely, colloquial feeling whereas the loan words
have a literary flavor and are used in allusions or stock expressions. The
former class of words occurs exclusively in Min dialects, but the latter
class also occurs in Mandarin dialects. Clearly, Southern Min speakers
adopted literary words from Mandarin, although it is difficult to pin down
exactly when the borrowing took place.

Of course, some semantic domains remain beyond the reach of non-
Min words. The table below shows Min words whose Mandarin equiva-
lents have not entered the Southern Min lexicon.[12]

[11]Lang ɪb 儂 is probably related to mang 氓 since both can be posited as going back to an
earlier form with the consonant cluster *ml-.

[12]厝 is the Min-unique word for "house." To be sure, the morpheme pang ɪb 房 also occurs in
the dialect, but it means "room," as in pang ɪb-king ɪa 房間 "room," or a division of a family,
as in toa 3b-pang ɪb 大房 "a large branch of a family." The term for "mother-in-law" in
Southern Min is ta ɪa-ke ɪa 乾家, not 婆婆 (the Mandarin term), not even in the literary

Min	*Pekingese Mandarin*	*gloss*	*page*
chhu 3a 厝	fang-tzu 房子	house	4833
ta ɪa-ke ɪa 乾家	p'o-p'o 婆婆	mother-in-law	4832
nng 3b 蛋 (<卵)	tan 蛋	egg	4741
o. ɪa 烏	hei 黑	black	4830
sim ɪa-pu 3b 媳婦 (<新婦)	hsi-fu 媳婦	daughter-in-law	4831

stratum. The word for "egg" is inevitably 卵 and it is so resistant to Mandarin influence that besides occurring in the Min stratum, as nng 3b-chhing ɪa 卵淸 "the white of an egg" and nng 3b-jin ɪb 卵仁 "yolk," it appears in such neologisms as koe ɪa-nng 3b-ko ɪa 雞卵糕 "cake" and nng 3b-peh 4b-chit 4a 卵白質 "protein" rather than tan 3b-ko ɪa 蛋糕 and tan 3b-peh 4b-chit 4a 蛋白質. The only exception I find is phi ɪb-tan 3b 皮蛋 "preserved egg." While wu 烏 and hei 黑 occur side by side in Mandarin, 烏 being more literary and surviving in compounds like wu-ya 烏鴉 "crow," wu-yun 烏雲 "dark clouds," and wu-tsei 烏賊 "ink-fish," "black" is denoted exclusively by o. ɪa 烏 in Southern Min. Hsi-fu 媳婦 means "daughter-in-law" and "wife" in Mandarin, whereas "daughter-in-law" is rendered as sim ɪa-pu 3b (<sin ɪa-pu 3b) 新婦 in Southern Min. Note that in the cited Taoist Southern Min text 媳婦 is used as a semantic loan for 新婦 sim ɪa-pu 3b, alternatively written as 心婦 in popular literature; sim 心 (<sin 新) acquires its bilabial ending from the initial of the second syllable. This semantic loan is also recorded in *Tai-nichi dai jiten* 台日大辭典 vol. ɪ, p. 732 where 媳婦 is given the pronunciation sim ɪa-pu 3b (Taipei: Chung-wen t'u-shu yu-hsien kung-ssu, 1981).

Loan words are a useful means for dating lexical borrowing. Documented evidence attests to the existence of 新婦 in the Old Chinese period and both senses of this word ("bride" and "daughter-in-law") date as early as the Han period or even earlier. (See the following citation, p. 1375). 媳婦 is probably later than the Middle Chinese period since its first occurrence is attested no earlier than the Sung (ibid., p. 1124). It is interesting to note that 新婦 in the sense of "bride" survives both in Sino-Korean and Sino-Japanese. This means that it must have been no later than the Middle Chinese period when 媳婦 and 新娘 came on the scene, ultimately supplanting 新婦 in Mandarin. Furthermore, the survival of 新婦 in the Min dialect indicates that a Middle Chinese or Old Chinese stratum in Min can be established with certainty only on the basis of lexical evidence. Shang-wu yin-shu kuan pien-chi pu, ed., *Tz'u-yuan* (Hong Kong: Shang-wu yin-shu kuan Hsiang-kang fen-kuan, 1984).

In some cases the Southern Min-Mandarin distinctions are quite subtle, but nevertheless obvious to a native speaker. For example, old Chinese texts give two senses of chin 緊: "rapid" and "tight."[13] As a free form, 緊 means "tight" in Mandarin, but when it occurs as a bound morpheme in literary compounds like chin-chi 緊急 or chin-p'o 緊迫 "urgent," the sense of "fast, rapid" is still preserved. In Southern Min, however, the semantic domain of kin 2a 緊 has narrowed down to "rapid" only and the sense of "tight" has been taken up by an 1b 絚. Again, in Old Chinese 細 has both the sense of "small" (vs. "large") and that of "thin, slender" (vs. "thick")[14] and both meanings survive in Mandarin, "thin, slender" in colloquial words such as hsi-t'ieh-szu 細鐵絲 "thin wire," and "small" in more literary words such as hsi-ku 細故 "trifle" and ts'u-hsi 粗細 "big and small." But in Southern Min, 細 means only "small," as in soe 3a-kiaN 2a 細囝 "youngest son" and soe 3a-i 1b 細姨 "concubine," while the meaning of "thin, slender" is rendered by iu 3a 幼.

Demotic Characters

Demotic characters, that is, characters that are unique to a dialect, can be used as a supplementary criterion for identifying the Min elements in a Taoist text. Such characters can also be found in local rhyme books such as that of Lin Fan chü-shih and in popular ballads.[15] The following is a list of some of the demotic characters found in texts in the Chuang-lin collection:

demotic	standard	sound	gloss	page
炁	氣	khi 3a	air; spirit	597
笋	筍	sun 2a	bamboo shoot	6004
皈	歸	kui 1a	go back	542
䗂	境	king 2a	place	563
坔	地	te 3b	earth	501
灾	災	chai 1a	calamity	6008

<hr>

[13]Ibid., p. 2439.
[14]Ibid., pp. 2414–15.
[15]For the ballads see Anonymous2, "Tsap 4b-geh 4b hoe 1a-thai 1a piN 3b-kiaN 2a koa 1a," and Anonymous3, "Khoan 3a-se 3a liau 2a-kai 2a koa 1a." For the rhyme book see Lin Fan chü-shih, *Tseng-pu shih-wu-yin*. (All cited n. 9.)

歆	歌	koa 1a	song	6004
箄	算	sng 3a	to count	6002
桸	桃	tho 1b	peach	6004
烌	秋	chhiu 1a	autumn	6006
帋	紙	choa 2a	paper	6108
蕊	蕋	lui 2a	flower blossom	6017
姐	姊	chi 2a	older sister	6108
孝	學	oh 4a	learn	4818

Many Min-unique dialectal characters in the Chuang-lin texts can also be found in an opera script written in the Ch'ao-chou and Ch'üan-chou dialects that may be as early as the mid-sixteenth century,[16] as shown in the following table:

		Chuang-lin	*Anon. 1*	*Gloss*
(1)				
卜	beh 4a	4823	6, 31	want to
袂	be, boe 3b	4830	28, 38	be unable to
許	hit 4a, hia 1a	4825	7	that, there
只	chit 4a, chia 1a	4825	24	this, here
共	kang 3b, kah 4a	4809	9, 41	comitative and patient marker
通	thang 1a	4815	6	may (deontic)
得桃	thit 4a-tho 1b	6996	12	amuse oneself
白賊	peh 4b-chhat 4b	4807	43, 58	liar, swindler
簡	kan 2a	4803	5	slave
厝	chhu 3a	4833	29	house
細二	soe 3a-ji 3b	4818	2	careful, gingerly
無賽	bo 1b-se 3a	6020	4	unrivalled, galore
查某	cha 1a-bo. 2a	4832	5	woman
某	bo. 2a	4833	9	wife

[16]*Li-ching-chi hsi-wen*, published toward the end of the Chia-ching era during the Ming

(2)

伶俐	leng 2a-li 3b	6996	27	clean and neat
冥	miN 1b	6022	29	night
翁	ang 1a	4833	9	husband
細	soe 3a	4830	9	small
著	tioh 4b	4830	40	should

(3)

乜	mih 4b	7407	10	what
咒咀	chiu 3a-choa 3b	6277	30	to swear
孝	oh 4b	4818	30	learn

The above Min-unique dialect words fall into three types: (1) phonetic loans, (2) words or compounds which also occur in other dialects but take on specific meanings in Min dialects, and (3) demotic characters. Such words, commonly found in opera scripts, are typical of local popular culture. In comparison with the long history of the dominant elite culture, local popular culture is a very important arena of literature that has long been neglected in the study of Chinese culture. In intellectual circles awareness of the popular aspects of culture has developed in the present century under the influence of western culture. The fact that so many vulgar words are shared by a sixteenth-century opera script and the Chuang-lin Taoist texts is an unmistakable sign of the adaptation of imported Taoist texts to the local Min culture.

Grammar

The Chuang-lin Taoist texts provide many examples of grammatical features that are unique to Southern Min, four of which will be given below.

1. *The marker of thematic roles (agent, patient, and benefactive markers):*

ho. 3b	被	agent marker	(p. 4822)
ho. 3b	乎	benefactive marker	(p. 4828)
ho. 3b	伏	patient marker	(p. 4810)
ka 3b	甲	patient marker	(p. 4827)

---

period. See Anonymous1, *Li ching chi hsi-wen* (cited n. 9).

Ho. 3b can be represented with three different types of graphs depending on which of the three grammatical functions shown above it has in a given sentence. Kei 給 and jang 讓 in Mandarin show a close resemblance to it. Ka 3b sometimes plays a similar semantic role.[17]

2. *Pronouns.* Plurality in pronouns is indicated by -men in Mandarin, but -n in Southern Min.

> lan 2a　　咱　(inclusive) "we"　(p. 4838)
>
> lin 2a　　您　"you"　　　　　(p. 4833)
>
> in 1a　　　伊　"they"　　　　　(p. 4833)

3. *Modals.* Modals are used to express a range of meanings but mainly the speaker's attitude regarding necessity, possibility, certainty, and the like. The dialectal flavor of Min modals can be appreciated by setting them off against Mandarin counterparts such as (1) yao 要, (2a) tei 得, (2b) pu-k'o-yi 不可以, (3a) pu-hui 不會 and (3b) hui/neng 會/能.

 (1) desiderative modal denoting desire and wishes

  (Mandarin yao 要):

  beh 4a 卜 "want to" (p. 4833)

 (2) deontic modals

  a. modal expressing obligation (Mandarin tei 得):

   tioh 4b 著 "should" (p. 4831)

  b. modal expressing prohibition (Mandarin pu-k'o-yi 不可以):

   m 3b-thang 1a 不通 "must not" (p. 4817)

 (3) epistemic modals

  a. modal expressing inability (Mandarin pu-hui 不會):

   be 3b 袂 "cannot" (p. 4830)

  b. modal expressing ability (Mandarin hui/neng 會/能):

   e 3b 個 (<解) "able" (p. 4832)

4. *Markers of Subordination and Coordination.*

 (1) subordinator of a conditional

  na 3b 那 (<若) "if" (p. 4824)

---

[17]For detailed treatment of ho. 3b see Tsao Feng-fu 曹逢甫, "The Functions of Mandarin Gei and Taiwanese Hou in the Double Object and Passive Constructions," in Robert L. Cheng 鄭良偉 and Huang Hsuan-fan 黃宣範, eds., *The Structure of Taiwanese: A Modern Synthesis* (Taipei: Wen-ho ch'u-pan yu-hsien kung-ssu, 1988), pp. 165–208.

(2) conjunction

ka 3b 甲 "and" (p. 4836)

5. *Interrogative Words.*

mih 4b 乜 (<物) "what" (p. 4824)

6. *Genitive Marker.*

e 1b 個 (p. 4832)

Prosody (Poetic Convention)

Rhyme is one of the surest indicators of the dialect a text was written in. If the rhyme-words in a poem do not rhyme in Mandarin, then we know that it was not composed in Mandarin. (I will ignore for the purposes of this paper the problem of poems composed in old forms of Mandarin.) If one knows that they rhyme if pronounced in Southern Min, the chances are obviously high that it was written by a Southern Min speaker. For example, in the seventh stanza of "Tsai-hua huan-tou ch'ang-hua ko" (栽花換斗唱花歌 "Flower-planting Ballad" (pp. 6019–25), the rhyme-words are miN 1b 冥, ki 1b 期, and thiN 1a 天, while in the eleventh stanza the rhyme-words are ki 1a 枝, siN 1a 生, and iN 1b 圓.

Anyone who knows that these words should rhyme in that particular ballad will also know at once that it was not written in Mandarin, and if further aware that nasalized vowels rhyme with oral vowels in Southern Min will see that it was composed in that dialect. (Although nasalized vowels are in phonemic contrast with oral vowels, I suspect that perceptually the nasalized element as a secondary articulation may be quite negligible and liable to be lost. Thus, it is phonetically natural for a nasalized vowel to rhyme with an oral vowel.[18] Of course, this intuitive observation has to be verified by experimental tests.)

Another example comes from a much longer ballad (pp. 6969–7058). A stanza on p. 6999 has ang 1b 紅, chang 1b 叢, and lang 1b 人 as the three rhyme-words. If the last character is read in Southern Min literary pronunciation, i.e. jin 1b, it will not rhyme with the others. But in colloquial

[18]Paul Jen-Kuei Li 李壬癸, "Rhyming and Phonemic Contrast in Southern Min," *Bulletin of the Institute of History and Philology* 57 (1986), pp. 439–64.

Southern Min it is a semantic loanword, read lang 1b. Here the informed reader can infer that the ballad was probably aimed at an audience with little education.

Sandhi Phenomena

Unless demotic characters are used (see above), or unless compounds are used that are unique to the dialect, it is impossible to tell which dialect isolated characters are intended to represent. But there is an interesting exception in the case of sandhi phenomena, that is, phonological modification of juxtaposed forms in connected speech. In certain cases sandhi can be used to identify dialects. For example, the word 石榴 "pomegranate" is represented by a script variant, 榭榴 (p. 6999). This tells us at once which dialect is involved. In isolation, 石 /siah 4b/ and 榭 /sia 3b/ are not homophones in Southern Min; the former is a Tone IV syllable characterized by the presence of a glottal stop whereas the latter is a Tone III syllable with no stop ending. But it is usually the case in Southern Min that a syllable with a glottal stop ending such as 石 drops its ending in sandhi form, i.e., when followed by another syllable. The sandhi form is therefore /sia 3b/ and this is why 榭 /sia 3b/ can be used in its place.

HYBRIDIZATION
IN TAOIST TEXTS

Hybridization as a type of language adaptation obviously is not limited to the evolution of Taoist texts. It seems to be a universal tendency in the development of written language. Although in China the written language parted company with the spoken language as early as the Han dynasty (206 B.C.–A.D. 220), the written language was not dead.[19] In the long history of China the written language as a means of communication followed its path of evolution in space and time and there is much evidence of the influence that the spoken language exerted on it. Many colloquial forms found their way into literary texts. For example, there are many colloquial elements in the prose of Han Yü, the T'ang dynasty champion of ku-wen

---

[19]See Chou Tsu-mo 周祖謨, "Han-yü fa-chan te li-shih," 漢語發展的歷史 [History of the development of the Chinese language] *Chung-kuo yü-wen yen-chiu*, I (1980), pp. 3–12.

or the pure ancient prose style.[20] By no means all texts couched in the highly codified classical idiom were free of the impact of spoken language and exclusively accessible to the classically educated literati.

There are two types of what I shall call hybrid texts in the Chuang-lin collection. The first is entirely non-Min, with an earlier literary stratum overlaid by later northern colloquial strata. The second consists of non-Min texts, which may have had both literary and colloquial elements, that were brought into the Min-speaking context and gradually incorporated Min elements—especially texts intended not for silent reading but for performance. Texts that exhibit both non-Min and Min elements are unmistakable evidence that the original text was adapted to meet the requirements of a new audience. An extreme case of this type are the texts that are modelled largely on Min folk songs or ballads. Clearly, the role of audience in the evolution of texts should never be overlooked.

The texts that are written solely in literary language have a greater time depth than texts of either hybrid type, while the hybrids that consist entirely of non-Min elements are older than those that contain Min elements. The focal point of the following discussion will be the hybrids containing greater or lesser amounts of Min elements.

The Taoist religion, like any religion, had to be preached in easily understandable language in order to spread. Religious Taoism as a way of life must have had an oral literature to start with. Otherwise, it would never have been able to make its influence felt among the populace and remain viable to this day. Of course, not all Taoist texts were intended to be understood by the common people. Some ritual texts could fulfill their functions without being intelligible to ordinary listeners, prayers and other messages addressed to the gods, for example. But when the pronouncements of the gods were issued through the priests to the people, they had to be couched in language that everyone could understand, and then the local tongue was inescapably the vehicle of communication.

The Taoist texts used in Taiwan that were imported from the mainland were originally written in a combination of literary Chinese and northern

---

[20]Tu Chung-ling 杜仲陵, "Lueh lun Han Yü te shu-mien yü-yen yü tang-shih k'ou-yü te kuan-hsi," 略論韓愈的書面語言與當時口語的關係 [On the relation between Han Yü's written language and the spoken language of his time], *Yü-yen yen-chiu* 4 (1959), pp. 55–63.

colloquials of various periods. Since Mandarin and Min are not mutually intelligible languages, one would expect that in earlier times Taiwanese Taoist priests, whose mother tongue was Southern Min, simply read the imported texts in local pronunciation. But it soon became crucial to incorporate local elements into the imported texts. I believe that the popularity of the heterodox hsiao-fa 小法 (pp. 5953–7496) is due to the incorporation of local elements, or, to put it another way, the frequency with which one encounters Min colloquial elements in the hsiao-fa materials is proof of their popular nature. These hybrid texts show that the Taoist religion had been integrated into the local culture.

At the other extreme, some texts in the Chuang-lin collection are written entirely in classical Chinese with no trace of colloquial elements, typically texts that were used in the pursuit of self-cultivation. These were intended for private use by highly educated priests or laymen whose classical education enabled them to understand their abstract ideas and elaborate and intractable idiom. Material taken over directly from the orthodox Tao-tsang, compiled in North China in the fifteenth century, also by definition did not have any Min elements. But texts whose purpose it was to communicate with ordinary people on issues of direct personal concern were written in simple and easy to understand language. It must be remembered that in pre-modern times people grew up in a local culture that was characterized by open-air theatricals, story-telling, and all the other traditional performance genres. This inevitably had an effect on Taoist texts that were intended to be readily accessible.

The heptametric chant in the "Fu-jen k'o" 夫人科 is a case in point. Some colloquial words steal into the song unobtrusively, as in kim 1a-si 1b bo 1b-hoe 1a thang 1a pi 2a-tui 3a 今時無花通比對 "At this moment [its brilliance] is unsurpassed by any flower" (p. 6021), where 通 /thang 1a/ is a colloquial word meaning "can," and in chhit 4a-geh 4b chhit 4a-jit 4b chhit 4a-siah 4b miN 1b 七月七日七夕冥 "in the seventh night of the seventh moon" (p. 6022), where 冥 /miN 1b/ is a Min word meaning "night."

The following section will provide detailed examples of both types of hybrid texts in the *Chuang-lin hsü Tao-tsang*: literary with non-Min colloquial, and non-Min with Min.

CASE STUDIES
OF HYBRID TEXTS

Non-Min Texts

In order to better appreciate the Min/non-Min hybrids that are my chief concern, I will first discuss a hybrid text that has no Min elements, i.e., one that is a combination of literary Chinese and Northern Chinese colloquials of various periods. I will also offer an explanation of why some texts have undergone adaptation and some have not.

The *Ch'ao-t'ien pao-ch'an* 朝天寶懺 (pp. 479–1258) consists of dialogues between the supreme Taoist god and his entourage. One can readily imagine occasions in the history of Taoism when this text was presented to large gatherings of laymen, to teach them about good deeds and bad, fate and retribution, merit and repentance. The language used is plain, unpretentious and easy to understand. The topics dealt with are down-to-earth with no admixture of the metaphysical. Even though the text is written for the most part in the literary language it contains many colloquial elements, as the following examples make clear.

literary		*colloquial*	
yueh 曰	complementizer (p. 572)	ts'ung . . . lai 從 . . . 來	preposition (p. 587)
che 者	agent marker (p. 572)	hui-huai 毀壞	destroy (p. 572)
chih 之	genitive marker (p. 561)	shang-hai 傷害	wound (p. 574)
hsien 咸	universal quantifier (p. 562)	mei-mao 眉毛	eyebrow (p. 582)
		hsiang-ts'ou 香臭	odor (p. 582)

It is significant that there are a host of compounds or disyllabic words in the text, since the use of such words is an important characteristic of colloquial Chinese. But there is no trace of Min colloquial elements in it.

The Chuang-lin version is unchanged from the original version except for some minor variations which may be due to scribal errors or natural variations in oral traditions. The text was probably designed to be understood by a Northern Chinese-speaking audience when it was first written down, and certainly would not have been readily understandable by a Min-speaking audience. Of course the characters could have been given Min pronunciations, but that is not the same thing as a discourse written in Southern Min. But in this case comprehensibility may not have been as important as one might think, since in Taiwan the text was not used to teach moral lessons to the laity but instead was chanted by the priest in rituals of repentance and blessing. The form had become more important than the content; the scripture had been subsumed in ritual.[21]

[21]Some of the texts in the Chuang-lin collection are practically identical to scriptures in the orthodox Taoist canon. With minor distinctions *T'ai-shang chin-lu ch'ao-t'ien pao-ch'an* 太上金錄朝天寶懺 in the Chuang-lin collection (pp. 479–1258) is the same as *T'ai-shang ling-pao ch'ao-t'ien hsieh-tsui fa-ch'an* 太上靈寶朝天謝罪法懺 as published in P'eng Wen-ch'in 彭文勤 et al., eds., *Tao-tsang chi-yao* 道藏輯要 (Taipei: Hsin-wen-feng ch'u-pan kung-ssu, 1977), pp. 9873–9916. Similarly, *T'ai-shang tung-hsuan tu-jen wu-liang shang-p'in miao-ching* 太上洞玄度人無量上品妙經 in the Chuang-lin collection (pp. 4109–41) is in most parts akin to *Yuan-shih wu-liang tu-jen shang-p'in miao-ching* 元始無量度人上品妙經 as published in P'eng Wen-ch'in et al., (eds.) *Tao-tsang chi-yao*, pp. 853–946. But there are omissions in the former showing that in the process of copying the scribes took the liberty to prune the more abstract parts and interpolate additional passages.

An interesting case of formulaic isomorphism is found between *T'ai-shang chin-lu ch'ing-chiao ch'ao-t'ien pao-ch'an* (volume 2) 太上金錄清醮朝天寶懺 卷二 in the Chuang-lin collection (pp. 557–637) and *T'ai-shang yeh-pao yin-yuan ching* (*O-pao p'in* 3) 太上業報因緣經 (惡報品第三) as well as *San-tung feng-tao k'o-chieh ying-shih* (*Tsui-yuan p'in* 1) 三洞奉道科戒營始 (罪緣品一). (See Yoshitoyo Yoshioka 吉岡義豐, *Dōkyō to bukkyō* 道教と佛教 [Taoism and Buddhism] [Tokyo: Kokusho kankokai, 1976], volume 3, pp. 117–33.) There are two set formulae that they share even though they differ in what fills in the slots:
1. . . . che 者, hsien-shih 見世 . . . , kuo-ch'ü sheng 過去生 . . . shen/chung 身 / 中.
2. . . . che 者, ts'ung 從 . . . chung lai 中來.

The meaning of the first construction is "that those (who commit such-and-such a sin or sins) will suffer . . . while alive, but will be reincarnated as/into . . ." The second construction means that "the present existence's suffering stems from . . . " It is claimed that *San-tung feng-tao k'o-chieh ying-shih* dates back to the Southern Liang period (A.D. 550). See Yoshitoyo Yoshioka, *Dōkyō to bukkyō*, volume 3, p. 78. If the claim is valid, the Taoist text should have a long history and the counterpart that survives in the Chuang-lin collection reflects more or less the original format of its source, though the contents are freely altered and augmented. The editing must have been done before the scriptures were brought to Taiwan since there are no Southern Min elements in them.

Min / Non-Min Hybrids

Unlike the text just discussed, these texts have been adapted for Southern Min-speaking audiences. They cannot be fully understood by those who do not know that dialect.

The Rite of Absolving the Deceased of Sins and Instructing the Slaves (Ling 1b-po 2a poat 4b-bong 1b kai 2a-choa 3b ka 3a-kan 2a kho 1a-gi 1b 靈寶拔亡解結教嬭科儀), no. 17, pp. 4743–4820.

This text has a literary part and a colloquial part. The first part, whose main concern is the freeing of the soul of the deceased from Hell, is in the literary language (pp. 4743–4801). The scenario is as follows. A flame is lit and divided into forty-nine magic lamps, symbolizing forty-nine wishes. The light is reflected on Heaven and Hell so that the soul of the deceased can break out of purgatory at once. Forty-nine Taoist supreme gods are entreated to save the soul from its present confinement and escort it to Heaven. The rescue of the soul from Hell is followed by the redemption of crimes committed while the deceased was alive. The sins of the deceased are confessed and forty-nine wishes made again. In conclusion, the soul is released from the burden of its sins and sent off to Heaven.

In the second part the language shifts to Southern Min (pp. 4803–4819). It is about the purchase of a lad and a maid to be the servants of the deceased. The servants (or slave-servants) are symbolized by constructions of paper and bamboo sticks which are "brought to life" by the Taoist priest. A series of moral injunctions is then issued exhorting them to provide their master the best service they can, the lad having responsibility for matters outside the home and the maid for domestic affairs. Since this part concerns the daily well-being of the deceased, family members must have paid close attention to it, and since it was performed in Southern Min, it certainly will have communicated with a local audience effectively.

The Rite of Inviting the Lady (ChhiaN 2a hu 1a-jin 1b kho 1a-gi 1b 請夫人科儀), no. 21, pp. 6031–6102.

This text is also characterized by the alternation of literary and Min colloquial elements. It opens with a literary preamble which consists of

verse in seven-syllable lines (pp. 6031–34) and ends with a coda in the
literary idiom (pp. 6095–6102). Here are some examples of literary terms:

fu	伏	empty word preceding a sentence	(p. 6031)
ch'ih	持	hold, take	(p. 6033)
chu	諸	every	(p. 6032)
chih	之	a genitive marker or nominalizer	(p. 6097)
chin-shang	金觴	a gold wine cup	(p. 6095)
ch'in-ch'en	芹忱	sincere feeling	(p. 6095)
fu hua-yen	赴花筵	attend a splendid banquet	(p. 6033)

Between the opening and closing sections, the text is written in Min colloquial, as the following expressions attest:

chhiu 2a-soh 4b	手鍊	flat armlets	(p. 6049)
thit 4a-tho 1b	敕桃	play	(p. 6049)
chui 2a-kiN 1b	水漧	the edge of the water	(p. 6069)
kin 2a-siN 1a	緊生	be delivered quickly	(p. 6073)
chhu 3a-au 3b	厝後	behind the house	(p. 6074)
chhing 1a-khi 3a	清氣	clean	(p.6077)
lam 1b-lui 2a	濫濾	tattered; slovenly	(p. 6077)
chhiN 1a-kiaN 1a	靑驚	be scared	(p. 6078)
o. 1a-hoe 1a	烏花	black flower	(p. 6084)
ka 3a kiaN 2a pha 1a-lin 3a-tau 2a	敎子跑連斗	teach the child how to do somersaults	(p. 6087)
ka 3a peh 4b-chhat 4b	敎白賊	teach the child to tell lies	(p. 6088)
hi 3b-kau 1a	耳鉤	earring	(p. 6092)

The Rite of Bridge-Crossing (Ke 3a-kio 1b k'o 1a-gi 1b 過橋科儀), no. 18, pp. 4821-39.

This is a ritual text about crossing the bridges to Heaven. The whole text is in Southern Min. It tells how a gold lad and a jade maid are sent by the Heavenly Master of Three Treasures to escort the deceased across the Gold Bridge, the Silver Bridge, and the Naiho Bridge on the way to Heaven. There is a ferocious baleful general blocking the way, but there are documents indicating that the soul was a good person in his previous existence and has confessed his sins and crimes. This saves him from abuse and torture and wins his passage to Heaven.

The "Song of the Ten Months of Pregnancy" is presented as an interlude, followed by a discourse encouraging listeners to perform good deeds to accumulate merit for happiness in the afterlife. All the injunctions concern topics such as family harmony, filial piety, the well-being of the family, and the like. The same topics are found in popular didactic ballads. After this interlude the soul is led home and established in the spirit tablet of the deceased. Paper money that is to be used for the soul's travelling expenses is then burned before the ancestral altar.

The language of the text is characterized by frequent repetition and the use of rhyme, further evidence that it was intended to instruct listeners and not merely fill a ritual function. Even though the words were spoken by the Taoist priest to the gods (on behalf of the soul of the deceased), it was supposed to be understood by the human audience as well.

The Rite of Sending Off a Boat (Sang 3a-tsun 1b kho 1a 送船科), no. 25, pp. 7387–7422.

This is also a text combining literary Chinese and Southern Min. It is mostly in an unadorned literary idiom virtually devoid of local Min elements. But it has been influenced by its Min milieu, as can be seen in its rhymes and its use of Southern Min vocabulary.

The final words of the first, third, and fourth lines of the second stanza, which are intended to rhyme, are 坤, 輪 and 船, pronounced khun 1a, lun 1b, and chun 1b in Southern Min (p. 7408). The rhyme words in the third stanza (p. 7409) are 波, 篙 and 桃, pronounced pho 1a, ko 1a, and tho 1b in Southern Min. If pronounced in modern Mandarin, or even Old Mandarin, not all these words would rhyme.

Expressions that are unique to Min, and Min demotic characters, can also be found, such as mih 4b 乜 (<物) "what" (p. 7407), thit 4a-tho 1b 敕桃 "amuse oneself; play" (p. 7410), and loh 4b 落, as in loh 4b-chun 1b 落船 "get on the boat."[22] In Southern Min the classifier for boat is chiah 4a 隻 rather than tiau 1b 條, and in the text we find the phrase leng 1b-chun 1b chit 4b-chiah 4a 龍船一隻 "a dragon boat" (p. 7411).

AN OVERVIEW OF THE DISTRIBUTION
OF COLLOQUIAL AND LITERARY
ELEMENTS IN THE *CHUANG-LIN HSÜ TAO-TSANG*

According to Saso[23] there are two kinds of Taoist priests: o. 1a-thau 1b 烏頭 "black-head" and ang 1b-thau 1b 紅頭 "red-head." The black-head Taoist priests belonging to the orthodox Cheng-i sect 正一派 use the following manuals in the Chuang-lin collection:

A. Chin-lu 金錄　　vols. 1–14　　chiao 醮 (curing of disease and
　　　　　　　　　　　　　　　　　purging of evil spirits)

B. Huang-lu 黃錄　vols. 15–18　chai 齋 (funeral service)

C. Wen-chien 文檢　vols. 19–20　mi-chueh 秘訣 (rubrical manuals)
　　　　　　　　　　　　　　　　　and fu 符 (talismans)

Most of the above texts can be traced back to much earlier Taoist canons which were written in classical Chinese.

The red-head Taoist priests on the other hand belong to the Shen-hsiao sect 神霄派. This is a heterodox order and uses more popular and recent texts called Hsiao-fa 小法, which date to the Sung dynasty or after:

D. Hsiao-fa 小法　　vols. 21–25　Shen-hsiao 神霄[24]

Our study of language types in the *Chuang-lin hsü Tao-tsang* confirms Saso's classification. In general, the language used in sections A, B, and C is literary and non-Min whereas the language used in section D shows

---

[22]The word /thit 4a-tho 1b/ can be dated back to the Ming period (fourteenth–seventeenth century). In *Li-ching-chi hsi-wen* (cited n. 16), p. 5, it is written as 得桃.

[23]*Chuang-lin hsü tao-tsang* (cited n. 1), pp. 1–33.

[24]Hsiao-fa 小法 belongs to the red-head orders. However, according to Saso, sections 1–17 of the Hsiao-fa are also used by the black-head Taoists, whereas sections 18–23 are used by exclusively the red-head Taoists.

various degrees of infiltration of non-Min and Min colloquial elements. In particular, many Min elements are found in the Hsiao-fa 小法 texts (vols. 21–25). However, Huang-lu 黃錄 (e.g. vols. 15 and 17) devoted to funeral service and Wen-chien 文檢 (vol. 20) also contain colloquial Southern Min features.

The texts or portions of texts discussed in this paper are as follows:

A. Chin-lu 金錄   *Ch'ao-t'ien pao-ch'an*, vol. 2 朝天寶懺卷二 (pp. 551–638);

Ch'ao-t'ien pao-ch'an, vol. 6 朝天寶懺卷六 (pp. 869–940);

Chiu-yu ch'an 九幽懺 (pp. 3437–3712).

B. Huang-lu 黃錄   *Yu-fu pan-she k'o-i* 玉府頒赦科儀 (pp. 4269–4326);

Ling-pao pa-wang chieh-chih chiao-chien k'o-i 靈寶拔亡解結 教媾 科儀 (pp. 4743–4820);

Kuo-ch'iao k'o-i 過橋科儀 (pp. 4821–40).

C. Wen-chien 文檢   *Chi-hua k'o-i* 祭花科儀 (pp. 5671–5703).

D. Hsiao-fa 小法   *Ch'ing fu-jen k'o* 請夫人科 (pp. 5953–6030);

Ch'ing fu-jen k'o-i 請夫人科儀 (pp. 6031–6102);

Ch'i-t'u k'ai-chin i 起土開金刈 (pp. 6103–68);

Piao-ch'ien tsao-chih 俵錢造紙 (pp. 6389–6428);

Chieh-lien miao-ching 解連妙經 (pp. 6187–6306);

Shang-chun k'o-i 賞軍科儀 (pp. 6481–6504);

Tsao-ch'ien i-tuan 造錢一段 (pp. 6637–6695);

T'ang-shan k'o-i 唐山科儀 (pp. 6969–7058);

Sung-ch'uan k'o-i 送船科儀 (pp. 7387–7422).

CONCLUSION

In this paper I have proposed a number of refinements in the way that we think about texts written in Chinese. First, it should be recognized that many texts, especially those that were intended to communicate with non-elite segments of the population, contain colloquial elements. Similarly, literary forms can be found in the spoken language (though I have not dealt with that in this paper). Second, there is not a single written colloquial, but as many as there are dialects. In the Chuang-lin Taoist texts, for example, we can find Southern Min colloquial but also older Northern Chinese colloquial elements. That is why non-specific references to "vernacular" elements in written texts can be misleading.

The identification of Min-specific local elements helps us to understand the evolution of Taoist texts in Taiwan. We can see more clearly how the Taoist texts that were brought to Taiwan evolved in dynamic interaction with audiences consisting mostly of illiterate or semi-illiterate Min speakers. Texts intended to communicate effectively are fully anchored in their social context. A corollary to this is that the form and transformation of texts must be considered in conjunction with the social context in which they are involved. This in turn means that one can reconstruct the mentality of a people in an earlier society by examining critically the texts which are inlaid in it, as argued in Johnson, Nathan, and Rawski.[25]

We have seen that in linguistic terms there are three types of texts in the Chuang-lin collection: those written in literary Chinese; those written in a combination of literary Chinese and Northern Chinese colloquials of varying periods; and those written in a combination of literary Chinese, non-Min colloquials, and Southern Min. I have called the second two types hybrids, and have concentrated on non-Min/Min hybrids in this paper.

The importance of hybrid Taoist texts cannot be overemphasized. Hybridization seems to be an inevitable step in the development of a new linguistic type from the amalgamation of two different types. The process can be imagined to consist of four phases: contact, interaction, selection, and hybridization.

A non-Min linguistic type will be compelled to adjust when placed in the Min context. Its viability will depend crucially on how well it adapts to the new setting. The evolution of Taoist scriptures in Taiwan shows this process in operation.[26] It involved not only the use of Southern Min words,

---

[25]David Johnson, Andrew J. Nathan, and Evelyn S. Rawski, (eds.) *Popular Culture in Late Imperial China* (Berkeley and Los Angeles: University of California Press, 1985).
[26]There is also a genre of secular vernacular literature characterized by the mixture of standard

pronunciation, and even grammatical patterns, but also the use of folk literary forms such as the ballads of blossoming and of pregnancy.[27]

In every locality there is a colloquial tradition. This tradition is conspicuous by its absence in elite literature. It is handed down by oral transmission generation after generation in ballads, stories, jokes, and the like, and in written form in popular religious texts, rhyme books, entertainment literature, and so on. This tradition can be extremely tenacious, as we saw above, when I noted the presence in a Ming dynasty opera script of many terms still current in Southern Min today. And it can also be very widespread, for religious texts, rhyme books, and ballad booklets in Southern Min have been found as far away as the Philippines.[28]

The hybridization of linguistic types as manifested in the evolution of religious Taoism in Taiwan is nothing new. In fact, the idea has been with us for a while; Stein,[29] for one, concludes in his study of religious Taoism and popular religion that the interaction between them is bidirectional.[30]

---

and local vulgar forms. Like Taiwan Taoist texts this genre reflects the adaptation of prestige kuan-hua colloquial texts to the local Min culture milieu. Take the following two novels. The first item was written in the Soochow dialect, a variety of the Wu group, in the late Ch'ing period and the second one in the Foochow dialect, a variety of the Min group, in the mid-Ch'ing period. In both works the narrative is written in the standard kuan-hua whereas the dialogues reflecting daily verbal exchanges are rendered in local dialectal forms. However, the conversations in the second item are only sporadically represented in local vulgar forms. Han Pang-ch'ing 韓邦慶, *Hai-shang-hua lieh-chuan* 海上花列傳 (Taipei: Kuei-kuan t'u-shu ku-fen yu-hsien kung-ssu, 1985); Kao Hsiao-yun, et al. 高嘯雲等, eds., *Min-tu pieh-chi* 閩都別記 (Taipei: Luo-hsing-t'a yueh-k'an-shê, 1986).

[27]The evolution of Taoist texts in Taiwan is analogous to that of the popular Wu Tzu-hsü story, in which history and myth (e.g., folkloric motifs) are fused into an organic whole. See David Johnson, "The Wu Tzu-hsü Pien-wen and Its Sources, Part I," *Harvard Journal of Asiatic Studies* 40 (1980), pp. 93–156, and "Part II," pp. 465–505.

[28]Piet van der Loon, "The Manila Incunabula and Early Hokkien Studies, Part I," *Asia Major*, New Series, 12 (1966), pp. 1–43, and "Part II," 13 (1967), pp. 95–185.

[29]Rolf A. Stein, "Religious Taoism and Popular Religion from the Second to Seventh Centuries" in Holmes H. Welch and Anna Seidel, eds., *Facets of Taoism* (New Haven and London: Yale University Press, 1979), pp. 53–81.

[30]As is evident in the above discussion, the concept of interaction between types of language also applies to phonological change. For further discussion see William S.-Y. Wang and Chinfa Lien, "Bidirectional Diffusion in Sound Change" in Charles Jones, ed., *Historical Linguistics: Problems and Perspectives* (London: Longman Group Limited, 1993), where contact-induced change in the Ch'ao-chou dialect is said to be accomplished in three steps: implanting of the non-Min stratum into the native stratum, interaction between them, and ultimate integration. Also see William S.-Y. Wang, "Theoretical Issues in Studying Chinese Dialects," *Journal of the Chinese Language Teachers Association* 22 (1990), pp. 1–34.

However, in this study I have focused on the unidirectional change of the texts, namely the incorporation of local Min elements into the orthodox Taoist texts.

In the light of previous studies I have proposed a model of the evolution of Taoist texts. The pattern of adapting Taoist texts in response to the local popular culture milieu seems to be an example of a universal phenomenon, and we should expect to find analogous patterns of adaptation in the evolution of other types of texts.

I also present a much-neglected heterogeneous view in the appreciation of Chinese culture underscoring the important role of local non-elite indigenous cultures vis-à-vis the prestige Mandarin colloquial tradition. In this perspective Chinese culture is viewed as a mosaic consisting of a prestige elite culture with a constellation of equally important local popular cultures represented by Min, Yueh, Wu, Hakka, Hsiang, and many other non-Mandarin colloquial traditions. It will lead to a poor understanding or even a distortion of Chinese culture if we are blind to the presence of local popular elements.

My main concern in this paper is, needless to say, texts. I have looked upon the texts as dynamic objects. They have a life of their own and are in constant metamorphosis as long as they still function in a social context and are brought into interaction with audiences. The notion of communication is a prerequisite for understanding the relationship among the texts, the audiences (patrons), the proxies (the Taoist priests), and the gods.